Pessimism of the

PESSIMISM
OF THE INTELLECT?

A History of
New Left Review

Duncan Thompson

MERLIN PRESS

© Duncan Thompson, 2007

First published 2007 by The Merlin Press Ltd.
96 Monnow Street
Monmouth
NP25 3EQ
Wales

www.merlinpress.co.uk

ISBN 9780850365566

British Library Cataloguing in Publication Data
is available from the British Library

Printed in Great Britain by Lightning Source, Milton Keynes

Contents

Preface   vii

Chapter One: The Two New Lefts   1

Chapter Two: The Moment of 1968   43

Chapter Three: Revolutionary Expectations   73

Chapter Four: From Rethinking to Retrenchment   106

Chapter Five: The End of History?   133

Notes   165

Bibliography   232

Index   251

Preface

Communism and Social Democracy were – for better or worse – the principal currents of twentieth century socialism, and it is thus unsurprising that, with the collapse of the former and the surrender of the latter to neoliberalism, the history of the New Left, determined to chart an alternative course for socialist politics after 1956, continues to generate interest and controversy; for it was the New Left that first consistently broached many of the central questions that any successful refoundation of the anti-capitalist Left today must seek to answer.

An extensive literature now exists concerning the history of the New Left prior to its frustration as a political movement in 1962/3, and to its various continuing endeavours thereafter. Less well documented, though hardly less significant, has been the career of a distinct group within the wider family of the New Left, the so-called 'second' New Left, who inherited the sole surviving institutional legacy of the original New Left, the bi-monthly journal the *New Left Review*, on the dissolution of the first New Left as a coherent group. Although such a history necessitates a brief resumé of the journal's pre-history in the period of the first New Left, my principal focus is the distinctive and neglected career of the post-1962 *New Left Review*, the 'new' or 'second' New Left.[1]

Forty years and 238 issues after the *New Left Review*'s first appearance, the launch, in the year 2000, of a 'new series' seems an appropriate moment to reflect upon that career. I hesitate to make any extravagant claims for such a study. To borrow (from a different context) a phrase of Peter Wollen's, the story of the post-1962 *New Left Review* might, with some justice, be described as but 'the passage of a few people through a rather brief period of time'.[2] However, these 'few people' include some of the best Left intellectuals of their generation, and the 'period of time' – some forty years – though historically brief, has been exceptional: a period in which a serious challenge was posed to the reign of capital in the advanced capitalist countries. The defeat of that challenge, and the triumph of a radicalised Right, shapes the world we inhabit today.

Despite well-grounded charges of esotericism and 'super-theoreticism',[3] the focus of the post-1962 *New Left Review* has, I would argue, consistently been upon questions of politics and political strategy. In terms of Raymond Williams' characterisation, the *NLR*'s Marxism deserves to be categorised as 'operative', rather than 'academic'.[4] Examining the politics of the second New Left is not, I hope, simply a matter of furnishing some missing episodes in the story of the wider New Left, a mere recovery of a finished history. Insofar as the making of an anti-capitalist politics remains, for some of us at least, as pressing today as in the past, the second New Left's distinctive engagement with many of the principal issues confronting socialist strategy over the last forty years is of great intrinsic interest and value. If an important sub-text of the question 'where are we now?' (the currently much debated meaning of capitalist 'globalisation') is 'how do we get out of here?', neither may be answered satisfactorily without adding the further question, 'how did we get here in the first place?' An understanding of our immediate past – too often lost in the fetish of the all-consuming present – might serve to help us find an exit from our current predicament.

While the larger part of this study narrates the journal's negotiation of the past forty years, my aim is also, in reflecting upon that past, to attempt to place, politically, the *New Left Review* today. For although it continues to prosper as an academic journal enjoying an international reputation, the *Review* has quietly abandoned its 'operative' character and original organising intellectual focus; namely, divining a politics capable of effecting a passage beyond capitalism. In launching the new series in 2000, Perry Anderson's editorial 'Renewals' poses a specific test for the continuing relevance of the *New Left Review* as a political journal: namely, its ability 'to decipher the course of the world'.[5] Let us leave aside for the moment the fact that deciphering the world used not to be enough; for the second New Left the point was once to change it. To anticipate, and to put the matter baldly, the *New Left Review*'s currently guarded – or, perhaps, not so guarded – pessimism ultimately results, in my estimate, from a misreading of the current conjuncture, an inability 'to decipher the course of the world': a misreading inscribed in, and inexplicable without an understanding of, its own evolution.

Although billed as a 'new *New Left Review*'[6] anyone led to expect from Anderson's editorial in the first issue of the new series a statement of new political direction, or overdue critical self-reflection upon the journal's past, would have been disappointed. Whilst Anderson judges that the journal has reached the point, as it enters its fifth decade, where its life must be extended 'beyond the conditions' and 'generations that gave rise to' it, the shape and direction of any such 'overhaul' is left curiously in the air.[7] The uncertainty of the project that will define the new series is a direct reflection of the *Review*'s reading of what Anderson calls the 'conjuncture of '89'; namely, 'the virtually uncontested consolidation, and universal diffusion, of neo-liberalism'.[8] Even under notionally centre-left 'third way' governments of the Clinton-Blair type, the 'hard core of government policies remains further pursuit of the Reagan-Thatcher legacy … now carefully surrounded with subsidiary concessions and softer rhetoric', the combined effect of which, 'now being diffused throughout Europe, is to suppress the conflictual potential of the pioneering regimes of the radical right, and kill off opposition to neo-liberal hegemony more completely'.[9] Thus, in Anderson's sweeping and downbeat estimate, for 'the first time since the Reformation, there are no longer any significant oppositions – that is, systemic rival outlooks – within the thought-world of the West'.[10]

If the principal response of the erstwhile Left, in Anderson's estimate, has been one of 'accommodation' to the triumph of neo-liberal capitalism, he is equally quick to warn against what he describes as the politics of 'consolation', the search for 'silver linings', inducing 'a propensity to over-estimate the significance of contrary processes, to invest inappropriate agencies with disinterested potentials, to nourish illusions in imaginary forces'.[11] Instead, Anderson advocates for the *NLR* an 'uncompromising realism', 'refusing any accommodation with the ruling system, and rejecting every piety and euphemism that would understate its power'.[12] Tellingly, however, and buried in a footnote, Anderson identifies a third response on the Left; namely, 'resignation': 'a lucid recognition of the nature and triumph of the system, without either adaptation or self-deception, but also without any belief in the chance of an alternative to it'.[13] Although a 'bitter conclusion', and one 'rarely articulated as a public position',[14] we may speculate that this is indeed, at least privately, the perspective of Anderson and his fellow editors.

What is missing from Anderson's editorial – consistent with the veil of secrecy the second New Left has drawn over its own affairs and the public reticence concerning its own evolution – is any critical reflection upon the *Review*'s past, a history, as I have already suggested, that is central to understanding the *Review*'s reading of, and response to, the 'conjuncture of 1989', and thus its ability or otherwise to illuminate the terrain on which we must contest capitalism at the beginning of the twenty-first century. Our task here is to excavate and examine that history.

∗∗∗

No full-length history of the *New Left Review* has previously been attempted. Robin Blackburn has provided a useful, if discreet, periodisation of the *Review*'s career; however, his brief synopsis avoids critical reflection upon its intellectual development ('A Brief History of *New Left Review* 1960-1990', in *Thirty Years of the New Left Review: Index to Numbers 1-184 (1960-1990)*, London, 1992, pp.v-xi). Other studies have a more restricted time-span, and/ or are broader in focus. These include Nigel Young's *An Infantile Disorder? The Crisis and Decline of the New Left* (Routledge and Kegan Paul, 1977), Lin Chun's *The British New Left* (Edinburgh University Press, 1993), Michael Kenny's *The First New Left: British Intellectuals After Stalin* (Lawrence and Wishart, 1995), and Dennis Dworkin's *Cultural Marxism in Postwar Britain: History, the New Left, and the Origins of Cultural Studies* (Duke University Press, 1997). In defining the New Left as essentially anarchist and pacifist, Young explicitly precludes consideration of the post-1962 *New Left Review*.[15] Lin Chun charts the careers of the *Socialist Register*, the History Workshop movement, and the Centre for Contemporary Cultural Studies, as well as that of the *New Left Review*. Moreover, she terminates, somewhat abruptly and arbitrarily, in 1977. Dworkin's focus is similarly broad, and concludes, more convincingly, in 1979-80. In any event, focusing on 'cultural Marxism', the history of the *NLR* is marginal to his account. Kenny's study, on the other hand, covers the period prior to the dissolution of the first New Left as a political movement in 1962, when the *Review* was a mere two years (or twelve issues) old.

In addition to Kenny's study, the history of the first New Left is also well-documented in personal recollections: John Saville, Mervyn Jones and Malcolm MacEwen have reflected on the events of 1956,[16] whilst a conference and subsequent collection of essays – including contributions from Stuart Hall, Michael Rustin, Raphael Samuel and Charles Taylor – has explored the experience of the early New Left.[17] Recent biographies of key figures include Bryan Palmer's *E. P. Thompson: Objections and Oppositions* (Verso, 1994), Fred Inglis' *Raymond Williams* (Routledge, 1995), and Michael Newman's *Ralph Miliband and the Politics of the New Left* (Merlin Press, 2002).[18] Primary documents are publicly available in the Saville papers at Hull and the Daly papers at Warwick.

In contrast to coverage of the first New Left, there is a striking absence of either personal recollections by, or comparable studies of, the second New Left. Two recent exceptions are Gregory Elliott's political biography, *Perry Anderson: The Merciless Laboratory of History* (University of Minnesota Press, Minneapolis and London, 1998)[19] and Paul Blackledge's *Perry Anderson, Marxism and the New Left* (Merlin Press, London, 2004), since Anderson, editor of the *Review* from 1962 to 1983, and again since 2000, necessarily looms large in any history of the *NLR*. Otherwise, reflections to date on the post-1962 *Review* have been both short and polemical. As early as 1964, Peter Sedgwick perceptively identified the emergence of a 'new New Left', 'rootless' and 'Olympian' in character.[20] It is a charge that has been repeated with numerous inflections, in, for example, Geoff Hodgson's 'The Antinomies of Perry Anderson' (1977), Michael Rustin's 'The New Left and the Present Crisis' (1980), Donald Sassoon's 'The Silences of *New Left Review*' (1981), Ian Birchall's 'The Autonomy of Theory' (1981), and Paul Hirst's 'Anderson's Balance Sheet' (1985).[21] In equally polemical vein, Ellen Wood has unfavourably contrasted the second New Left's 'fairly extreme kind of intellectual substitutism' with the first New Left's commitment to popular politics.[22] Interventions since the launch of the new series include acerbic commentaries by James Petras (2001) and Boris Kagarlitsky (2000), and, in less hostile vein, by Gilbert Achcar (2000).[23] Perhaps the most fulsome critiques – 'The Peculiarities of the English' (1965) and *The Poverty of Theory* (1978)[24] – have been penned by Edward Thompson, sharpening the contrast between the so-called 'first' and 'second' New Lefts. These are themes to which we will return in due course.

The greater coverage of the history of the first New Left partly reflects its inherently more transparent character as a political movement, which the 'new' New Left showed little interest in seeking to resurrect. Writing in the *Review* in 1965, Perry Anderson reflected that 'the hope of becoming a major political movement haunted' the first New Left, 'and ended by dissipating its initial assets'. Henceforth, accordingly, the *Review*'s focus was the '[t]heoretical and intellectual work … sacrificed' by the first New Left 'for a mobilising role which perpetually escaped it.'[25] Its model was Sartre and de Beauvoir's *Les Temps Modernes*.[26] Moreover, the journal has been characterised by a notoriously secretive internal regime, seeking to maintain, in the words of a confidential 1982 editorial report, 'a certain opacity capable of keeping casual Carlisle [Street]-watchers guessing'.[27]

Save for the unseemly semi-public spectacle of periodic schism, what went on within the editorial walls of the *Review*'s Soho offices has been notoriously difficult to monitor. The apparent determination of those most centrally involved to draw a veil over the *Review*'s affairs – neither accounts of their past involvement in the *NLR*, nor critical reflections upon the journal's history, have been forthcoming from anyone intimately involved in the post-1962 *Review* – effectively precludes a balanced reconstruction of its internal life. Only an incomplete and one-sided account would be possible from the limited available sources. Instead, I shall attempt to construct – with reference to unpublished editorial documents – what is essentially a history of the *Review*'s intellectual development via its published record. If this misses one dimension of its history, half-a-history (and the more rewarding half, I'm sure) appears better than none given the salience of the *New Left Review* in the culture of the Left in the English-speaking world and beyond.

The fact that one may attempt to write such a history of a journal 'underscores the extent to which the internal life of the *NLR* assimilated certain features of the *modus operandi* of a semi[-]clandestine revolutionary organization'[28] – what one far from hostile commentator reputedly designated a 'common-law variety of democratic centralism'. In the unusual case of the *New Left Review*, certain key texts may be treated less as individually authored essays than as collective pronouncements – at least in its heyday, which one may date, approximately, from the mid-sixties to the mid-eighties. One has only to think of, say, the *Socialist Register* (a journal of broadly comparable political provenance) to acknowledge the *New Left Review*'s distinctiveness in this respect. It is much more like a party journal, tied to the fortunes of the parent organisation – save that for the *NLR* there was no such organisation beyond the romance of the proto-party, embodied in the 'fantasy politburo' of the editorial committee. Today's pluralism – where even the editorials, Anderson now tells us, will be written 'without presumption of any automatic agreement'[29] – is but one index of the 'normalisation' of the *Review*'s journalistic life, the abandonment of a driving political project, the dropping of the mask of a collective *NLR persona*. Although the *New Left Review* continues in existence, and any history of the journal is thus necessarily provisional, the history of the second New Left as a group of intellectuals committed in earnest to a shared political project with the *Review* as its principal vehicle is, one may safely surmise, at an end.

***

I have organised the book into five broadly chronological parts. Chapter 1 begins with a brief account of the rise and fall of the first New Left, and the emergence of the 'new' New Left at the helm of the *New Left Review*. The new editorial team's disparagement of the 'corporatism' of the labour movement, and its commitment to 'high theory' and the role of ideas through the importation and naturalisation of continental Marxism in the light of its dismissal of native intellectual resources, is examined via the controversy with Thompson over the 'Nairn-Anderson theses'. The 'left turn' induced by the events of the French May in 1968 effectively re-founded the second New Left, inaugurating a decade of revolutionary expectations in which the *Review* developed a clear identity and strong collective *persona* on the basis of its affiliation to Trotskyism, the subject of Chapter 2. Chapter 3 entails a more detailed examination of the *Review*'s strategic thinking during this self-confidently *Trotskysant* phase. Chapter 4 covers the period from the *Review*'s attempted 'reanchorage' in domestic politics after 1980 in the context of a concerted political and ideological offensive by the New Right, to its 'retrenchment' against the rising tide of the 'new revisionism' on the British and wider Left in the mid-eighties. Chapter 5 focuses on the *Review*'s over-investment in the chances of reform in the East, inducing, following the 'fall' of 1989-91, a profound pessimism about the prospects for socialism and an abandonment of its erstwhile revolutionary politics.

***

In citing unpublished material, I have followed the convention established in Elliott's *Perry Anderson: The Merciless Laboratory of History* (Minneapolis and London, 1998), p.xvii; namely, quoting directly from documents that 'bear no signature and possess an institutional character', and paraphrasing from signed papers.

***

Acknowledgements

Escaping the world of 'regular work' I took a degree at Brighton Polytechnic in my late twenties. Finding myself in the unusually fortunate position of being in the right place at the right time, I picked up some teaching work and then, as polytechnics became universities, there opened up the prospect of undertaking a doctorate with British Academy funding. It was thus that I embarked on a history of the *New Left Review*.

Undoubtedly, by far the largest debt is owed to Gregory Elliott, who supervised my Ph.D. It is questionable whether I would have taken even the first step without his encouragement and guidance, let alone reach any conclusion for which Gregory himself is, of course, entirely blameless. A big thanks also to Mike Hayler and Tom Hickey for their support and encouragement during my first degree and after; and both to my brother David and to Johnny Denis, who were called upon more than once, as draft succeeded draft, to rescue me from my early misadventures with computers.

Having completed the doctorate in 1997, and with teaching having dried up, various odd-jobs intervened. With new adventures on the horizon – dropping out for good on five acres of deepest, wettest Brittany – I took advantage of a few spare months late in 2002 to dust down the Ph.D., substantially re-work it, and post it to Tony Zurbrugg and Adrian Howe at

Merlin Press. (Some thoughts on the subject have also been published in the journal *Socialist History*.)

Aside from the stimulus of degree, doctorate and teaching at Brighton Polytechnic/University, I also owe a great deal to my involvement in the Red-Green Study Group and in the uncountable round of protests and projects in Lewes, where I lived for twenty years prior to our move abroad.

Above all I would like to thank Debbie, Becky and Hannah, and my parents Ann and Derek, for their love and support.

Duncan Thompson, Landelo, Breiz Izel, 2006

Chapter One
The Two New Lefts

1. The frustration of the first New Left

The prospects for the Left in Europe had never stood so high as in 1945. With the Right discredited by its association with authoritarianism and collaboration, and the era of liberal capitalism seemingly drawn to a close following its descent into depression, fascism and world war, there was every prospect that the lately reunited Left might effect a decisive break with capitalism. In the sudden and dramatic eclipse of this favourable conjuncture lay the seeds of the New Left.

The political polarisation resulting from intensifying international rivalry between the United States and the Soviet Union with the onset of the Cold War in 1947 destroyed unity on the Left, throwing the careers of Communism and social democracy into sharp relief, tightening the hold of Stalinism over the former and Atlanticism over the latter. This was the era of High Stalinism in the Soviet Union, of Zhdanovism, Lysenkoism and the 'Doctors' Plot'. In the new 'People's Democracies' broadly-based governments of the Left succumbed to an authoritarian 'Sovietisation' accompanied by show-trials of dissenting Communists. Meanwhile, in western Europe Keynesian techniques of economic management, underpinned by substantial investment via Marshall Aid funds from the United States, rescued and stabilised a modified capitalism. The commitment of social democracy to a recycled, 'managed' capitalism, achieving full employment and enhanced social provision, blunted its erstwhile socialist ambition – Anthony Crosland influentially argued against further instalments of socialisation in seminal 'revisionist' texts[1] – and sealed its adhesion to anti-Communism. The Communist Parties of western Europe withdrew into intransigent isolation.[2] In Britain, the Atlanticist Right held sway in the Labour Party, while the Communist Party, after its two most successful years (boasting two Members of Parliament, 256 local councillors[3] and some half a million voters),[4] 'fell back into useless obedience' to Moscow.[5]

In the judgement of the early New Left, '[b]etween Stalinist Russia, and the "welfare-state – no-further" jungle of the mixed economy, there seemed to be nothing but an arid waste. In these tight compartmentalised worlds, buttressed by bans and proscriptions, suspicions and fears, supported by texts from Lenin and Stalin, mottoes from Burke and Bagehot, protected by massive armies with nuclear stockpiles and mutually exclusive military pacts, British socialism suffered moral and intellectual eclipse'.[6] In the dramatic events of 1956 those who rallied to the prospective 'new Left' saw the opportunity, and the urgency, of rekindling a socialist politics that had been all but extinguished in the frozen years of the early Cold War. If suppression of the Hungarian rising by Soviet force of arms 'brought to an end a certain kind of socialist "innocence"'[7] and induced a profound crisis within international Communism, the Anglo-French attack on Suez revealed the latent imperialism of the Western powers and questioned social democratic complacency about the character of post-war capitalist society. Thus, in Stuart Hall's recollection, 1956 was 'not just a year', but 'a conjuncture'.[8] Under the twin impact of these events, the New Left was born, opposed alike to the Stalinist corruption of Communism and the 'Natopolitan' and revisionist seduction of social democracy.

Although aspiring to the role of a political movement, the organised New Left never numbered more than a few thousand at most and eschewed a centralised organisation or leadership. Such coherence and wider influence as it had was therefore disproportionately shaped by its two sister quarterly journals, the *New Reasoner* and *Universities and Left Review*, and it was late in 1959, at the organisational peak of the New Left, that these two journals merged to found the bimonthly *New Left Review*. Yet within two years the New Left was in dissolution, and the *New Left Review*, beset by organisational and financial difficulties, was relinquished by its founders into the untried hands of new editors and owners grouped around Perry Anderson. Whilst the history of this 'new' or 'second' New Left is our principal theme, understanding its evolution and character fully makes sense only by way of contrast to its forbears. A brief resumé of the history and ultimate frustration of the first New Left is where our story begins.

The origins of the *New Reasoner* lay in the 'democratic opposition' in the British Communist Party. The restricted debate within the party on issues arising from Khrushchev's denunciation of Stalin at the Twentieth Congress of the Soviet Communist Party in February 1956 prompted two prominent members of the Communist Party's Historians Group – John Saville, a lecturer in economic and social history at Hull University, and Edward Thompson, an extra-mural teacher at Leeds University – to publish a self-styled discussion journal, the *Reasoner*.[9] Initially Saville, Thompson and those associated with the *Reasoner* had no intention of breaking with the Communist Party.[10] After Hungary, however, 'ideas of accommodation and compromise', wrote Saville, 'were no longer practicable'.[11] Prospects of reform at a discount, anything up to an estimated third of the membership left the party,[12] among them the *Reasoner* dissidents, who regrouped around the *New Reasoner*.

The second of the New Left's sister journals, the *Universities and Left Review*, also launched in the spring of 1957, originated in the student Left milieu of Oxford University (its four editors – Stuart Hall, Gabriel Pearson, Raphael Samuel and Charles Taylor – were all Oxford graduates), and the more youthful and somewhat cosmopolitan character of its London-Oxford axis contrasted with the provincial base and labour movement orientation of the *New Reasoner*. With less of a stake in the past, and future prospects, of international Communism, it was more alert to domestic social change and more comfortable in its engagement with the themes of affluence and consumerism.

Michael Kenny has gone so far as to argue that '[i]ncreasingly, the two journals operated as poles of attraction for differing types of politics and organisation' and that these 'tensions were accentuated when the New Left began to cohere as a movement in late 1959.'[13] Undoubtedly there were differences of emphasis. For the present, however, diversity and controversy invigorated the nascent movement, determined as it was to re-think socialist politics from first principles. Above all, in rejecting the mood of 'apathy' (a key early New Left theme) – apparent fatalism in the chances of nuclear annihilation and complacency in the benefits of capitalist affluence – the New Left sought to place a sense of moral purpose at the heart of the socialist project, convinced that socialism would be won because it was consciously desired, not vouchsafed as the end-point of an unfolding historical process.

The Cold War appeared the principal barrier to the renaissance of a socialist politics freed from the dead-hand of Stalinism and Atlanticism, duly condemned as 'the greatest effective cause of apathy, inhibiting or distorting all forms of social growth',[14] and of 'actively poisoning the political, intellectual and cultural life of Europe'.[15] The New Left were thus keen adherents to the Campaign for Nuclear Disarmament, launched in 1958 following, amongst other events, Britain's hydrogen bomb tests on Easter Island and Nye Bevan's dramatic disavowal of the unilateralist cause at the Labour Party Conference the previous autumn. In its style of politics and scale of mobilisation CND became something of a surrogate for the movement to which the New Left aspired. However, in Peggy Duff's estimate, CND did the New Left 'no good. It swallowed them up as a political force in Britain',[16] effectively binding them to the fortunes of CND and the attempt to convert the Labour Party to unilateralism.

Domestically, meanwhile, Harold MacMillan was assuring the British people that they'd 'never had it so good' and secured, in 1959, the re-election of the Conservative government with a significantly increased majority. As affluence and consumerism, and social and geographical mobility, began to touch the working class, the New Left was quick to recognise that a socialist critique could no longer rest on capitalism's inability to meet the material needs of the mass of the people (at least in the West). The shift in emphasis to a qualitative and cultural critique of capitalism – that it was humanly undesirable even if economically viable – is thus unsurprising. The New Left's critical fire was directed at capitalist affluence, at a 'Business Society … uncomfortable with any philosophy more searching than that of material success. It does not offer any civilising mission, any moral Utopia. It offers consumer goods.'[17] 'Has the Labour Movement come through the fire and brimstone of the last fifty years', asked Stuart Hall incredulously in 1960, 'to lie down and die before the glossy magazines? Has Labour no sense of the capacities, the potential of a society, more various, more skilled, more literate, less cramped and confined, less beaten down and frustrated? So that now, we are going to fade away in front of the telly and the fri[d]g[e]?'[18] The editorial to the first issue of the *New Left Review* argued that people have to be called 'to the "society of equals" … not because they have never had it so bad, but because the "society of equals" is better than the best soft-selling consumer-capitalist society, and life is something *lived*, not something one passes through like tea through a strainer.'[19]

Moreover, far from seeing the recomposition of the working class as a hindrance, or quietus, to the goal of socialism (or even the election of a Labour government), as the sociological and psephological convention of the time would have it, the New Left saw the potential for a new working-class consciousness instilled by the expansion of technical or 'intellectual' labour – one 'broader and more generous' and 'less "class-bound"' than that of the thirties.[20] This new consciousness, Thompson trusted, would shape 'a revolutionary critique of the entire capitalist *system*', judging that '[t]he demands which will be made – for common ownership, town planning, or welfare, or democratic access to control of industry or mass media – cannot be met by a wage increase here and a ladder there.'[21]

The New Left's principal recruits were, unsurprisingly, from among these newer fractions of the working class, the better-educated and the young, dislocated from traditional class loyalties, and simultaneously stimulated and dissatisfied by the broader horizons glimpsed via greater educational and career opportunities. The Left Clubs, the organised New Left on the ground, made relatively little headway – the exceptional case of Lawrence Daly's Fife Socialist League in Scotland aside[22] – in traditional working-class communities, and was (much like CND) disproportionately represented in rather unlikely wealthier southern towns and suburbs; Left Clubs could be found, for example, in such places as Tunbridge Wells, High Wycombe, Hemel Hempstead, Woking, Richmond-on-Thames and Blackheath. Although the early *New Left Review* worried that 'the distant wariness between intellectual and industrial workers' was 'one of the most dangerous aspects of the present plight of the socialist movement,'[23] the New Left seemed unable to bridge the gap between the two. According to a contemporary estimate, it was 'quite clear that the original impulse behind the Clubs came in the main from the universities',[24] and while Samuel later considered that 'our strongest local support came from the new towns', he also concurred in the centrality of young people to the movement: 'we came to think', he reflected, 'that there was an elective affinity between protest politics and generational revolt.'[25] For Peter Sedgwick, '[y]outh was more than another partner in the bloc of claims, it was the banner of the whole confederacy, the source of positives.'[26]

At the end of 1961, in a valedictory 'note to readers', the original editors of the *Review* wrote that in the winter and spring of 1959-60 the New Left had 'almost made a breakthrough'.[27] In addition to the popular *Universities and Left Review* Club at the Partisan Coffee Bar in Soho (which attracted on average some 200-300 people to its meetings), provincial Clubs flourished. The second conference of Left Clubs in May 1960 boasted sixty delegates from thirty clubs – the year before there had been just six – which established a Left Clubs' Committee with a three-person secretariat. By October 1960 there were forty-five clubs comprising some 3,000 paid-up members.[28] An expectant Edward Thompson enthused that 'the gulf which is opening between the young socialist generation and traditional Labour politicians ... is a gulf as deep as that which opened in the 1880s between the Lib-Lab politicians and the new unionists and socialists.'[29]

The proposed merger of the New Left's two journals, which occurred at the peak of this mobilisation, was not without its opponents – Ralph Miliband voiced the strongest doubts [30] – but was ultimately, in Dorothy Thompson's words, 'a financial and logistical necessity'.[31] Presented as 'an organic growth out of the two different traditions from which we began',[32] the union was duly cemented, and the *New Left Review* launched at a public

meeting on 14th December 1959, at St. Pancras Town Hall. Speakers included the novelist Iris Murdoch and the philosopher Alfred Ayer, alongside
Edward Thompson, Stuart Hall and Raymond Williams. The first issue, under Stuart Hall's editorship, was dated January/February 1960.

However, within a year, the *New Left Review* was soon to admit, 'the tide
was already receding', and the winter of 1960-61 'was a thin time for the Left
Clubs'.[33] By 1961 the New Left and the *Review* were in crisis, and tensions
that had lain dormant or been left unresolved now came to the fore. Stuart
Hall, as editor, was overburdened with work and conflicting expectations
from an unwieldy and increasingly unworkable board,[34] and there were organisational tensions between the informality of the local Left Clubs and
the need for some sort of national lead. Moreover, there was a certain crisis
of identity: 'Was this, at root, an intellectual milieu, an independent political movement or a lobbying group of the Labour Party? Alternately, as Hall
asked in 1961, was this a movement of people or ideas?'[35]

At the root of the New Left's dilemma was its relationship to the Labour
Party. Too small to act alone, and in any event divided on the issue of being
'in' or 'out', the New Left largely trailed in the wake of the larger battalions of
the Left: the commitment of the Tribunites – regrouped, following Bevan's
defection, as 'Victory for Socialism' – to the Labour Party was never in serious doubt, while CND had become wedded to the prospect of converting
Labour to unilateralism. Even as the Labour leadership sought to steer the
party rightwards into an abandonment of socialism – such as in its presentation of the 'Industry and Society' document at the 1957 conference, endorsing key Croslandite analyses, and concluding that private corporations
'are as a whole serving the nation well' – it proved contentious within the
New Left to advocate an independent political platform. Lawrence Daly's
independent candidature at West Fife in 1959, for example, caused no inconsiderable controversy within their ranks.[36] In Raymond Williams's estimate, the New Left simply 'broke on the usual rock of majority loyalties and
the centralizing pattern of British politics'.[37]

The New Left fell between two stools: those who sought to work within
the Labour Party and those whose focus was primarily outside it. Flawed
though it might be as a coherent strategy, there was little alternative but to
pursue both courses. 'One foot in and one foot out', reflected Mike Rustin
subsequently, 'was never going to be a strong position to push from, and the
revealing physical absurdity of this image never seemed to be noticed at the
time.'[38] That this 'physical absurdity' was never noticed at the time is not
quite true: the second issue of the *NLR* acknowledged that 'one foot in, one
foot out' was 'a difficult position to stand in for any length of time'.[39] It was

less the patent absurdity of the position than the lack of viable alternatives that was the problem.

After Labour's third successive electoral defeat in 1959 the energies of the Left were, unsurprisingly, further absorbed in the struggle for the party's soul. But the successful defence of section four, clause four of the party's constitution merely fostered illusions about Labour's socialist commitment, while the vote in favour of unilateralism at the 1960 Scarborough conference a year later was to prove short-lived: in the teeth of the leadership's implacable opposition, the vote was overturned the following year.

'What is *wrong* with the New Left?', asked a troubled *Review* in 1961. 'Everyone has an answer. The journal: too glossy, too detached, too Cuban, too much. The Board: too big, too windy, too incompetent ... The Clubs: too few, too gimicky, too much talking-shops, too little hard organisation. Too much Old Left. Too little culture. You can take your pick.'[40] What was wrong had largely to do with the political conjuncture. The failure to sustain Labour's commitment to unilateralism did much to sap the energy of CND – already weakened by the divisions over strategy with the launch of the direct action 'Committee of 100' – and the New Left.[41] The Cuban Missile Crisis of October 1962, emphasising as it did Britain's diplomatic irrelevance as the world came close to nuclear war, induced a sense of helplessness; rather than acting as a spur to CND, it further dissipated the Campaign.[42] The Partial Test Ban Treaty in August 1963 took more wind out of the Campaign's sails. With Gaitskell's sudden death that year, the Labour Party rallied to its new leader, Harold Wilson, who managed to transcend the deep left-right divide that had dogged the party for more than a decade by a modernising sleight-of-hand. The 'old Left' had demonstrated a stubborn resilience and the Labour Party proved immune to either change or decomposition,[43] whilst even the Communist Party had recouped its lost membership by 1964.[44] Compounded by these disappointments, more mundane commercial difficulties, and personal exhaustion and friction, had surfaced. 'Much of the steam had gone out of the people who had launched the two magazines six years before. The *NLR* was plagued by financial problems and the inevitable inefficiency of a voluntary outfit. A gap was opening between Edward Thompson and the younger academics.'[45] As early as the eleventh issue, September/October 1961, the *Review* was announcing that a 'considerable reconstruction' was in hand, affecting both journal and movement.

Following Hall's resignation, it was proposed to install a new, smaller core of editors: a mixed bag comprising Raphael Samuel, Mervyn Jones (who soon dropped out), Gabriel Pearson, Denis Butt and Perry Anderson. There was to be a New Left Board, to replace the existing editorial board, chaired by Edward Thompson. However, this arrangement did not last. The belated double issue *NLR* 13-14 proved 'a project motivated more by intellectual purism than financial responsibility. The issue ran to over two hundred pages, took five months to prepare and went £1000 over budget.'[46] The editorial team was subjected to severe criticism at the March 1962 board meeting. Butt and Samuel (who was held primarily responsible) resigned, leaving Anderson to recruit a new, younger team.

However, differences soon developed between Anderson's new editorial team and some of the 'old guard', notably Edward Thompson. At a decisive board meeting held over the weekend 6-7 April 1963, the New Left Board – which Anderson found a 'constitutional built-in irritant and distraction'[47] – was dissolved and 'the entire legal and financial, as well as editorial, responsibility for the *Review*' transferred to Anderson's new team.[48] This 'process of elimination'[49] was, however, clearly not as smooth a process as Anderson later portrayed it, and '[a]t one point there was even a move to exercise legal copyright to prevent the revised journal calling itself *New Left Review*'.[50] Undeniably different interpretations have been read into these events, and where Thompson insinuated that there had been an 'editorial coup', Anderson restated his conviction that there 'was no usurpation in the process of succession: in the strict, neutral sense of the term, there was an abdication'.[51]

Whatever the rights and wrongs of the case, by 1963 Edward Thompson could justifiably write 'that the movement which once claimed to be The New Left ... has now, in this country, dispersed itself both organisationally and (to some extent) intellectually. We failed to implement our original purposes, or even to sustain what cultural apparatus we had. What purposes the review which now bears its name will fulfil remains to be seen.'[52] Intellectually, in fact, the New Left continued to flourish, and key figures of the first New Left were soon pursuing what might be described as broadly new leftist projects elsewhere – Stuart Hall was recruited by Richard Hoggart to the Centre for Contemporary Cultural Studies at Birmingham University in 1964; John Saville and Ralph Miliband launched the annual *Socialist Register* in the same year, embodying (in Miliband's later judgement) 'the spirit which had informed *The New Reasoner*';[53] Raphael Samuel instigated the History Workshop at Ruskin College, Oxford, in 1966; and Raymond Williams, Edward Thompson and others oversaw what was, in effect, a regrouping of the first New Left in the *Mayday Manifesto* project of 1967-8. However, Thompson's 1963 judgement, shared by Anderson and the new editorial team,[54] was a sound one: the history of the first New Left

had drawn to a close, and the survival, let alone the role, of its sole institutional legacy, the *New Left Review*, remained an open question.

2. The emergence of a 'new' New Left

In contrast to either 1956 or the *Review*'s launch in 1960, the inauguration
of the new editorial regime at the *New Left Review* took place at a moment
of defeat and uncertainty. Consequently, the political identity of the 'new, or
'second', New Left took some time to take shape, and if it can be said to have
had a 'founding', or perhaps more accurately a 're-founding', moment it occurred only later, in 1968, when, radicalised by events, it took a pronounced
'left turn'. Nonetheless, there was a sufficiently significant change of direction prior to its re-founding, highlighted in the very public controversy over
the issue of Britain's 'peculiar' history and the political prescriptions drawn
from such diagnoses, that permits us to speak of the making of a distinctive
'second' New Left soon after Anderson's assumption of editorial control.

The advent of a new team at the helm of the *NLR* initially offered no
outward sign of a change in editorial content or political direction.[55] More
critical, in this period, was the question of the journal's very survival. An
apologetic 'Note to Readers' at the end of 1962 regretted the late appearance
– by over a month in each case – of the previous three issues, and the loss
of an entire number (a loss repeated the following year, when again only
five issues appeared). In a retrospective editorial account, '[p]rospects for
the survival of the review were extremely bleak': the 'NLR was bequeathed
as a virtually empty husk … The material situation … was in every respect
lamentable.'[56] Circulation had more than halved[57] and large debts were inherited.

Perry Anderson, born to relatively wealthy Anglo-Irish parents and en-
dowed 'with significant private means',[58] personally bank-rolled the *Review*
through this transitional period.[59] His father (who died when Perry was sev-
en) spent almost his entire adult life working as a custom's official in China,
where Perry's older brother Benedict was born (in Kunming, Yunan province), though Perry himself was, 'by accident', actually born in London in
1940. Infancy in China was followed by a war-time childhood in California
and school years divided between London and Ireland, entering Oxford
University via Eton in September 1956 on the very eve of the formation
of the New Left.[60] Robin Blackburn, born in 1941, took a similar route to
the *NLR* via Oxford and its new-leftist student journal *New University*. The
two would prove key figures in the history of the *Review*, sharing between
them the role of editor-in-chief to date: Anderson 1962-1983, succeeded
by Blackburn to 1999, and reverting to Anderson at the outset of the 'new

series' in 2000. A third key figure in these early years was Tom Nairn, born in Scotland in 1938 (and now living in Ireland), also Oxford-educated, co-partner of the 'Nairn-Anderson theses', and today foremost analyst of the drawn out death of the UK state, dubbed 'Ukania'. Nairn, however, would soon drop out of the *Review*'s core '*aktiv*'. In divining nationalism as the driving force of the modern world, and politically identifying with Scottish 'civic' nationalism, his work and politics developed at a considerable tangent to the main line of the *NLR*'s evolution, and he formally broke editorial links with the journal in 1983.

Early recruits to the editorial committee included Juliet Mitchell, Roger Murray, Gabriel Pearson, Mike Rustin and Tom Wengraf; while important additions through the mid-sixties included Anthony Barnett, Ben Brewster, Alexander Cockburn, Ronald Fraser, Quintin Hoare, Gareth Stedman Jones, Nicolas Krassó, Branka Magaš, Bob Rowthorn and Peter Wollen.[61] A 1974 editorial report judged that this group 'functioned with a remarkable collective élan, perhaps never later recaptured'.[62] Such was the commercial success of the *Review* that it achieved its first annual surplus in 1967.[63]

Perhaps the most significant ingredient that went to the making of the new model *New Left Review* was its unambiguous commitment, in direct contrast to the first New Left, to a self-consciously intellectual role. In 1965, in a settling of accounts with the *Review*'s immediate past, Anderson contended that the principal failing of the first New Left was that it had sought to substitute itself – a grouping of intellectuals – for 'the range of forces which it can properly only link … [o]nce it had ceased to be a purely intellectual grouping, the hope of becoming a major political movement haunted it, and ended by dissipating its initial assets … Theoretical and intellectual work were sacrificed for a mobilising role which perpetually escaped it.'[64] By contrast, the 'new' New Left's model was *Les Temps Modernes*, under the editorship of Sartre and de Beauvoir.[65] Its goal was not to mobilise a political movement, but to slowly transform British culture as a precondition for the making of a socialist politics.[66]

This orientation contrasted not just with the first New Left in Britain, but with the self-proclaimed 'New Left' elsewhere – permitting Nigel Young, for example, to refuse to accept the post-1962 *NLR* as part of the New Left at all.[67] In America the New Left was a broadly based activist movement, originating in the campaigns for free speech at the universities and for civil rights in the South, largely identified with 'Students for a Democratic Society' (SDS), founded 1960, and adopting the famous Port Huron statement at its first convention in 1962. In West Germany the *Socialistische Deutsche*

Studentbund (also, confusingly, bearing the SDS initials) – expelled from the parent SPD in 1961 for its continued opposition to the Bad Godesberg 'turn' (abandoning the party's historic commitment to socialism) – was similarly rooted in a student activist constituency.[68]

In a perceptive critique that appeared in *International Socialism* in the summer of 1964, Peter Sedgwick identified in this highly distinctive 'new New Left' a group of intellectuals that was 'not so much uprooted … as rootless', 'an openly self-articulated, self-powered outfit' without even the original New Left's 'notional or umbilical link … with extra-intellectual sources of action in British society', a group of 'roving postgraduates that descends at will from its own space onto the target terrains of Angola, Persia, Cuba, Algeria, Britain …'[69] His characterisation of the 'new' New Left's 'Olympianism' has become something of a cliché.

In its own retrospective estimate, the new editorial team 'represented a sharp break with the previous New Left' and 'conceived its own aim as that of effecting a radical left turn … by means of a drastic internationalisation of the review.'[70] There is little evidence in this period of any 'sharp break' or 'radical left turn' – this is a reading back of later changes, misleadingly attributed to the very outset of the post-1962 *Review*. A 'drastic internation-alisation' is better attested, and was, indeed, a second major ingredient in the mix that constituted the new *NLR*. Such an 'internationalisation' may seem paradoxical, given, as we shall see, the unusually strong focus on Britain in this period, with the extensive space afforded both to the Nairn-Anderson theses and the more immediate preoccupation with the election and per-formance of a new Labour government. This 'internationalisation' was to be less one of *coverage* than of *perspective*, the placing of Britain in a wider geo-political field of reference, and the attempt to see it, in some sense, 'as a foreign country'.[71] Whether such detachment proved politically debilitating, and whether this was an acceptable price to pay for analytical clarity, must be reckoned with in due course.

Without doubt it was the series of essays that collectively earned the title of the 'Nairn-Anderson theses' that signalled the emergence of a distinc-tively 'new' New Left, not least, because in Anderson's reply to the sharp response they elicited from Edward Thompson, they 'provided the occasion for the first clear self-definition'[72] of the post-1962 *Review*. It is to these es-says and ensuing controversy that we now turn.

3. The Nairn-Anderson Theses

The exhaustion of the first New Left, and the emergence of the new team at the *NLR*, occurred just as the Conservatives 'thirteen wasted years' were drawing to a close. The immediate political difficulties of the government were compounded by deeper anxieties over the manifest under-performance of the British economy, for the prosperous self-confidence of the fifties following the long years of depression and austerity could no longer mask its relative fundamental weakness. Annual rates of growth compared unfavourably with all major competitors and were in especially marked contrast to the rapidly recovered post-war economies of Germany and Japan. Penguin Books launched a whole series around the theme of 'what's wrong with Britain?'[73] The parallel disarray in the Conservative administration, headed since late 1963 by the '14th Earl of Home', prompted a revival in Labour's fortunes. Their new leader, Harold Wilson, adopted a forward-looking agenda, pledging to harness 'the white-hot heat of technology' to the goal of industrial modernisation.

Appearing in the wider context of this 'condition of Britain' debate, Tom Nairn and Perry Anderson, in a series of essays commencing in the first issue of 1964, produced the *Review*'s most original and distinctive work of this period. Detailed substantive reflection upon the specific contours of the British state and society as it has developed over some four centuries would take a volume in itself and clearly lies beyond our scope. All we can do here is to introduce the main themes of the 'theses' so as to draw out the distinctiveness of the 'new' New Left' analysis, not least its disparagement of native resources in the making of a socialist politics and its attachment to the importance of ideas.

In answering how it was that this 'Prometheus' – once the 'workshop of the world' – 'inexplicably dozed off some time last century',[74] they sought to trace the *origins* of the 'present crisis'.[75] '[T]heir intention was not to write the history of the previous three hundred years, but to quarry it, using new concepts and asking different questions, for information which would help explain the *present* crisis. They wanted to "think" the present crisis "historically".'[76] While self-consciously Marxist in inspiration, the essays drew from outside the orthodox canon – principally upon Gramsci's as yet largely untranslated writings on Italian history.[77] The 'first source'[78] of these ideas was Tom Nairn, fresh from the Scuola Normale in Pisa. Indeed, the analyses developed in the theses were rehearsed in the PCI journals *Il Contemporaneo* and *Critica Marxista*[79] – 'La Nemesi Borghese' appearing in the former in 1963. Anderson's intellectual formation, on the other hand, had 'a major element in … Sartre; a minor one [in] Lukács'.[80] Heterodox in both idiom and argument, the essays and ensuing controversies can be taken in two parts: first, an analysis of the exceptional, pre-modern character of the ruling bloc; and second, prescriptions thus derived for the pursuit of a socialist politics.

The English Revolution of 1640, Nairn and Anderson argued, was not simply early, but *premature.* Consequently, England experienced the 'most mediated and least pure bourgeois revolution of any major European country'.[81] Fought out largely between fractions of the landed classes, 'it was a "bourgeois revolution" only by proxy.'[82] Nevertheless, the Revolution did win sufficient space for the uninterrupted development of agrarian and mercantile capital, shattering 'the juridical and constitutional obstacles to rationalised capitalist development', while the Glorious Revolution of 1688-9, that 'decorous epilogue' to the Revolution proper, provided 'the official, radiant myth of creation in the collective memory of the propertied classes'.[83] Crucially for Nairn and Anderson, the emergence of the industrial bourgeoisie issued in no further political revolution. Why? If in the first instance the cause was conjunctural, a more complete answer was to be found in the proto-capitalist orientation of the landed patrician elite.

The industrial revolution coincided with the French Wars (1793-1815), in which Britain fought on behalf of international reaction against revolutionary and Napoleonic France whilst the ruling elite was simultaneously facing down the domestic challenge of the plebian radicals of the early working-class movement. 'The French Revolution and Napoleonic expansion froze propertied Europe with fright. For twenty panic-stricken years the new English manufacturing class rallied to the aristocracy; in that time it developed habits and attitudes it has never lost.'[84] Frightened by the revolutionary excitements witnessed across the Channel, the new industrial bourgeoisie opted for an accommodation within the existing ruling bloc rather than risk heading an inevitably confrontational and volatile political movement of its own – a movement that might readily pass out of its control to more radical popular forces and raise the spectre of an English Jacobinism. Such an accommodation was possible because '[t]here was … from the start no fundamental, antagonistic contradiction between the old aristocracy and the new [i.e., industrial] bourgeoisie. English capitalism embraced and included both. The most important single key to modern English history lies in this fact.'[85]

> [T]he English middle classes chose an organic 'alliance' with the pre-existing forms of society, from fear of a radicalism that might over-reach itself, and because their easily attained economic domination of the world permitted them to bear the cost of the operation. In their peculiar historical situation, the advantages outweighed the disadvantages: the hegemony of a ruling caste was 'efficient' enough, it brought

with it social stability in spite of the general, pseudo-feudal conservatism which it also clamped permanently onto bourgeois society.[86]

In this new ruling bloc the senior partner remained the established landed patrician elite: 'the landlords kept control of the state and its main organs, as a governing elite trusted (on the whole) by the bourgeoisie'.[87] In
Anderson's summary: 'Undisturbed by a feudal state, frightened by the
French Revolution and its own proletariat, subdued by the prestige and authority of the landed class, the bourgeoisie won two modest victories [i.e.,
the 'Great Reform' of 1832 and the repeal of the Corn Laws in 1846], lost
its nerve and ended up losing its identity.'[88] Thus, 'by a singular paradox of
Victorian capitalism, the aristocracy became – and remained – the vanguard
of the bourgeoisie.'[89] The formal Empire-building of the late nineteenth-
century 'not merely preserved but reinforced the already personality type
of the governing class: aristocratic, amateur, and "normatively" agrarian'[90]
– characteristics transmitted to the present century via an unreformed Civil
Service and in the critical nexus between the Treasury, Bank of England
and City. The durability of this hybrid ruling bloc was assured by a fortui-
tous succession of external successes. In its recent history Britain had suffered neither invasion nor defeat – a principal catalyst of domestic upheaval
and social change in twentieth-century Europe. 'Alone of major European
nations, England emerged undefeated and unoccupied from two world
wars, its social structure untouched by external shocks or discontinuities.'[91]
Limited in scope and unmodernised, the state was imprisoned within its
original cast, remaining unreformed from either above, below or without.
    Central to Nairn and Anderson's account, given the weight they afforded
to ideas, was the enduring ideological ascendancy of the landed patrician
elite. '[T]he ideological legacy of the [English] Revolution was almost nil',[92]
for, being pre-Enlightenment, it embodied none of the radical rationalism
that coloured the French Revolution, and thus bequeathed to English political culture no revolutionary language or legacy. 'Never was a major revolutionary ideology' – i.e., militant Puritanism – 'neutralised and absorbed
so completely'.[93] The way had been opened for the progress of capitalism
without the accompanying ideological spur of Enlightenment *philosophes*
or a revolutionary remaking of society in the name of a rational modernity. During the period of early industrialisation a Burkean conservatism
prevailed, conveniently blending respect for traditional hierarchy with the
needs of a developing capitalism. 'The English capitalist class, because of
the peculiar circumstances attending its birth, was conservative from the
outset.... The perfect model of social conservatism was before its eyes, in

the social order of the English agrarian world.'[94] Crucially, at no point in the drawn-out transition to modernity was the industrial bourgeoisie compelled to marshal its strength, articulate a comprehensive critique of an *ancien régime*, and offer a modernising prospectus of its own. Sociology, 'the great achievement of bourgeois social thought in the late 19th and early 20th century',[95] was strikingly absent in Britain – the 'lumpen-bourgeois, crackpot empiricist philosophy of Utilitarianism'[96] being the sole weakling example of a bourgeois ideology aspiring to 'universal claims'. This shortcoming had been compounded and reinforced by the 'non-hegemonic' perspective of Labourism: a bourgeois sociology might latterly have been stimulated, as elsewhere, by an encounter with Marxism. In Anderson's summary – a rehearsal of the more substantive essay, 'Components of the National Culture' published in 1968:

> the momentous, overwhelming fact of British intellectual history in the last 50 years has been *the simultaneous failure to produce either a Marxism or a Classical Sociology of any serious kind* … It is unique among European nations … Britain alone has produced *neither* a Lenin, a Lukács, a Gramsci – *nor* a Weber, a Durkheim, a Pareto. That is to say, it has not participated in either of the two great traditions of synthetic social thought which superseded discrete 'political theory', 'economics' and 'history' at the turn of the century.[97]

So pervasive was this conservative culture that the nineteenth-century 'Romantic Revolt' – although recognised by Anderson as 'a remarkably far-reaching critique of Victorian capitalism'[98] – could be couched only in terms of a backward-looking nostalgia for a mythical 'golden' past. A lament for a lost past spoke of an uneasy and reluctant accommodation to modernity: a striking lack of confidence in the culture of the first industrial nation in a modern, urban, industrial future. The 'landowning civilisation survived … as a mode of living, a culture and language, a type of personality and psychology, a whole dominant ethos'.[99] Industrialists were quick to find themselves a country seat, enjoying the status of landed gentry, lamely acquiescing in the notion that it was 'uncultured' to dirty one's hands in trade, and sending their sons to the new Public Schools to learn Latin and Greek classics in preference to setting them on technical or engineering careers.

Contemporary Britain, Nairn and Anderson argued, continued to bear the stamp of its aristocratic inheritance, with a social hierarchy that remained deferential, where birth counted for more than ability, where tradition was fetish-worshipped – contrasting British moderation with foreign extremism[100] – and where the political and business elite was marked by a patrician aloofness.[101] That this should have compared unfavourably with America went without saying; that it now did so even with continental Europe served to highlight Britain's economic and social 'backwardness'.

The essays sparked a wide-ranging debate. No response, however, had quite the impact of Edward Thompson's fierce polemic 'The Peculiarities of the English', published in the 1965 *Socialist Register*,[102] to which Anderson fired an equally sharp riposte, 'Socialism and Pseudo-Empiricism' (1966). The points in historical dispute need not unduly detain us: suffice to register Thompson's insistence that a full passage to capitalist modernity had been achieved, rejecting any notion of enduring aristocratic ascendancy: the character of the capitalist ruling class, he argued, far from being '"fragmentary" or "incomplete" … would appear to be unusually fulfilled'.[103] For our purposes, the primary significance of the exchange is that it made public for the first time the divergence of political perspective between Thompson and the 'new' *New Left Review*. Whereas Thompson had written of Britain being '*over*-ripe for socialism',[104] accusing Nairn and Anderson of misdirecting their energies in 'hunting … an aristocratic snark',[105] Nairn and Anderson argued, that, on the contrary, Britain, far from being ripe for socialism, had yet even to complete a successful transition to bourgeois modernity. This was, of course, not merely at odds with Thompson, but with almost all the received wisdom of the Left, Marxist and non-Marxist alike, which judged Britain the first, paradigmatic industrial-capitalist country with an unusually unified and class-conscious proletariat.

Moreover, in disparaging the weakness of the indigenous socialist tradition, imprisoned within an irredeemably conservative and 'empiricist' national culture, the 'new' New Left looked to Franco-Italian Marxism in a bid to furnish a 'total' analysis of British society as a necessary precondition of effecting meaningful political change – signalling the *Review*'s determination to explore and naturalise key currents of Western Marxism. Thus Thompson's opening salvo blasted Anderson, as editor of the *Review*, for being 'a veritable Dr. Beeching of the socialist intelligentsia. All the uneconomic branch-lines and socio-cultural sidings of the New Left ... were abruptly closed down. The main lines ... were electrified for the speedy traffic from the marxistentialist Left Bank.'[106] Thompson lampooned what he saw as the simplistic, schematic approach of Anderson and, particularly, Nairn: 'We hold our breath in suspense as the first Marxist landfall is made upon this uncharted Northland. Amidst the tundra and sphagnum moss of English empiricism they are willing to build true conventicles to convert the poor trade unionist aborigines from their corporative myths to the he-

gemonic light.'[107] Thompson railed against the 'stridency in the way our authors hammer at class and tidy up cultural phenomena into class categories',
which alongside the 'ruthlessness in their dismissal of English experience
… stirs uneasy memories'[108] – implicitly equating the new direction of the
NLR with a return to doctrinaire Stalinised Marxism. Thompson concluded
belligerently, alluding to the need to 'man the stations of 1956 once again'.[109]
It is no wonder that Anderson accused Thompson of speaking 'in a voice
choking with anger', 'warped with paranoia and bad faith', to say nothing of
'reckless falsification'.[110]

Little ground was conceded by either of the two main protagonists.[111] So
far as the *NLR* was concerned, more substantial issues than the points in historical dispute with Thompson were raised by others who entered the fray,
questioning Nairn and Anderson's 'idealist' emphasis, and thus challenging their characterisation of 'hegemony'. Whilst Thompson harried Nairn
and Anderson for their allegedly 'economistic' excesses, the evidence they
had presented in support of a landed patrician ascendancy was in fact almost entirely 'superstructural': cultural, ideological and political. Nairn and
Anderson mistook the outward appearance of aristocratic power for the real
thing. Anderson was quick to acknowledge the objections raised by James
Hinton,[112] replying to Thompson's charge of reductionism that, if anything,
the original theses were too idealist. He added, by way of self-criticism, that
Althusser might offer a corrective to the influence of Lukács, Sartre and
Gramsci.[113]

One such Althusserian corrective was offered by Nicos Poulantzas, in an
essay that first appeared in *Les Temps Modernes* in 1966. He raised a more
fundamental difficulty: how in Marxist terms to explain the fact of a capitalist social formation in which bourgeois ideology has never been dominant.[114] Furthermore, Poulantzas reminded Nairn and Anderson that 'there
may be sizeable disjunctions between the politically dominant class and the
objective structures of the state.'[115] Nairn and Anderson recognised that in
mid-nineteenth-century Britain the landed elite continued to rule on behalf of the bourgeoisie, but such a 'disjunction' might be less exceptional
than they supposed[116] – a point Anderson would later acknowledge (in 'The
Figures of Descent', 1987). It should not, of course, be forgotten that the
emergence of 'normal' bourgeois, liberal democratic forms of the capitalist
state, even in the advanced capitalist countries of western Europe, had only
been achieved since the war – and in southern Europe would not be won
until the seventies.

The state, particularly one with a record of longevity as remarkable as
the British, may mystify, often with deliberate intent, the real processes of

power. This was, of course, Bagehot's famous interpretation of the British constitution, highlighted by Thompson,[117] where the theatrical show of the monarchy and Lords – the 'dignified part' of the constitution – was a facade behind which lay a 'disguised republic'. For Thompson and others, Nairn and Anderson had failed to see through this 'theatrical show', and thus, according to Richard Johnson, their 'main explanatory notion (aristo-cratic hegemony) turns out to be nothing more than the principal themes of English Liberal ideology … The *New Left Review* analysis conforms to this very English tradition of radical liberalism: it does not surpass it, still less unmask it.'[118] Nairn and Anderson might be read as suggesting that the political agenda consisted less of an immediate advance to socialism than in completing 'the unfinished work of 1640 and 1832';[119] that the problem was not so much capitalism, as its incompletion.[120]

Having established for the *Review* a distinctive research programme and prompted a lively debate that extended to continental Europe, the project was abruptly abandoned. Anderson's 'Components of the National Culture' appeared in 1968 and Nairn's 'The Fateful Meridian' in 1970, but while Nairn has written prolifically (at something of a tangent from the original theses) on 'Ukania' and nationalism, this was conducted outside the *Review*'s prin-cipal intellectual and political focus.[121] It would be a full two decades be-fore Anderson revisited these themes, in 'The Figures of Descent' in 1987.[122] While some detected 'a radical re-weighting'[123] of the original thesis, the main line of argument – incorporating a greater emphasis on the role of the City and the predominance of commercial capital – remained largely unchanged.[124] What is noteworthy, though, is that Anderson returned to a serious interest in the pre-modern character of British state and society – extolling, for example, the programme of constitutional reform advanced by Charter 88 – only once the orientation to revolutionary socialism in the years following 1968 had been abandoned.

4. Labourism and Socialism

The 'new model' *NLR*'s distinctive political perspective was further devel-oped in Nairn's and Anderson's analysis of Labourism. For them, the British labour movement had remained 'corporatist' in character, mirroring an un-ambitious industrial bourgeoisie: in Anderson's words, 'a supine bourgeoisie produced a subordinate proletariat'.[125] Where the first New Left saw the in-stitutions of the labour movement as encompassing, in Thompson's words, 'the immanent community of socialism',[126] Nairn and Anderson saw only 'incorporation' and subordination. While the British working class enjoyed a sociological cohesion unmatched almost anywhere else in the world – indeed, in this limited sense, an 'excess' of class consciousness[127] – it had failed to mount a 'hegemonic' challenge to the existing order. How was it that such an homogeneous working class, with such a density of organisational strength, had remained so unambitiously 'corporatist'? And how could a corporatist Labourism be transformed into a hegemonic socialism?

Historically, the British working class, in the words of both Nairn and Anderson, had suffered a particular 'tragedy'.[128] Its early formation occurred prior to the advent of modern socialism, and thus '[i]ts greatest ardour and insurgency coincided with the least availability of socialism as a structured ideology'[129] – note the importance attached to ideas – '[i]n England, in contrast to countries that industrialised afterwards, Marxism came too late: the *Communist Manifesto* was written just two months before the collapse of Chartism.'[130] The lack of a modern – Marxist – socialist politics was compounded by the absence of any recent revolutionary mobilisation and any revolutionary ideological inheritance from the bourgeoisie (in contrast to the French example). The revolutionary temper of working-class politics in the first half of the nineteenth century was succeeded thereafter, according to Nairn and Anderson, by an unrelieved reformism. Although Thompson's famous account of *The Making of the English Working Class* ends in 1832, the formative moment of the modern proletariat post-dated the Great Reform Act, and was stamped by the defeat of Chartism in 1848 and a subsequent accommodating quietism. It was the conjuncture of this 'fateful meridian' in the nineteenth-century that accounted, in the estimate of Nairn and Anderson, for the reformist character of the modern labour movement, for it was here that the institutions of Labourism originated: principally the 'new model' craft trade unions and the Co-operative movement. Antipathy to the 'theatrical show' of apparent aristocratic political power served to integrate this re-made labour movement into the broad church of Gladstonian Liberalism. The belated socialist 'revival' of the 1880s and beyond failed to win over the labour movement; the modern Labour Party was little more than a trade union party that inherited the social liberalism of the disintegrating Liberals.

There is no denying that the mid nineteenth century marked a fundamental divide in the evolution of the British working class. However, Thompson rejected the disparaging label of 'corporatism', contending that 'once a certain climactic moment is passed, the opportunity for a certain *kind* of revolutionary movement passes irrevocably … because more limited, reformist pressures, from secure organisational bases, bring evident returns'.[131] His conclusion – that 'the workers, having failed to overthrow capitalist society, proceeded to warren it from end to end'[132] – was less convincing. Did the institutional strength of the labour movement, and the Labour Party itself, speak of the imminence of socialism? Anderson and Nairn were certain that it did not. On the contrary, they equated 'Labourism' with what Lenin defined as 'trade union consciousness': a caste consciousness at the level of economic class ('them and us') that falls short of a socialist desire to remake society anew. In Britain, it was only when the trade unions – in defence of their own interests following the Taff Vale decision of 1901 – lent their support that the nascent party of the working class attained political weight. On the continent, by contrast, the roles were reversed: the ideas of socialism came prior to, and were instrumental in helping to found, the parties of classical social democracy. The consequence was, in Anderson's analysis, that in Britain 'the working class has developed over a hundred and fifty years an adamantine social consciousness, but never a commensurate political will. The very name of its traditional political party underlines this truth ... a name which designates not an ideal society ... but an existent interest'.[133]

Displaying 'the indigenous nature of all its roots', the labour movement, wrote Nairn, had proved 'empirical' and 'undoctrinaire' from the outset.[134] He denounced the 'practicality' which 'turns into wilful short-sightedness, a ritual pragmatism wielded to exorcise the sort of theoretical thinking socialism requires'.[135] Labour's acquiescence – the price of 'respectability' – in an 'aristocratic embrace' confirmed its corporatism: its station as an estate within an archaic hierarchy, 'occupying its proper place in the British firmament midway between the House of Lords and the Boy Scouts',[136] rather than as the potential agency of a new society.

What stands out in Nairn and Anderson's account is the centrality afforded to *ideas*; ideas, moreover, derived from *outside* the working class. Whilst the co-option of the industrial bourgeoisie into a counter-revolutionary ruling bloc during the French Wars and the consequent political isolation of the early labour movement imparted to the British working class a striking sociological and institutional cohesion, the absence of any radical, intellectual middle-class leadership deprived it of any 'global' outlook. Anderson was explicit: intellectual leadership tends to come from outside the working class. 'The division of culture in the nineteenth century meant that the development of socialist thought was bound in the main to be the work of non-working-class intellectuals ... Thus everywhere it tended to come to the proletariat from the outside.'[137] Fabianism they judged a 'leaden legacy'. The architects of Labour's one moment of measureable reform – namely Keynes and Beveridge – were both liberals, whose proclaimed intent was the reconstruction, not the abolition, of capitalism. Such diagnoses held good for the present; Nairn argued that if the modern labour movement was to overcome its corporatism, it stood in need of leadership from 'an intellectual stratum torn adrift from the social consensus with sufficient force and capable of functioning as catalyst ... against the consensus'.[138] In 'Problems of Socialist Strategy' in 1965, Anderson wrote that 'a purely working-class party, tends, by its very nature, towards either corporatism or outright subordination ... It is enough to say that the relationship between the working class and culture, decisive for its consciousness and ideology is *inevitably* mediated through intellectuals, the only full tenants of culture in a capitalist society'.[139] For Anderson, the key task ahead was to transform the 'trade union consciousness' of the working class into a socialist consciousness, a battle that 'can ... only be won on the plane of ideology'.[140] Again, in 1967, he argued that '[t]he corporate character of trade union consciousness does not derive from the nature of trade union action ... It has a cultural-political basis. Trade unions represent only the working class. A revolutionary movement – a party – requires more than this: *it must include intellectuals and petit bourgeois who alone can provide the essential theory of socialism.*'[141]

The bourgeoisie had succeeded, after a fashion, without needing to articulate a world-view of its own. Capitalism, given the all-embracing reach of its social relations – tending towards commodification of all resources and transactions – requires little more than an everyday, 'common-sense' acquiescence in its inordinate 'logic'. Capitalist relations of production could evolve slowly within a decaying feudalism, quietly undermining the latter through an inexorable economic momentum. However, 'the working class possesses no corresponding foundation within capitalist society', and therefore 'cannot hope for the same sort of victory'.[142] Thus, whereas it had been demonstrated that capitalism can prosper without the accompaniment of an ascendant 'totalising' bourgeois ideology – an implicit, though initially unacknowledged conclusion of the Nairn-Anderson theses – the feat was not repeatable by the working class. The transition to socialism was qualitatively different: not the transformation of one type of class society into another, but the supersession of class society altogether. There could be no quiet erosion of existing productive relations from within, no comparable evolution, only a decisive and *conscious* break:

> Consciousness, theory, an intellectual grasp of social reality – these cannot occupy a subordinate or fluctuating place in the socialist transformation of society, no empirical anti-ideology or trust in the 'natural' evolution of affairs can substitute for them. Consequently ... the working class had to become what the bourgeoisie had never been – what

it had renounced, what it had found effective replacements for, what it desired *not* to be with all its force of instinct. That is, a class dominated by reason. To become a new hegemonic force, capable of dominating society in its turn, the English working class absolutely required a consciousness containing the elements ignored by, or excised from, the consciousness of the English bourgeoisie ... The English working class, immunised against theory like no other class, by its entire historical experience, *needed* theory like no other. It still does.[143]

The distinctiveness of the *Review*'s politics derived from Anderson's rejection, in 'Problems of Socialist Strategy' (1965), of both Leninism and social democracy. He argued that they shared a fundamental misconception: 'They both polarise their whole strategies on the state: civil society remains outside the main orbit of their action.'[144] Given the weakness of civil society in backward Russia, 'Leninism represented a sombre but genuine adaptation to its world'.[145] The appeal of Leninism was a real one outside the West; 'it is precisely in backward, inchoate societies, dominated by scarcity and integrated only by the state, that such a strategy has its meaning'.[146] The developed civil society of the First World dictated an entirely different approach; one less preoccupied with the direct conquest of state power. Here the moment of Leninism had long since passed: 'it is important to emphasise that a Leninist strategy in the West is fundamentally *regressive*: it threatens to destroy a vital historical creation [i.e. 'democracy'], when the task is to surpass it.'[147] In Anderson's definition, hegemony was exercised through 'the dominance of one social bloc over another, not simply by means of force or wealth, but by a wider authority whose ultimate resource is cultural'.[148] Anderson's conclusion was that, if revolutionary Leninism might still be appropriate in the Third World, 'in western Europe ... capitalist hegemony is first and foremost entrenched in civil society, and must be beaten there':[149] 'Socialist strategy must aim at entering and inhabiting civil society at every possible point, establishing an entire alternative system of power and culture within it.'[150]

Writing in 1964, Peter Sedgwick thus characterised the *Review* as 'Jacobin in its inclinations towards the "Third World" of radical scarcity', whereas it 'veers toward Fabian methods nearer home'.[151] It was a characterisation that, in part, Anderson privately accepted; revolutionist in the former, the *Review* projected a 'policy of presence' in the First World.[152] The charge of Fabianism, however, was one that Anderson would have rejected. Although social democratic 'names' were prominent in the *Review* in the transitional period 1962-4, this soon gave ground to perspectives explicitly rooted in continental Marxism. In 'Problems of Socialist Strategy', Anderson was, in effect, counterposing a Gramscian war of position in civil society to both Leninist revolutionary 'insurrectionism' and Fabian reformism.

Moreover, ideas – the development of socialist theory and ideology – were judged central because, in the *Review*'s reckoning, hegemony was principally exercised ideologically in civil society. If, as Anderson argued, capitalist hegemony in Britain 'was founded on an ideology of stupefied traditionalism and empiricism, an anti-ideology which is the enemy of all ideas and all calculation,'[153] the challenge for the *Review* was 'to create theory in an environment rendered impervious to rationality as such'.[154] Thompson's recurrent appeals to the 'common people' or 'ordinary men and women', for example, spoke to Anderson of just such a failure of structural analysis. He charged the first New Left with being 'populist and pre-socialist', its inability to produce 'a systematic sociology of British capitalism' resulting in 'a major failure of nerve and intelligence, an inability to name things as they were'.[155] Nairn and Anderson's prescription was the creation of a socialist intelligentsia via the importation and naturalisation of such 'systematic sociology' and totalising theory from abroad, principally in the shape of Western Marxism – a project first adverted to as early as 1963[156] and upon which the *NLR* now embarked in earnest.

The tone of the *Review* became unapologetically theoretical. A large helping of sociology with a pinch of psychology and anthropology were the initial ingredients of a totalising synthesis intended to challenge a compartmentalised and empiricist British culture. Thus, for example, articles by R. D. Laing and assessments of both C. Wright Mills and Lévi-Strauss appeared in the *NLR*,[157] prior to the commitment in 1966 to begin a series of presentations of 'some of the major Marxist thinkers'.[158] The essays, though appearing for the first time in English translation, were often of considerable vintage: Lukács' critique of Bukharin – 'Technology and Social Relations' – was first published in 1925. Also included were Walter Benjamin's 'Paris, Capital of the 19th Century', written in the thirties, and a collection of 1919-20 articles by Gramsci, 'Soviets in Italy'.[159] Of the contemporary texts, Althusser's 'Contradiction and Overdetermination' (1967)[160] was perhaps the most significant, for it promised to rescue a materialist Marxism from economistic orthodoxy, without (or so it was held) repeating either the 'superstructural' biases of the principal Western Marxists or the 'moralism' of the first New Left. However, these were explicitly 'presentations'; what was absent at this stage was anything much by way of critical appraisal.

Anderson and Nairn's recognition of the necessity of a 'hegemonic'-socialist, as opposed to a 'corporatist'-Labourist, politics was salutary. However, their analysis was flawed in several key respects. In identifying civil society as the central site of struggle Nairn and Anderson neglected the entrenched power of the capitalist state, an error Anderson was soon to acknowledge, rejecting the reading of Gramsci in 'Problems of Socialist Strategy' that counter-posed him to Lenin. Thompson, in turn, it should be noted, mis-read Anderson's interpretation of Gramsci. Thompson was right to argue that in Britain, within obvious limits, reformism had produced results, be-cause capital has usually been in a strong enough position to make suffi-cient concessions to labour to ensure relative social peace – highlighting one key *structural* factor in determining the character of Labourism. But he was wrong to infer that hegemony stood for 'revolution' and corporatism for 're-form', and to counterpose one to the other.[161] Anderson reckoned hegemony to be exercised in civil society, encouraging him to adopt, at this stage, a clearly reformist – not a revolutionary – perspective. 'Problems of Socialist Strategy' was not reproduced in the subsequent collection of Anderson's work on Britain – evidence of his later distance from the analyses it con-tained. Indeed, it was privately referred to in 1974 as 'certainly the worst text produced by any e[ditorial]/c[ommittee] member throughout this period',[162] emphasising the sharp break in the evolution of the *NLR* under the impact of the events of 1968. Its errors were traced 'to a Gramscianism that was not tempered or corrected by any comparable control of classical Marxism'.[163] Thus,

> the confusions and ambiguities of Gramsci's own characteristic con-cern with 'hegemony' in bourgeois democracy and its primary exercise in the arena of 'civil society' rather than the State, led imperceptibly but fatally towards compromises with reformism – via the notion that proletarian hegemony could gradually be won in civil society, without any direct confrontation and abolition of the capitalist State.[164]

Moreover, in equating hegemony with simply ideological dominance, Nairn and Anderson misunderstood how hegemony is exercised; failed to register the permanently incomplete and contested character of hegemony; overestimated the role of ideas and thus of the making of a socialist intelli-gentsia; and undervalued the transformatory potential of the working class as embodied in the institutions of the labour movement.

In Poulantzas' critique, 'the dominant ideology is … only *one aspect* of … [the] … organisation of the hegemonic class or fraction'; rather, 'hegemony designates the *objective* structuration of the *specific* "interests" of a class or fraction as representative of a general *political* interest' – a wider, less purely ideological, definition than that underlying Nairn and Anderson's analysis.[165] It is simply wrong to expect that a single dominant ideology – a 'pure' ruling-class consciousness – could be derived from the complex, and often contradictory, unity of a given social formation. Poulantzas traced this error to a Lukácsian reading of social reality, in which a 'total' correlation is reckoned to exist between a given economic base and its ideological, superstructural reflection. In addition, a thorough reading of Gramsci should have taught Nairn and Anderson that hegemony is in fact always in a process of tension and reconstruction.

Perhaps most fundamentally of all, Nairn and Anderson thus exaggerated the role of ideas and the 'high' ideological and cultural component of hegemony, and simultaneously undervalued the solidaristic, anti-capitalist character of working-class culture and the transformatory potential of the labour movement. In Richard Johnson's reading, Nairn and Anderson's working class was 'fooled in the head by ideas but not exploited and governed in the factory'.[166] No doubt a lively socialist intellectual culture would have a part to play in the winning of socialism, but alone it would amount to very little. The principal weakness in Nairn and Anderson's analysis was to under-rate the strength and character of the actual organised working class. Writing in the *Review* in 1965, Raymond Williams argued that whilst, in one sense, working-class allegiance to Labourism was indeed 'an obstacle to militant socialism' … in another sense it keeps open the possibility of putting socialism on the political agenda without civil conflict or violence'. He concluded that there was a 'balance, here, of strengths and weaknesses, which is our real political context.'[167] Nairn and Anderson failed to balance the strengths against the weaknesses. Given their culturalist conception of hegemony, they identified the making of a socialist intelligentsia versed in a global, 'totalising' theory, via the importation of Western Marxism, bringing ideas *to* the working class, as the principal route to political advance. Hence they disregarded the prospect of a radicalisation from within the ranks of organised labour itself, such as, for example, in the shop stewards movement and the Institute for Workers' Control, which only fleetingly captured their attention and played little part in their strategic calculations.

Crucially, whilst, as we have seen, the *Review* would revise its position in important ways, these two fundamental character traits – overstating the role of ideas, understating the capacity of the labour movement – would be reinforced rather than abandoned with the impending sharp break in the *Review*'s evolution after 1968.

5. Wilsonism and the Prospects for 'Structural Reform'

Expectations of a Labour government in Britain rested less on the party's immediate programme or the inclinations of the Wilson leadership than on the perceived opportunities presented by structural changes in post-war capitalism. Organised 'neo-capitalism' (or, more optimistically, 'late capitalism') was perceived by many on the Left as heralding a decisive stage in the evolution of capital, in which increased state intervention, judged an unavoidable corrective to the instability and anarchy of the free-market, tended towards a politicisation of economic decision-making, hinting at an 'encroaching' social control and tabling the prospect of a strategy of 'structural reform' – that could only (so it was thought) be advantageous to the Left.

The apparent failure and obsolescence of free-market doctrine was paving the way to greater levels of economic socialisation and democratisation. Joan Robinson had written in the *NLR* of 'the final end of laissez-faire',[168] while Serge Mallet, analysing French planning under the Fifth Republic, argued that 'capitalism ... is attempting to preserve its position by the use of socialist techniques.'[169] A similar confidence was expressed across a wide spectrum of the Left, including contributions to the *Review* on this theme in the period 1962-4 from Mallet of the French new leftist PSU; Barbara Castle of the British Labour Party; Lelio Basso, a leading left-wing member of the Italian PSI; Ernest Mandel of the Fourth International; an unlikely panegyric on the Labour Party under Wilson by the PCI representative in Britain, Giorgio Fanti; and, from a first New Left perspective, two essays by John Hughes detailing a programme of reforms that might be enacted by a Labour government.[170]

With a more relaxed domestic political climate in western Europe as Cold War tensions receded, it appeared legitimate to envisage the formation of centre-left administrations committed to deepening the economic socialisation and democratisation of the Western parliamentary democracies. The debate around the opening to the Centre-Left in Italy, involving the participation of the PSI in a modernising coalition government, brought this endeavour into strategic focus, providing a parallel with the concerns of the British Left given the imminent prospect of a Labour government pledged to vigorous state-led modernisation.

Mainstream Labourites were afforded considerable space in both the *Review* and the *Towards Socialism* collection of 1965, which included contributions from Thomas Balogh and Richard Crossman, prominent figures in the Wilson administration. Writing in 1964, Peter Sedgwick contrasted the efforts of the first New Left to build a grassroots movement with the second New Left's 'tactic of theoretical entry':[171] a lobbying or 'Fabian' approach, seeking to permeate the inner circles of the Labour leadership,[172] and the *Review* later acknowledged its 'unmistakeable accommodation to Wilsonism before the advent of [the] Labour Government'.[173]

Thus, somewhat at odds with Nairn's withering dismissal of historic Labourism, the Labour Party's return to government – narrowly elected in October 1964, and subsequently re-elected with a substantial majority in 1966 – was greeted with cautious optimism by the *NLR*. Anderson's pre-election essay, a 'Critique of Wilsonism', spoke with warmth of the Labour Party as 'the dynamic left-wing of European Social-Democracy', and said of Wilson himself, that 'the Labour Party has at last, after 50 years of fail-ing, produced a dynamic and capable leader'.[174] However, Anderson was not unmindful of the weaknesses of 'Wilsonism'. He recognised that Wilson's 'trenchant criticisms of English capitalism ... conceal a consistent dis-placement of attention from essential to the inessential'; in consequence, 'Labour's present programme is radical, within limits which are always short of a serious confrontation with the power structure of British soci-ety.'[175] While Wilson's 'modernisation' involved a forthright critique only of unproductive capital – 'the Bourbons of the economic establishment'; 'serious-minded industrialists' were to be encouraged[176] – and the labour movement was 'incapable of tabling a socialist transformation in any imme-diate future',[177] Anderson nevertheless argued that 'between this perspective and the role of executor of bourgeois reform and stabilisation ... there lies a wide gamut of choices'.[178] Anderson concluded that Wilson's programme 'is not at any point socialist; but nor is it, unlike its predecessor, inherently incapable of debouching onto socialism'.[179]

Labour in power, however, failed to fulfil even the most modest of expec-tations, and the *Review*'s disillusionment was soon complete. After the first few months in office, it could write that the 'Labour Government ... has won the virtually universal contempt of the Left, both in this country – and even more so – abroad (contrasting inaction over Rhodesian UDI with the intervention in Aden in 1967 and supine backing for America's escalation of the war in Vietnam). Few regimes have so immediately lost all credit or re-spect.'[180] The *NLR*'s call for Labour to radicalise and polarise debate, follow-ing the indecisive election of 1964, was always likely to fall on deaf ears.[181]

Nonetheless, the *NLR* maintained its commitment – in, for example, Anderson's 'Problems of Socialist Strategy' – to a policy of structural re-form in the First World. Such a perspective is perhaps difficult to square with the self-proclaimed 'sharp left turn' in the *Review*'s centre of gravity, and the avowed Marxism of the post-1962 *New Left Review*.[182] However, the *Review*'s Marxism was coloured in this period by, for example, both the Italian Communist Party's (PCI) and Ernest Mandel's endorsement of a strategy of structural reform within neo-capitalism. The PCI currently served as something of a model socialist party, its 'hegemonic' ambition implicitly contrasted with the Labour Party's 'corporatism';[183] its positive stance towards an 'opening to the Left' in Italian politics undoubtedly influenced the *Review*'s own perspective on the promise of a new Labour government. The turn to *revolutionary* Marxism came in 1968, effecting a much sharper break with the politics of the first New Left and with the *Review*'s proto-Euro-Communism of the mid-sixties.

In sum, the strategy of 'structural reform' involved a bargain between capital and labour. Increased levels of state intervention were deemed unavoidable in modern capitalist economies: even the Conservative government in Britain had tentatively introduced the first rudiments of planning in the form of the National Economic Development Council and the National Incomes Commission. The basis for such a bargain between capital and labour in Britain rested on wage restraint, for conventional wisdom held that industrial modernisation would only succeed with a non-inflationary increase in productivity. Thus, the willingness of the trade unions, as the institutional representatives of labour, to participate in such bargaining was essential. A debate on the Left arose around this central issue. Did such an accommodation involve the incorporation of the trade unions into a state-led rationalisation of capitalism? Or did it present an historic opportunity to encroach upon the prerogatives of capital? And if the latter, in what form was such an encroachment best effected?

Beset by a balance of payments crisis from the day it entered office, Labour adopted traditional Treasury prescriptions, imposing wage controls and accepting levels of unemployment that, though modest by later standards, seemed at the time almost unthinkable. Deflationary measures in defence of an overvalued pound sterling had wrecked its programme of industrial expansion and modernisation from the outset.[184] The question, long debated within the first New Left, as to what a Labour government might offer the trade unions in return for their support of an incomes policy, became something of a dead letter; *nothing* was on offer from Wilson.[185] Amidst the ruins of his economic strategy Wilson pinned the blame for Britain's ills on the trade unions. Vilification of the seamen during the 1966 strike was followed by proposals for anti-union legislation – inappropriately misnamed 'In Place of Strife' – provoking a sharp confrontation between the Labour government and the trade unions that cut right through the labour movement and into the Cabinet itself.

If nothing was on offer from above, what might be wrested from below? Rejecting, in any event, the statist tripartism of, for example, Sweden and Austria, the *NLR* looked for inspiration to the experience of workers' control in Yugoslavia, and to the more limited experiments in *autogestion* in Algeria and 'co-determination' in Germany;[186] an altogether more positive option: 'the only negotiable exchange for an incomes policy', Anderson argued, for 'it alone offers a genuine counterpart – powers and not pence'.[187] The advocates of 'workers' control' argued that a new stage had been entered in the contest between capital and labour, in which the simple struggle for better wages had been superseded by the increasing number of strikes over working conditions and practices, optimistically seen as presaging a more profound challenge to the rule of capital. A radicalisation of shop-floor demands might both limit the sway of the bureaucratic leaderships within the trade unions and initiate a process of 'encroachment' upon the role of management (seen, in turn, as a 'school' for full self-management in a planned, socialised economy). Thus, in the period 1966-7, the *New Left Review* was encouraged to examine the new, combative trade unionism, politicised by the struggle over the impending industrial relations bill, in which shop-floor militancy and advocacy of workers' control found influential voice in new left-wing union leaderships. It was also drawn into friendly contact with the Communist Party – given its influential presence in many trade unions – including the establishment of an 'informal discussion group' at the Marx Memorial Library, Clerkenwell Green, in the summer of 1967.[188]

'The unions have never needed to be more militant, and they have never had to confront such a systematic attempt to confiscate their rights', wrote the *NLR*, with a pinch of exaggeration, early in 1967.[189] In the same year the *NLR* published, under Robin Blackburn's inspiration[190] and in association with Penguin Books, *The Incompatibles*, a collection of essays on the new trade unionism. More militant in tone than the *Towards Socialism* volume of 1965, it identified an awakening tension that promised to tear the unions from their allegiance to 'the dry schemas of the Fabian and Keynesian right wing' of the Labour Party.[191] 'There is no escape', the editors concluded: 'The unions must – they are being forced to, they will continue to be forced to – seek for *a new political identity*.'[192] In the past the unions had been a negative influence on the Labour Party – 'the dead souls of Labourism',[193] in Nairn's phrase – holding the Labour Party, through the block vote, to a rightward course against the wishes of left-leaning constituency parties. A series of union election victories for the Left – most notably Jack Jones, Hugh Scanlon and Clive Jenkins – promised both a leftward shift in the Labour Party and a radicalisation of the unions themselves.

These questions of trade unionism and workers' control shifted the *Review*'s attention, albeit briefly, from the preoccupation with culture and ideology to capitalist economic relations and the transformatory potential of the labour movement – a potentially fruitful re-focusing of priorities. Anderson nonetheless remained sceptical. His concluding essay in *The Incompatibles*, 'The Limits and Possibilities of Trade Union Action', stressed the limitations of trade unionism, and argued that a socialist consciousness was only possible if mediated via intellectuals through a socialist party. 'Trade unions represent too limited a sociological base for a socialist movement. By themselves they inevitably produce a corporate consciousness'; '[o]nly a revolutionary party, not a trade union, can overthrow capitalism'[194] – consistent with the conclusions drawn in 'Problems of Socialist Strategy': trade unionism was an important elementary stage in developing class consciousness, but the struggle 'to convert the natural sociological shape of society into its political shape, in a new popular hegemony', could only 'be won on the plane of ideology'.[195]

By the time the *NLR* carried an interview with Hugh Scanlon (newly elected President of the Engineering Union) in late 1967,[196] a more conducive front for the New Left had opened in the student movement; and despite the further politicisation of the trade unions in the campaign over the industrial relations bill 'In Place of Strife', the *Review*'s skittish attention had already drifted away from organised labour. The defeat of the bill in 1969 received no coverage in the *Review*.

6. International Perspectives

As we have noted, and somewhat curiously given all the space devoted to domestic history and politics in this period – the Nairn-Anderson theses and the prospects and performance of the Labour government – the new editorial team set itself the goal of 'a drastic internationalisation of the review'.[197] Such an 'internationalisation' was largely one of *perspective*, the attempt to see Britain 'as a foreign country',[198] and was widely commented upon by the *Review*'s critics, notably in Sedgwick's characterisation of the 'new' New Left's 'Olympianism'. But this internationalisation also entertained the prospect that the greatest challenge to global capitalism might lie outside the developed countries, opening the *Review* to the charge of an incipient Third Worldism.

Early in its career, in the context of an atypical collective editorial, 'On Internationalism' in *NLR* 18 (January/February 1963), the new team charted an international landscape constituted by the triangular relationships be tween the First, Second and Third Worlds, and amounting to something of a manifesto of its geo-political expectations:

> Socialism was born into a world whose limits were those of capitalism itself … Inevitably, socialist thought itself was influenced by this unique supremacy: the liberation of society would be inaugurated in the capitalist countries themselves … Events proved this belief both right and wrong. Socialism remains the vocation of our time; the dethronment of capital has proved both possible and necessary. But the revolutions were not made in Europe … The Russian and Chinese revolutions resulted in a continuous Communist world stretching across the length of Eurasia, numbering one-third of mankind. And since 1945, a third world has emerged, in violence and war. The decolonisation of Asia, Africa and Latin America, which is forcing capitalism back upon its homelands of the nineteenth century, has created an immense community of newly or imminently independent nations. Today these three great zones structure the contemporary world. The triangular pattern of the relations between them will shape the next decades. Their competitive confrontation already conditions and accelerates the internal evolution of each of them … World history is now immediately single and indivisible as never before; but its agents have become multiple.[199]

Recognition of this interconnectedness did not, however, lead the *NLR* to conceive of 'capitalism as a single, undifferentiated phenomenon'.[200] A wide ranging 'country study' series – of specific social formations within a global context – was inaugurated at the same time, commencing with the Third World, but with the intention of extending this to the advanced capitalist countries. The series included essays by Perry Anderson on Portugal and the Portuguese colonial empire, 'Lucien Rey' on Persia, Roger Murray and Tom Wengraf on Algeria, and Ernest Mandel on Belgium.[201] The editorial preface to the first study of an advanced capitalist country in 1963 acknowledged, in Gramscian vein, that 'respect for the density and irreducibility of the many different historical experiences of capitalist accumulation is a precondition of any serious theory of capitalism as a type of human society. A general model is not denied, but enriched by the diversity of the forms which it integrates.'[202] Such studies would also, the editorial continued (signalling the forthcoming Nairn-Anderson theses), serve 'to deepen our understanding of the fundamental structure of capitalism by exploring all its contingent possibilities, and so, reciprocally, to perceive more clearly – by contrast and similarity – the specific nature of British society today'.[203]

As we have seen in 'Problems of Socialist Strategy', Anderson had contrasted a Gramscian 'war of position' in the West, amounting to a contest for 'structural reform' and a strategy of cultural hegemony, to a Leninist 'war of movement' in conditions of scarcity in the Third World. Despite the contrasting strategies appropriate to each zone, he was convinced that the First and Third Worlds held the key to political advance; the former because it offered the material conditions for a mature democratic socialism, the latter because it constituted a weak link in the chain of global capitalism.[204] The Second World, by contrast, was a low priority for the *Review*, offering as it did a model of 'socialism' unlikely to inspire Western socialists, while being too conservative to support revolutionary movements in the Third World.[205]

The chances of a reformed Communism – though not the causes of the degeneration of the October Revolution into Stalinism – had been a principal preoccupation for the 'New Reasoners' of the first New Left, and this interest (following a lapse) seemed set for a revival under the new editorship. The transitional double number 13-14 (January/April 1962) carried a substantial report of the PCI's Central Committee debate on the 22nd Congress of the CPSU, whose importance was summed up in Anderson's introduction as constituting 'a liberated, unintimidated interrogation of the whole structure of Communist political practice for 40 years'.[206] Thereafter, however, coverage was slim.[207] The 22nd Congress of the CPSU in 1961 proved to be the high-point of Khrushchevite de-Stalinisation. The Cuban missile crisis of 1962 weakened Khrushchev's position, and his fall from power in 1964 – an event that effectively terminated de-Stalinisation – passed without comment in the *Review*.

On the subject of the Soviet Union, the new editors deferred to the authority of Isaac Deutscher, who produced two essays and two interviews for the *NLR* in this period.[208] In Deutscher's analysis, the October Revolution had succeeded in abolishing private property relations in the principal means of production. However, war and civil war had devastated 'backward' Russia's underdeveloped economic infrastructure and decimated the ranks of the revolutionary proletariat. In these circumstances, as a 'besieged revolutionary elite' isolated by the failure of revolution in the West, the party was compelled either to abdicate or sustain the revolution by acting as 'locum tenentes'[209] until such time as a new working class could enter its inheritance. 'The single party system became for the Bolsheviks an inescapable necessity ... They had not aimed at it with any premeditation. They established it with misgivings as a temporary expedient.'[210] Herein lay the seeds of the Stalinist bureaucratic dictatorship. However, in Deutscher's analysis, Stalinism had not reversed the principal 'gain of October': the abolition of private property. The potential of contemporary Soviet society was based on this profound transformation, emphasising the 'continuity of the revolutionary epoch'.[211] The internal conservatism of the Soviet bureaucracy, in Deutscher's analysis, was matched by its cautious – but not, as Trotsky argued, counter-revolutionary – foreign policy, exemplified by its Khruschevite policy of 'peaceful co-existence' with the West.

> The Soviet leaders see in the preservation of the international *status quo*, including the social *status quo*, the essential condition of their national security … They are therefore anxious to keep at a 'safe distance' from the storm centres of class conflict in the world and to avoid dangerous foreign entanglements. On the other hand, they cannot, for ideological and power-political reasons, avoid altogether dangerous entanglements … Sooner or later the moment of crisis comes and the contradiction explodes in Moscow's face. Soviet policy must then choose between its allies and protégés working against the *status quo*, and its own commitment to the *status quo*. When the choice is pressing and ineluctable, it opts for the *status quo*.[212]

Since the Sino-Soviet split of the early sixties, China had, by contrast, emerged as an alternative pole of attraction within international Communism – with a revolutionary experience and orientation closer to the conditions of the Third World. Deutscher himself was not immune to the appeal of Maoism. Writing in the *Review* in 1964, he argued that the breakdown of a monolithic Stalinism had revived healthy debate, stifled since the twenties, within the international Communist movement: the new right-centre-left configuration of Tito/Togliatti-Khrushchev-Mao paralleling that of Bukharin-Stalin-Trotsky forty years earlier (providing an otherwise unlikely and tenuous linkage between Trotskyism and Maoism). Deutscher judged that 'the Maoists, whatever their ulterior motives and limitations, are now impressing the ideas of revolutionary internationalism on the minds of millions, as no one has done since Lenin's days'.[213]

Although Deutscher retracted his Maoist sympathies sooner than most,[214] the appeal of Maoism to many Western socialist intellectuals – including the *NLR* – grew rapidly, denoting to some extent a substitution of China for the Soviet Union as their reference-point in the politics of the Second World,[215] indeed, effectively substituting the Third World, and China's place within it, for the Soviet Union and the Second World as the revolutionary focal point of world politics. As a conservative neo-Stalinism followed the fall of Khruschev, the *NLR* increasingly distanced itself from any favourable assessment of the Soviet Union in its strategic calculations. A reappraisal of the role of the Second World (and the restoration of a quasi-Deutscherite perspective on the Soviet Union) came later, with the onset of the 'Second' Cold War in 1978-9, when the appeal of Maoism had waned with China's own, far more blatant abandonment of 'socialist internationalism'.

The Cold War stalemate of the fifties served, in some minds, to indicate the emerging 'Third World' as a hopeful source of political and social trans-formation. The strategic outlook of the first New Left and CND, hostile to the bi-polar Cold War divide, often ran parallel to that of the non-aligned 'Bandung powers'. Some on the New Left were unduly optimistic about the socialist and anti-imperialist character of decolonisation and national liber-ation, a stance that was accompanied by a pronounced pessimism as to the prospects of initiating change in the decadently prosperous West. While such 'Third Worldism' was later denounced by the *Review* as entailing 'regressive and mythic counterpositions of "poor" and "rich" countries, the peasantry of the underdeveloped versus the proletariat of the developed worlds',[216] it certainly opened itself, early in its history – and under the influence of war and revolution in Algeria, Vietnam and Cuba – to such a charge. Nowhere was this more explicit than in the 1963 editorial 'On Internationalism', which not only counted the Third World as a distinct (and mistakenly ho-mogenous) force in world affairs – 'an immense community of newly or im-minently independent nations' – but also implicitly portrayed the emergent Third World as non-capitalist, arguing that the process of 'decolonisation … is forcing capitalism back upon its homelands of the nineteenth century'.[217]

The *Review* also carried distinctly Third Worldist texts, notably those by Keith Buchanan in 1963.[218] He argued that 'we may expect the countries of the Third World' – united, despite their differences, in a 'fellowship of the dispossessed', a 'commonwealth of poverty' – to move increasingly towards a pattern of peasant-based socialisms';[219] achieved by their own efforts, for 'the Western working class and their leaders have averted their faces and be-come increasingly Europocentric in their vision'.[220] 'The *fellaghas* of Algeria, the Pan-Africanists of South Africa, the guerillas of South Vietnam or of Venezuela may … be a more decisive factor for change in the capitalist world than all the Left-wing parties combined.'[221] Sartre, an important influence on some of the 'new' New Left, famously gave credence to 'Third Worldism'.[222] 'Europe is at death's door' – and so too was 'that super-European monstrosity, North America'[223] – he wrote emphatically in the Preface to Frantz Fanon's *The Wretched of the Earth* (1961). Fanon himself concluded:

> Leave this Europe where they are never done talking of Man, yet murder men everywhere they find them, at the corner of everyone of their own streets, in all the corners of the globe ... Come, then, comrades, the European game has finally ended; we must find something different. We today can do everything, so long as we do not imitate Europe, so long as we are not obsessed by the desire to catch up with Europe. Europe now lives at such a mad, reckless pace that she has shaken off all guidance and all reason, and she is running headlong into the abyss; we would do well to avoid it with all possible speed.[224]

Despite the attraction, Third Worldist perspectives were ultimately at odds with the thinking of the new team at the *NLR*, and met with a ready response in the pages of the *Review*. Both Michael Barratt Brown and, in a later essay, Ernest Mandel rejected any suggestion of an inherent conflict between the proletariat of the First and the poor of the Third Worlds,[225] and Anderson was privately critical of the Buchanan texts.[226] They argued that development through equitably planned world trade would be universally beneficial: it was not the self-sacrifice or charity of the European workers, 'still less the violent self-mortification of Sartre's latest writing, that the developing lands require; it is quite simply our machines and tools and our cooperation on the common task of developing world trade'.[227] Peter Worsley's suggestion of a quasi-'Narodnik' transition to an African socialism based on village communalism was equally rejected by Victor Kiernan, wary of too indiscriminate a disavowal of the European experience.[228]

A better gauge of the views of the *NLR* editors may be found in their response to the Cuban revolution, registered by Robin Blackburn – who in 1962 was working at Havana University and researching the island's history[229] – as 'an event of world-historical importance'.[230] For by the time Blackburn's essay 'Prologue to the Cuban Revolution' appeared in 1963, Cuba was already an exceptional case, not merely professing socialism – this was the norm for most ex-colonial regimes – but displaying its commitment by social transformation at home and militant anti-imperialism abroad. It was the failure of other revolutionary and national liberation movements to live up to the Cuban ideal that shattered the *Review*'s incipient faith in any purely 'generic' Third Worldism. The struggle for national independence in the Third World was necessarily anti-imperialist, yet it was not intrinsically socialist; it was the social composition and political leadership at the head of the revolutionary and independence movements that shaped their character.

In a damning critique, 'Second Thoughts on Ghana' (1967), Roger Murray located 'the willing self-deception and anaesthetisation of the critical function' among socialists with regard to the inherently anti-capitalist orientation of the Third World in 'a misinterpreted application of revolutionary responsibility and commitment', 'embattled and defensive reflexes', and the 'acute tension and distortion of "socialist internationalism" brought about in the historical process of Stalinism, cold war, and volatilisation of socialist experience ... carried over and transposed on to the post war anti-colonial liberation movement'.[231] The case of Ghana – where Kwame Nkrumah, erstwhile pan-Africanist and socialist revolutionary, had fallen from power in 1965 – was far from exceptional. The disappointments multiplied; 'pretensions to an occult steering of history in the Third World', Murray concluded, 'have ... been shattered on the rocks of hard experience.'[232] High hopes of social revolution were deferred and neo-colonialism imposed, whether through a stalling conservatism (India), military intervention or coup (Indonesia and Algeria), or outright US invasion (the Dominican Republic).[233] An emotive portrayal of the idealised and incorruptible poor of the Earth redeeming a socialism debased by affluence in the First World was untenable, however attractive to a New Left at odds with social democracy and Communism. However, with the Western working class sunk in the torpor induced by the long post-war boom, and its parties largely paralysed by Cold War divisions or pursuing timid reformism, it was still to the Third World that socialists looked, perforce, for inspiration. The 'weakest links' in the chain of global capitalism lay outside the metropolitan core of western Europe and North America. It was perhaps here, in the 'three continents' of Africa, Asia and Latin America, that class tensions, aggravated by questions of national dependency, could be expected to be at their most acute. But after the disappointments in Ghana and elsewhere, the post-1962 *NLR* was more discriminating, embracing specifically revolutionary socialist states and movements in the Third World, rather than the concept of a generically anti-capitalist Third Worldism.

Such an affiliation was made explicit in 1967 – again in the context of the Cuban revolution, which remained something of a touchstone for the *NLR* – via the writings of Régis Debray, extolling 'Fidelism' or 'Guevarism' in three major essays: 'Latin America: The Long March', which originally appeared in *Les Temps Modernes*, and was published for the first time in Britain in the *NLR* in 1965; 'Problems of Revolutionary Strategy in Latin America', which also appeared in the *Review*, in 1967; and *Revolution in the*

Revolution? (1967). (In addition, Robin Blackburn edited a collection of Debray's writings, *Strategy for Revolution*, published by Jonathan Cape in 1970). The editors of the *NLR* were unstinting in their praise, confirming their conviction in the prospects for socialist revolution in the Third World: 'Together, they unquestionably constitute one of the most brilliant examples of Marxist-Leninist analysis to have appeared in many years. What above all distinguishes Debray's writings is their relentlessly Leninist focus on *making the revolution*, as a political, technical and military problem'.[234]

In part such fulsome commendation derived from an expression of solidarity with Debray, who, having made contact with Che Guevara in Bolivia, had been captured, imprisoned and threatened with summary execution; Anderson and Blackburn (together with Tariq Ali, Lothar Menne and Ralph Schoenmann) went to Bolivia in 1967 on behalf of the Bertrand Russell Peace Foundation to secure, by their presence, Debray's safety, and to attend his forthcoming trial. But it also confirmed an earlier conviction, following the rapid disillusion with the prospects for advance in the First World, that '[g]uerilla war has become at once the most successful and the most typical mode of revolutionary struggle in the contemporary world … [F]or the time being, the jungle and the mountain side, the swamp and the paddy field have replaced the barricade as the main locus of combat'.[235] The disappointing sequel to decolonisation in Africa and Asia could only be avoided by resisting amorphous cross-class alliances in which conservative and neo-colonial elements tended quickly to dominate, once independence had been won. Debray evinced an intransigent distrust of such coalitions. His programme, reflecting the Cuban experience, was an uncompromising revolutionary socialism prosecuted by a militant vanguard of guerilla cadres.[236]

'Under an autocratic regime', argued Debray, 'only a minority organisation of professional revolutionaries, theoretically conscious and practically trained in all the skills of their profession, can prepare a successful outcome for the revolutionary struggle of the masses';[237] '[n]o political front which is basically a deliberative body can assume leadership of a people's war; only a technically capable executive group, centralised and united on the basis of identical class interests, can do so; in brief only a revolutionary general staff'.[238] Debray drew three basic conclusions for the struggle in Latin America: first, that it was possible for a disciplined, mobile guerilla band, operating from a secure base or '*foco*', to defeat the army; secondly, that a determined group of revolutionary guerillas could create the conditions for revolution – that a 'small motor' (the guerilla band) could spark the 'large motor' of suppressed discontent (Castro had initiated the revolutionary war in Cuba with a party of twelve); and thirdly, that the terrain of struggle would be the countryside.

The Cuban experience, however, proved unique and not repeatable. A cult of militarist *machismo*, where 'the mountain proletarianises the bourgeois and peasant elements',[239] was ultimately fruitless – witness the fatal recklessness of Che's doomed Bolivian adventure – though one might admire, from a safe distance, such uncompromising commitment. The 'large motor' of popular discontent in Latin America proved insufficiently flammable to be lit by the spark of guerilla action.

In 1974 the *Review* confidentially reflected that its political outlook in this period resulted from 'a combination of illusions: undue pessimism about the First and optimism about the Third Worlds due largely to Sartre … and undue optimism about the development of the Second World, due to the influence of Deutscher'.[240] But a 'generic' Third Worldism, though forcefully expounded by influential figures such as Sartre, and provoking significant debate within the pages of the *NLR*, never struck firm root in the mainstream thinking of the 'new' New Left. Solidarity with the Cuban and Vietnamese revolutions was based on their militant socialist orientation. Though much more critical of the capacities of the labour movement and sceptical of the prospects for socialism in Britain than the first New Left, the new model *NLR* nonetheless recognised the centrality of the First World both in terms of political strategy – as the engine-room or metropolitan core of global capital – and as furnishing the material basis for socialism. In 1965, for example, Anderson wrote that whilst 'in Asia, Africa and Latin-America, men will still struggle to create a socialism of privation and duress', only 'in the advanced capitalist countries' would it be possible to create 'a socialism of liberty and privilege'.[241]

However, the performance of the Wilson government, and the evident failure of structural reform and centre-left experiments, prompted the second New Left to look selectively beyond the First to the Third World for revolutionary inspiration. The general outlook of Anderson's 'Problems of Socialist Strategy' in 1965 – insurrectionism in the Third World, cultural contest and structural reform in the First – was not explicitly disavowed. But there was, by 1967, with the presentation of the second of Debray's two essays in the *Review*, a significant change in register. Insurrectionism in the Third World was no longer disparaged as a second-best option, applicable solely in conditions of scarcity and an underdeveloped civil society. On the contrary, the Leninist prospectus was embraced with some enthusiasm. With the failure of the 'policy of presence' in the First World, and the evaporation of optimism in the trajectory of the Second World with the advent of Brezhnev, for the time being militant injunctions on guerilla war in the Third World appeared the most promising strategic option on offer.

7. Contrasting the Two New Lefts

That a significant split divides two distinct New Lefts; that it originated in the change of editorial regime at the *NLR* in 1962; and that it was made public by the controversies of the mid-sixties – these have become commonplaces. Yet whilst Michael Kenny's recent study stresses the tensions between the two wings of the first New Left (the *New Reasoner* and *Universities and Left Review* groupings) – arguing that the formation was 'characterised, from its inception, by internal divisions which were impossible to resolve'[242] – he argues that the 'notion of a complete break' between the first and second New Lefts 'is a fanciful reconstruction which has suited both antagonists and their supporters'.[243] With one or two significant caveats, it is a judgement that I would broadly share.

The exchange over the Nairn-Anderson theses, for instance, was essentially conducted through the ill-tempered polemics of Thompson and Anderson; and although these two were, arguably, the respective driving forces in each of the two New Lefts, they were scarcely their sole representatives. Raymond Williams' perspective of a long cultural revolution, of which Thompson was sharply critical, was not radically dissimilar to Anderson's strategic outlook (a contest for cultural hegemony) in this period, and reminds us there were clear differences of opinion within the original New Left. Nor did all those associated with the first New Left necessarily see the controversy – at this early stage – in terms of a dispute that demarcated a first from a second New Left. For example, John Saville and Ralph Miliband – launched the *Socialist Register* in 1964 less as a regrouping of the first, as opposed to the second, New Left, than of the *New Reasoner* as opposed to the 'culturalist' *Universities and Left Review*, and its continuation, as they saw it, in the pre- *and* post-1962 *New Left Review*.[244] Moreover, it is hard to avoid the conclusion that the intemperance of the exchange was over-determined by a residual bitterness on Thompson's part, and a defensiveness on Anderson's, concerning the change in editorial control of the *Review*.

However, it would be wrong to ignore the very real substantive issues that demarcated the two New Lefts from the outset. The most obvious were, first, their contrasting estimates of the value of indigenous resources in shaping a socialist politics; and secondly, the post-1962 *NLR*'s insistence on the priority of ideas, tending to an intellectualism and distance from the labour movement and the perceived 'populism' of the first New Left.

While Thompson and others of the first New Left admired the strength of native socialist and progressive traditions, and tended to write of the imminence of socialism,[245] Anderson and Nairn reprehended the corporatist character of the labour movement, insisting, in Anderson's words, that the first New Left's 'almost complete failure to offer any structural analysis of British society ... automatically made the New Left's ambition to furnish a new socialist synthesis impossible',[246] and looking to continental Marxism to overcome the limitations of English moralism and empiricism. Their exchange pitted Thompson's 'social patriotism' – and subsequent disparagement of the 'new' *NLR*'s preoccupation with the experience of 'Other Countries'[247] – against Anderson and Nairn's 'national nihilism';[248] what Richard Johnson has characterised as 'a rather self-indulgent Anglophobia'.[249]

In his retrospective *Arguments Within English Marxism* (1980), Anderson traced the differences between the two New Lefts to their distinctive political-generational formations (a distinction which also accounts for the uneasy relationship between the *New Reasoner* and younger *ULR* wings of the first New Left).[250] Whereas, in 1965, Anderson had denounced Thompson's 'messianic nationalism' and 'maundering populism',[251] Thompson's 'patriotism' was now portrayed in a more generous light, recognised as having been shaped by the anti-fascist mobilisations of the thirties and the war years, and reinforced by the Communist Party's Cold War populist anti-Americanism. (John Callaghan writes of the party's 'super-patriotism' of the period 1941-47).[252] Anderson recognised that Thompson's repeated emphasis on Britain's special or leading role should not, for example, obscure the genuine internationalism of his politics and outlook. Anderson excused his own animus against all things indigenous by reference to his own political formation, for the conditions that had formed the political outlook of the younger editors of the post-1962 *NLR* were strikingly different: '[t]hey were colder. Untouched by the afterglow of the War, we never knew the popular elan of the 40s. It was the reactionary consolidation of the 50s that dominated our consciousness'.[253] The Cold War mobilisation, whilst never unleashing committees for the investigation of 'unBritish activities', was intent on consolidating British culture in a deeply conservative light: 'its major idiom was glutinously chauvinist – reverent worship of Westminster, ubiquitous cult of constitutional moderation and common sense, ritualised exaltation of tradition and precedent'.[254]

The sharpest divergence between the two New Lefts arose over the post-1962 *NLR*'s insistence on the priority of ideas. Whereas the first New Left had welcomed the emergence of a 'new' working class – with the growth of technical and scientific employment (the moment of Wilson's 'white hot heat of technology') and the expansion of higher education – seeing in this the development of a less economistic, and more broadly politicised, working class – the 'new' New Left, with its conception of hegemony confined to the realm of ideology, judged that an as-yet-to-be-made socialist intelligentsia, drawn in the main from outside the ranks of the working class, would prove the principal partisans of the socialist project. Miliband's judgment that 'the *New Reasoner* people were intellectuals *of* the labour movement', while 'the *ULR* people were intellectuals *for* the labour movement',[255] is a characterisation of the latter that applies more forcefully to the post-1962 *NLR*. In contrast to the preoccupations of the continuing New Left with the detailed *minutiae* of popular culture and the recovery of working-class 'history from below' (in the work of History Workshop, the Centre for Contemporary Cultural Studies, etc.), the post-1962 *Review* was oriented to 'high' theory and increasingly attuned to thinking in terms of 'epochs and continents'.[256]

Nonetheless, these important differences aside, the broad political perspective of the two New Lefts was not, at this stage, by any means wholly dissimilar. Writing in 1981, Ian Birchall argued that whilst the change in editorial control marked 'a significant shift in style and personnel … as far as politics was concerned there was no clear break'.[257] Anderson's 'Problems of Socialist Strategy', for example, was not ultimately incompatible with the strategic outlook of the first New Left; Anderson himself later critically reflected that it exhibited the 'illusions of Left Social-Democracy',[258] and the *Review*'s 1974 'Decennial Report' identified its 'quasi-reformist illusions' as 'the most vulnerable aspects of the Nairn-Anderson theses'[259] – a 'weakness' ignored, because shared, by Thompson.

There were, in fact, as many continuities as discontinuities between the two New Lefts in this period. Blurring the distinction between the two New Lefts, for instance, Kenny, following David Forgács, has identified the 'brokerage role' of the first New Left in laying the basis, through its development of cultural studies, for the ready reception of Gramscian ideas – more usually associated with the 'new' New Left – in the sixties and seventies, writing of the 'proto-Gramscian conclusions which some within the first New Left had reached'.[260] In terms of a 'national-popular' project, constructing a vernacular socialist politics, the first New Left was clearly closer to Gramsci,[261] a continuation, argues Bill Schwarz, of the work of the Communist Party's Historians' Group – of which Saville and the Thompsons were members[262] – in its attempt 'to reactivate a national-popular consciousness', and in which 'the Group cultivated a profound sense of *Englishness*'.[263] Thompson was surely right to argue that 'England is unlikely to capitulate before a Marxism which cannot at least engage in a dialogue in the English idiom'.[264] Similarly, Anderson's insistence that a socialist intelligentsia would be drawn from outside the working class is difficult to square with Gramsci's concept of 'organic intellectuals'. Curiously, the first New Left thus in some ways demonstrated a greater proximity to Gramscian emphases than Nairn, Anderson et al, and yet it was the latter which explicitly adopted Gramsci to examine the specifities of the British social formation, and to contrast what it perceived as the 'hegemonic' project of the PCI with the 'corporatism' of the Labour Party.

In sum, a brief recapitulation of the politics of the two New Lefts illustrates the far from complete character of the break effected either by the transfer of editorial control in 1962-3, or the polemics over the 'peculiarities' of the English in 1964-6. Substantive issues did divide the two New Lefts in this period; and Anderson's 'Conspectus' of late 1964 consciously demarcated a new chapter in the history of the *Review*. But a more decisive break occurred only in 1968, with the turn to revolutionary socialism, which was as much a discontinuity within the career of the 'new' New Left as a break between it and its forebears. This latter break has been read back into the editorial changeover in 1962-3, simplifying what was initially a less decisive, less neat, rupture between the two formations.

Chapter Two
The Moment of 1968

When the new editorial team inherited the *Review* in 1962 it was at the moment of the exhaustion and dispersal of the first New Left as a political movement. The West lay becalmed in the last years of the 'long boom' and a gloomy *NLR* editorial of 1967 noted that there 'is no major area of the non-Communist world where armed counter-revolution, executed or endorsed by the United States, has not registered a triumph in the last few years'.[1] In the Soviet Union the fall of Khrushchev in 1964 had effectively foreclosed the prospects of a de-Stalinising 'reform from above' (a cherished hope of the first New Left). Third Worldist anticipations had been similarly disabused. Frictions between the three worlds mapped by the *NLR* in 1963 had, to a considerable extent, stabilised. The Cold War had given way, if not to warmth, then at least to a grudging acknowledgement of the status quo: peaceful co-existence and the division of Europe had become accepted features of the international landscape. Soviet-American rivalry had been displaced to distances safe enough to preclude direct confrontation: to the Olympic Games, the 'space race', and self-contained wars-by-proxy. The era of colonial wars, and thus the sharpest period of confrontation between the First and Third Worlds, had largely passed, removing the principal cause of antagonism – national independence – without upsetting the global predominance of the West or the rule of capital.

The 'sharp left turn' envisaged in the 1964 'Conspectus' becomes evident only from around 1967, with the first examinations of the question of 'student power', and the *Review*'s forthright endorsement of Regis Debray's 'Guevarism'. But it was the events of 1968 that confirmed and deepened the *Review*'s left turn – in marked contrast to the first New Left, which temporarily regrouped around the *May Day Manifesto* and subsequent Convention of the Left.[2] Whereas the latter continued to seek a third way *between* social democracy and Communism, after 1968 the second New Left stood to the *left* of them both.

1. The Return of the Repressed

1968 may not have been a revolutionary year of the order of 1848, 1917 or even 1989. Existing regimes, though shaken, did not fall. However, while '1968' should not be mythologized, nor should its political impact be underestimated. The advantage of historical hindsight allows more sober judgement, but to hopeful revolutionaries and fearful conservatives alike it genuinely seemed that a new world might be in the making. Without warning, the relative social peace of the advanced capitalist countries was shattered. Suddenly, spectacularly history was on the move.

Between 1953 and 1966 'West Germany, France and Italy trebled, and the U.S. and Britain doubled, their gross national products'.[3] The majority of people in the West had indeed 'never had it so good'. Yet beneath the surface of unprecedented post-war economic growth and material prosperity, the half-hidden strains of industrialisation and urbanisation, of unsolved inequalities and new-found conflicts and contradictions – and not least, as we shall see, a rapid expansion of higher education – were about to be exposed, placing unbearable pressure upon archaic and illiberal structures of authority, from the governing bodies of universities to the 'Jim Crow' states of the American South.

A generation that had not known the privations of depression and war, born instead to rising expectations and widening horizons, was coming to maturity. Moreover, this was an exceptionally large generation, swollen by the post-war 'baby boom': in the USA more babies were born in 1948-53 than in the previous thirty years;[4] while André Glucksmann considered it politically significant that by 1971 one French worker in four would be under twenty-five.[5] This profound generational shift lent the moment of 1968 much of its edge and élan – aggravated, for example, in Germany by parental refusal to acknowledge and come to terms with the Nazi past, and especially marked in America, where the new generation had to largely reinvent the Left following the reactionary Cold War years of the late forties and fifties; and underlined and made strikingly visible by the burgeoning counter-culture, with its challenge to everyday mores of dress and social conduct. Alarmed conservatives no doubt felt the emergence of long-haired, colourfully-clothed, sexually-'liberated', dope-smoking youngsters to be as corrosive of bourgeois society as the more distant threat of Vietnamese-in-arms.[6]

While 1968 is sometimes mistakenly equated with student revolt, there can be no doubt that students and young people were often at the forefront of struggle, from America to Germany and France, from Belgrade to Mexico City, from Prague to the north of Ireland, from Madrid to Tokyo.

In response to the needs of modernising economies, students were being enrolled in unprecedented numbers. In pre-war Britain students had never numbered more than 70,000. The roll for 1954-5 numbered 122,000; for 1962-3, 216,000; and for 1965-6, 300,000. By 1967 students accounted for 11 per cent of their age group.[7] Between 1950 and 1964 student numbers doubled in Germany and trebled in France.[8] By 1967 there were six million university students in the United States (outnumbering the five-and-a-half million farmers and their employees),[9] two-and-a-half million in western Europe and one-and-a-half million in Japan.[10] To some, it seemed that the necessary expansion of higher education would prove an explosive, perhaps even fatal, contradiction at the heart of modern capitalism. In any event, such a rapid increase in numbers was disruptive in itself: facilities and resources failed to match the increased numbers, while subjection to the archaic paternalism of the university authorities (acting *in loco parentis*) was a common point of conflict.

If there was a single thread that linked the events of 1968, a trigger that set off the explosion, it was undoubtedly the war in Vietnam. It was, writes David Caute, the 'greatest evil of the age … Many other furies surfaced in the late sixties, but it was the systematic destruction of a people and its habitat, the moral collusion of European governments, which "over-determined" the fusion of other angers, political and cultural, into the international insurrection [of 1968].'[11] The Vietnam war unmasked the shocking illiberalism of the 'free world', thereby apparently blocking the path to meaningful reform – from the frustration of Johnson's 'Great Society', the limitations of Wilson, to the SPD's entry into a 'grand coalition' with the Christian Democrats in Germany. Might revolution be the only answer?

The Johnson administration matched its prosecution of an increasingly vicious war in South-East Asia with an inability, or unwillingness, to challenge the institutionalised racism of the Deep South. The pressing need and shrinking chances of winning the Democratic Party to a programme of reform undermined the civil rights movement's strategy of non-violence, resulting for example in the growth of the militant Black Panther Party, proclaiming the taking up of arms in self-defence against police violence, and an orientation to the more flammable Northern black ghettos: 34 died in the Watts riot in Los Angeles in 1965.[12] The 'Students for a Democratic Society' (SDS), principal organisational forum of the American New Left, was itself radicalised by the tide of events, paralleling the shift of the frustrated civil rights movement towards a politics of revolutionary intransigence.

To many in America, the mood in 1968 was apocalyptic. Despite the presence of half a million US troops, the Tet offensive – marking the Vietnamese

New Year, 31 January – brought the fighting into the very compound of the American embassy in Saigon. The war had no end in sight. Badly beaten in early Democratic primaries, Johnson withdrew from the forthcoming Presidential contest. The assassinations of Martin Luther King in April (sparking riots in '167 cities',[13] involving 75,000 National Guardsmen on the streets, and leaving 39 dead)[14] and Robert Kennedy (having just won the Democrat's California primary) in June, and the police riot at the Democratic Party's August Convention in Chicago (at which the party machine secured Hubert Humphrey's nomination over the principal anti-war candidate, Eugene McCarthy), beating protestors, journalists, and McCarthy's staff alike on the 15th floor of the Hilton Hotel, seemed to draw a line against reform and to sound the death-knell of American liberalism. The 'promise of redemption' seemed to have passed out of US politics.[15]

The American New Left appeared to be caught between an 'impossible revolution'[16] and the lengthening shadow of counter-revolution: by May 1970, 14 students had been shot dead on American campuses by the police and para-military National Guard;[17] a concerted FBI campaign to eliminate the Black Panther Party was to lead to the shooting dead of 44 militants in the period 1970-5.[18] These were years, recalls Todd Gitlin (a leading SDS activist), lived like a 'cyclone in wind tunnel'.[19] 'It was not a moment for thinking small'.[20]

In western Europe, the storm-centre was initially over West Germany. As in America, the apparent blocking of the path to reform – the SPD's governing coalition with the Right and its pending Emergency Powers Act – left an increasingly militant student-led New Left (the *Socialistische Deutsche Studentbund*) as the principal, and by now self-proclaimed revolutionary, opposition. A confrontational International Vietnam Congress, held in the Cold War citadel of West Berlin in February 1968, was followed by the attempted assassination of Rudi Dutschke, one of the principal student leaders, resulting in five days of violent confrontation with the police over Easter 1968, leaving two killed and 400 injured.[21] But it was when the eye of the storm passed through Paris that revolutionary change appeared, albeit fleetingly, a tangible prospect. For France proved different in one highly significant respect: student protest sparked and paralleled – though never quite integrated into a single movement – the revolt of the working class, in an unprecedented wave of strikes and occupations.

As if to prove Mao's adage that a single spark could truly ignite a prairie fire, mounting student protest, inflamed by the repressive measures of the university authorities and police brutality, erupted in a night of violent confrontation on the Left Bank (10-11 May). In protest against police violence, and to demand the release of arrested students, the main trade union confederations held a one day general strike on 13 May (coincidentally the tenth anniversary of de Gaulle's coup), and the biggest demonstration Paris had seen since the end of the war. Unexpectedly, and against the intentions of the trade union leaderships, the buoyant mood spilled over into a widening rank-and-file led movement of strikes and factory occupations. Within days 10 million workers were on strike – the biggest strike in history. It was a bolt from the blue, catching everyone off balance. Even for an 'old leftist' such as Eric Hobsbawm, it 'seemed to demonstrate what practically no radical over the age of twenty-five, including Mao Tse-tung and Fidel Castro, believed, namely that revolution in an advanced capitalist country was possible in conditions of peace, prosperity, and apparent political stability.'[22]

With the government paralysed, France stood on the brink of revolution. On 29 May De Gaulle left Paris to take refuge at Baden-Baden in Germany with the French Army of the Rhine. Revolution, however, was the last thing on the minds of those capable of giving the movement leadership and direction, namely, the Communist-led CGT and the PCF itself. The trade unions sought to channel the strike movement towards negotiable economic demands, while the political parties of the Left, the PCF included, manoeuvred to form a government entrusted with settling the crisis.

However, reinforced by General Massau's assurance of the Army's loyalty, de Gaulle returned to Paris, mobilising the Gaullist party machine for a massive counter-demonstration and, abandoning the earlier plan for a referendum that would have issued in his resignation if defeated, instead called a snap parliamentary election. Eager to demonstrate their democratic respectability, the PCF and CGT demobilised the strike movement. Red May turned to white June, to de Gaulle's renewed parliamentary mandate; the employers' offensive, attended by police violence and several deaths, that brought a piecemeal end to the strikes and occupations; the banning of the organisations of the far left; and the symbolic release of General Salan, leader of the far-right terrorist OAS, from prison.

Despite the denouement of June, it was the experience of May – alternately heady or alarming, depending on one's perspective – that stayed at the forefront of most people's minds. Coming so unexpectedly 'out of the blue', when or where might it strike next?

The defeat of the French May did not induce disappointment. On the contrary, arising so unexpectedly, it was seen as the harbinger of a new revolutionary epoch. In Tom Nairn's account, it 'did not fail because it was too weak and secondary an event … It failed because it was too big, too novel, and inevitably dwarfed most of the circumstances around it. It was heavy

with a significance too great for our times to bear, a premonitory significance which the events of May could only sketch in outline, like a vivid,
troubled dream experienced just before waking'.[23] Although the revolutionary moment was lost, a rude shock had been dealt to liberal, social democratic and, indeed, Communist complacencies, for 'the spectre of revolution
demonstrated in the streets that it still haunts Europe'.[24]

Moreover, for the *NLR* this was to be a revolution of a distinctly classical
type. The special issue on the French May, number 52, November/December
1968 (carrying the banner heading borrowed from Lenin, 'Festival of the
Oppressed'), marked the *NLR*'s unambiguous affiliation to the revolutionary Left. On the central issue of the May Events, the role of the Communist
Party in demobilising the movement, the *NLR* was unequivocal. Instead of
seeking 'a return to normality, to the idyll of bourgeois politics and capitalist
parliaments, to the dream of an electoral majority', the PCF's 'motto should
have been that of Danton: "Audacity, more audacity, still more audacity!"'[25]
For 'the choice was not simply between two kinds of tactics but between
two kinds of consciousness and, ultimately, two kinds of society', argued the
Review (in Sartrean vein): 'The voter in the polling booth is pre-eminently
private, atomised, serialised ... In the occupied factory, in the Soviet-style
assembly, political life is public, collective; individuals form fused groups ...
The context determines the consciousness'.[26] Thus, as the old order broke
down, the 'revolution demanded the prolongation of abnormality, the production of a new order of consciousness: latent aspirations and ideas, suffo-
cated by ordinary life, would become manifest and dominant – an authentic
new majority would inaugurate a new epoch'.[27]

While Britain was touched only by the outer ripples of the year's principal events, echoing them in minor key, it was far from insulated from
the global drama. There were student occupations (at the LSE, Essex, and
Hull, among others) and the marches of the Vietnam Solidarity Campaign
(VSC), with attempts to break police lines and storm the American embassy
in Grosvenor Square, culminating in a 100,000 strong demonstration in
October 1968, prior to which *The Times*, on 5 September, in witness to the
feverish atmosphere induced by the May Events in France, carried a front
page story claiming that during the demonstration key buildings in London
would be seized as the signal to revolution!

The *New Left Review* was in no doubt that 1968 signalled (in uncharacter-
istically Freudian terms) the welcome 'return of the repressed' in the West.[28]
Writing in the one hundredth issue of the *Review* in 1977, the editorial collective reflected that it 'was not until the May Events in 1968 that the idea of
the actuality of the revolution transformed political consciousness through-

out the capitalist world.'[29] So far as the *New Left Review* was concerned, the question of the transition to socialism in one or more of the advanced capitalist countries had been placed firmly on the political agenda, framing its intellectual and political endeavours for a decade or more.

Despite its more limited bearing on the evolution of the *NLR*, we should not let 1968 pass without reference to the third great convulsion of that year, namely the Prague Spring, which was about to enter its moment of crisis as the dust began to settle in France. The most economically advanced country in the Second World, Czechoslovakia arguably contained the most acute contradictions of 'actually existing socialism' and potentially the most advantageous prospects for a mature – post-Stalinist, post-'primitive accumulation' – socialist democracy.[30] A programme of economic reforms, including a 'price mechanism' responsive to a liberalised market, were not in themselves markedly radical, being implemented by a technocratic reform group within the Communist leadership. It was the coincidence of demands for political liberalisation and the invasion by Soviet and allied troops on 20 August that raised the stakes, prompting a general strike, the disaffection of prominent intellectuals, and student occupations of the universities. An Extraordinary Congress of the Czechoslovak Communist Party was held, in defiance of the invaders, on the initiative of the Party in Prague. However, the Party leadership's unwillingness to countenance resistance to the invasion doomed the Prague Spring to a slow death, confirmed by Dubcek's capitulation to the 'Moscow Protocols', and his demotion in April 1969. The intervention demonstrated the decisive ascendancy of authoritarian conservatives over reformers within the Soviet leadership, and entrenched the neo-Stalinist course pursued by Brezhnev in the Soviet Union, although the suppression of the Prague Spring won near-universal condemnation from the Communist Parties of western Europe. So far as the *NLR* was concerned, the Soviet action attested to the counter-revolutionary character of official Communism, radicalising its anti-Stalinism and reinforcing its gravitation towards the revolutionary Left.[31]

In the First World modest openings to the centre-left, 'structural reform', or the implicit 'war of position' in civil society advocated by Anderson in 'Problems of Socialist Strategy', were abandoned. Revolution was now on the agenda, though the agency (or agencies), strategy and tactics, and even the goal of such a transformation were far from settled questions. In the Second World, hopes of reform from within the bureaucratic dictatorships of the ruling Communist Parties were abandoned. Again, revolution appeared the only way forward. Illusions in any inherently progressive vocation on the part of the Third World had, as we have seen, already been renounced by the

NLR. Even where significant social forces could be mobilised under revolutionary leadership, the prospects of a meaningful transition to socialism in conditions of relative scarcity appeared bleak.

Insisting that primacy should be accorded neither to the proletariat of the West, the peasantry of the South, nor the states of the East, the *NLR* judged, in Althusserian vein, that global productive relations constituted a complex dynamic; even though its ultimate determination was to be found in the contest between capital and labour in the advanced capitalist countries, the dominant contradiction might today lie in the Third World.[32] The decisive factor in Third World struggle would be its impact on the global balance of class forces, but particularly in the core countries of metropolitan capitalism. In this, argued Göran Therborn in 'From Petrograd to Saigon' in the *NLR* in 1968, the Vietnamese revolution was exemplary – an analysis that, in Anderson's later judgement, 'provided what arguably remains to this day the best synthesis of the historical meaning of this signal moment'.[33]

In Therborn's estimate, the Cold War confrontation between an affluent capitalism and a backward 'socialism' (of sorts) had resulted in 'a long penalisation of socialism'.[34] The Western working class 'was by and large mobilised in the anti-Communist crusade, because of its fear of the Soviet model, symbolised by a regime of shortages and repression',[35] putting the Left on the defensive. The war in Vietnam was of a different order: one in which a national liberation movement confronted the barbarous excesses of US militarism. 'Socialism here is no longer a dull, harsh austerity threatening the consumers of the West, but a heroic fight by exploited and starving peoples for a human existence.'[36] It placed the contest between rival social systems and forces in a qualitatively different light:

> whereas … the Cold War *blocked* the contradictions within capitalism, the Vietnamese conflict has *detonated* the contradictions within US capitalism itself … The Vietnamese Revolution has … done what no other economic or political force in the world has achieved for 30 years – it has shattered the cemented unity of American society and at last *reactivated* its internal contradictions … Imperialism is today on the defensive. The social peace installed by the Cold War is disintegrating in the vortex of the Vietnamese War. The tranquil conscience of 1949 has become the brutalised demoralisation of 1968.[37]

Therborn underlined the dialectical relationship between Third World revolution and the challenge to metropolitan capitalism, for if revolutions were more likely in poorer countries on the periphery of the global capitalist system – where social contradictions were more explosive, and a 'national-popular' identity readily forged into a progressive weapon against the dominant capitalist-imperialist states – they would inevitably be faced with almost insurmountable difficulties in sustaining their momentum in conditions of isolation and scarcity. Their principal impact would be measured in terms of their effects on the core countries of metropolitan capitalism, whose own social contradictions tended to be more muted and relatively stabilised. In this sense the Vietnamese revolution was of fundamental significance: its successes achieved a decisive, if temporary, weakening of the United States.

> When some half a million American troops with enormous technological superiority are no longer capable of keeping even the US embassy in Saigon safe, the most rabid spokesmen of imperialism have temporarily lapsed into a stunned silence. The incredible heroism of the Vietnamese militants has awed the world. They have proved, once and for all, that revolutionary peoples, not imperialism, are invincible.[38]

Ultimately, the American Left was unable to seize the moment. As in Germany, and unlike France and Italy, the working class remained quiescent. The Democratic Party proved unwilling to embrace a platform of reform and opposition to the war in Vietnam. The faction-torn New Left imploded. Yet Nixon's escalation of the conflict to neighbouring Cambodia and Laos, and violent repression of opposition (for example, the shooting dead of four students at Kent State University, Ohio, by the National Guard in May 1970), intensified anti-war sentiment in America. The prosecution of a hopeless war appeared increasingly irrational, not least because of its divisive domestic impact, and the demoralisation of the army – including the breakdown of military discipline, desertion, extensive drug-taking, and 'fragging', i.e., the killing of unpopular officers (official figures list a minimum of 788 incidents and 86 deaths for the period 1969-72).[39] Meanwhile, the scandal of the Watergate affair first paralysed the Presidency and finally brought a premature end to Nixon's second term in 1974.

America's liberal credentials, and its geo-political standing, had never, in the post-war period, stood so low. This, in spite of the eclipse of the American New Left, was central to the coming conjuncture, which would end, far from coincidentally, with the determined reassertion of American power in the late seventies.

2. 'Combat Bourgeois Ideas'

If revolution was indeed on the agenda in the West, the *NLR* was initially attracted, in the first rush of the events of 1968, to the student movement as its principal bearers, both because militant student organisations were unquestionably at the forefront of the struggles of that year, and, perhaps more significantly, in the words of the *Review*, because higher education might prove 'the weakest link in the chain, the most vulnerable point' of modern capitalist society.[40]

As early as 1960, C. Wright Mills – in a 'Letter to the New Left' critical of the British New Left's attachment to the working class as '*the* historic agency' of social change – had identified the radicalism of the 'young intelligentsia' as pivotal.[41] Indeed, in the United States students were in the vanguard of the civil rights and anti-war movements of the sixties. The SDS, numbering perhaps as many as 100,000 members at its peak in 1968-9,[42] was, as we have noted, the organisational focus of the American New Left. A similar part was played by the German SDS in West Germany. The May Events in France brought to prominence, together with the looser March 22nd Movement initiated by the students at Nanterre (in which 'Danny the Red', Daniel Cohn-Bendit, was a leading figure), the Trotskyite *Jeunesse Communiste Révolutionnaire* (the JCR) and the Maoist *Union des Jeunesses Communistes - marxistes-léninistes* (the UJC), both originating in groups recently expelled from the Communist Party's student organisation. These organisations remained small, however, as did their British counterparts – though here, too, the combined strength of the largely student-based International Socialists and the smaller (Fourth Internationalist) International Marxist Group, though no more than a few hundred, soon eclipsed the doctrinaire *groupuscules* of the existing far left, such as the Healyite Socialist Labour League and Militant.

It was to this milieu that the *New Left Review* swiftly gravitated, hailing the 1967 'revolt' at the London School of Economics as 'an important stage in the formation of student consciousness in this country';[43] the occupation was 'an extraordinary achievement. It should not remain unique.'[44] Further occupations – principally at Hull, Essex, Hornsey Art College, London, and the LSE again – during 1968 led to a radicalisation of the student movement. A short-lived Radical Students Alliance (embracing the Labour Left, Communists and Young Liberals) was superseded by the formation of the Revolutionary Socialist Students' Federation (RSSF) in June 1968. The *NLR* 'collectively participated as a group' in its founding conference at the LSE, 'where it won a leading position in the organisation'.[45] The RSSF's uncompromising eleven-point manifesto, committed 'to the revolutionary overthrow of capitalism and imperialism and its replacement by workers power',[46] was reprinted in full in the *Review*. For the *NLR*, the RSSF and the Vietnam Solidarity Campaign represented 'the first, embryonic expressions' of a 'united revolutionary organisation' in Britain.[47]

The revolutionary mood was infectious. 'Everybody was terribly young', recalls Anthony Barnett, 'and didn't know what was going on. One had a sort of megalomaniac attitude that by sheer protest and revolt things would be changed …. The desire to do something became tremendously intense …'[48] The *NLR* embraced the temper of the times, reflected in the romantic, unflinching and voluntarist icons of the moment: Mao, Ho and above all the martyred Che, whose unbending – and unhelpfully simplistic – injunction (proclaimed in the Second Declaration of Havana, 1962) captured the moment perfectly: 'The duty of the revolutionary is to make the revolution'. The *Review*'s revolutionary intransigence may be gauged by its endorsement of urban guerillas in Brazil, 'imaginatively reviving the Leninist tactic of "partisan war in the towns"';[49] a generous appraisal of Blanqui on the centenary of the Paris Commune, and the publication of his 'Instructions for an Uprising';[50] and the republication in 1970 by the newly created New Left Books of the Comintern handbook, *Armed Insurrection*.[51]

The generational divide that was so much a part of '1968' is nowhere more in evidence than in the contrasting reactions to the student revolt. While the *NLR* was fully committed to the student strikes, demonstrations and occupations, those of an older leftist generation – including some of the first New Left – kept a wary, and sometimes hostile, distance, at odds with the militant bravado of student politics, and often finding themselves, as tenured staff, on the opposite side of the institutional fence to the student insurgents.[52] The exceptions – Herbert Marcuse in America, Jean-Paul Sartre in France – merely underscored the general rule.

For those at the *New Left Review* there would be a high personal price to pay for their part in the revolt. Robin Blackburn and Tom Nairn lost their academic posts, Blackburn as assistant lecturer in sociology at the LSE, Nairn as lecturer in the history of art at Hornsey College.[53] Anthony Barnett, Ben Brewster (at the LSE), and David Fernbach (recently recruited to the *Review* via the agitation at the LSE) were all penalised in different ways.[54]

The *NLR*'s infatuation with the possibilities of the student revolt was nowhere better illustrated than in its call to turn the universities into 'red bases'. Acknowledging the classical claim that 'the only social class in industrial countries capable of making the revolution is the working class', the RSSF manifesto nevertheless judged 'that the institutions of higher education are a comparatively weak link in British capitalism.'[55] It proposed that 'correctly waged struggles for student control and for universities of revolutionary criticism' would yield 'red bases',[56] providing 'embryos of a new social order', which might, as in France in May 1968, detonate wider social conflict and act as 'strategic pivots' in the development of a revolutionary dual power.[57]

The distinctly Maoist banner headline 'Red Bases' carried by *NLR* 53 (January/February 1969) was only partially qualified by the accompanying question-mark: no such restraint was shown by the four contributors on the subject of student tactics, who uniformly emphasised the call of the RSSF to 'build red bases'. The articles – by 'James Wilcox' (i.e., Robin Blackburn), David Triesman, David Fernbach and Anthony Barnett – were liberally peppered with slogans that spoke to the mood of the moment: 'guerilla strategy', 'raising consciousness', 'the mass line', 'popular assemblies', 'red democracy', 'focos', and 'protracted people's war'.[58] 'In the face of threats to close a college', wrote Fernbach, 'we must show that we are prepared to run it – as a Commune.'[59] Mao, Lenin and Debray were quoted at length, and analogies with guerilla warfare much in evidence. 'We must ask ourselves', wrote 'Wilcox', 'whether the complex structures of late capitalism do not contain areas, *sociologically* inaccessible to the repressive forces of the ruling class, which can become growing points of revolutionary power?'[60] His answer was in the affirmative: 'The Red Base concretely incarnates one aspect of the *maximum* programme of the revolution – popular power.'[61]

However, the RSSF had but a brief life, barely surviving its first 'plenary conference' at the Round House (Chalk Farm, London) in November 1968; by all accounts a chaotic affair, dogged by Maoist intransigence and 'Situationist comedy': 'If several people weren't on the CIA payroll', David Widgery concluded, 'they deserved to be'.[62] The two dominant groups within the RSSF, the International Socialists and those grouped around the *NLR*, patched together a constitution that kept the RSSF alive into 1969.[63]

The *NLR*'s part in the student movement was complemented by a commitment to political journalism. Sharing the same Carlisle Street building in Soho, the fortnightly *Black Dwarf* was launched in June 1968, the cover of its first issue uncompromisingly emblazoned, 'PARIS, LONDON, ROME, BERLIN. WE WILL FIGHT, WE SHALL WIN.' As a broadly based paper of the revolutionary left (backed by Clive Goodwin, a well-connected socialite and 'left-wing literary agent who was' its 'driving force'),[64] under the editorship of Tariq Ali, unwittingly designated student 'leader' by the media, the *Black Dwarf* had a print-run of 30,000.[65] Fred Halliday[66] of the *Black Dwarf*'s editorial committee joined the *NLR* late in 1968, and the link between the two journals was formalised in 1969 when Anthony Barnett and Robin Blackburn joined the *Black Dwarf* 'with the official sanction of

NLR',[67] with the aim of 'creating a revolutionary weekly, in parallel to the review'.[68] However, signalling tensions within the *Review*'s editorial collective between those oriented to the classical Trotskyite tradition and others embracing a broader, libertarian, and more contemporary perspective, Robin Blackburn and Branka Magaš departed the *Black Dwarf* in 1970 to found the IMG-affiliated *Red Mole*, leaving Anthony Barnett and Fred Halliday at the *Black Dwarf*. Neither paper was destined to last, though the attempt to sustain a weekly newspaper in tandem with the *NLR* would soon be attempted again.

Equally ambitious in scope, and more successful, was the launch in 1970 of the *Review*'s publishing house, New Left Books (NLB, later Verso), under the direction of Ronald Fraser. Its remit was not merely 'to further *New Left Review*'s established policy of making available to English-language readers major works of the European Marxist tradition', but to help fashion an indigenous Anglo-Marxism: 'to make possible the extension of the work of the NLR's editors and contributors as authors in their own right … so as to help create an English-language sector of Marxist work eventually comparable in concentration to NLB's European Marxist translations'.[69] Emblematic of the times, the *Review* also embarked on a major project in collaboration with Penguin Books: a paperback 'Marx Pelican Library' under the general editorship of Quintin Hoare. It included the first English edition of the *Grundrisse*, heralded by its translator Martin Nicolaus in the *Review* in 1968 as a 'work … of epochal significance';[70] three volumes of political writings, edited and introduced by David Fernbach; a volume of *Early Writings* introduced by Lucio Colletti; and a new translation (by Ben Fowkes and David Fernbach) of the three volumes of *Capital*, introduced by Ernest Mandel.

Meanwhile, the *NLR* was keen to explore wider, and arguably momentous, questions about revolutionary prospects in the advanced capitalist countries. In the introduction to a special collection on *Student Power*, produced jointly by the *NLR* with Penguin Books in 1969, Alexander Cockburn argued that '[t]he emergence of the student movement promises a renewal of revolutionary politics as well as the arrival of a new social force.'[71] The belief that the affluent societies of the advanced capitalist West were immune to social revolution had been exploded by the French May. Far from muting the conflict between capital and labour, contemporary capitalism had apparently heightened it. The expansion of higher education was the inescapable consequence of the increased demand for technical and intellectual labour in the reproduction of capital. Cockburn argued that in modern capitalist society, where 'work is robbed of meaning … [t]eams of work study engineers, ergonomists, labour relations experts, industrial psychologists and sociologists' are required 'to ensure that the maximum surplus labour is extracted with the minimum of trouble.'[72] Equally, 'market researchers, media planners, account executives, copywriters and so forth' are needed to 'alleviate the curse of over-production', and fuel the 'process of the *spectacle* and spectacular consumption'.[73] Whereas the old industrial working class was necessarily constrained by its atomised experience and conception of the world, the new technical and intellectual fractions of the working class were capable of perceiving the overall character of bourgeois society, and mounting a more comprehensive challenge to it, tabling more global demands that could not simply be bought off with higher wages. Moreover, it was becoming increasingly difficult to 'conceal from the masses the fact that the material preconditions for social liberation already exist'.[74] The expansion of technical and intellectual labour, capable of challenging capitalism as a *system*, was thus potentially an explosive contradiction at the heart of capitalism. In classical Marxist terms, 'the increasing integration of manual and mental labour, of intellectual and productive work' heralded the revolutionary moment when, in the words of the RSSF manifesto of November 1968, 'this productive force comes into sharpening conflict with the institutional nature of capitalism'.[75]

In similar vein, if more apocalyptic in tone, in a text which, despite being closer to anarchism than Marxism (and complementing Angelo Quattrocchi's prose-poem to the glory of Paris '68), the *Review* considered an 'essential complement'[76] to its special issue on the May Events, Tom Nairn judged that this 'Utopic generation is *by far* the most revolutionary one the system has ever produced': '[c]apitalism is generating its negation, and its fate, within its nerve-centres, because it is helpless to do anything else.'[77] For Nairn, 'civilisation', commencing in 'the era of the Neolithic villages ... has attained something like its natural goal':[78] communism was now materially feasible. Moreover, 'the development of mental production', he argued, 'rather than the tensions inherent in the matrix of material production, becomes the directly "revolutionary" agent which will finally compel the transformation' of society in the direction of communism.[79]

Such expectations – sharing much in common with early New Left themes on the emergence of a 'new working class' – were to prove misplaced. Moreover, neither the expansion of technical and intellectual labour nor relative material abundance would pose any inherent threat to the production and reproduction of capital (any more than so transient a social stratum as students were capable of constituting a new 'social force'). Capital's remorseless commodification of life and its small pleasures, its propensity to fashion new ever-expanding 'needs' should not be underestimated. Its

rapid colonisation and 'marketisation' of the music, clothes and other trap-
pings of the counter-culture is a case in point.

As the more extravagant hopes invested in 1968 proved illusory, a small,
frustrated minority turned to violence. Parallel with the disintegration of the
student New Left as an organised force in America came the Weathermen's
'Days of Rage' and bombings.[80] In Germany, frustration at the failure to win
the trade unions or rank and file to a worker-student 'Extra-Parliamentary
Opposition' to the Emergency Powers Act (passed by the Grand Coalition in
1969), led to the terrorist campaign of the Red Army Fraction (the 'Baader-
Meinhof gang'). Even in Italy, where stronger student-worker links were
forged during the upsurge of the 'hot autumn' of 1969, and the far left won
more adherents than elsewhere, the 1972 Fanfani government's strategy of
tension, carrying the threat of authoritarian rule, found a response in the
'armed actions', bombings and kidnappings of the Red Brigades. The formation of the Provisional IRA was very much of this moment. In Britain,
where the impact of 1968 had been less momentous, its fall-out was com-
mensurably less dramatic, the Angry Brigade being but the faintest of echoes of the tendency to armed violence.

The *Review*'s revolutionary expectations did not diminish after 1968, despite the waning of the student insurgency, 'to which so much' of the *NLR*'s
'hope and energy had been committed'.[81] Even at the height of its attraction
to the student revolt the *NLR* maintained an ultimate, if admittedly distant,
commitment to the working class as the agency of socialist transformation.
As the student movement went into sharp decline, and the goal of making
'red bases' of the universities proved patently untenable, attention re-fo-
cused on the working class as the historic agency of revolutionary change.
Such an orientation was not exceptional. For some of the student Left, it
meant taking up work in factories (or at least selling papers at the factory
gates), winning recruits from amongst the workers, and attempting to build
militant rank-and-file organisations to challenge the trade union bureauc-
racies. For the *NLR*, however, this commitment was largely to labour in the
abstract, to the proletariat as the *deus ex machina* of socialist revolution. It
made no attempt to make a strategic analysis of the labour movement (or
even make much contact with it). Indeed, coverage of domestic politics, the
greatest strike-wave and industrial unrest since the General Strike notwithstanding, was, as we shall see, all but abandoned.

Above all, the *NLR* was committed to the centrality of ideas and intellectuals. The *Review* argued that while 'the May events vindicated the fundamental socialist belief that the industrial proletariat is the revolutionary
class of advanced capitalism', a crucial and revealing caveat was added: the

French May 'has, at the same stroke, made indisputable the vital revolution-ary role of intellectuals, of all generations', judging that the 'student revolt in France achieved an international peak, at least partly because – with all their faults – French intellectuals have in the last 10 years created perhaps the most advanced Marxist culture in the world.'[82]

No-one better attests the commitment to theory than Perry Anderson. Temperamentally attuned to the 'longer durées',[83] he was, of all those at the *NLR*, most immune to the excitements of the moment, wary of the transient nature and political fragility of the students as a social force.[84] Appropriately – though no doubt more by chance than design – Anderson's 'Components of the National Culture', magisterially above the fray, appeared in the fiftieth issue of the *Review* to the background of unrest at Hull, Essex and the LSE. Carrying on its cover the Maoist injunction to 'Combat Bourgeois Ideas', there is no mistaking the *Review*'s primary focus in prosecuting a war of ideas, a struggle against the dominant bourgeois ideology, where the 'stu-dent movement obviously has special responsibilities'.[85] In 'Components', Anderson concluded that if a 'revolutionary culture is not for tomorrow … a revolutionary practice within culture is possible and necessary today', discerning in the 'student struggle … its initial form.'[86]

Although surveying the 'Components of the National Culture' discipline by discipline, Anderson's motive was not to map them in isolation, but to 'achieve a *structural* analysis of them … located in the inter-relationship between the disciplines which compose it … It is not the content of the individual sectors that determines the essential character of each so much as the ground-plan of their distribution'.[87] British culture was characterised above all by its 'absent centre', lacking as it did the synthesising theory that would have been capable of capturing 'the "structure of structures" – the social totality as such',[88] whether classical sociology or Marxism. The natu-ralisation of just such a revolutionary theory was Anderson's remedy to the 'deadly' and 'chloroforming effect' of a British culture that operated 'against the growth of any revolutionary Left' by depriving it 'of any source of con-cepts and categories with which to analyse its own society, and thereby at-tain a fundamental precondition for changing it'.[89]

It was to the making of just such a 'synthetic', 'totalising' 'revolutionary culture' that the *NLR* would thus devote its energies. For if creating a rev-olutionary culture was *the* central precondition for the development of a socialist politics, then intellectuals would be its privileged bearers, the *New Left Review* its vehicle – and its editors, perhaps, its vanguard. (Ironically, the decisive mediating role apportioned to intellectuals drew much from the earlier influence of Sartre, and the model of *Les Temps Modernes*, just at the moment that Sartre himself was proclaiming 'a self-flagellating anti-intellectualism',[90] adopting instead, along with many of the *gauchistes* of '68, a Maoist-populist faith in the elemental class-consciousness of the workers.)

We shall turn to this question of a revolutionary culture shortly. But first, how did Anderson account for this 'absent centre'? Grounding his argument in the historical analysis presented in the Nairn-Anderson theses, Anderson argued that the industrial bourgeoisie, 'traumatised by the French Revolution and fearful of the nascent working-class movement',[91] had acquiesced in the continued pre-eminence of the landed elite. Thus the British bourgeoisie 'never had to recast society as a whole, in concrete historical practice. It consequently never had to rethink society as a whole, in abstract theoretical reflection. Empirical, piece-meal intellectual disciplines corresponded to humble, circumscribed social action.'[92]

This initial absence was subsequently challenged neither by an indigenous Marxism, nor by the wars, occupations and revolutions that marked European history in the first half of the twentieth century. Exposure to a 'White Emigration' from the troubled continent only deepened the conservatism of British culture. An extraordinary preponderance of expatriates was registered by Anderson: Popper and Berlin in social and political theory; Wittgenstein in philosophy; Namier in history; Malinowski in anthropology; Klein in psychoanalysis; Eysenck in psychology; and Gombrich in aesthetics, to name only the most prominent. The *émigrés* served to reinforce the native propensity to reject synthesising 'continental' doctrines. Namier, for example, considered England peculiarly blessed, 'a land built on instinct and custom, free from the ruinous contagion of Europe – general ideas'.[93] 'Established English culture', wrote Anderson, 'naturally welcomed these unexpected allies. Every insular reflex and prejudice was powerfully flattered and enlarged in the convex mirror they presented to it'.[94]

In two disciplines only did Anderson discern an attempt to construct a totalising perspective. The first was anthropology, which, practiced at a safe temporal and geographical distance, was 'useful to colonial administration and dangerous to no domestic prejudice'.[95] The second was literary criticism, which, through Leavis, had sought to establish itself as pre-eminent among the humanities: a claim that 'should be seen, not as a reflection of megalomania on the part of Leavis, but as a symptom of the objective vacuum at the centre of the culture'.[96] Wittgenstein's reorientation of philosophy to the 'technical' study of language licenced literary criticism's forays into 'ethics', allowing Leavis to claim for English Literature the crown of moral and social criticism. However, the design, in Anderson's estimate, failed because Leavis either could or would not defend his literary judgements theoretically – he constructed no *system*. 'The paradox of this great critic is that his whole oeuvre rested on a metaphysic which he could never expound or defend. Empiricism here found its strangest expression.'[97] Nonetheless, given the void where sociology should have been, the achievements of literary criticism counted for something: 'It was logical that it should finally be the one sector capable of producing a synthetic socialist theory'[98] – namely, the work of Raymond Williams.

Reaffirming his conviction that a successful challenge to bourgeois culture would be of decisive importance, Anderson wrote that a 'political science capable of guiding the working-class movement to final victory will only be born within a general intellectual matrix which challenges bourgeois ideology in every sector of thought and represents a decisive, hegemonic alternative to the cultural status quo'.[99] However the essay, bearing the stamp of Althusser in addition to that of Gramsci, signalled a significant departure from the reformist premise of the mid-sixties: a cultural contest in civil society was no longer seen as a sufficient strategy for attaining socialism. The success of such a contest was an all-important *pre-condition*, but not a substitute, for the revolutionary transfer of political power. Whilst this presented a surer analysis of the revolutionary task to hand, Anderson continued to confine the construction of a socialist counter-hegemony to the realm of culture and ideology, effectively sealed off from the world of organised labour and its existing institutions.

3. A Revolutionary Politics

What would be the precise character of the revolutionary theory that the *NLR* desired to occupy the absent centre? In an unpublished editorial discussion document, 'The *Coupure* of May' (1968/9), the *NLR* identified three principal sources and component parts of contemporary Marxism, examining each in turn: Western Marxism, Trotskyism and Maoism.

Western Marxism had 'occupied the front stage in the whole intellectual history from 1922 of the European Left',[100] and as 'an indigenous and authentic reflection of the advanced and stabilised societies of Europe during the past four decades'[101] it had been central to the *Review*'s own project of naturalising Marxism in Britain. However, it had one critical flaw (rehearsing Anderson's later judgement in *Considerations on Western Marxism*, 1976), for it had 'advanced via an unending detour from any revolutionary political practice', reducing it to 'an esoteric discipline'.[102]

Meanwhile, two other major currents within Marxism had 'erupted into the centre of political attention with the French upheaval'; namely, 'the work of Trotsky and the thought of Mao Tse Tung'.[103] There is no doubt that the

NLR was more attuned to the latter than the former. Trotskyism, rooted in the 'tremendous mass upheaval' of the October Revolution, 'always had a direct relationship to it'.[104] As such, it displayed at times an 'archaism'; the product of a 'delayed birth', for 'it precisely *post-dated* the Revolution, when the experience that made it possible had already disappeared', and was thus in 'a sense ... not a theory but a *memory* of mass practice'.[105] In Tom Nairn's damning account, the Trotskyites 'remained the guardians of the flame, in a world that would not catch fire': a 'profoundly conservative' task.[106]

By contrast, Maoism 'was and is the systematic theory of the largest mass revolutionary practice history has ever seen'.[107] Thus it was judged 'of an order comparable to Lenin', indeed 'in certain respects it surpasses Lenin'.[108] The document concluded that Maoism 'clearly ... has a long future in front of it'.[109] The 'fundamental determinant' that differentiated the Russian and Chinese Revolutions was that the latter 'was based on the enthusiastic support of the majority class of the country – the peasantry ... whereas the civil war in Russia largely destroyed the working class and alienated the peasantry'.[110] Although China could not escape 'the universal determinations of any transition to socialism in conditions of scarcity', it had 'avoided the fate of the October Revolution'.[111]

Meanwhile, the document judged that the Cultural Revolution, launched in 1966, had awakened 'the egalitarian initiative and creativity of the masses', and thus acted as a check on 'manifestations of bureaucratic privilege and authority'.[112] It went so far as to suggest that this 'was the solution advocated by Lenin on the eve of his death for the rescue of the October Revolution'.[113] Even when doubting that the 'initiative and creativity' of the Chinese masses could really 'overcome ... the objective limits imposed by scarcity' tending to bureaucratisation, the *NLR* held that a cultural revolution was perhaps 'more possible in the advanced countries of the West'.[114] Accordingly, it concluded that 'China today – in contrast to the USSR – acts as a major revolutionary pole throughout the world.'[115] As it would later acknowledge, the *Review* 'slid towards an uncritical substitution of China for Russia in its ... political orientation', in which the 'record of the Chinese Revolution ... functioned as a kind of absolution for the disasters of the Russian Revolution'.[116]

In judging that 'Mao Tse Tung's thought is the only contemporary theory of a mass practice' – in contrast to Western Marxism as 'the theory of a renunciation of any political practice' and Trotskyism as 'the theory of past political practice' – this endorsement was qualified by the recognition that it had 'emerged in a social formation radically distant and distinct from West European capitalism'.[117] Thus although Maoism was registered as the dominant component among the three legacies, this final qualification pre-cluded any straight-forward affiliation given the *Review*'s primary concern with a breakthrough to socialism on the terrain of the advanced capitalist countries.

Registering the limitations of contemporary Marxism should have been the basis for the development of a modern revolutionary politics. Tellingly, however, the *Review*'s gravitation away from Maoism led it to Trotskyism – previously the least regarded of Marxism's three components parts – via 'a new debate on the twenties'.[118] The exchange on the defects and merits of Trotsky's historic legacy initiated by Nicolas Krassó was of international significance, and, aside from its impact in determining the *NLR*'s evolution, is worth detailing in its own right.

Writing prior to the events of 1968, and, following his mentor Lukács, displaying a more indulgent attitude to the Soviet Union that would soon be the case for the majority of those at the *NLR*, Krassó argued, in sum, that Stalin's course of 'socialism in one country' had been vindicated, and thus that Trotsky had been mistaken in pinning the fate of Soviet Russia upon the successful outcome of revolution in the West. He concluded that 'the su-periority of Stalin's perspective over Trotsky's is undeniable', for the vindica-tion of Stalin's 'basic strategic line … by the course of political events'[119] not only frustrated Trotsky in the inner-party struggles of the twenties, but also disabled the career of the 'International Left Opposition' and, subsequently, the Fourth International.

Krassó traced the roots of the fundamental and recurrent flaw in Trotsky's outlook to the pre-war debates within the Second International. For where the 'right' was guilty of 'economism', the 'left', including Trotsky and Luxemburg, was equally in error – guilty, in Krassó's terms, of 'sociolo-gism':

> Here it is not the economy, but *social classes*, which are extracted from the complex historical totality and hypostasised in an idealist fash-ion as the demiurges of any given political situation … Economism naturally leads to passivity and tailism; sociologism, on the contrary tends to lead to voluntarism … In … [Trotsky's] writings, mass forces are presented as constantly dominant in society, without any political organisations or institutions intervening as necessary and permanent levels of the social formation. Lenin's Marxism, by contrast, is defined by the notion of a complex totality, in which all the levels – economic, social, political and ideological – are always operational, and there is a permutation of the main locus of contradictions between them.[120]

Trotsky's isolation and ultimate downfall were due, in Krassó's estimate, to this weakness in 'the theoretical character of his Marxism'.[121] Thus, during the political manoeuverings and inner-party duels of the twenties, Trotsky 'was always interpreting the political positions adopted by the various participants as merely the visible signs of occult sociological trends within Soviet society' – hence 'his constant under-estimation of the autonomous power of political institutions' and individual figures such as Stalin.[122] For Krassó, the 'only thing that could have defeated Stalin' was 'a bloc of the Left and Right against the Centre',[123] whilst for Trotsky it was the Bukharinite Right – seeking to placate the capitalist kulak farmers and favouring 'socialism at a snail's pace' – who posed a greater threat of capitalist restoration than the Stalinist Centre.[124] It was this 'lack of any ... theory of the political level' which, in Krassó's estimate, 'led to disastrous practical mistakes in the prosecution of Trotsky's own struggle'.[125]

The death of Deutscher, which chanced to coincide with Krassó's essay, meant there could be no reply from the man whose 'greatness of ... achievement', in Krassó's words, had previously 'seemingly overpowered any other potential contributor's to a debate, within Marxism, on Trotsky's true historical role'.[126] Instead, Ernest Mandel, a leading figure within the Fourth International, responded. He threw back Krassó's charge and unequivocally defended Trotsky's assertion of the paramouncy of social forces, arguing that Krassó had overstated the autonomy of politics and individuals, writing of history as if it were 'just an arena for "power politics" in a social vacuum'.[127] The evolution of Soviet Russia in the twenties and thirties was overwhelmingly determined by the 'growing political passivity of the working class and growing strength of the bureaucracy in the state apparatus and society, accompanied by the growing bureaucratisation of the party apparatus itself'.[128] Lenin was well aware of this: in 1921 he spoke of Russia as 'a workers' state with bureaucratic deformations'.[129] For Mandel, the failure of the other party leaders to respond soon enough to the bureaucratic danger was 'the basic explanation for the apparent ease' with which Stalin assumed 'absolute power as representative of the Soviet bureaucracy'.[130] Trotsky made tactical errors and miscalculations; but similar criticisms could be made of Lenin – for example, his conflation of state and party, the suppression of tendencies within the party, and the failure to oppose Stalin's election as General-Secretary. 'Socialism in one country', argued Mandel, far from expressing the independent political force and determination of the Communist Party under Stalin, was merely an accommodation to the uncomfortable fact of scarcity and primitive accumulation, in which a party-bureaucracy ruled *in lieu* of an absent – or, at least, numerically small and politically immature

– working class. Far from being the political or institutional master, Stalin became the 'unconscious tool of social forces'[131] – that is, of the bureaucracy.

In the circumstances, Mandel argued, a bureaucratic deformation was largely unavoidable. But he insisted that the programme of the Trotskyite Left Opposition would have tempered its worst effects – strengthening the proletarian character of Soviet society through industrialisation, weakening the hold of the kulaks by winning the mass of the peasantry to collectivisation, reconstituting soviet democracy as a counter-weight to the bureaucracy, and committing the Comintern to a revolutionary internationalism that would, in time, have rescued Soviet Russia from isolation and hostile encirclement. Moreover, it was only by recognising the objective basis for, and character of, the bureaucratic dictatorship that any meaningful assessment could be made of the nature of Soviet society.

Mandel defended Trotsky's thesis that the 'triumph of the bureaucracy over the masses' had resulted in a 'Soviet Thermidor'.[132] This bureaucracy constituted a 'ruling stratum', but not, according to Mandel, a new social class. Although instinctively conservative, and with no commitment to furthering the cause of world revolution, it was nonetheless 'fundamentally attached to collective ownership of the means of production and opposed to capitalism'.[133] Although productive relations had been socialised, their administration had, in effect, been confiscated by the bureaucracy. These provisional arrangements were, in Trotsky's judgement, far from being in a stable equilibrium: 'a further development of the accumulating contradictions can as well lead to socialism as back to capitalism,… on the road to capitalism the counter-revolution would have to break the resistance of the workers,… on the road to socialism the workers would have to overthrow the bureaucracy'.[134]

Replying to Mandel, Krassó wrote that Trotsky in exile had become the embodiment of a romantic, yet politically impossible, myth and symbol of how the October Revolution 'ought' to have been: '[r]eality, however, is never merely a matter of principles … Marxism is not a beatific optimism: it is the intelligence of an intolerable era and the movement to transform it.'[135] The presence of the Soviet Union and the Communist International, for all its errors, was a fact of great political weight. That this historical record entailed so many disappointments did not warrant Trotsky's impossiblist condemnation, or the pursuit of a new – largely fantasy – International.

What was new in Krassó's reply, 'more heavily processed than the first essay in the review office'[136] and bearing ('to the discomfiture' of Krassó himself)[137] a distinctly Althusserian-Maoist stamp, was an emphasis on

the importance of the Chinese Revolution – 'the vortex of world revolution at mid-century' – which 'spectacularly disproved' Trotsky's contention
that there could be 'no revolution within the ranks of parties loyal to the
Third International'.[138] As far as China was concerned, 'no more obvious
instance of Trotsky's sociologism may be conceived', for he disregarded and
condemned Mao's reliance on the peasantry as the mainstay of the Chinese
revolution: 'this was his judgement of the decisive political phenomenon of
the epoch'.[139]

Mandel's second reply, published in 1969, was stalled by the editorial committee 'for more than eight months after it was submitted – far the longest
delay in the history of NLR',[140] and demonstrates the continuing resistance
of the majority at the *NLR* to Trotskyism. 'Paradoxically', and alone amongst
the editorial committee, Perry Anderson's thinking was 'permanently altered' by Mandel's two replies.[141] We may surmise that within the editorial
collective it was Anderson – from the outset least impressed by Maoism (a
rare point of disagreement between Anderson and Blackburn)[142] and always
attuned to the 'longer durées' – who took the lead in directing the *NLR* towards Trotskyism.

For others the shift from Maoism to Trotskyism, when it came, was as
much a question of temper as politics. The passing of the more optimistic
expectations invested in '1968' helped to induce an unmistakeable shift of
emphasis from the voluntarist impatience of Mao to the more sober, longer-
term perspective of Trotsky, with its greater appreciation of the weight of
objective conditions. Two events further assisted the passage of the *Review*.
The first was the discrediting of the Soviet bureaucracy over the invasion of
Czechoslovakia; the second, more decisive instance was the disillusionment
with Maoism, following the sudden right turn in Chinese foreign policy
after 1971.

After the invasion of Czechoslovakia, an altogether less indulgent characterisation of the Soviet bureaucracy was propounded – one closer to Trotsky
than Krassó or Deutscher. The bureaucratic dictatorship in the Soviet Union
was not amenable to reform from above, but could only be displaced by a
political revolution from below. 'The fate of socialism in one country', wrote
the *Review* in 1970, 'was conclusively sealed, not in the isolation and mis-
ery of the USSR in the twenties, but in its "power" and "prosperity" of the
sixties.'[143] The Soviet bureaucracy, and the battalions of 'official', Moscow-
oriented Communism carried little weight in the *Review*'s strategic audit of
1968/9. In contrast to Deutscher's contention that the bureaucratic dictatorship might be reformed from within, the *Review* now concluded, in orthodox Trotskyite vein, that socialism could only be achieved in Russia with its

overthrow.[144] This appeared to be confirmed by the confrontation in Poland in the winter of 1970-1 – more explosive than the Prague Spring, initiated 'from above' – which from the outset was led by the workers themselves: 'the only class', in the estimate of the *NLR*, 'that can bring to an end the long dominion of bureaucratic oppression … to which they are condemned by a ruling class that usurps their name'.[145] The *Review* perceived in the Baltic strike movement 'the elemental directness and power of the *class consciousness* of the shipyard workers'.[146]

As late as 1971 the *Review* carried, in its first number of that year, Mao's 'Letter to Lin Piao' (dated 1930), and a laudatory introduction by Bill Jenner. However, before the year was out Maoism's reputation had been decisively tarnished by the abrupt right turn in Chinese foreign policy. China's support for the military regime in Pakistan during the struggle for independence in Bangladesh, and for the Bandaranaike government in Ceylon during the JVP rising, was sharply denounced in *NLR* editorials and articles by Tariq Ali and Fred Halliday. A 'Holy Alliance for the victory of counter-revolution in Ceylon', involving 'an unprecedented and infamous coalition of powers: USA, USSR, Britain, China, India, Pakistan and Yugoslavia', was held up 'to socialist militants' as 'a grim warning' and 'ominous precedent'.[147] Chou En-Lai's message backing Bandaranaike and promising material support was reprinted in the *Review* in order to publicise and denounce China's new international line.[148]

The break with Maoism induced 'an acute internal crisis' within the *NLR*,[149] and resulted in the resignations of Ben Brewster and David Fernbach (since 1970 a leading activist in the Gay Liberation Front) from the editorial committee in 1971.[150] There was, however, no immediate reckoning with the domestic character of Chinese Communism or evaluation of the Cultural Revolution.[151] A pair of short articles at the beginning of 1975[152] were deemed to have 'formalised the emancipation of NLR from any residual influence of Maoist ideology',[153] though it was fully two more years before Fred Halliday's more substantive piece in the hundredth issue of the *NLR* drew a definitive line under the *Review*'s affair with Maoism.[154]

By now, Robin Blackburn, Quintin Hoare and Branka Magaš were involved in the IMG. However, continuing resistance within the editorial collective to the *Review*'s orientation to Trotskyism meant that the first unambiguous public affiliation to the Trotskyist tradition was not made until 1976, in Perry Anderson's *Considerations on Western Marxism*. His argument, and the response it drew from some within the editorial collective, is worth reflecting upon in some detail.

Although the *Review* had been consciously more critical in its appraisal of Western Marxism in the years after 1968,[155] *Considerations* was the first explicit public break with a tradition with which the *NLR* had once been closely associated. The long separation of theory from practice that, in Anderson's judgement, had imposed such penalties on Western Marxism, appeared to be nearing its end – signalling that its 'intellectual course' had 'probably already been run'.[156] The upsurge in working-class militancy in the advanced capitalist countries after 1968, combined, in 1974, with the 'first major synchronised recession' of the world capitalist economy since the war, had increased the 'chance of a revolutionary circuit reopening between Marxist theory and mass practice, looped through real struggles of the industrial working class'.[157]

Thus discarding Western Marxism, what would be the principal source of this 'Marxist theory'? Anderson was unequivocal: a 'tradition of an entirely different character' from Western Marxism had developed 'off-stage': Trotskyism.[158] Its 'politico-theoretical heritage', wrote Anderson, provided 'one of the central elements for any renaissance of revolutionary Marxism'.[159] This emphatic declaration was not, however, sustained by any supporting analysis. Anderson's survey of Trotskyism amounted to barely five pages at the end of a 100-page essay.

To the core text – written in 1974, discussed and criticised at length by colleagues on the *New Left Review*,[160] and eliciting strong reservations from some quarters[161] – Anderson added a somewhat chastened 'Afterword', reflecting upon 'difficulties peremptorily evaded or ignored'.[162] Aware of Trotskyism's weaknesses, Anderson's affiliation was more forthright than his own reservations warranted. For if, as Anderson accepted, Trotskyism was equally 'subject to the ultimate dictates of the long epoch of historical defeat for the working class in the West', did its legacy really make a 'polar contrast' to that of Western Marxism?[163] Was it really of an 'entirely different character' from Western Marxism?

Anderson conceded that an 'enforced isolation from the main detachments of the organised working class', and the 'protracted absence of revolutionary mass upsurges in the central lands of industrial capitalism', had inevitably left their mark on this tradition.[164] If the varied practioners of Western Marxism became immersed in philosophical abstractions, the Trotskyist response involved its own penalties, not least a certain conservatism: '[t]he preservation of classical doctrines took priority over their development. Triumphalism in the cause of the working class, and catastrophism in the analysis of capitalism, asserted more by will than by intellect, were to be the typical vices of this tradition in its routine forms'.[165] Moreover,

Anderson conceded, Trotskyism had yet to resolve 'the formidable scientific problems posed to the socialist movement' by the question of revolutionary strategy in the West.[166]

Certainly, Deutscher, Rosdolsky and Mandel – the three figures cited by Anderson in his brief examination of the Trotskyist tradition – 'filled no chairs in universities',[167] nor were they primarily moved by philosophical or aesthetic concerns. However, Sartre and Althusser, for example, were arguably less divorced from political practice, even if the practice they were engaged in tended towards reformism. Deutscher and Rosdolsky, on the other hand, although they held no 'university chairs', were as much isolated intellectuals as any Western Marxist. Trotskyism's greater interest in politics and economics was salutary, but, as Gareth Stedman Jones noted, such a distinction made for an altogether more modest claim than that advanced by Anderson.[168]

The key for Tom Nairn was the precise character of the defeat that had sundered theory from practice for two generations. Was 1917 the starting-point to which revolutionaries should return for guidance? For Nairn, August 1914 was the more decisive date.[169] The origins of the revolutionary failure in the West had to be traced at least as far back as 1870. The central problems confronting any successful socialist strategy in the West, he argued, were representative bourgeois democracy and its twin, nationalism – it was the latter that created the possibility of the former.[170] This was the terrain of the advanced capitalist countries: Trotskyism and the moment of 1917 in Russia were thus an inadequate basis for a revolutionary socialism appropriate to the West. The Leninist-Trotskyite heritage upon which Anderson sought to base a contemporary revolutionary politics was, in Nairn's judgement, already largely redundant in western Europe by 1917.

Anderson's 1976 'Afterword' sat awkwardly with the main text. In it he was more critical of the entire Marxist inheritance, including the 'classical tradition' of Marx, Lenin and Trotsky, arguing that there were certain key areas 'where the heritage of classical Marxism appears inadequate or unsatisfactory'.[171] Its principal failing was an undeveloped theory of the state: 'Marx never produced any coherent or comparative account of the political structures of bourgeois class power at all';[172] whilst Lenin compounded the problem, for by 'failing to delimit a feudal autocracy unequivocally from bourgeois democracy', he 'involuntarily permitted a constant confusion among later Marxists, that was effectively to prevent them from ever developing a cogent revolutionary strategy in the West'.[173] Also included in Anderson's formidable list of 'the main theoretical weaknesses of classical Marxism'[174] were the labour theory of value;[175] the question of nationalism;[176] the character of socialist democracy; Trotsky's theory of permanent revolution; and his analysis of the 'bureaucratised workers' state'.

Anderson concluded that these 'numerous and insistent' problems should not diminish 'respect for the greatness' of the key figures of the classical tradition.[177] This may be so, but Anderson's confident conclusions as to the value of classical Marxism – Trotskyism included – hardly squared with such a balance-sheet. Such an allegiance, in spite of the weaknesses highlighted, suggests, perhaps, an unwarranted over-identification with the tradition of 1917 on Anderson's part. Although he recognised the specificity of the obstacles confronting revolutionary strategy in the West, this over-identification was more of a hindrance than an aid when it came to surmounting them. Instead of drawing universal conclusions from the contingent success of the October Revolution – one that, moreover, was effected on the terrain of absolutist dictatorship – a better starting point historically would have been the contemporaneous failure of the German revolution, 1918-23, in the admittedly precarious, but otherwise more typical conditions for western Europe of parliamentary democracy.

For their part, in critical responses to Anderson's text, Anthony Barnett, Fred Halliday, Tom Nairn and Gareth Stedman Jones doubted that Trotskyism provided a sufficient basis for a contemporary revolutionary politics. An upturn in revolutionary practice today would gain little by excavating the debates of fifty years ago: it would provide its own starting point and bear its own name.[178]

That some of the *Review*'s editors were indeed open to an exploration of a contemporary, more pluralist and libertarian socialist agenda, uninhibited by the classical tradition, may be evidenced, for example, in the production of *Seven Days* – billed (in a promotional flyer) as a 'socialist photo-news weekly' – for an all-too-brief six months in 1971-2. In many ways a successor to the *Black Dwarf*, it was a collaborative venture involving Anthony Barnett, Alexander Cockburn, Fred Halliday, Gareth Stedman Jones and Peter Wollen from the *New Left Review* alongside colleagues from the Women's Liberation Workshop, *Idiot International*, and Gay Liberation. Unlike the *Review*, *Seven Days* was closely attuned to the themes of the libertarian Left. Its proclaimed aim was 'to help people to discover the truth of capitalism for themselves, and to realise their own ability to take political power'.[179] Its coverage included mental health issues; claimants' unions; the commune movement; imprisoned militants of the Angry Brigade; 'kids lib'; and hunt saboteurs. In contrast to the *Review*, both the women's movement and the conflict in the north of Ireland, including the events of Bloody Sunday in Derry, featured prominently.

The confidential Decennial Report of 1974 concluded that the sudden end of *Seven Days* had 'dealt the morale and cohesion' of the *NLR* editorial committee 'the worst blow in its history'.[180] Such dissenting libertarian socialist voices never reached the pages of the *Review* itself, and the opportunity for a potentially fruitful debate was missed. Dispersal and activity elsewhere removed from the *Review*'s immediate orbit such as Alexander Cockburn and Peter Wollen, both working in the USA; Ronald Fraser, preoccupied at New Left Books (whose volume of output was beginning to overshadow that of the *NLR* itself);[181] Tom Nairn, relocated to Scotland; and Juliet Mitchell, the 'first major exponent of socialist feminism' in Britain,[182] whose 'Women: The Longest Revolution', published in the *Review* in 1966, remained an isolated text.[183] In 1980 it was reported that '[l]ess than half of those listed in the journal play any active role in producing it'.[184] This loss, as much by chance as design, allied to the earlier resignations of Brewster and Fernbach,[185] deprived the *Review* of many of those open to a more diverse agenda, and undoubtedly contributed to the hardening of the *NLR*'s Trotskyite position (none of the *Review*'s IMG contingent had been directly involved in *Seven Days*) – despite the fact that the IMG was itself 'heavily influenced by the anti-bureaucratic thrust of the women's movement, student radicalism, community politics, the squatters' and claimants' movements'.[186]

Perhaps the most serious omission was any reflection upon, or engagement with, the women's movement, 'both a product and a repudiation of male-dominated radicalism in the late sixties'.[187] Sheila Rowbotham, briefly on the editorial board of the *Black Dwarf*, which carried her seminal intervention, reproduced as the pamphlet 'Women's Liberation and the New Politics', in a special women's issue in January 1969, has hinted at the far from untypical chauvinism of the male-dominated *NLR* group at this time.[188] It was here, in the women's movement that emerged as an organised force after 1970, that sixty-eightist themes of participatory grassroots democracy and 'the personal is political' were most developed, suggestive of novel forms of organisation, contestation and political strategy.

For a period in 1974 the *Review*'s active core had been reduced to Perry Anderson, Robin Blackburn and Fred Halliday, and 'the last vestiges of a formal e/c structure disintegrated'.[189] The addition of Francis Mulhern (born Ireland, 1951, today Professor of Critical Studies, Middlesex University) in 1975 and Norman Geras (born Zimbabwe, 1943, educated at Oxford University, and since 1967 teaching at Manchester University) in 1976 helped to create a healthy quorum 'for the first time in many years', and to establish 'a more compact and reasoned political consensus within NLR than at any time in its past'.[190]

Of the editorial committee's eight identifiably active members in the late seventies[191] – Perry Anderson, Anthony Barnett, Robin Blackburn, Norman Geras, Fred Halliday, Quintin Hoare, Branka Magaš and Francis Mulhern – there is no doubting the *Trotskysant* character of the *Review*'s new-found 'political consensus'; with perhaps only Barnett, Halliday and Mulhern defending a somewhat alternative position. No less than four were members of the IMG: Blackburn, Geras, Hoare and Magaš.[192] In addition, Ernest Mandel, a leading figure in the Fourth International, became a major contributor to the *Review*.[193] His *Revolutionary Marxism Today*, published by New Left Books in 1979, was, to all intents and purposes, a manifesto of the Fourth International.[194]

It should be noted, however, that the *Review*'s organisational independence was closely guarded – the overlapping of membership with the IMG and Fourth International involved no formal linkage with the *NLR*. Indeed the involvement in the IMG was not an entirely happy one, and by 1974 the *NLR* contingent were an 'isolated minority' within the organisation.[195] Robin Blackburn had been 'eliminated from a leading position in it' and Quintin Hoare 'deprived' of the editorship of its theoretical journal.[196] For 'those who joined it, the IMG was largely confiscated'.[197]

For all its faults and missed opportunities this *Trotskysant* phase was the most outwardly self-confident in the history of the *Review*: a period in which it pursued a clear project and enjoyed a strong political identity. In its own estimate, the 'NLR might be said to have finally attained relative ideological maturity – a stabilisation of its outlook on the basis of an open and critical revolutionary marxism',[198] with an identity that derived from being 'both more meticulously edited, and more collectively produced' than any comparable journal[199] (for example, the editorial committee met twice monthly on average in the four years 1976-9).[200] It judged that 'no other [comparable] journal has taken so much trouble in writing up articles submitted to it', nor in producing so large a part of the journal from within the editorial collective.[201]

Less kindly one might argue that in the baggage of the classical revolutionary tradition came a vanguardist mentality, and a creeping Leninist model of organisation, fashioning the *NLR*'s editorial committee into something of a fantasy politbuto-in-the-making.[202] This excessive desire to display an outward unity of purpose, largely driven, by all accounts, by Anderson's overbearing presence, did much to poison the *NLR*'s internal life.[203] Differences of view tended to turn into explosive disputes, often magnified, in such a small circle, into highly personalised confrontations – such instances included sharp disagreement over Tom Nairn's 'The Modern Janus' (on nationalism), published 1975, from which Quintin Hoare and Robin Blackburn 'in particular ... expressed strong divergence';[204] Terry Eagleton's sharp critique of Raymond Williams, published 1976, to which Anthony Barnett made reply, following 'a long period of tension' with others on the editorial committee, in which 'personal relations deteriorated'; dissension over Norman Geras' article on Leon Trotsky (eventually published in 1979); and a conflict over direction and control of New Left Books, 'precipitated' by Perry Anderson, leading to walk-out by NLB employees and the resignation of Ronald Fraser in their support late in 1977, described by a confidential editorial report as 'the worst crisis in the history of the [R]eview';[205] (though such 'worst crises' were becomingly increasingly frequent). At the root of all these disputes was the central issue of 'handling public differences' within the editorial committee. Acknowledgement of the need 'for greater liberty and candour of publication by e[ditorial]/c[ommittee] members in disagreement with each other' failed to find satisfactory resolution and continued to be suppressed for fear of 'centrifugal risk'.[206] .

Chapter Three
Revolutionary Expectations

1. Considerations on Western Communism

'The imperialist world today', reckoned a 1972 *NLR* editorial, 'is everywhere subjected to the fourfold pressures of the class struggle of the industrial proletariat within its homelands, international rivalry between its main metropolitan centres, the assault of national liberation movements, and the burdens of defense against the Communist countries.'[1] Of these four co-ordinates, the first was, at this time, undoubtedly most central to the *Review*'s strategic thinking.

Working-class militancy intensified across the industrialised world, whilst Ernest Mandel judged that the end of the post-war boom would be succeeded by a 'long wave' of economic stagnation. Indeed, it was Mandel – whose *Late Capitalism* (translated from the German original) was published by New Left Books in 1975 – who furnished the *NLR* with much of its economic analysis in this period. This was a field in which the members of the *Review* itself were largely ill-equipped. The one exception was the Cambridge economist Bob Rowthorn, who, although contributing to the debate in the pages of the *Review* (and penning a broadly sympathetic review of Mandel's *Late Capitalism*),[2] remained outside the orbit of the *NLR*'s core *aktiv*, having, uniquely from the *NLR* milieu, gravitated since 1968 via the Mayday Manifesto and the short-lived Left Convention to the Conference of Socialist Economists (the publishers of *Capital and Class*) and the Communist Party.

The main co-ordinates of the crisis of profitability and accumulation that marked the end of the long boom developed by Mandel and others need not detain us unduly. The fall in post-tax profits was largely ascribed to the relative defensive strength of labour in conditions of near-full employment, aggravated by sharpened inter-capitalist competition and inter-state rivalry between the major capitalist powers (the economic decline of the United States vis-à-vis Europe, principally Germany, and Japan).[3] Although the economic down-turn, especially the recession of 1974-5, provided the backdrop to this period – encouraging the *NLR* to argue that it was 'only now, in the mid seventies, with the demise of the post-war boom and economic recession throughout the capitalist world, that the historic scale of the political crisis of the world imperialist system can be fully appreciated'[4] – the *Review* never adopted a 'catastrophist' perspective. Ultimately, it was simply less interested in economics and more attuned to politics and questions of political strategy.

The fall of the Saigon regime and the reunification of Vietnam in 1975, symbolic of the decisive weakening of the pre-eminent capitalist power, the United States, was greeted by the *Review* as a 'victory of … profound significance', which will 'stimulate the struggles of the exploited and oppressed everywhere'.[5] Lukács, for example, quoted in the *NLR*, optimistically forecast that the 'defeat of the USA in the Vietnamese War is to the "American Way of Life" rather like what the Lisbon earthquake was to French feudalism'.[6]

While the developing countries were displaying a new-found assertiveness buoyed by rising commodity prices and reflected in the political muscle demonstrated by OPEC in the wake of the 1973 Arab-Israeli war (imposing a selective embargo on Israel's Western backers) and the calls for a 'new International Economic Order' (proposed at the 1973 Algiers summit of non-aligned countries, and tabled at a special session of the UN General Assembly in 1974) bidding for a global redistribution of economic power at the expense of the increasingly divided 'West' – more threatening still to Western dominance was the number of countries attempting to subtract themselves entirely from the circuits of global capital, principally in southeast Asia and southern Africa, enhancing Moscow's geo-political standing into the bargain. Nowhere was the new global balance better exemplified than the intervention of Cuban troops in defeating an invading column of South African forces in the civil war in Angola in November 1975.

Althusser relayed to the *NLR* a critical yet unmistakably confident message from the PCF's 22nd Congress of 1976: 'it can be said that imperialism, for the third time in its history, is today in a pre-revolutionary crisis … [D]espite all the anti-crisis mechanisms set up and "adjusted" by the bourgeois states after 1929, a "link" may give way, somewhere, at the weak point of the "chain"'.[7] Whilst revolutionary forces came to power in Indo-China and the crumbling Portuguese colonial empire in Africa, the *Review* judged that it was 'above all in Western Europe' that this crisis 'of the world imperialist system … is likely to be concentrated'.[8] Perry Anderson in turn contrasted the stable northern zone of western Europe, where social democratic parties – often with substantial governmental experience – held the allegiance of the working class, and a more unsettled southern zone, encompassing France, Italy, Spain, Portugal and Greece.[9] It would be these weaker capitalist states, least able to respond to growing international competition and thus with less room for manoeuvre, that, in the *Review*'s reckoning, would prove the weak links in the chain of metropolitan capitalism.

France, the most populous and economically advanced of these countries, occupying a pivotal geographical location straddling southern and northern Europe, was, since the May-June events of 1968, the most likely proving ground of revolutionary expectations. A breakthrough here could not but have the most profound consequences, perhaps sufficient to galvanise popular social forces in its near neighbours. If Italy had not experienced anything as intense as the French May, the post-1968 'protest movement was the most profound and long-lasting',[10] and its 'revolutionary groups … the largest new left in Europe',[11] challenging the vulnerable hegemony of the sclerotic Christian Democrat ruling bloc. The 'hot autumn' of 1969 radicalised the Communist, Socialist and Catholic trade union confederations alike, bringing them into closer unity and greater autonomy from their parent parties. Moreover, Italy witnessed more sustained student-worker alliances than elsewhere in Europe, and burgeoning social movements addressing a wide range of issues from women's rights to housing and prison conditions.

Potentially more explosive still were the cases of Spain, Portugal, and Greece, where dictatorships (two of classically fascist pre-war vintage) testified to the fragility of bourgeois rule. In Spain, Franco's last years were marked by an increasing tempo of strikes and the radicalisation of opposition in the Basque country (and the campaign of political assassinations, including that of the prime-minister Carrero Blanco, carried out by ETA) which sharp repression failed to suppress. In post-Salazar Portugal, costly and unsuccessful colonial wars issued in a coup by aggrieved and radicalised junior army officers, unleashing the complex dynamic of the 1974-5 'revolution of carnations'. In Greece, burdened by the unresolved legacy of the bitter civil war of 1944-8, openly fascist Colonels headed by Papadopolous seized power in 1967, yet with little legitimacy appeared vulnerable to popular revolt, such as the bloodily suppressed student-worker rising in Athens in November 1973.

Moreover, in southern Europe – in contrast to northern Europe – the mass parties of the working class were Communist; indeed, in Spain and Portugal the clandestine Communist Parties were almost the only effective opposition. It was this fact above all else that registered the decisive significance of southern Europe in the *Review*'s strategic calculations.

Should the Communist Parties be characterised as reformist or revolutionary organisations? If the former, could they be displaced by new parties of the revolutionary Left? If they continued to retain the allegiance of the mass of the workers, what part, positive or negative, might they be expected to play in the pursuit of socialism? In seeking an answer to these questions, between 1968 and 1971 the *Review* examined the contemporary political complexion of no less than seven Western Communist Parties[12] – Lucio Magri's left-critique of Italian Communism being in notable contrast to the *Review*'s earlier identification of the PCI as something of a model socialist party. In addition, Perry Anderson devoted an unpublished manuscript, 'The Founding Moment', to an appraisal of Western Communism.

Anderson argued that the parties of the Communist International were born too late, missing the revolutionary opportunity of 1918-20.[13] They were, in effect, subsequently refounded as leaders of national resistance movements to Nazi occupation[14] – the roots of which lay in the Popular Front strategy adopted at the Seventh Congress of the Comintern in 1935.[15] Although reflecting a genuine desire for anti-fascist unity on the Left,[16] the Popular Front was sanctioned by the requirements of Soviet diplomacy (whose goal was collective security against Hitler), and viewed as 'liquidationist' by Trotsky – who in response founded the Fourth International to carry the banner of the revolutionary Comintern. Writing in the *Review* in 1972, Claudin echoed Trotsky's verdict that the role of the Spanish Communist Party in the Popular Front government during the Civil War had amounted to 'the subjugation of … revolution … to the reasons of state of the Soviet Union'.[17] The comparable cases of Greece and the Philippines were also explored in the *Review*.[18]

The chief consequence of their 'refounding' was the acclimatisation of the Western Communist Parties to the terrain of parliamentary democracy. Their Popular Front and Resistance reincarnation led them to abandon revolutionary Leninism. Instead, they became absorbed in electoral politics and committed to building an 'advanced democracy' on the basis, rather than the ruins, of the parliamentary-democratic state. But they remained, in Anderson's estimate, distinct from social democratic parties in two principal respects: in their democratic (in fact, bureaucratic) centralist organisational structure (significantly, counted a positive attribute by Anderson); and, notwithstanding a growing independence,[19] in their origins in an international movement that still retained a residual affiliation to Moscow, historic adversary of the capitalist West.[20]

Crucially, were the Western Communist Parties reformist or revolutionary organisations?[21] Had they undergone a social democratic metamorphosis? Despite the fact that the PCF had rejected revolution in 1968, Anderson characterised the Western Communist Parties as 'centrist': for although non-revolutionary, they nevertheless remained anti-capitalist. This, he wrote, was a contradictory position, untenable in revolutionary situations, when centrist organisations must choose between revolution and counter-revolution or split. The context and the scale of popular pressure would determine their course. In circumstances comparable to the French May, the PCI, for example, might split. In favourable conditions a Communist Party might yet opt for revolution. In Cuba, for example, the Communist Party belatedly threw its weight behind the revolutionary movement once the tide of events had turned decisively in favour of Castro's partisans. But Anderson took care not to write off even the PCF: although it had not acted as a revolutionary force, neither had it acted as a classically social democratic force. Through its trade union wing, the CGT, it had called a general strike to protest at the police violence against the students, and it had sanctioned the occupation of the factories. The events in France were thus of a qualitatively different character to the purely student agitation in Germany and America.[22]

Whilst far Left groups (involving, of course, some at the *NLR*) were busy projecting new revolutionary organisations in the aftermath of 1968, how realistic was it to expect that the allegiance of the mass of the workers could be won from the Communist Parties? Anderson looked for an answer in the experience of the birth of the Communist International – a period in which revolutionaries sought a similar displacement of loyalties. He judged this a moment of extraordinary social and political fluidity, involving a decisive break with the Second International over the issue of war in 1914, and the example of the Russian Revolution, combined with a new revolutionary theory, namely Leninism.[23] He stressed the difficulty of affecting a transfer of loyalties even at such a moment: by the mid-twenties the new Communist Parties were everywhere smaller than their social democratic rivals.[24] Any comparable displacement would be in danger of suffering the same fate: witness the career of the Fourth International. He concluded that only a major revolutionary upheaval could effect such a displacement.[25] The continuing loyalty of the French workers to the PCF after 1968 led Anderson to conclude that the Western Communist Parties would not be displaced in the immediate future,[26] registering once again, and in contrast to many of his colleagues at the *NLR*, Anderson's eye to the longer durées, and his softer stance towards Communism. Thus in southern Europe, where the principal parties of the labour movement were Communist, they would continue to hold a pivotal position in any calculations concerning the passage to socialism.

Meanwhile, with the advent of 'Euro-Communism' in the mid-seventies, the mass Communist Parties of France, Italy and Spain (the PCF, PCI and

PCE respectively) clarified their break with Leninism; a break that, though implicit since at least the war, was now made explicit for the first time. In this the experience of Chile was paramount, for it demonstrated the pressures that a reforming government of the broad Left, committed to the parliamentary road to socialism, would encounter; and posed key issues concerning the nature of socialist strategy in the West.

Chile enjoyed, by Latin American standards, a relatively stable parliamentary democracy. In September 1970 Salvador Allende, heading a 'Popular Unity' coalition that included the Communist Party, won election to the Presidency. Tugged leftwards by a popular mobilisation from below, and its hand strengthened by a strong poll at the March 1973 legislative elections, the government nonetheless took an extremely cautious line in a sharply polarised political climate, acutely aware of the danger of a right-wing backlash or the intervention of the army. In this they failed; the Popular Unity government was overthrown in a bloody military coup in 1973 (the 'other' 11th September). The *NLR* recognised, in the fate of Allende and the Popular Unity, the lethal constitutional illusions of reformism, arguing for a bolder strategy of confrontation: 'revolutions which do not advance rapidly are crushed'.[27]

The leaderships of the three principal Western Communist Parties, however, took a diametrically opposite view, firmly nailing their colours to the mast of constitutional legality and political moderation. It was in the weeks immediately after the fall of Allende that Enrico Berlinguer raised the prospect of an 'historic compromise' between the PCI and the Christian Democrats (DC) in a seminal Euro-Communist text, 'Reflections after the events in Chile'.[28] He argued that the forces of reaction could be contained and neutralised only by a programme that 'does not drive broad strata of the middle classes into positions of hostility'.[29] In addition, the PCE, PCI and PCF were keen to distance themselves from what passed as 'actually existing socialism', entailing a more explicit commitment to parliamentary democracy and the abandonment of the discredited concept of the 'dictatorship of the proletariat'. Socialism, argued the PCI and PCF in the Rome declaration of November 1975, will guarantee the 'development of all freedoms which are a product both of the great bourgeois-democratic revolutions and of the great popular struggles of this century'.[30]

Moreover, parliamentary democracy was a gain of popular struggles currently deemed to be threatened by 'monopoly capital' and an increasingly authoritarian bourgeois state. Had not the Communists been the staunchest defenders of parliamentary democracy in the period of the Popular Front and the war-time Resistance, when the bourgeoisie had been quick to resort to outright dictatorship? Was not the lesson of Chile that today, as in the past, the bourgeoisie would resort to dictatorship whenever threatened? 'Democracy is not only not consubstantial with capitalism', wrote Santiago Carillo, General-Secretary of the PCE, 'but ... its defence and development require the overthrow of that social system; ... in the historical conditions of today, capitalism tends to reduce and in the end destroy democracy'.[31] Socialism, argued the Euro-Communists, was the fullest expression of democracy; moreover, the institutions of parliamentary democracy could be continuously developed towards socialism. Such a transition would be a long and protracted process, rather than a sudden revolutionary leap. 'Our conception of the path to socialism', argued Giorgio Amendola, leading advocate of Euro-Communism in the PCI, 'is founded on a historicist understanding of social revolution as a process which has come a long way and is going a long way'.[32] If the state was benign, or at least neutral, parliamentary democracy a central component of socialist democracy, and the transition to socialism prolonged, it followed that the construction of a 'historic bloc' or electoral coalition was fundamental to the Euro-Communist strategy. This bloc, led by the Communist Party, would be a coalition held together by the ideological and cultural hegemony of the working class and its commitment to socialist democracy.[33]

In 1969, Anderson had characterised the Western Communist Parties as 'centrist'. Did the advent of Euro-Communism mark their social-democratisation? In the seventies, France, Italy and Spain shared one common characteristic: they were 'societies with no deep or long experience of reformist governments by workers' parties'.[34] It was quite possible, wrote Anderson in 'The Strategic Option' in 1978, that Euro-Communism might herald the transformation of the parties of the Third International into social democratic managers of capitalism – a fate that had befallen the parties of the Second International in northern Europe after the First World War. Would Euro-Communism 'lead to a repetition of the impasse of the Northern labour movement which, after having demonstrated a frequent ability to win elections, and after repeated experience of government, has ... totally failed to transform any of the North European societies in the direction of socialism?'[35] Although couched in terms of an open question, the trend was clear.

The *Review* nonetheless held that the advent of a Left government with Communist participation in western Europe – however moderate its programme, and despite reservations as to the trajectory of Euro-Communism – would dramatically alter the political climate. It might excite popular expectations, as in France in 1936, and polarise political forces, as in Chile at

the time of Allende's Presidency. In Robin Blackburn's words, the formation of governments based on the 'major workers' parties', the Socialists and
Communists, would prove 'an unprecedented test for the bourgeois political system in a string of important states'.[36] While such governments might
'be absorbed by the political system ... in a context of capitalist instability
and awakened popular aspirations it is also highly possible that they will
lead to a widespread extra-parliamentary mobilisation of both the bourgeoisie and the working class',[37] provoking a genuine revolutionary crisis,
in which the options on offer would be socialist revolution or revanchist
counter-revolution.

In Greece the Colonels' regime – having backed the coup against Makarios
in Cyprus, prompting a Turkish invasion of the island and the threat of war
between Greece and Turkey – was supplanted in 1974 by a new military
government effecting a smooth passage to conservative civilian rule. Yet, simultaneously, at the opposite end of the Mediterranean, expectations were
heightened by the dramatic revolutionary upsurge in Portugal.

The fall of Salazar's successor, Caetano, to the 25 April coup in 1974 by
junior army officers, pitched the country into a prolonged revolutionary
crisis. The strength of the popular movement, witnessed in strikes and occupations, and land seizures in the militant south, the mobilising role of
the parties of the Left and far Left, and the radicalisation of key army units
was sufficient to face down two abortive coups from the Right in September
1974 and March 1975, entrenching and deepening the revolution in the
process. Elections to a Constituent Assembly in April 1975 gave the Left a
substantial majority, with the Socialists (PS) emerging as the largest single
party with 38 per cent of the vote, the Communist Party, PCP, (and its allies)
scoring 17 per cent, and the independent and far Left 4 per cent. However,
with the Socialist Party under Mario Soares committed to the institutionalisation of parliamentary democracy, frictions and a conflict of legitimacy
soon emerged between the PS and the ruling Revolutionary Council of the
Armed Forces Movement (MFA), resulting in the withdrawal of PS minis-
ters from the provisional government of Vasco Gonçalves, whose base of
support shrunk to the radical wing of the MFA and the PCP, and finally fell
in September 1975 under pressure from moderates within the army. Such
divisions and lack of clear political strategy blunted the impetus of the revolution, leaving it exposed to the 25 November coup by the recently installed
government of Pinheiro de Azevedo, instituting a purge of radicals within
the MFA and a restoration of discipline to, and de-politicisation of, the
armed forces. With the popular movement deprived of the support of the
governmental or radical army units, the tide of the Portuguese revolution

turned. With the election, under the new constitution, of a minority government under Mario Soares on the second anniversary of the revolution in
April 1976, the way was open for the normalisation of bourgeois rule.

2. The State and Revolution in the West

Notwithstanding the failure in Portugal – where 'arguably the best single chance of a socialist revolution in Western Europe was spectacularly
missed'[38] – the upheaval itself appeared to confirm the 'actuality of the
revolution' in the West. Might Spain, where Franco's death in 1975 and an
unprecedented strike-wave promised the disintegration of the old regime,
provide the revolutionary breakthrough? In France, the PCF and the re-
founded Socialist Party, espousing radical rhetoric, had signed a common
programme in 1972 as the basis for a Union of the Left, gaining ground at
the 1973 legislative elections, coming within a whisker of electing Mitterrand
to the Presidency in 1974, and making such gains at the 1977 local elections
to suggest it would sweep to power nationally within a year. In Italy, on the
back of the Divorce Referendum of 1974 (voted by a substantial majority,
despite Christian Democrat opposition), the PCI made major gains at the
1975 regional and local elections, polling a record 33 per cent (up from 27
per cent at the 1972 legislative elections). With the Socialists, favouring an
orientation to the Left, taking 12 per cent of the vote, almost every major
Italian city passed under left-wing administration.[39] With national elections a year away, the prospect of ending the long ascendancy of Christian
Democracy appeared within sight.

A transition to socialism in one or more of the advanced capitalist countries of western Europe would, wrote Althusser, herald 'a genuinely democratic popular socialism'; its example – revealing 'a different form of socialism from the "grey" form of constraint and even repression' exhibited in the
Communist countries[40] – would prove a stimulus to the Left the world over.
'This historical opportunity', he urged, 'must be seized'.[41] Although alive to
the 'historical opportunity' afforded by this favourable conjuncture, the
Review was keenly aware of the unanswered questions concerning an appropriate revolutionary strategy in the West:

> The stakes will be extremely high in the class struggles of the new
> phase: if the present level of proletarian militancy is not developed
> to challenge bourgeois power at the political level, then there could
> be a historic defeat for the European working class and a new epoch
> of capitalist stabilisation … Unfortunately, alarmist and inaccurate
> pronouncements from bourgeois commentators have too often been

matched by euphoric generalisation and over-simplification on the left. Such questions as the nature of a genuine revolutionary bloc, the cohesion of the armed forces, the problem of regional disparities, the difficulty of projecting a model of proletarian democracy that is at once radically opposed to Stalinist bureaucracy and evidently superior to – more democratic than – bourgeois democracy, have been persistently ignored or evaded.[42]

Cognisance of the parliamentary-democratic nature of the political regimes of advanced capitalism lay at the heart of the *Review*'s concerns with regard to the transition to socialism in the West.

No single phenomenon in the contemporary world has been so central a barrier to socialist revolution, and yet so little engaged or explored by Marxist theory, as the bourgeois-democratic state. The paradox of stable rule by capital combined with universal right of suffrage was unknown in the epoch of Marx; still incomplete or peripheral in the world of Lenin; apparently in regression during the exile of Trotsky and the imprisonment of Gramsci. Yet since 1945, bourgeois democracy has become the normal and general form of state system throughout the advanced capitalist countries.[43]

In Portugal, as in Russia in 1917, the autocratic state had proved fragile at a moment of crisis. The parliamentary democracies, by contrast, were less vulnerable. Here, where the state apparatus was more broadly entrenched, and popular acquiescence in the rules of the electoral mandate were more deeply rooted, bourgeois rule was more stable. Nonetheless, Althusser was convinced that the new, post-1968 balance of forces suggested that 'for the first time in history the transition to socialism may be peaceful and democratic in some places'.[44] But was a Euro-Communist 'democratic transition' to socialism possible? What was the character of the parliamentary democratic state? How universal was the Bolshevik model of revolution? What sort of revolutionary strategy was appropriate in the conditions of advanced capitalism? These were among the key questions that focused the attentions of the *NLR* in the mid-seventies.

Unsurprisingly, given the fixation of key *NLR* figures with the historical 'moment of 1917', it was the controversies of the early twenties that the *Review* took as its starting-point in its analysis: 'the last great strategic debate in the European workers' movement' on the development of a 'revolutionary strategy in metropolitan capitalism that ... had any direct contact with the masses'.[45]

Claudin, for example, revisiting in the pages of the *Review* the sharp exchange between Kautsky and Lenin following the October Revolution, contrasted Kautsky's insistence that socialism was the culmination of a social and economic process (thus denouncing '1917' as a forcing of events)[46] with Lenin's analysis of social revolution as resulting from a breakdown of the old order, in which the existing state had to be 'smashed' and new institutions of political power – the direct democracy of the soviets – would arise. The polemical character of the exchange was shaped by the urgency of the subject under scrutiny, for the fate of the Russian Revolution appeared to hang on the success of the German Revolution. The strategy of Kautsky and German Social Democracy threatened to forestall such a prospect, leaving the Bolsheviks isolated and beleaguered. Kautsky and Lenin, argued Claudin, were both right and wrong at the same time: 'It seems ... that history is playing one of its tricks. It justifies Lenin against Kautsky and Kautsky against Lenin'.[47] How was this so? Their separate analyses each possessed a kernel of truth: the social and political conditions of the West were – and are – distinct from those of the East. According to Claudin, both were mistaken to abstract a universal model of socialist revolution from their specific analyses and concrete experience. Lenin was right to criticise Kautsky: an electoral evolutionism was insufficient to dismantle the capitalist state. Kautsky was right to criticise Lenin for the lack of democracy in post-revolutionary Russia, not all of which could be blamed on the exigencies of civil war. A similar critique of Lenin was made from the left by Rosa Luxemburg – a 'full reappraisal and recovery' of whose work, incidentally, the *NLR* judged 'indispensable today for the development of a socialist theory capable of guiding a proletarian revolution, based on workers' democracy, in the West'.[48]

In the controversies of the twenties, it was Gramsci who recognised the specific difference that distinguished East from West: the presence of representative political democracy in the latter, and its absence in the former.[49] 'The great theoretical merit of Gramsci', in Anderson's judgement, 'was to have posed the problem of this difference far more persistently and coherently than any other revolutionary before or since'.[50] Gramsci was pivotal because the Euro-Communists justified their break with Leninism by an appeal to his theoretical legacy – an appropriation which the *NLR* rejected, endorsing Colletti's 'sharp repudiation of attempts to portray Gramsci as some kind of precursor of the Popular Fronts and hence to establish a continuity between him and the current policies of the Italian Communist Party'.[51]

The Miliband-Poulantzas exchange on the state, whilst more contemporary and 'widely noted' internationally,[52] had little apparent bearing on the *NLR*'s own evolution; no-one from within the editorial collective, for example, joined the debate. The exchange contrasted Miliband's empirical approach to Poulantzas' desire to construct a theoretical framework, initially Althusserian in inspiration, in which to ground analysis of the capitalist state, but on the central question preoccupying the *Review* – effective political strategy – both refused to be drawn[53] (though Poulantzas would contribute to the later strategic debate in the pages of the *Review*, see below).

In acknowledging the distinct *terrain* of parliamentary democracy, the *Review* did not subscribe to a *parliamentary road* to socialism. It retained an affiliation to the tradition of classical Marxism, but recognised that the tactics of Leninism, though applicable to the conditions of Russia in 1917, could not be directly transplanted to western Europe. Nevertheless, the terrain of liberal democracy did not sanction a parliamentary or electoral *road* to socialism, but posed the question of the 'type of revolutionary strategy ... capable of overthrowing this historical form of State – so distinct from that of Tsarist Russia'.[54] Indeed, Anderson undertook a major historical survey to trace what he perceived to be the fundamental divide that distinguished the state-forms of western from eastern Europe: a divide whose distant origins, he maintained, lay in classical antiquity.[55]

Returning to Gramsci in the principal seventy-plus page essay – 'The Antinomies of Antonio Gramsci' – of the *Review*'s one hundredth issue in 1977, Anderson sought to clarify some of the strategic questions posed by the issue of the 'state and revolution in the West'.[56] Gramsci's innovation in the *Prison Notebooks* had been to demonstrate the 'hegemonic' character of capitalist class rule in the West: that in large measure the bourgeoisie sustained itself in power by the consent of the masses. However, Anderson concluded that, for all his insights, a solution to the puzzle of revolution in the West had eluded Gramsci: 'In the labyrinth of the notebooks Gramsci lost his way'.[57]

From Gramsci's inevitably opaque *Notebooks* Anderson deciphered three alternative models of class power, rejecting each in turn. In the predominant variant, the state embodied 'domination' and 'coercion', and civil society 'hegemony' and 'consent'. Thus, 'the preponderance of civil society over the State in the West can be equated with the predominance of "hegemony" over "coercion" as the fundamental mode of bourgeois power in advanced capitalism. Since hegemony pertains to civil society, and civil society prevails over the state, it is the cultural ascendancy of the ruling class that essentially ensures the stability of the capitalist order'.[58] Such an analysis, argued Anderson, was mistaken. Bourgeois power was not exercised ideologically in the realm of civil society – such were the 'illusions of Left Social-Democracy'.[59] Socialist strategy could not consist of a 'long revolution', a cultural conquest of civil society. A cultural confrontation with the bourgeoisie was important, but an insufficient substitute for a political confrontation with the bourgeois state.[60]

Anderson's own conclusion was that the Western capitalist democracies combined consent with a reserve of repressive power held by the state apparatus. 'Gramsci's primary formula was mistaken', he wrote, for the cultural and ideological hegemony of the bourgeoisie was located *both* in civil society *and* the state – it was 'impossible to partition the ideological functions of bourgeois class power' between the two.[61] It was the parliamentary-democratic institutions of the state themselves that provided the ideological lynch-pin of bourgeois class power. The 'fundamental form of the Western parliamentary state', Anderson argued, was 'itself the nub of the ideological apparatuses of capitalism … The novelty of this consent is that it takes the fundamental form of a belief by the masses that *they exercise an ultimate self-determination* within the existing order'.[62] Thus the capitalist state in the West was stronger than Tsarist autocracy: 'it rested not only on the consent of the masses, but also on a superior repressive apparatus … The keys to the power of the capitalist state in the West lie in this conjoined superiority'.[63]

Moreover, it was not the counterposition of 'war of position' and 'war of manoeuvre' – which 'in the end becomes an opposition between reformism and adventurism'[64] – but their combination, that Anderson considered critical. A 'war of position' was a *preparation* for a decisive 'war of manoeuvre'. This, in Anderson's mind, furnished the 'correct theoretical and temporal order in which Gramsci's concepts should have been applied'.[65] In the meantime, 'the prime agenda of any real socialist strategy today' was to win 'the conviction of workers' to revolutionary socialism: the 'imperative need remains to win the working class, before there can be any talk of winning power'.[66] To this end Anderson endorsed the tactic of the 'United Front' – adopted by the Comintern in 1921 – as the best means of winning the workers from the reformism of the leadership of the established workers' parties.[67]

Concrete strategic and tactical questions, insofar as they related to specific social formations, were left unanswered. These were, for example, 'workers' who, in Geoffrey Hodgson's critique of Anderson, remained 'abstract, diffuse, unstructured, unorganised, unrelated to their historical institutions and those of the alien world around them'.[68] Tellingly, the *NLR* remained fixed on the classical debates of the twenties, producing no revolutionary socialist equivalent to Anderson's reformist 'Problems of Socialist Strategy' of 1965. How would such a transition be effected?

Anderson remained wedded to the Leninist insistence that the capitalist state, even a parliamentary-democratic one, could not be reformed from within and must be displaced. The state was the embodiment of class rule, and the institutions of the parliamentary-democratic state could not readily be emptied of their class content. A representative assembly was but one aspect of the capitalist state, whose 'apparatuses' included the repressive armoury of the army and police, and an unelected administrative bureaucracy and judiciary, all of which operated as a shadow government at arm's length from the control of parliament. To win an electoral majority was by no means the same thing as neutralising these repressive apparatuses, let alone exercising authority over them.

Although the *Review* rejected the concept of a parliamentary road to socialism, Robin Blackburn renounced the 'anti-parliamentary cretinism' of much of the far Left that had emerged in Europe since the late sixties.[69] The task of the revolutionary Left was to participate in the election of a workers' government of the broad Left, without sowing illusions in the parliamentary road; to expect and, where possible, induce a polarisation of political forces in the event of such a government coming to office; and to prepare the workers for a decisive break with the bourgeois-democratic state during a period of revolutionary crisis.

Ernest Mandel, also writing in the hundredth issue of the *Review*, shared Anderson's recognition of the 'far greater *intrinsic* strength and stability of the bourgeois state and social order in the West, *in normal times*'.[70] However, he was convinced that moments of political crisis – perhaps induced, as in the past, by the election of a Left government with Communist participation – would demonstrate the universal applicability of certain key features of the Russian Revolution: the decomposition of the existing state and, marking the arrival of a genuine revolutionary crisis, the emergence of alternative institutions of workers' democracy.[71] Anderson considered that such a period of overlapping dual power was a critical precondition for socialist revolution in the West, which 'will only occur ... when the masses have made the experience of a proletarian democracy that is tangibly superior to bourgeois democracy. The sole way for the victory of socialism to be secured in these societies is for it to represent incontestably more, not less, freedom for the vast majority of the population ... [T]he exhibition of a new, unprivileged liberty must start before the old order is structurally cancelled by the conquest of the State.'[72]

But Anderson was less certain of the character, even the viability, of the 'proletarian democracy' that must prove itself superior to bourgeois democracy during the anticipated period of dual power presaging such a revolutionary rupture. The Paris Commune and the Russian soviets were taken as the models of socialist democracy,[73] yet Anderson recognised that the workers' councils that emerged in Russia and central Europe during the revolutionary era immediately after 1917 were 'ephemeral experiences'.[74] In 1971 Ben Brewster was posing the question of what form dual power would take in the 'imperialist countries today',[75] but by 1978 Anderson was acknowledging that '[s]o far little work has been done in exploring how – in what forms – there could occur a resurgence of a soviet-type state, soviet in the classical and genuine sense of the word, in the quite different social and historical conditions of contemporary Western Europe. The result is that a large question mark still remains suspended over the … classical tradition of revolutionary socialism.'[76]

If the question of democracy was so central, why the eagerness to abolish existing representative institutions? Was this not a case of tipping the parliamentary-democratic baby out with the capitalist-state bathwater? Why not maximise the legitimacy offered by a parliamentary majority, which in countries with a long parliamentary democratic tradition could be crucial in facing down any counter-revolutionary threat? As Arghiri Emmanuel sensibly argued, winning an electoral majority compelled the bourgeoisie to 'shoot first', and thus allow revolutionaries to act in 'self-defence' to make the revolution: 'the question is not one of legality for the sake of legality, but of fighting on the legal terrain in order to oblige one's adversary to abandon it'.[77] The *combination* of representative and direct democracy might prove the best means of navigating the difficult passage to socialism, and a better guarantee of socialist democracy in a post-revolutionary society. This was the perspective adopted by Left Euro-Communists such as Claudin, Poulantzas and Trentin, who advocated an alternative to both mainstream Euro-Communism and Leninism.[78]

However, so its critics argued, the Euro-Communist conception of the transition to socialism – in both its 'Left' and 'Right' variants – fatally (witness Chile) misunderstood the dynamics of social revolution: a revolutionary moment, however peaceful in intent, is also, unavoidably, a counter-revolutionary moment, in which class conflict is *heightened* not reduced. If political power is to be wrested from the bourgeoisie, it had better be done swiftly, while popular mobilisation is at the peak of its strength. The advocates of Euro-Communism, wrote Henri Weber, 'imagine that if the elements of the revolutionary break are dissociated and spaced out from one another, the chances of success will be greater than if an attempt is made to pass the point of no return through a head-on trial of strength. But they forget that the class relationship of forces is always changing; that the opportunity to inflict decisive defeats on the dominant class only arises in certain critical conjunctures; and that, in between, the bourgeoisie manages to stabilise its system and throw the workers onto the defensive.'[79] Anderson, presenting the *NLR*'s understanding of revolution, argued that when the 'unity of the bourgeois state and the reproduction of the capitalist economy are ruptured, the ensuing social upheaval must rapidly and fatally pit revo-lution and counter-revolution against each other in violent convulsion … In this end-game situation, socialists will seek to avoid a conclusion by arms, but will not sow illusions as to the probability of a resort to them.'[80]

The Left Euro-Communists viewed any such confrontation with trepi-dation. They – like Anderson – had doubts concerning the character and viability of 'proletarian democracy'. Without a directly elected representa-tive assembly, how could the organs of proletarian democracy be prevented from withering on the vine, giving way, as in the past, to a revolutionary dictatorship? Poulantzas insisted that 'socialism will be democratic or it will not be at all'; and whilst reflecting that 'if democratic socialism has never yet existed', this might be because it was 'impossible', he opted for the risk of de-feat entailed in a democratic road to socialism in preference 'to massacring other people only to end up ourselves beneath the blade of a Committee of Public Safety or some Dictator of the Proletariat'.[81]

However, leading advocates of the Fourth International could express no great optimism either. 'Who today would deny', wrote Henri Weber in the following issue of the *Review*, in 1978,

> that the Leninist theses on democracy and socialism present certain excesses and lacunae? When they first proclaimed these positions, the Bolshevik leaders were doing their utmost to resist social democracy's Europe-wide collaboration in re-establishing bourgeois order, under the banner of defending democracy. Seen in this light, Lenin's denun-ciation of 'bourgeois democratism' and his symmetrical apologia for 'proletarian democracy', according to an unhappily familiar (and to some extent inevitable) procedure, 'bent the stick in the other direc-tion'.[82]

Weber argued that the 'struggle to defend and enlarge democratic freedoms is certainly a key strategic axis of the struggle for socialism in the West. This is not the point in dispute with Eurocommunist theoreticians'.[83] But whilst rejecting the gradualism of Euro-Communism, in both its Right and Left variants, he concluded, honestly if rather lamely, that 'the strategy of transition to socialism ... has still largely to be invented in the advanced capitalist countries with a long democratic tradition'.[84]

Despite its revolutionary affiliations, the *Review* expressed a certain equivocation, presenting both revolutionary Marxist critiques of Euro-Communism and Left Euro-Communist responses – Mandel and Weber on the one hand, Claudin and Poulantzas on the other, being the main protagonists of each camp.[85] The *NLR* appeared unwilling, or perhaps unable, to adjudicate on the debate, and privately lamented that 'favourable significantly outweighed critical treatment of Eurocommunism', while what criticism there was tended to reiterate 'classical tenets', rather than develop 'new revolutionary strategies'.[86] Was it possible to avoid the twin pitfalls of the passage to socialism: either a revolutionary adventure, with disastrous and deadly consequences; or, in an effort to forestall the blows of reaction by maintaining the support of the broadest mass of the people, a fatal caution, demobilising the popular movement and assisting the restabilisation of bourgeois rule? At what point, precisely, did one advance from a 'war of position' to a 'war of manoeuvre'? Would the popular forces be prepared to go on the offensive as a unified bloc? Even if the moment were clear, and the movement united, the popular forces must still confront a state with considerable latent repressive power.

Critiques abounded, but little progress was made in divining a satisfactory solution. Symptomatically, Anderson's manuscript 'state and revolution in the West' remained unpublished, perhaps unfinished, and Mandel was unable to produce a promised strategic study of *Revolution in Western Europe*.[87] Although the *Review* retained its affiliation to the classical tradition, by 1978 Anderson was voicing his disappointment at the failure of the Fourth International to respond convincingly to the strategic impasse.[88]

Meanwhile, in Italy, Spain and France events were moving apace. The course of the PCI appeared the most timid of the Euro-Communist parties, provoking Magri to lament that Berlinguer, architect of the historic compromise, 'is to Togliatti what Napoleon III is to Napoleon I'.[89] Instead of being radicalised by the student and working-class militancy of the years following the hot autumn of 1969, the PCI inclined towards greater moderation, frightened by the prospect of a confrontation with the Right, and its menacing talk of a 'strategy of tension' (underscored by neo-fascist bombings linked to the security services).[90] At the 1976 polls the PCI consolidated its electoral advance (34.4 per cent), but in a squeeze on the smaller parties, the DC vote held firm, and the PCI failed to outscore it. In seeking to win over progressive elements of Christian Democracy, the PCI supported, but did not enter, Andreotti's DC government. However, in manoeuvring at the level of 'high' politics rather than in a mobilising from below, the PCI underestimated the cohesiveness of the DC, proving unable to win sections of it over to a new hegemonic bloc of the Left. Meanwhile, the Socialists, antagonised by the PCI's orientation to the DC, passed under the leadership of Bettino Craxi, intent on an anti-Communist 'centre-left' coalition with the DC, which would exclude the PCI from any prospect of government.

Pursuing a Spanish version of the Italian road, the PCE under Santiago Carillo sought its own historic compromise with the liberal bourgeoisie, assisting the passage to a stable parliamentary democratic order in signing up to the Moncloa Pact with the reformist Suarez government. In the first post-Franco elections in 1977 and 1979, the PCE scored a disappointing 10 per cent of the vote, strongly outvoted by the Socialists under Felipe Gonzalez, who, as in neighbouring Portugal, proved the architects of capitalist modernisation and entry to the European Economic Community.

As the political defeats of the seventies multiplied, the seriousness of the strategic blockage was forcefully underlined. The defeats were particularly damning in that they illustrated 'a spectrum of different types of blockage or error': from the bureaucratic 'sectarian putschism' of the Portuguese Communist Party, compounded by the failure of the Fourth International, to the 'fawning accommodation' of the historically compromised PCI and the electoral misadventures of the PCE.[91] 'The dearth of strategic inspiration proved universal': what was common to all these experiences was 'the complete absence of any coherent strategy for a transition to socialism across and beyond the barrier of a bourgeois-democratic state'.[92] The revolutionary Left, meanwhile, had failed even in the preliminary task of winning the workers in any number to the cause of revolutionary socialism.

It was the electoral defeat of the French Left in March 1978 – outwardly less conclusive and dramatic than, say, events in Chile or Portugal – that effectively closed the decade of revolutionary expectations opened in 1968, following the breakdown of the Union of the Left between the PCF and PS. It was not simply that the 'French working class, which in May 1968 showed itself capable of a far higher degree of coordinated mobilisation than any of its peers in the advanced capitalist world since 1945, has been – at least temporarily – demoralised and disoriented'.[93] More critically the *NLR*, convinced of the centrality of ideas, detected a 'significant rightward shift at the ideological level' in France attested by the ascendancy of the *nouveaux philosophes*, 'a flight from Marxism on the part of certain layers of the "generation of '68", and a progressive rightward drift of most social-democratic and Communist parties'.[94] Althusser, until recently so confident in his public pronouncements, spoke darkly of 'the crisis of Marxism'.[95] In the aftermath of the break-up of the Union of the Left and defeat at the polls in 1978, the PCF retreated to its workerist bunker, outmanoeuvred by the more tactically astute Mitterrand. The PS now emerged as the larger of the two parties of the Left for the first time, and although a patched up electoral arrangement with the PCF delivered presidential and legislative election victories to the Left in 1981, the dynamic between the two parties, and the wider political conjuncture, had altered decisively. As the prospect of a transition to socialism in one or more of the advanced capitalist countries receded, the unanswered questions confronting revolutionary strategy in the West slipped from the *Review*'s immediate agenda.

3. Silences and Criticisms

What did the *NLR*'s left-turn of 1968 involve in terms of its analysis of British politics and its ties with the British Left? With its attentions focused on southern Europe as offering the most likely prospect of a revolutionary breakthrough, sustained interest in and coverage of Britain almost vanished from the pages of the *Review* in the seventies. So far as the 1970 election was concerned, for example, Robin Blackburn was content to 'let it bleed', arguing, in the first issue of the *Red Mole* (3 April 1970) that 'the only principled course for revolutionary socialists ... will be an active campaign to discredit both of Britain's large capitalist parties'.[96] Aside from the short-lived interest in the brief period of industrial militancy in 1971-2, the principal exception to this silence was Tom Nairn's series of interventions on nationalism and the UK state, developing at a considerable tangent to the core trajectory of the *NLR*.

In 1972 the *Review* registered the recent 'dramatic rise in the intensity of the British class struggle', led principally by the miners, in which the 'most militant tactics have been taken up on a mass scale for the first time in the history of British trade unions'.[97] This prompted articles by both Robin Blackburn and Anthony Barnett,[98] and suggested a possible re-drawing of Anderson's summary distinction between southern and northern Europe. In 1972 the *Review* wrote that 'the new map of the Common Market contains something like two separate sectors: a central bloc of territory comprising France, Benelux and Germany, marked by unbroken growth and high per-capita income, with the laggard and relatively low-income zones of Britain and Italy on either flank'.[99] The Heath and Andreotti governments (in 1972 the DC broke its long-standing 'centre-left' coalition with the Socialists and opted to rule alone) represented 'the two most extreme right-wing regimes in the EEC, reflecting the gravity of the problems facing the bourgeoisie of each country'.[100]

For Anderson, 1972 marked the launch 'of the most successful industrial offensive'[101] in the history of the British working class, and the *NLR* hoped that the intensification of class conflict would 'disrupt political patterns that have long been an obstacle to the spread of revolutionary politics in Britain'.[102] However, given the weak implantation of a revolutionary socialist politics in the labour movement, Blackburn feared that industrial militancy would result only in a 'quasi-syndicalism'. An interview with Arthur Scargill, leader of the Yorkshire miners, served to underline the distance between even the most militant figures in the labour movement and the commitment to socialist revolution espoused by the *NLR*.[103]

Working-class resistance, and the nervousness of big business and the bourgeois press over the Conservatives' confrontational course, was charted by Barnett in 1973, signalling Heath's 'U-turn' to a more conventional interventionist approach. The relative industrial peace that followed the fall of the Heath government, and the diversion of the Labour Left's energies into opposition to the EEC, were sufficient to re-focus the *Review*'s attentions elsewhere. There was no coverage at all of the fall of Heath, the two elections in 1974, the performance of the Wilson and Callaghan governments, or the rise of the New Right within the Conservative Party.

Writing in 1977, Geoff Hodgson judged that Anderson and co. had become 'the lost sheep of the labour movement',[104] too remote from the institutions of organised labour and the problems confronting any realistic political strategy for the attainment of socialism in Britain. The *NLR*'s detached intellectualism was central to Edward Thompson's critique in *The Poverty of Theory* (see below); and in 1980 Mike Rustin condemned the *NLR* for 'deliberately severing it[s] ties with the reformist and consensual politics of Labourism, where the earlier new left and the *May Day Manifesto* had always sought to keep these connections open', deploring the fact that 1968 had 'marked the watershed of a politics of radical separatism of the left'.[105] Even in the absence of the 'control' constituted by links with a genuine movement, it would not have been beyond the *Review*, had it so wished, to devise a mechanism for a closer, and more interactive, relationship with its readers. Paul Hirst considered 'its failure to establish any political or democratic relation to its own "constituency"' as one of the *Review*'s main weaknesses,[106] and the establishment of readers' groups would be one of the unacceptable demands tabled by Barbara Taylor et al. when invited to join the editorial committee in 1984. This lack of 'control' partly explains the sudden shifts of commitment – from Wilson to trade unions, for example, or from students to the revolutionary Left – without any reflection upon, let alone explicit disavowal of, earlier editorial perspectives. '[P]revious positions', wrote Ian Birchall in 1981, 'were simply abandoned as though they had never existed.'[107]

In similar vein to Hodgson and Rustin, Donald Sassoon argued in 1981 that any 'analysis of British political life and political struggles would force' the Review 'to confront the problem of articulating plans and projects which must be rooted in contemporary reality', necessarily 'beginning ... at the level of existing struggles, the existing movements, the existing organisations, the existing framework of reference of ongoing politics'.[108] Moreover, it 'would lead it towards the domain of politics, which is the domain of compromises, historic or temporary, and of alliances'.[109] Whereas Anderson had lamented in 1980 that 'the absence of a truly mass and revolutionary movement in England, as elsewhere in the West, has fixed the perimeter of all possible thought in this period', Paul Hirst replied: 'Yes, how true. But we live in this period and no other, we must face this fact and not live in the hope of revolutions to come.'[110] The continuing work of Ken Coates and others in the Institute for Workers' Control, the tabling of an innovative alternative workers' plan at Lucas Aerospace, and the wide-ranging debate on an alternative economic strategy, for example, all went unexplored in the pages of the Review.

Wedded to the revolutionary paradigm of 1917, the NLR maintained a somewhat simplistic prognosis that crisis equals class polarisation equals revolution (or counter-revolution). Symptomatic of the NLR's commitment to 'labour' in the abstract – to 'the universal class standpoint of the proletariat',[111] to take one quote from the Review at random – and its lack of interest in domestic politics was that no updated equivalent of Anderson's 'Problems of Socialist Strategy' was ever produced. Was the 1921 strategy of the 'united front', as Anderson advocated, really adequate or appropriate? Where were the revolutionary parties that were to win the workers from reformism? Why did reformism have such a strong hold? Who precisely were these 'workers' – in what meaningful sense could they be treated as an homogenous whole, given the fault-lines that differentiated skilled from unskilled, industrial from service workers, the private from the public sector, to say nothing of divisions based on gender or race?

Developing a concrete analysis of the social and political forces at play in contemporary capitalist societies would, moreover, have required looking beyond 'labour' – abstract or actual – to social movements not directly reducible to class, not least the women's movement. The Review carried a brief three-page report of the 1970 conference at Oxford that effectively launched the women's liberation movement in Britain,[112] but thereafter devoted bare-ly a handful of theoretical articles to questions posed by feminism and none to the movement itself.

The one intervention by a member of the *NLR* collective – an extended review and critique of Germaine Greer's *The Female Eunuch*, Eva Figes' *Patriarchal Attitudes*, and Kate Millet's *Sexual Politics* (all originally pub-lished in 1970) – was by Branka Magaš in 1971. Magaš charted the limita-tions of feminism, and 'the overwhelmingly non-Marxist' and 'often explic-itly and bitterly anti-Marxist ... ideology which characterises the women's liberation movement'[113] – although she admitted that this owed much to the failure of Marxism to provide an 'adequate theory of the role of the family ... or the specifity of women's oppression in the advanced capitalist countries'.[114] Divisions within the editorial collective were such that reply and counter-reply quickly followed. Peter Wollen (writing as 'Lucien Rey') asserted, *contra* Magaš, that the 'process of Marxising feminism can only take place *pari passu* with the process of feminising Marxism',[115] though seemingly placing greater emphasis on the latter. He also defended the in-dependent organisation of women (rather than as merely 'auxiliary' to the revolutionary party). In addition, the later exchange on domestic labour was the occasion for a short half-page 'communication' to which Fred and Jon Halliday, Peter Wollen ('Lucien Rey'), and Gareth Stedman Jones put their names, defending, against the implied tone of a recent introductory 'Themes', the validity of Marxist feminism as 'an important and fruitful theoretical and political current within the women's and proletarian move-ments', arguing that it was not simply a matter of affirming 'the validity of ... the questions being raised by the feminist movement', but that these questions demanded a criticism and development of 'Marxism itself'.[116] For Branka Magaš and Robin Blackburn, on the other hand, the 'notion of a "feminised Marxism" or a Marxised feminism" is an absurdity': [117] feminism is an 'ideology', Marxism a 'science', therefore 'Marxism is the only possible starting point ... for a theoretical understanding and for a revolutionary in-tervention in the current women's liberation movement'.[118] They denounced the idea of separate women's organisation as un-Leninist,[119] and asserted the primacy of class politics.

Perhaps as with the case of Ireland (see below), it was divergent political positions within the editorial committee that enforced a tactical silence in the interests of maintaining an outward show of unanimity. But if so, given the centrality of the theoretical and strategic questions posed by feminism and the women's liberation movement, it was a silence that did much to thwart the *Review*'s proclaimed goal of divining a passage to socialism in conditions of advanced capitalism.[120]

Unimpressed by a labour movement wedded to reformism, and dismissive of such as the women's movement, some at the *Review* judged that a more potent threat to the UK state appeared to be posed by the 'national question' in its various aspects: by the near civil war in the six counties comprising Northern Ireland; by the issue of Britain's membership of the European Economic Community; and by the demands for independence in Scotland and Wales.

The most dramatic, though localised, challenge to the UK state in this period arose in the north of Ireland – 'British capitalism['s] ... nearest vassal territory'[121] – where the civil rights movement met the intransigent hostility of the Loyalist Stormont statelet, and escalating inter-communal violence led to the dispatch of British troops to the province in 1969. The *NLR* conducted an interview with five leading members of the socialist-oriented People's Democracy movement, including Bernadette Devlin, who had just been elected an MP at the age of 22, and Liam Baxter, member of the short-lived Revolutionary Socialist Students' Federation.[122] However, 'People's Democracy' failed to detach the Protestant working class from its Unionist loyalties, and the conflict returned to the well-worn grooves of sectarian animosity. Despite the continuing state of 'full-scale civil war' in one of the UK's four provinces, 'involving the most complex and tortuous case of the problems posed by the national question in Europe', the *Review* conceded, confidentially, that a 'tacit impasse' developed within the editorial committee on the question of Ireland – a subject that, 'by common consent', was 'avoided within NLR';[123] a silence that would not be broken for a full twenty-five years.[124] The IMG gave unconditional support for the IRA in the early seventies – calling for 'Victory for the IRA' and establishing the Irish Solidarity Campaign on the model of the VSC – and many on the far Left continued to see in the conflict the prospect of a revolutionary upheaval, attested by Tariq Ali's extravagant claim in 1972 that 'Ireland could ... turn out to be the Achilles heel of European capitalism, a Cuba in Europe'.[125] Most of those at the *NLR*, however, remained sceptical towards IRA terrorism. Fred Halliday, for example, as a principal speaker at the second Troops Out Movement conference in 1974, distanced himself from the IRA campaign.[126]

Nowhere was the *NLR*'s distant relations with the British Left in this period better attested than in Tom Nairn's heterodox intervention on the question of British entry to the European 'Common Market' – negotiated by Heath in 1972, and confirmed by referendum on the advent of the Wilson

government in 1975. While 'the ruling class', the 'architect and chief ben-
eficiary of nationalism', was uniting 'on a policy of abandoning old-style
national sovereignty', Nairn was deeply sceptical of the Left's mobilisation of
'the working class – principal victim of nation-state oppression throughout
history ... in a rigid defence of nationality, virgin self-determination, the
English constitution and the New Zealand dairy farmers'.[127] Indeed, in 1972
the *Review* devoted an entire issue – 'The Left Against Europe?' – to Nairn's
120-page critique of the British Left's response to EEC membership.[128] In its
preface, the *NLR* denounced the Labour Left's anti-Market campaign as a
'providential distraction from the painful choices of the real class struggle
raging outside the conventicles of the Labour Party'.[129] Moreover, the attempt
to marry the labour movement to 'the potent forces of popular nationalism',
lauded by many on the Left, was regarded as full of 'perilous consequences',
instanced in 'the Labour Party's capitulation to the racist hysteria surrounding the arrival of the Ugandan Asians'.[130]

The readiness of British capital to seek an answer to its long-term decline,
and recent precipitate drop in profitability,[131] in membership of the EEC
confirmed the trend of global internationalisation and the weakened significance of the nation-state in economic affairs. It was, according to Nairn,
a logical choice. 'The great "national" party put class before nation, while
the "class" party put nation before class.'[132] While capital adjusted to the new
international order, Nairn deplored the fact that the Left remained 'penned
... within the old frontiers'.[133] Supporting entry to the Common Market
did not, he argued, 'imply surrender to or alliance with the left's enemies.
It means exactly the opposite. It signifies recognising and meeting them as
enemies, for what they are, upon the terrain of reality and the future. It im-
plies a stronger and more direct opposition to them, because an opposition
unfettered by the archaic delusions of Europe's *anciens régimes*.'[134]

Critically for Nairn, British nationalism lacked any *popular* component:
'the People' had been mobilised neither from below nor above in the making of the modern bourgeois state, inducing a 'spurious conservative unity'
that 'is the bane of modern British politics'.[135] For Nairn, Scots and Welsh
national identity provided an escape route from an irredeemably regressive
'UK nationalism'. It was the emergence of these separatist Celtic national-
isms in the late sixties that Nairn identified as the most likely dissolvent of
the archaic UK state: as early as 1968 he was writing that 'in the slow, fester-
ing decay of British State and society, they are the most important forces of
disintegration to have appeared yet'.[136] English identity, however, was less
easily separable from the conservatism of 'UK nationalism', informing a
're-heated romanticism' that shaped a 'Disney-like English world where the

Saxon ploughs his fields and the sun sets to strains by Vaughan Williams'.[137] 'The fall of the old system must force a kind of national self-definition upon all the British peoples. This process is most important, but also most difficult, for the English metropolis where all the main roots of the British state are located. There, the very strength of those bases means that it is far harder for system-directed resentment and loss of allegiance to find tolerable expression.'[138] This disfigured identity was expressed, for example, in Powellism, and various ugly manifestations of populist racism – a constituent element in the rise of the New Right.

These questions raised wider issues about the nature of nationalism in the modern world, which represented, in Nairn's words, 'Marxism's great historical failure'.[139] The *Review* judged that in 'the twentieth century the defeats of the workers' movement have owed much to the unsuspected, and often unacknowledged, power of nationalism – an ideology that has also coloured many of its victories'.[140] Nationalism had proven 'to be one of the great elemental forces of twentieth-century history, bending bourgeois and proletarian politics alike to its particularisms … Marxism has manifestly failed to develop a serious theory of nationalism, commensurate with the formidable scale and gravity of its impact on the course of international class struggle'.[141] The deficiency of Marxist theory in respect of nationalism was reiterated by others. Anderson identified it as one of the key weaknesses of Marxism in *Considerations on Western Marxism*;[142] whilst in the *NLR* Michael Löwy recognised that 'Marx offered neither a systematic theory of the national question, a precise definition of the concept of a "nation", nor a general political strategy for the proletariat in this domain.'[143]

In 'The Modern Janus' in 1975, Nairn argued that nationalism was the product of the impact of uneven development; its origins 'are located not in the folk, nor in the individual's repressed passion for some sort of wholeness or identity, but in the machinery of world political economy … [T]he most notoriously subjective and ideal of historical phenomena is in fact a by-product of the most brutally and hopelessly material side of the history of the last two centuries'.[144] As capitalism spread in concentric circles from its north-west European heartlands, peripheral elites were compelled to mobilise a populist nationalism to resist outright domination by the more advanced capitalist states. Marx had been mistaken to envisage the erosion of national identity with the advent of free trade and global capitalism. On the contrary, nationalism was enhanced, and the nation-state had become the principal political unit of the bourgeoisie: 'The new middle-class intelligentsia of nationalism had to invite the masses into history; and the invitation had to be written in a language they understood ... This is why a romantic culture quite remote from Enlightenment rationalism always went hand-in-hand with the spread of nationalism'.[145]

'[O]nce the advanced states took over the doctrines of "nationalism" they were certain to give these ideas real muscle'[146] – culminating, ultimately, in fascism. The abstract internationalism of the 'universal' proletariat project- ed by Marx had been over-ridden by the potency of nationalism: national identity had persistently proved to be stronger than class identity – often the flawed and limited prism through which class conflict has itself been crudely articulated. In any anti-imperialist struggle, which was the context for most socialist revolutions in the twentieth-century, 'nationalism was simply incomparably superior to what was contained in a still rudimen- tary (often, one should say, a merely nascent) class consciousness'.[147] But nationalism was a double-edged weapon. Nairn's 'modern Janus' had both a progressive and regressive aspect, and thus no straightforwardly progressive vocation could be allotted to an anti-imperialist nationalism: there are not 'two brands of nationalism, one healthy and one morbid ... [A]ll national- ism is both healthy and morbid. Both progress and regress are inscribed in its genetic code from the start'.[148] He judged that nationalism was 'the pathology of modern developmental history, as inescapable as "neurosis" in the individual, with much the same essential ambiguity attaching to it, a similar built-in capacity for descent into dementia, rooted in the dilemmas of helplessness thrust upon most of the world (the equivalent of infantilism for societies), and largely incurable'.[149]

There was far from unanimity within the *NLR* on Nairn's emphasis on the centrality of nationalism.[150] In a critical review of Nairn's 'The Break-Up of Britain' published in the *NLR* in 1977, Eric Hobsbawm acknowledged 'the relative decline of the medium-to-large nation-state and "national econo- my" as the main building block of the world economy',[151] and the growth of small-nation nationalism. Hobsbawm recognised that where the 'main road' had 'been blocked or destroyed', Scots and Welsh nationalism might, in Nairn's words, produce 'a detour on the road to revolution', but he feared that 'the detour will become the journey.'[152] He remained sceptical about the progressive potential of nationalism, and reckoned that 'in its own Marxist terms, the Connolly Marxist-nationalist policy must be regarded as a fail- ure. There is no reason to suppose *a priori* that Scots and Welsh revolution- ary Marxists have a good chance of transforming the SNP or Plaid Cymru into some kind of Vietcong merely by offering their services and leadership to the nationalist cause.'[153] He wondered whether the temptations of Scots and Welsh nationalism might be an undue pull 'for Marxists who wanted to be on the winning side for a change',[154] and remained convinced that it was mistaken for Marxists to welcome or seek an accommodation with nationalism, 'rather than realistically to accept it as a fact, a condition of their struggle as socialists'.[155] Undoubtedly echoing the concerns of some at the *NLR*, Hobsbawm heeded Lenin's injunction: 'Do not paint nationalism red'.[156]

The 1980 editorial report recognised the 'brilliance' of Nairn's intervention – 'the most comprehensive and significant development of the original NLR theses on Britain since the mid-sixties'[157] – but judged that Nairn had 'overpitched the degree of condensation of the contradictions of the British social formation into the national question'.[158] However, it acknowledged that this 'misreading of the balance of forces in the periphery was … very much in the tradition of NLR', for '[e]ver since the early sixties, the review had looked with hope to one potential agent after another to unhinge the ruling political order in England – each time overstating its radicalism or staying-power'; citing 'the credence lent' to the Labour Party in 1964, the trade unions in 1967, and students in 1968-9, in addition to the 'national revolts of 1974-8'.[159]

Looking to the future, the 1980 editorial report went on to advocate a 'reanchorage' in the British Left, in a political context transformed by the recent defeats experienced by the Left in southern Europe, and the rise of the New Right to governmental power in Britain and America.

4. The Two New Lefts, or Edward Thompson and Perry Anderson: reprise

On the eve of this new, unfavourable conjuncture, Edward Thompson's *The Poverty of Theory* was published in 1978. Although ostensibly a frontal assault on the work of Althusser, Thompson's intervention was much wider in scope. Perry Anderson considered it 'the most sustained exposition of Thompson's own credo, as a historian and socialist, that we have to date'.[160] It could be said that Anderson's reply to Thompson, *Arguments Within English Marxism*, was, in turn, the most sustained exposition of the *NLR*'s own credo to date, for Anderson used the opportunity to summarise the *Review*'s perspective at what was arguably the moment of its greatest direction and self-confidence.

The 'controlled hysteria'[161] of Thompson's polemic in *The Poverty of Theory* amounted (in Anderson's words) to 'the declaration of a general jehad against Althusserianism'.[162] Thompson wrote that 'Althusserianism *is* Stalinism reduced to the paradigm of theory':[163] Althusser's project should be seen 'as a manifestation of a general police action within ideology, as the attempt to reconstruct Stalinism at the level of theory'.[164] Much of the sting of Thompson's assault had been drawn prior to publication, for the identification of Althusser as arch-Stalinist proved untimely. *The Poverty of Theory* appeared just after Althusser had issued his damning critique of the PCF, 'What Must Change in the Party',[165] of which Anderson could with some justice write: 'it is probably safe to say that Althusser's manifesto of April 1978 is the most violent oppositional charter ever published within a party in the post-war history of Western Communism'.[166] Thompson, somewhat wrong-footed, sought to redirect his fire in an Afternote, claiming that his target was as much contemporary British Marxism in general, including the post-1962 *NLR*, as Althusser in particular.

Thus Althusser's particular claims need not unduly detain us – his star was already waning in Paris, and though near its zenith in Britain would soon experience a precipitous decline. In any case, the *Review* had sufficiently distanced itself from Althusser, publishing no less than four critical appraisals of his work prior to Thompson's outburst; the first, by Norman Geras, as early as 1972.[167] It was Althusserian*ism*, symbolic of all that he found most objectionable in contemporary Marxism, which provoked Thompson's ire. He inveighed against the whole generation of *gauchiste* 'sixty-eighters', including British 'import agencies' such as the *NLR*,[168] in his sweeping polemic.

Expanding upon themes first broached in the 1976 Postscript to the second edition of *William Morris* (reproduced in the *Review* in the same year),[169] Thompson contended that Marxism had experienced a determinist closure in the 1880s and 1890s, in part due to the contemporary ascendancy of positivism. The failure to respond to Morris' utopianism and moralism was, in Thompson's account, a decisive missed opportunity in the early career of Marxism, which thereafter proved unable to escape the economistic framework of *Capital*. In Thompson's reading of the history of Marxism, this determinist imprisonment had been shaken by the 1914-18 war and the advent of fascism. The evolutionist optimism of the earlier period gave way to an 'heroic period', which Thompson dated to 1936-46, with its emphasis on commitment and sacrifice, marked by the Spanish Civil War and the Resistance to fascism and occupation. It was, of course, in this 'voluntarist' period that Thompson was recruited to the ranks of Communism. The Cold War, he argued, brought this 'heroic period' to an end: the emergence of two entrenched blocs heralded an era of political and cultural immobility, in which history 'seemed to congeal in an instant into two monstrous antagonistic structures'.[170] Thus, in the structuralist imagination, history could appear as a 'process without a subject'.[171] The intervention of the first New Left, in Thompson's reckoning, had been precisely to rescue Marxism from the consequences of this closure – with 'Althusserianism' portrayed as the latest, paradigmatic, attempt to restore it.

In Thompson's judgement Althusserianism, and the tendency within Marxism of which it was the contemporary representative, amounted to 'Stalinism' in one key aspect: it reflected and justified a divorce between theory and practice. Moreover, this 'weird apparition, a freak of intellectual fashion' sanctioned an ultra-leftist posturing.[172] 'In general', he argued, 'it may be said that there has never been a generation of socialist intellectuals in the West with *less* experience of practical struggle, with less sense of the initiatives thrown up in mass movements, with less sense of what the intellectual can learn from men and women of practical experience, and of the proper dues of humility which the intellectual must owe to this.'[173] This was in contrast to the first New Left, whose *raison d'etre* had been to build a popular movement. Herein lay the real target of Thompson's polemic, for he saw in this wilful separation of theory from practice and experience the imprint of 'Stalinism':

> [T]he intellectuals – a chosen band of these – have been given the task of enlightening the people. There is no mark more distinctive of Western Marxisms nor more revealing of their profoundly anti-democratic premises ... [T]hey are marked by their very heavy emphasis upon the ineluctable weight of ideological modes of domination – domination which destroys every space for the initiative or creativity of the mass of the people – a domination from which only the enlightened minority of intellectuals can struggle free ... Such a theory, if ever afforded any power, so far from 'liberating' the working class would, in its insufferable arrogance and pretensions to 'science', deliver them into the hands of a bureaucratic clerisy: the *next* ruling-class, waiting on the line.[174]

Although a polemicist's licence may excuse some of the exaggeration of Thompson's intervention, the polemical style itself was not conducive to a constructive exchange – witness the notorious 'gladiatorial combat'[175] over these and related issues at a History Workshop debate between Thompson, Stuart Hall and Richard Johnson in Oxford in December 1979. But Thompson was surely right to highlight the incipient elitism of too great a distance between socialist theory on the one hand, and the practice and experience of working people on the other. Norman Geras had made the same criticism of Althusser in the *Review* in 1972.[176] It was this very separation that, in Anderson's judgement, had condemned Western Marxism to an 'esoteric' existence. However, the *NLR* cannot escape the charge of 'elitism' quite so easily, reflecting as it did something of the esotericism Anderson had condemned in Western Marxism, identified by Lin Chun as a certain 'super-theoreticism',[177] witness, in Ellen Woods words, to a 'loss of interest in popular struggles in general, and the labour movement in particular', and the 'conviction that the central terrain of socialist struggle was from now on intellectual'[178] – themes to which we shall return in due course.

Whilst the *Review*'s *Trotskysant aktiv* awaited the return of a revolution-ary practice of the masses to rejoin theory to practice, Thompson, by con-trast, preferred that theory recognise the inherently pragmatic and reform-ist practice of the labour movement in the advanced capitalist countries. The 'revival of Marxism' in Britain, he argued, had produced 'a mountain of thought', but 'not yet given birth to one political mouse. Enclosed within the intelligentsia's habitual elitism, the theorists disdain to enter into any kind of relation with a Labour movement which they know (on *a priori* grounds) to be "reformist" and "corporative"'.[179] We have seen that similar critiques were penned by Geoff Hodgson, Mike Rustin, Donald Sassoon and Paul Hirst.[180]

In *Arguments Within English Marxism*, Anderson responded to Thompson's salvo with a remarkably measured appraisal, dispassionately adjudicating Thompson's claims in marked contrast to the polemics over the 'Nairn-Anderson theses' in the mid-sixties. Of the substantive issues raised in *The Poverty of Theory*, Thompson's version of the history of Marxism, and his attempt to locate Althusser within it, was swiftly dismissed by Anderson. The purported period of determinist closure included some of the most voluntarist of all currents within the history of Marxism: the triumph of the Chinese Revolution and Mao's 'Cultural Revolution'; the Cuban Revolution and Guevarism (one of whose most articulate exponents was Régis Debray, student of Althusser); and, not least, the unquestionably 'heroic' struggle of the Vietnamese. 'An explanation of Althusser's thought in terms of plan-etary doldrums', concluded Anderson, 'is without worth.'[181]

Nonetheless, Thompson's critique of Althusser's unyielding structural-ism and self-referential verification – 'the child of economic determinism ravished by theoreticist idealism'[182] – was, by and large, upheld. Anderson recognised the amoral consequences of a theoretical endeavour such as Althusser's that sought to seal itself off in a self-validating realm immune to the world of human practice. The due balance between structure and agency was identified by Anderson as the key point in dispute, with Althusser and Thompson located at opposite and equally mistaken poles: structuralism on the one hand and voluntarism on the other.[183] Where Althusser stressed 'the overpowering weight of structural necessity in history',[184] Thompson was a passionate advocate of the potential of human agency, 'in defiance of the millennial negations of self-determination in the kingdom of necessity'.[185]

The essence of Thompson's 'socialist humanism' or 'libertarian communism' was a faith in ordinary men and women as the 'ever-baffled and ever-resurgent agents of an unmastered history',[186] mediated through the key Thompsonian category of 'experience'. But quite different lessons can be drawn from 'experience', as Anderson demonstrated. To take, for example, a case close to hand: Thompson could write of the seventies that it 'is a bad time for the rational mind to live: for a rational mind in the Marxist tradition it is a time that cannot be endured.'[187] His fellow first New Leftist, Raymond Williams, by contrast, offered a strikingly different judgement, experiencing in this period a remarkable flowering and opening up of Marxism.[188]

Anderson rejected both Althusserian and Thompsonian polarities, and sought to strike a balance between structure and subject: a balance in which men and women were seen as potential agents in a conscious, collective transformation of society, whilst at the same time recognising the structures and relations shaping their consciousness and militating against such endeavours. In effect, Anderson sought to locate in an historical context the ongoing tension between structure and subject in the pursuit of social transformation:

> The area of self-determination ... has been widening in the past 150 years. But it is still very much less than its opposite. The whole purpose of historical materialism ... has been precisely to give men and women the means with which to exercise *a real popular self-determination for the first time in history*. This is, exactly, the objective of a socialist revolution, whose aim is to inaugurate the transition from what Marx called the realm of necessity to the realm of freedom.[189]

Thus, Thompson's moralism was no substitute for strategy. Whilst Anderson acknowledged the importance of Thompson's emphasis on the moral dimension to socialism, on utopianism and 'the politics of desire'[190] – forcefully conveyed in Thompson's 1976 Postscript to his biography of Morris – he was convinced that 'a humane socialism equipped only with an ethic against a hostile world ... is doomed to needless tragedy'.[191]

Anderson's central conclusion was that 'Thompson's strictures on NLR largely mistake their object ... No great chasm seems to exist between his position and ours on any of the ... questions he raises.'[192] But what lay at the heart of the dispute was not, as Anderson acknowledged, a 'rather tedious bill of particulars'.[193] It might be traced, as Anderson sought to explain, to a remaining grievance on Thompson's part, or nervousness on his own, over the circumstances of the change in editorship of the *Review* in 1962-3. However, there was indeed a significant political divide between Thompson and Anderson – although this should not be taken as representative of the positions of even the majority of the personnel of the two New Lefts. For while the New Left as a whole rejected Stalinism as a matter of course, Thompson and Anderson parted company over their respective characterisations of, and responses to, it.

In Anderson's judgement, Thompson remained transfixed by an 'uncritical cult of 1956'.[194] That year did not mark the solitary, defining moment of anti-Stalinist dissent. There was an earlier tradition – that of Trotsky, Serge, Deutscher *et al.* – which Thompson chose to ignore. Nor was the year of 1956 especially momentous. To Thompson's charge, "Where was Althusser in 1956?", Anderson asked, "Where was Thompson earlier?" – 1956 conferred 'no special historical privilege or exemption on' him.[195] Why should not the 'Doctor's Plot' of 1952, or the Slansky trial of 1951, be equally significant? Or, for that matter, the Nazi-Soviet Pact, or the Purges, or even the banning of tendencies within the Bolshevik Party in 1921? Where Thompson claimed that the post-1962 *NLR* had lost its way, and was in danger of returning to the doctrinaire Marxism of the Third International, Anderson stood the argument on its head: it was Thompson's strategic conceptions – 'national roads' to socialism and parliamentary reformism – that marked a continuity with the Stalinised Comintern.[196] The themes of 1956 – the humanism of the Young Marx, national distinctiveness, and a consensual popular politics – 'had become the standard slogans of the official Communist leaderships themselves'.[197] Thompson's national-reformist politics might be designated Left-social democratic (by this time he had joined the Labour Party). It was a perspective increasingly shared by the Western Communist Parties. It amounted, to put it a little schematically, to a 'right-wing' critique of Stalinism: its antidote to Stalinism was an adhesion to liberal democracy of the Western parliamentary type.

Anderson, by contrast, rooted his 'left-wing' critique of Stalinism in the revolutionary and internationalist socialism of classical Marxism. However, his rejection of Thompson's reformism and parliamentarianism in *Arguments Within English Marxism* was couched less in terms of the classical heritage than in the words of someone closer to Thompson's heart: William Morris. Anderson taxed Thompson with neglect of Morris' stringent rejection of a reformist and parliamentary road to socialism.[198] He added that Morris' strategic perspective was, in this respect, an advance upon both Marx and Engels. Morris was credited with developing a 'fundamental and novel' analysis 'which cannot be found in Marx';[199] and with being 'intellectually much tougher and more clairvoyant in his assessments of the choices before the nascent labour movement than Engels'.[200] Thus, in their differing response to Stalinism, Thompson and the Andersonian *Review* drew diametrically opposite strategic conclusions.

In keeping with the tone of *Arguments Within English Marxism*, Anderson struck a conciliatory note by way of conclusion. In a mood of confidence in an expanding 'Anglophone' Marxism, Anderson stressed that 'the Left as a whole … *benefits* rather than suffers from a diversity of interests and outlooks … A certain one-sidedness is inherent in all intellectual production as such: the important thing is that there should be many sides'.[201] An olive branch was proffered: 'Thompson's identity and our own are unlikely ever to be confused … But need they still be counterposed?[202] … [i]t would be good to leave old quarrels behind, and to explore new problems together'.[203]

The rapprochement with Thompson was, as we shall see, part of a conscious attempt to 'reanchor' the *Review* within the domestic Left. One of the first fruits of this new direction was the publication in the pages of the *Review* in 1980 of Thompson's 'Notes on Exterminism, The Last Stage of Civilisation', which followed his return to active politics in a revived CND and in European Nuclear Disarmament (founded in 1980). It opened a major international debate on the character and origins of the renewed Cold War of the late seventies and early eighties; and although the *Review* differed from Thompson in its interpretation, Anderson later reflected that the 'rift' between Thompson and the post-1962 *Review* 'was over'.[204]

Chapter Four
From Rethinking to Retrenchment

The *Review*'s Decennial Report in 1974 had concluded that the 'chances of the Left are now much greater than at any time since the start of the Cold War, in the advanced and ex-colonial countries alike'.[1] However, surveying global prospects six years later, the *NLR* conceded that '[n]o such confidence is possible in 1980'.[2] The revolutionary decade, opened in Europe on the streets of Paris in May 1968, had come to a close. The successive failures of the Left in Portugal, Spain, France and Italy resulted in the stabilisation of bourgeois rule at what had been perceived its weakest links in southern Europe. 'The historical defeat of the European labour movement in these years was a momentous one … quelling … any short-range prospect of progress towards socialism in this central zone of imperialism.'[3]

The succeeding period was, by contrast, to be marked by a sustained ideological and political offensive by an invigorated 'New' Right, determined to reverse the growing challenge posed to Western capitalism in the seventies and restore capital's profitability with an assault upon the domestic post-war gains of labour; the subordination of the global South to metropolitan capital; and a calculated escalation of the geo-political contest between the West and the Soviet Union, issuing in a 'second' Cold War.

The passing of the moment of 1968, with its expectations of a transition to socialism in one or more of the advanced capitalist countries, and the entering of this new, far less favourable conjuncture, would, unsurprisingly, have a major impact on the evolution of the *NLR*. The second Cold War – involving a reappraisal of the Soviet Union and expectations of the renewal of socialism with the advent of Gorbachev – would prove central to this evolution (see chapter five). First we shall examine the strategic impasse and general crisis of socialist politics in the West.

1. A 'Crisis of Marxism'?

If the political advance of the New Right was largely confined to Britain and the United States, with the successive election victories of Thatcher and

Reagan in 1979 and 1980, the looming crisis of socialist politics was initially registered with greatest force in France. Here, where expectations were highest, the break-up of the Union of the Left, and the electoral defeat of March 1978, were decisive blows, issuing in a sharp ideological shift to the Right. Marxism, the dominant reference-point for the French post-war intelligentsia, suffered in the late seventies a sudden and precipitous collapse, a veritable 'crisis' in Althusser's words, accompanied by the rise of the clamourously anti-Marxist *nouveaux philosophes*. By 1983 Anderson could write that 'Paris today is the capital of European intellectual reaction, in much the same way that London was thirty years ago'.[4] The *Review* noted that 'the massacre of ancestors' had been 'impressive', as the roll-call illustrates: 'Sartre a disabled anarchist, Colletti an embittered liberal, Claudin an aspirant social-democrat, Heller a whitening émigré, Gorz an ecomane, Glucksmann a cold war crusader, Althusser a purveyor of the "crisis of Marxism", Poulantzas a suicide'.[5]

Addressing this challenge to Marxism in *In the Tracks of Historical Materialism*, published by Verso in 1983,[6] Anderson argued that the 'master-problem' at the root of the purported 'crisis of Marxism' was 'the nature of the relationships between structure and subject in human history and society',[7] (themes highlighted, as we have seen, in *Arguments Within English Marxism*) which had, he conceded, generated an 'inveterate tension – at times lesion – within historical materialism'.[8] Classical Marxism, 'even at the height of its powers, provided no coherent answer',[9] causing a permanent tension in the history of Marxism between determinism on the one hand, and voluntarism on the other. In France in the fifties, Sartre had sought a resolution of this tension in attempting to marry Marxism to existentialism. However, when Levi-Strauss, assimilating Saussure's linguistic model to anthropology, launched a general critique of his project, 'Sartre, so agile and fertile an interlocutor, so indefatigable a polemicist hitherto, made no answer … When a Marxist reply finally came, in 1965' – from Althusser – 'it was no repudiation, but a counter-signature of the structuralist claim'.[10] However, Althusser's Marxism, 'in which subjects were abolished altogether, save as the illusory effects of ideological structures', was 'bound to be outbid' in such 'an objectivist auction'.[11] In the subsequent passage from structuralism to post-structuralism, which had led, in Anderson's words, from a 'rhetorical absolutism' of the structure to a 'fragmented fetishism' of the subject, no advance was made in developing a theory of the '*relations*' between structure and subject – a theory that required 'a dialectical respect for their interdependence'.[12] Thus, the hypothesis that Marxism had been intellectually defeated by Parisian structuralism or its sequels, Anderson concluded, was 'implausible'.[13] The problem of the relations between structure and sub-ject that constituted the 'formal battle-field between the two ... was never occupied in sufficient depth by structuralism to present any real challenge to a historical materialism confident of itself'.[14]

Thus unimpressed by the 'intrinsic' theoretical challenge posed by struc-turalism, post-structuralism and 'the jejune irrationalism of the New Philosophy',[15] the *NLR* privately reflected that 'most of this bric-a-brac' was due to 'the general servility to sheer fashion of most Western intellectuals', to 'a "nihilism" that ostensibly lights funeral-pyres for every philosophical con-vention in sight, while comfortably leaving everything material as it is', and 'the convenience of its rancour or renegacy towards socialism to the bour-geois political order'.[16] Unwilling to be distracted from its preoccupation with the politics of navigating a passage to socialism by the philosophical siren-voices emanating from Paris, the *Review* was happy simply to wait for post-structuralism 'to self-destruct in the next spin of the wheel of vogue'.[17]

The causes of the retreat of French Marxism were judged to be 'extrinsic', explicable in terms of the political conjuncture – namely, the recent defeats suffered by the Left in southern Europe, allied to the ideological offensive of the Right that accompanied the advent of the Second Cold War. In the words of the 1980 editorial report, the 'European bourgeoisies' had been 'genuinely and deeply scared by the successive conjunctures of 1975-77. In response, they unleashed a concerted ideological campaign of the utmost violence, whose essential organising themes were the equation of Marxism with Stalinism, and Stalinism with totalitarianism, totalitarianism with per-manent terror and genocide, bureaucracy and penury.'[18] The 'orchestration' of this 'Gulagism' was a 'preemptive strike against the dangers it perceived in the possibility of Union of the Left style governments'.[19] It had a particular impact in southern Europe, for whilst these anti-Soviet themes had been 'the classic tropes of the Cold War in the Anglo-Saxon and German zones of imperialism' in the fifties, their 'lesser penetration in Latin Europe in that epoch left it relatively unimmunised against the second wave of bombard-ment' in the late seventies.[20]

In southern Europe it was the 'double disappointment' in Maoism and Euro-Communism as alternatives to 'actually existing socialism' that had induced, in Anderson's argument, the purported 'crisis of Marxism'.[21] Whereas 'Maoism appeared to debouch into little more than a truculent Oriental Khruschevism', Euro-Communism 'lapsed into what looked in-creasingly like a second-class version of Occidental social-democracy'.[22] In the context of the Second Cold War, it was but a short passage from the anti-Sovietism of Maoism and Euro-Communism – especially virulent in the former – to outright anti-Communism and anti-socialism. Nonetheless, one might fairly doubt that this constituted a crisis of Marxism as such. In Francis Mulhern's words, the 'less sensational but better attested hypothesis of a crisis of Maoism, or of culpably lingering illusions in Stalinism, was less enthusiastically bruited, being not so flattering to the renegades or ideologically so serviceable to their new allies'.[23]

In France, Spain and Portugal reminted 'Socialist' parties eclipsed their Communist counterparts as the principal parties of the Left. In Italy – where the defeat of the FIAT strike in 1980, the 'hot autumn in reverse',[24] presaged an era of retreat for organised labour in all the major industrialised countries – Craxi's rightward-moving PSI entered governmental coalition with the Christian Democrats. Having won presidential and legislative elections in 1981 against a divided Right, and initially embarking upon an ambitious programme of economic modernisation through nationalisation and interventionism, it was the retreat of the French Socialists in 1982-3 that set the pattern for southern European 'Euro-Socialism'. Coming to power at an unpropitious moment, the Mitterrand-Mauroy government soon succumbed to pressure to abandon *dirigisme* and Keynesian reflation, with the diminished PCF unable to provide any counter-weight to the PS's rightward trajectory. Modernising, secular, youthful in appearance and cross-class in appeal, 'Euro-Socialism', though electorally successful, accomplished little more than a capitalist rationalisation, an economic remodelling on neo-liberal lines: 'Reagonomics with a socialist gloss', as James Petras put it in the *NLR* in 1984.[25] Displacing Communist Parties at a strategic impasse, Euro-Socialism enthusiastically endorsed Atlanticism, the Cold War and anti-Communism (Spain under Gonzalez joined NATO in 1986).[26] The *NLR* commented acidly on 'the dismal record of capitulation to capitalist austerity and Cold War politics which has marked the Euro-Socialist experience of Government in France, Portugal, Spain and Italy. Euro-Socialist leaders have performed feats of political disorientation and demobilisation beyond the capabilities of other bourgeois politicians.'[27]

In *In the Tracks of Historical Materialism* Anderson contended that the 'crisis of Marxism' was historically conjunctural and geographically confined: it could be quarantined as a merely localised 'crisis of Latin Marxism'.[28] Meanwhile, in northern Europe the previously dismissed social democratic parties were undergoing a certain radicalisation, in large part under the pressure of the peace and anti-nuclear movements mobilising thousands on the streets (particularly in West Germany, Britain and Holland) in protest against the deployment of a new generation of American missiles – in marked contrast to the rightward and Atlanticist trajectory of the southern

European Euro-Socialist parties. Ideologically, too, the 'crisis of Marxism' was less pronounced. In Germany, for example, Habermas pursued similar theoretical problems to the Parisian structuralists and post-structuralists, but nonetheless retained some filiation to the Marxist tradition and 'his own version of a Frankfurt-style socialism'.[29] Moreover, what characterised the period since *Considerations on Western Marxism* – where Anderson had written that Marxism would remain incomplete 'until it is finally at home in the mature imperial bastions of the Anglo-Saxon world'[30] – was a remarkable flowering of Marxism in the English-speaking world, most especially in Britain, where the absence of a mass Communist Party, as elsewhere in northern Europe, had rendered 'domestic gulagism rather marginal'.[31] This was 'a truly astonishing metamorphosis', reversing the 'traditional relationship between Britain and Continental Europe … Marxist culture in the UK for the moment proving more productive and original than that of any mainland state'.[32] Thus, far from experiencing a 'crisis', Marxism had, in Anderson's judgement, undergone 'a period of overall growth and emancipation'[33] which represented 'a remarkable renaissance of its intellectual vitality and international appeal'.[34]

In Britain, the 'paramountcy of … Marxist historiography reached its peak'[35] in the continuing output of Eric Hobsbawm, Christopher Hill, Rodney Hilton, Victor Kiernan et al; whilst the field of literary criticism included the work of Raymond Williams, Terry Eagleton and Francis Mulhern. Significant achievements had been registered in the fields of economics, political theory and philosophy. G. A. Cohen's *Karl Marx's Theory of History* was singled out by the *Review* as 'arguably the most important work of Marxist philosophy to appear in the last decade'.[36] The renaissance charted by Anderson was impressive (and was something for which the *NLR* and NLB/Verso could take no small credit), and importantly, given his critique of the 'esoteric' preoccupations of Western Marxism, there had been a marked return to the themes of classical Marxism: in economics, for example, in the work of Ernest Mandel, Harry Braverman, Michel Aglietta and Bill Warren, in politics, that of Ralph Miliband, Nicos Poulantzas and Göran Therborn.

2. The riddle of the Sphinx

However, reviewing the 'hopes and hypotheses' expressed in *Considerations on Western Marxism*, Anderson acknowledged that the 'reunification of Marxist theory and popular practice in a mass revolutionary movement signally failed to materialise'.[37] His assessment of the renaissance of Marxism was therefore curiously 'bibliocentric'.[38] Although these intellectual gains were undoubtedly impressive, Anglophone Marxism suffered the same divorce between theory and practice that had been the very basis of Anderson's critique of Western Marxism. His confident appraisal of the health of Marxism contradicted his earlier conviction that it would remain incomplete until it was rejoined to a revolutionary practice. This public confidence was also somewhat at odds with the *Review*'s private reflections: an editorial report of late 1982 recognised that Britain and America have 'now also been infected by local variants of the continental virus'.[39] Earlier expectations that Britain might become 'the leading producer of Marxist theory in the advanced capitalist world', the *NLR* conceded, had derived from 'an unduly optimistic assessment of the dispositions and directions of the English-speaking left intelligentsia'.[40] Indeed, as early as 1981 Anderson was warning that in Britain the decomposition of Euro-Communism was threatening a similar rightward movement to that experienced in southern Europe.[41]

Although publicly pronouncing the overall vitality of Marxism, Anderson identified 'two striking deficits' in *In the Tracks of Historical Materialism*.[42] The first was 'geographical' – namely, the reverses it had experienced in southern Europe. The second was 'topical': the unresolved impasse of political strategy.[43] How was the transition to socialism to be effected in the advanced capitalist countries? The resolution of this central problem remained as elusive as ever: the 'dearth of strategic resource or invention' had not been 'seriously remedied, from any quarter'.[44] 'The problem of such a strategy', wrote Anderson,

remains today, as it has done now for fifty years, the Sphinx facing Marxism in the West. It is clear that the freedom of capitalist democracy, meagre but real with its ballot or bill of rights, can only yield to the force of a qualitatively greater liberty of socialist democracy, exercised over work and wealth, economy and family as well as polity. But how are the supple and durable structures of the bourgeois state, endlessly elastic in adjustment of the consent on which it immediately rests and infinitely rigid in preservation of the coercion on which it ultimately relies, to be overpowered? What bloc of social forces can be mobilised, in what ways, ever to undertake the *risks* of disconnecting the cycle of capital accumulation in our intricately integrated market economies?[45]

The question was an insistent one, and Anderson's final sentences betray a real sense of doubt as to the very feasibility of such a task.

In *Considerations on Western Marxism*, Anderson had maintained that Trotskyism, hitherto a neglected tradition within Marxism, might provide 'one of the central elements for any renaissance of revolutionary Marxism'.[46] In the seventies there was no doubting the *Review*'s *Trotskysant* affiliation. In contrast to Western Marxism, wrote Anderson, 'the distinctive theoretical heritage of the Trotskyite tradition gave it obvious initial advantages in the new conjuncture of popular upsurge and world depression, that marked the early seventies'.[47] However, in 1983 he judged that 'the promise it contained' had not been 'fulfilled', for whilst the 'conceptions and evasions of Eurocommunism met their most effective critiques from the literature of Trotskyism ... these negative demonstrations ... were not accompanied by any sustained positive construction of an alternative scenario for defeating capitalism in the West'.[48] 'The Fourth International', Anderson concluded, had 'lost its way at the cross-roads of the Portuguese Revolution'.[49] Unable to escape an inclination (as Anderson put it in 1976) 'towards conservatism',[50] Trotskyism's particular blockage 'stemmed from too close an imaginative adherence to the paradigm of the October Revolution, made against the husk of a feudal monarchy, and too distant a theoretical concern with the contours of a capitalist democracy the Bolsheviks never had to confront'.[51]

Notwithstanding these significant reservations concerning Trotskyism and the unresolved question of socialist strategy in the West, Anderson argued that Marxism's weaknesses were in large measure due to 'its very preeminence within the intellectual universe of socialism. As a theory, it has been – one might say – *too* powerful for its own good. Precisely because of its inordinate assets, its marginalisation of contestants from the Left was often unduly easy, its victory over critics from the Right unprofitably cheap.'[52] This enduring strength, derived from 'its sheer scope as an intellectual system', its explanatory power 'as a theory of historical development', and 'its radicalism as a political call to arms'.[53] Despite 'errors and misdirections', Marxism would not be displaced within socialist theory 'so long as there is no superior candidate for comparable overall advance in knowledge. There is no sign of that yet.'[54] However, new pressures and challenges to Marxism, argued Anderson, heralded 'a change that can only be welcomed'.[55] The *Review* proposed working 'to reassert the *centrality* of historical materialism within socialist culture, while at the same time affirming without inhibition its *non-exclusivity*'.[56]

Of the new challenges to Marxism, Anderson highlighted the issues raised by gender, ecology and war – issues that he considered 'have now become unevadable.'[57] Despite Engels' innovative work, feminism was a subject largely unexplored by classical Marxism, whilst the concerns of the ecological movement, posing the question of the 'relations between nature and history',[58] were, in Anderson's judgement, 'unpostponable in their urgency',[59] and heralded 'the long overdue moment of socialist morality'.[60] Meanwhile, the idea 'of a military conflagration that could wipe out every form of human society never occurred to Owen or Fourier, Marx or Engels, Morris or Lenin'.[61] It was, wrote Anderson, 'impossible to imagine the basic structures of their thought remaining unaltered had this been historically conceivable in their time'.[62]

Although Anderson recognised their importance, he considered that the very universality of the issues surrounding gender, ecology and war provided no specific leverage to effect the far-reaching social transformation necessary to their resolution; a transformation that would entail the overthrow of capitalism. As a social force, women, for example, were 'molecular and dispersed', and therefore 'insufficiently operational as a collective agency, actual or potential, ever to be able to uproot the economy or polity of capital'.[63] Similarly, whilst the 'benefits of arresting the drive towards' nuclear war 'can only be universal … the forces capable of securing them will necessarily be particular'.[64] Socialism was the precondition for women's emancipation and the abolition of war; the only agency capable of effecting such a transition was the 'collective labourer'. The 'decisive advance' of Marxism, Anderson argued, had been to identify 'the site of a particular social agency … as the Archimedean point from which the old order could be overturned – the structural position occupied by the industrial working-class created by the advent of capitalism'.[65] However, the 'working class in the West', Anderson continued, 'is currently in disarray, in the throes of one of those far-reaching recompositions that have periodically marked its history since the Industrial Revolution'.[66] Although 'much less defeated and dispersed than it was during the last Great Depression',[67] what the cause of socialism required was a rekindling of the proletariat's revolutionary spirit. Herein lay the value of the issues raised by the women's, peace and ecological movements, for in their own emphases they highlighted that the conscious desire for a better society would be a critical component of any successful anti-capitalist politics.

The 'utopian' dimension to socialism was central to Edward Thompson's politics, and had been responded to positively by Anderson in *Arguments Within English Marxism*. The *Review*'s 1980 editorial report had recognised that 'it is now necessary to put a quite renewed emphasis on socialism as a future society, that exists nowhere in the world today, or even seems very close, yet whose articulated forms it is essential to debate at once as imaginatively and as concretely as possible'.[68] Prefacing the *Exterminism and Cold*

War collection in 1982, the *NLR* argued that whilst socialism still needed a perspective indicating 'particular agencies and strategies for its realisation',[69] the 'long-separated traditions' of 'utopian' and 'scientific' socialism must 'be rejoined … today'.[70] The point was reinforced by Anderson, who recognised that '[n]o working class or popular bloc in a Western society will ever make a leap in the dark, at this point in history, let alone into the grey on grey of an Eastern society of the type that exists today. A socialism that remains incognito will never be embraced by it.'[71]

Was Anderson's claim of a 'remarkable renaissance' of Marxism's 'intellectual vitality and international appeal' justified? Did the productivity of Anglophone Marxism outweigh the setbacks experienced by Latin Marxism? What of the continuing failure to present a convincing resolution to the impasse of political strategy in the West, or the question-mark over the revolutionary vocation of the working class as the principal agency of socialist transformation? Reviewing *In the Tracks of Historical Materialism* in 1985, Ronald Aronson argued that Anderson 'ends up bridging today's doubts … by dint of a remarkable *tour de force* which denies Marxism has fallen into crisis. This denial is its weakness'.[72] Aronson argued that the 'crisis of Marxism' had to be faced squarely if it was to be overcome; and that this did indeed require a radical reconsideration of some of the basic tenets of socialist politics, not least regarding the question of agency. He was convinced that there should be 'a new and more fruitful relationship between historical materialism and the various non-working-class movements that have shaped our generation and vice versa',[73] for 'whatever its centrality, the direct conflict between capital and labour has not been dominant over the past twenty years. Imperialist war, national liberation, feminism, ecology, anti-nuclearism, student movements, domestic struggles against racism – these have occupied the centre-stage in most places, for most of the time.'[74]

Even if, as Anderson argued, post-structuralism had been unable or unwilling to provide any satisfactory resolution of the tension between structure and agency in social transformation, the problems posed by the relationship between the two – 'the province par excellence of socialist strategy'[75] – remained unsolved within Marxism. Was a resolution of this tension possible within the terms of classical Marxism? These challenges were far from inconsiderable, and appeared to cast graver doubts on the overall health of Marxism than Anderson and the *NLR* were willing to entertain. Nonetheless, the *Review*'s public recognition of the limits of the classical revolutionary tradition, and its apparent willingness to engage with the utopian and pre-figurative themes raised by new social currents and forces, was potentially of great significance – promising, after the long detour of the years after 1968, the exploration of a genuinely contemporary revolutionary politics.

3. Reanchorage

There had long been a certain tension between the post-1962 *Review*'s self-perception as an international journal, an 'intangibly offshore periodical',[76] whose readers were, by 1980, 'heavily concentrated overseas',[77] and the fact that it was published in London, with historic roots in the British New Left, and thus with an expectation that it should be attuned to national politics. However, in 1980 the *Review* judged 'there may be less structural tension' between its 'two vocations than ever in the past', for 'the major *international* resources of Marxist culture lie for the first time very largely within the *national* ambit of the UK. In this sense, a concerted turn towards Britain by the NLR would no longer mean an isolation from wider debates within historical materialism, but on the contrary one of the most fruitful means of promoting them.'[78] Initial confidence in the health of Anglo-Marxism, a certain radicalisation on the British Left, and recognition of the impasse that had been reached in developing political strategies appropriate to the conditions of advanced liberal-democratic capitalism, combined to bring to an end the *NLR*'s long aloofness from domestic politics, signalled in its conscious 'reanchorage in Britain' after 1980.[79]

While the commitment to a more active engagement with the British Left than at any time since the demise of the first New Left was, first and foremost, a reflection of the *Review*'s perception of the strength of Anglo-Marxism, it may also be taken as an index of the need to explore new avenues of strategic debate in a refreshingly ecumenical spirit. The 1980 editorial report suggested 'a conscious policy of publishing at least one significant article, on any topic, by representative figures of British socialism – whether from the former New Left, the Communist Party, the Labour Left, the IMG, the SWP, the Militant or other currents – in every issue'.[80] In addition the *NLR* proposed 'a steady cross-flow of contributors and collaborators' with 'fraternal publications' such as *History Workshop, Capital and Class, Economy and Society* and *Feminist Review*.[81] Of all these currents, it was adherents of the first New Left that the *NLR* worked with most successfully: in 1980 alone, Stuart Hall, Mike Rustin, Raphael Samuel, Edward Thompson and Raymond Williams all appeared in the pages of the *Review*.[82] Largely as a consequence of his own intellectual trajectory, Raymond Williams was perhaps the closest to the *NLR* in this period, and the most favourable in his assessment of the record of the *New Left Review*. Indeed, it was the rapprochement with Williams via the volume of interviews *Politics and Letters* (published by NLB in 1979) that provided the initial stimulus to the whole process of 'reanchorage'.[83] Close relations were also established with Ralph Miliband, particularly through collaboration in the work of the Socialist Society.

The domestic political scene within which the *NLR* was seeking reanchorage was in the throes of a sharp polarisation. The post-war Keynesian consensus was under assault from the newly installed Thatcher government. The monetarist shock of 1979-81 induced a spectacular collapse in manufacturing output – the largest ever one-year decline was recorded in 1980[84] – and unemployment that spiralled to three million. So steep was the fall in the government's popularity, with voices of dissent even within the Cabinet, that it seemed unlikely that so disastrous an experiment could long continue. (Just as Heath had abandoned his proto-monetarist 'Selsdon Man' stance in 1972, so a similar 'U-turn' was expected of Thatcher – despite her determination that 'the lady's not for turning'). It was left to others to search the meaning and menace of 'Thatcherism'. Largely undaunted by the prospect of a 'Thatcher counter-revolution', the *Review*'s over-riding preoccupation at this time was with the acrimonious soul-searching within the Labour Party, and the socialist potential of its resurgent left wing. The dismal performance of the Callaghan government, that had itself abandoned Keynesianism and opted for monetarism in 1976, stirred an inner-party rebellion – with Tony Benn as its focus – that sought to answer Thatcher's attack from the right with a left response to the exhaustion of the post-war settlement. Recognising the inadequacy of Keynesianism (to which the Labour front bench had returned in opposition) in the context of the increasing internationalisation of manufacturing and finance, a *dirigiste* 'alternative economic strategy' was advocated by the Bennite Left, embracing controls on imports and the international movement of capital, expansion of public ownership (especially in the sphere of banking and finance), statutory planning agreements and meaningful industrial democracy. Whilst successive party conferences endorsed just such a programme, the central problem remained committing the parliamentary party to conference decisions, issuing in a bitter struggle for intra-party democracy and accountability.

'The crisis of British capitalism', wrote the *Review* in 1981, 'has also become the crisis of the labour movement. A new Labour Left with impressive rank-and-file strength is engaged in pitched struggle with the quasi-dynastic authority of the parliamentary party.'[85] The Bennite insurgency was reaching a crescendo. In the 1981 deputy leadership election Benn received 83 per cent of the votes of constituency party members,[86] narrowly defeated only by the weighted voting of the parliamentary party and the trade unions.

Combined with defections to the newly formed and vociferously Atlanticist Social Democratic Party (SDP) early in 1981, there was the promise of a significant realignment of the Labour Party – even to the point where it could be considered socialist. The *NLR* was thus convinced of the 'need to take stock of the phenomenon of Bennism, as a new constellation within the ranks of Labourism'.[87]

In pursuit of its reanchorage in the British Left, the *Review*, with Robin Blackburn to the fore, took the initiative in launching the 'Socialist Society' – first mooted at the 'Beyond the Fragments' conference, 1981 – in London on 23-24 January 1982. From the outset, those closest to the *NLR* were convinced that the necessity of securing the 'inter-denominational basis'[88] of the Society meant that whilst there should be an unambiguous commitment to socialism, the question of whether this would be achieved via a revolutionary or parliamentary road should be left deliberately open.[89] The Socialist Society venture was perhaps the most public expression of the *Review*'s attempt to situate itself within the milieu of the British Left, and a certain common purpose was quickly established between the *NLR* and representative figures of the first New Left prominent within the Society, such as Raymond Williams and Ralph Miliband.

However, the commitment to a dialogue with the broader Left was mixed with considerable scepticism, and 'the Socialist Society won no unanimity of adhesion within the *aktiv*'.[90] Reanchorage reflected a certain tension and ambiguity in the *Review*'s strategic thinking now that the expectations of the mid to late seventies – election of Left governments with Communist participation in southern Europe equals sharp polarisation equals pre-revolutionary crisis – had proven false. Politically – and, one might add, emotionally – committed to a revolutionary socialism, yet compelled to acknowledge its limited prospects, the *Review* was willing, at least tentatively, to explore the prospects of a radicalised social democracy promising, in the words of the French PS (which swept to power in 1981), a 'rupture with capitalism'.

Questions of political strategy echoed, in minor key, the debate of the late seventies between Euro-Communists and their critics, and, as then, the *Review*'s editors made no intervention themselves. Nonetheless, we may surmise that they shared David Coates' doubts that a determined radical-reformist programme could succeed in national isolation and a hostile international climate without alarming capital and thus inducing a profound economic and political crisis.[91] While Geoff Hodgson rejoined that there was no 'zero-sum' game between capital and labour – it would be possible to raise wages and profitability through higher productivity, compensated for by greater industrial democracy; a structural strengthening of labour that did not immediately endanger capital[92] – Coates was unconvinced. He doubted 'whether … "space for reform" still exists in the downturn of late capitalism and in the context of a competitively weak national capital'.[93] The real danger was, that in retaining illusions in the possibility of fundamental reform without provoking capital, social democracy was unprepared for facing down the opposition of capital, and, ultimately, the inevitable choice between revolution and counter-revolution. The *Review* endorsed Adam Przeworski's 'particularly timely'[94] reminder that '[s]ocial democrats will not lead European societies into socialism … [T]he process of transition must lead to a crisis before socialism could be organised. To reach higher peaks one must traverse a valley, and this descent will not be completed under democratic conditions'.[95]

However, the scenario of a radicalised social democracy *à la* Mitterrand coming to power in Britain seemed increasingly unlikely to be put to the test. Support for Labour remained strong during the first two years of the Thatcher government (an opinion poll in October 1980, for example, gave Labour 50 per cent to the Conservatives 34 per cent),[96] and it performed well at the May 1981 local elections – gaining the Greater London Council in the process, which under Ken Livingstone's leadership rallied many of those working towards the new politics of the Labour Left.[97] However, Benn's challenge for the deputy leadership of the party in 1981 proved the highwater mark of the Left's advance. The Foot-Healey leadership, rallying the Tribunite 'soft' left and backed by the trade union king-makers, began to re-consolidate the authority of the parliamentary party. Moreover, by the end of 1981 opinion polls and spectacular by-election successes suggested that Conservative unpopularity might rebound not to the advantage of the Labour Party, but to the newly formed alliance of the SPD and the Liberals.

Thus a more limited, though more immediate, question was posed: was there a real chance of fashioning a socialist party out of the 'crisis of Labourism'? The IMG, for one, believed so and, reconstituted as the Socialist League, now practised entryism. In the *Review*, Quintin Hoare and Tariq Ali (who was to join the editorial committee in 1983) argued that the decision whether or not to join established workers' parties was a purely 'tactical' one, based on an acknowledgement that 'it is necessary to state clearly that the attempt to construct revolutionary parties in Western Europe in this period, with the aid of the new vanguard radicalised since 1968, bypassing the historic mass parties of the working class, has failed.'[98] 'For us', wrote Quintin Hoare and Tariq Ali, 'there is an overwhelming case in the present conjuncture for socialists to be in the Labour Party',[99] because there existed 'the possibility for the first time in this country of [forming] a mass socialist party … [T]hough this could only be a left-leaning or at best centrist formation, its appearance would represent a significant advance for the working class and the Left as a whole.'[100] Tariq Ali was barred from membership of the party – witness to the entrenched strength of the Labour Right and the swift turning of the tide against the Left.

The clearest collective response to Bennism was conveyed in the series of interviews conducted with Tony Benn himself and published by Verso in 1982 as *Parliament, People and Power*. Benn's faith in the Labour Party was not in doubt, claiming that it was 'too strong, too deeply rooted in the trade unions and in socialism and too self-confident ever to be taken too far away from its real purpose of transforming society'.[101] To which the interviewers responded incredulously: if the Labour Party's 'objectives are those proclaimed in Clause Four, the main difficulty seems to lie in getting it anywhere *near* them'.[102] And where Benn talked of 're-converting the Labour Party to socialism', the *NLR* interjected that 'the party … has never been socialist'.[103] The interviews confirmed that the *NLR* was, on significant matters, considerably at odds with Benn's non-revolutionary perspective. In the *Review*, for example, David Coates had rebuked the autarkic conception of the Labour Left's 'Alternative Economic Strategy'. Critical of the latent nationalism of Bennism – such as its opposition to the EEC – Coates argued that the 'Labour Left too often suggests that the problem faced by British workers is one of *foreign* capital rather than capital as such'.[104] Even Benn's radical democratic credentials were flawed, for he adhered to the 'first-past-the-post' electoral system and a reformed Westminster model of democracy – in Anderson's reckoning, reputedly a 'smugglers' road' to socialism.[105] For the *Review*, its difficulty in engaging with Bennism arose from trying to

> define a stance that is at once *politically* supportive of Benn and Bennism, as the major moving force of the Left as a whole, while at the same time being *intellectually* intransigent about the nature of the Labour Party. The problem in this respect is manifest: how do we propagate the perspective of a break-up of Labourism, as the decisive precondition of any serious political change in the UK, without weakening the fortunes of the only healthy elements within it, upon whose successful exit from the old order the immediate future of any socialist project depends?[106]

Stuart Hall was right to fear that the task of democratising the Labour Party would prove 'too traumatic', and that forces representing the status quo would prove 'too rigid, deeply entrenched, and historically binding to be overcome'.[107] Exhausted and ultimately frustrated in its efforts to win effective democratic reform and accountability within the party, the Labour Left was never in a position to campaign for its political and economic programme in the country at large.

Meanwhile the Falklands War of April-June 1982 had profoundly changed British politics, throwing all recent calculations into doubt. 'Thatcher's bid to reflate her collapsing popularity with a jingoistic sideshow', was swiftly denounced by the *Review*: 'it is the first duty of British socialists to unite massively and unconditionally against Thatcher's war'.[108] In response to the war and Thatcher's new-found ascendancy within the Conservative Party, the *NLR* devoted a whole issue to Anthony Barnett's extended essay, 'Iron Britannia' – an intervention whose 'popular wit and ease' was far from the *Review*'s 'traditional diction'.[109] The Falklands Islands themselves, wrote Barnett, were of little moment and Britain's claim under international law suspect, to say the least. The war drew blank astonishment among Britain's European allies, gravely damaged her reputation in the world (Latin America in particular) and, according to Barnett, aroused no measurable enthusiasm from the Falkland Islanders themselves. Alternative solutions were to hand, not least to offer the Island's inhabitants ample resettlement in a more hospitable clime. The principle of self-determination for a community so small – 1300 native-born residents[110] – was, in Barnett's estimate, hardly viable. Nor was it particularly convincing coming from a country that had recently deported the entire population of Diego Garcia in the Indian Ocean so as to furnish the United States with a military base. For Thatcher, however, the war was a 'miraculous advent',[111] and laid the basis for her, until then far from certain, political ascendancy. With the opposition divided and wrong-footed by the episode, Thatcher's position was ensured by the silencing of dissent within her own party. 'Under her leadership', argued Barnett, 'petty-bourgeois militancy has taken over from the old, semi-cultured patrician elite'.[112] The 'one-nation' Conservatives – the 'Wets' who had nervously voiced their concerns as doctrinaire monetarism wrought extraordinary damage to British industry – were sidelined. (The cull was far from over: 'During the three months of the Falklands War 226 companies went into liquidation every week, while a torrent of capital cascaded into overseas investment'.)[113]

It was this shift within the ruling bloc that was potentially of the most profound consequence. For anyone schooled in the 'Nairn-Anderson theses', an obvious question arose: did Thatcher presage a rigorously bourgeois solution to the endemic and by now near-terminal 'British crisis'?

The 'whigs' may finally have succumbed. The country house has at last been captured. But it has not been stormed by an aroused rabble of gardeners, against whom it was well fortified. It has not been taken over by the disgruntled servants, who have always been closely policed. It has not been seized by a radicalised scion of the mansion who had the misfortune to be repelled by its inequality and attracted to theory. It has not even been overrun by the proletariat, who are kept a good distance away. Assault from all these likely quarters had been foreseen and was defused. Instead, the pillar of rectitude and narrow-minded-ness, the governess whose loyalty had never been questioned, who na-ively *believes* in the whole thing and regards it as virtuous, has decided to run it herself.[114]

The contest between the 'Wets' and the Thatcherite 'Drys' for the leader-ship of the Conservative Party was, in Barnett's summary, 'a struggle be-tween a supra-bourgeois and a sub-bourgeois stratum; between stricken pa-tricians and over-confident *arrivistes*'.[115] However, the Thatcherite ascend-ancy amounted only to 'a shift in the balance of power within the same class bloc. The squire may have been superannuated, to return to the metaphor, but he is still allowed to poke the embers from the comforts of his armchair. He has not been ejected, nor has the house been burnt down.'[116]

The Falklands War brought a reversal of the Conservatives' previously dim electoral prospects, and the rout of Thatcher's opponents within the party meant that she could no longer be deemed something of a passing ab-erration, 'an extremist in a country that has always worshipped at the cult of moderation'.[117] Opinion polls prior to the war demonstrated an almost equal three-way split of electoral preferences between Labour, the Alliance and the third-placed Conservatives; by its end the Conservatives had established a full twenty point lead over Labour, with the Alliance trailing behind.[118] The *NLR* recognised the prospect of a more permanent reconfiguration of British politics to the advantage of a radical 'new Right', writing that the war 'promises to be a watershed in British politics, giving a virulent new lease of life to Margaret Thatcher's authoritarian populism, adding a sharp twist to the eclipse of the Left and the division of the Labour movement'.[119]

Even prior to the 1983 election, it was evident that the crisis of socialist politics, which Anderson had initially hoped would be contained to south-ern Europe, had escaped its Latin quarantine: in Britain expressed as a crisis of the labour movement rather than of Marxism. Although the *Review* pri-vately judged that a 'collapse of epidemic proportions such as occurred in

France or Italy is a long way off',[120] it was on its guard: 'one can well imagine the Book of Lamentations that a second Thatcher victory might induce in an already semi-defeatist Left'.[121] A 'far greater caution', 'even vigilance',[122] was urged in respect of certain elements of the British Left, and with the Communist Party's revamped theoretical journal, *Marxism Today*, in particular.

In the absence of any vehicle for serious theoretical debate within the Labour Party itself, *Marxism Today* became the standard-bearer of what the *NLR* soon labelled the 'new revisionism', enjoying an influence that stretched well beyond the Communist Party itself.[123] While considering that it had been 'the success-story of the British intellectual Left in these years',[124] and commending its 'skilful editing and sure-footed timing',[125] an editorial report in 1982 judged that 'the final product is curiously without any hard cutting-edge of challenge or confrontation with any reigning intellectual orthodoxy; ideas are banalised, and issues mollified, in a smooth emulsion whose net effect is usually well to the right of the official C[ommunist] P[arty] line itself, and far to the right of the Bennite current in the Labour Party'.[126]

In 1985, Anderson lamented that the *Review* had been unwittingly responsible for promoting the new revisionism in publishing, through Verso in association with *Marxism Today*, the collection of essays *The Forward March of Labour Halted?*, opening with, and taking its title from, Eric Hobsbawm's seminal lecture of 1978.[127] In its assessment of the limitations of Labourism, and in the unwritten assumption that a socialist politicisation of the labour movement would be required before the forward march of labour could be resumed, the *NLR* would not have violently dissented from Hobsbawm's initial thesis. The tone of the debate, however, was a disappointing one from the perspective of the *Review* – of the editorial collective, only Robin Blackburn contributed (a mere six pages) to the published volume – and the *Review* privately regretted that it had been 'instrumentalised to the right by our partners when it appeared'.[128]

It was the second of Hobsbawm's two replies to the debate that indicated with greater clarity the trajectory of his thinking. Troubled by the marked shift to the left in the Labour Party in 1980-81, he argued that 'the best and most left-wing party is not enough, if the masses won't support it in sufficient numbers'.[129] Whilst 'capturing the Labour Party for the left ... could in theory be achieved pretty well entirely by a smallish minority of a few tens of thousands of committed socialists ... by means of meetings, drafting resolutions and votes', it was an 'illusion' to imagine 'that *organisation* can replace politics'.[130] Whilst, again, the *Review* would have had some sympathy with Hobsbawm's critique of such a 'smugglers' road' to socialism, it rejected his underlying message: the call for a 'Popular Front' minimalism around which the divided anti-Tory majority could unite, spelt out clearly after the 1983 general election,[131] and privately condemned as 'a shrunken and frightened latter-day Browderism'.[132]

4. Crisis and Retrenchment

Meanwhile, a storm was about to break over the *NLR*, in which many of the unresolved tensions of the recent past were distilled. In pursuit of the intended reanchorage in the British Left, Anderson had proposed, as far back as 1980, to step down as editor.[133] As he himself put it, in a candid conclusion to the confidential 1980 editorial report, the project of 'reintegrating the [R]eview into the common milieu of the Left in Britain' required a 'different kind of editorial temperament' than that demanded by the (self-imposed) 'conditions of isolation and beleaguerement', and 'the stockade mentality', of the *NLR*'s past.[134] Robin Blackburn, consistently more attuned than others to the need to work with the wider British Left, duly assumed editorial responsibility for, and overall direction of, the *New Left Review* in 1983.

However, by the time this had been put into effect, confidence in the disposition of the Left intelligentsia – the basis for reanchorage – was proving harder to sustain. The fall-out from the 1983 election was much as Anderson had predicted. Determined that the *Review* should stand firm against the sort of conclusions being drawn by Hobsbawm and propagated by *Marxism Today*, Anderson, who was far from about to take a back seat in the affairs of the journal, issued furious dispatches to Blackburn and the *NLR* on the *Review*'s handling of Thatcher's re-election, favourably contrasting Benn's unyielding critique of the British Left's defeatism with the *Review*'s own coverage of post-election politics.[135]

Anderson's interventions proved the catalyst for a sharp exchange within the editorial committee, largely focused on grievances concerning the covert internal life of the *Review*, reputedly characterised as a 'fantasy Politbureau' operating under a 'common-law variety of democratic centralism'. The resignation of ten members of the editorial committee was met by a typical outward show of calm, no doubt due to the *Review*'s continuing desire to maintain 'a certain opacity capable of keeping casual Carlisle [Street]-watchers guessing'.[136] It received one short paragraph in the *NLR*, at the end of 1983: the only explanation offered being 'disagreements over the management of the *Review*'.[137]

Immediately prior to the dispute, active participants in the editorial work of the *Review* numbered some seven of the nominal editorial committee:

Perry Anderson, Robin Blackburn, Anthony Barnett, Fred Halliday, Francis Mulhern, Norman Geras and the recently recruited American-born Mike Davis[138] (whose endeavours would make good the *Review*'s previous neglect of the United States as a distinct capitalist social formation).[139] The only members of this *aktiv* to resign were Anthony Barnett and Fred Halliday. The remaining eight had, for the most part, ceased to play any immediate role in the affairs of the *Review*: Jon Halliday, John Merrington, Juliet Mitchell, Roger Murray, Tom Nairn, 'Lucien Rey' (Peter Wollen), Bob Rowthorn and Gareth Stedman Jones.[140]

Although it is hard to discern any clear-cut political fault-line, those who resigned may be largely identified with the disparate grouping least disposed to the *Review*'s *Trotskysant* direction (and, more contentiously, Anderson's over-bearing presence). The recomposition of the editorial committee certainly did not preclude working with the wider Left, but it did make it more likely that in the current conjuncture the 'conditions of isolation and beleaguerement' and accompanying 'stockade mentality' would be resorted to once again. As some on the Left, 'pink Professors and their even paler house-journals',[141] rallied to a moderating 'realism', where did this leave the *Review*'s determination to reanchor itself in domestic politics? The 1982 editorial report, while not wishing to 'warrant a retreat to the isolationism of the review in the past', nonetheless suggested 'a greater measure of reserve towards our immediate environment'.[142] It was such a perspective that would guide the *Review* through the mid-eighties, ultimately frustrating it in its efforts to resolve the strategic riddle of the Sphinx confronting socialist politics in the West.

If the working class of the advanced capitalist countries was indeed undergoing a period of 'far-reaching recomposition' (as Anderson wrote in *In The Tracks of Historical Materialism*) – one in which 'new patterns of class formation' were 'undermining' the labour movement's 'social base'[143] – what did this portend for socialist politics? How radical a reformulation of socialist politics was required to accommodate the issues raised by the questions of gender, ecology and war? To what extent did they challenge the central role previously allotted to the working class in the transition to socialism? If the working class did indeed remain the agency of socialism, it clearly stood in need of an injection of revolutionary purpose. There was no denying that, for the present, it was new formations, such as the contemporary peace movement, mobilising hundreds of thousands on the streets of Europe, that displayed a far greater radicalism than the traditional labour movement, including its Communist detachments. All the contributors to the contentious post-1983 election issue of the *Review* – including Raymond Williams,

Ken Livingstone and Eric Heffer – referred to the importance of 'new social constituencies', citing in particular CND, the women's movement, ethnic communities, young people and ecology.[144] In 1982 the *NLR* had recognised the German Green Party (*die Grünen*) as one of the most promising new leftist formations in Europe.[145]

Some of these issues were aired in an exchange over the role of the women's movement in the immediate aftermath of the 1983 resignations, when the *Review* sought to recruit new blood to the editorial committee. The proposed expansion of the editorial committee immediately went awry when four of the five women invited to join – Cathy Porter, Lynne Segal, Barbara Taylor and Hilary Wainwright – tabled demands which the existing rump editorial committee found unacceptable.

The 1980 editorial report had belatedly suggested that the *Review* 'should … have a conscious programme for the integration of gender into class debates within the socialist culture it seeks to develop. A sexual – as well as ecological – politics will clearly be salient parts of any late 20th century socialism.'[146] In *In the Tracks of Historical Materialism*, Anderson conceded that '[s]exual domination is much older historically, and more deeply rooted culturally' than class exploitation, and would thus require a 'far greater egalitarian change … than would be necessary to level the difference between classes'.[147] If this were ever achieved in a capitalist society, it was 'inconceivable that it could leave the – more recent and relatively more exposed – structures of class inequality standing'.[148] However, posing the question, 'could the struggle against sexual domination ever provide the main impetus for a wider human liberation, tidally sweeping class struggle along with it to common victory?', Anderson answered: 'plainly no'.[149] The women's movement was 'insufficiently operational as a collective agency, actual or potential, ever to be able to uproot the economy or polity of capital', for 'women do not possess either the same positional unity or totalised adversary' as workers.[150] An effective primacy was reserved for the working class because of the structural position it occupied: the 'Archimedean point from which the old order could be overturned'. Consequently, the *Review*'s 1983 Charter stated that socialism and feminism were distinct. The labour and women's movements should certainly work in alliance; but socialism and feminism could not be merged or absorbed into one another: 'Just as NLR is not a peace journal, but a socialist journal that supports the peace movement, so it is not a feminist journal but a socialist journal that supports the women's movement'.[151]

In reply to their invitation to join the *Review*, Porter, Segal, Taylor and Wainwright specifically rejected the perspective expressed in the Charter.

They argued that a gender-neutral workers' struggle was an insidious illusion, since, in the first instance, it failed to challenge existing inequalities within the labour movement and organisations of the Left. They did not believe that feminism could be simply tacked on to existing socialist theory and political practice: it was not an alliance of feminism with socialism they sought, but a feminist reformulation of socialist politics. Their demands – the designation of the *NLR* as a Marxist-feminist journal, and an equal number of women to men on the editorial committee – proved unacceptable.[152] However, it might be argued that it was to some extent less the substance of the argument than the peremptory manner in which the demands of Porter, Segal, Taylor and Wainwright were presented, which led to their rejection.[153]

Was it possible for the *NLR* to open its pages and its editorial committee to broader currents on the British Left without threatening its identity? The tension between widening its political base on the one hand, and guarding its independence on the other, dogged the internal life of the *NLR* through the eighties and into the nineties. It was perhaps unsurprising that when the editorial committee was expanded early in 1984, a clear majority of the new recruits could be said to share the *Review*'s more traditionalist perspective: Victoria Brittain, Patrick Camiller, Peter Dews, 'Oliver MacDonald' (Peter Gowan) and Ellen Wood. Nonetheless, coverage of feminism and the women's movement increased significantly. In 1984 Angela Weir and Elisabeth Wilson's survey of 'The British Women's Movement'[154] inaugurated a country-by-country series, collected as *Mapping the Women's Movement* and published by Verso in 1996.[155] Thus, despite opposing the four women's specific demands with regard to their co-option onto the editorial committee, the *Review* did, for the present, retain an interest in evaluating the significance for socialist politics of the women's and other social movements.

Not the least of the *Review*'s interest in the new social movements was their relative radicalism in contrast to organised labour that appeared, for the present, to have lost its combativity. In 1985 the *Review* acknowledged that the current political scene was 'a much harsher one than anything the Left has known since the 30's'.[156] The domestic Left was in undisguised disarray. Of its main detachments, the miners had been defeated in their year-long strike, and left-wing local government either abolished (the fate of the GLC) or isolated and disowned by the rightward-moving Kinnock-Hattersley leadership of the Labour Party. Internationally, a 'new imperialist cycle of Cold War is pushing the nuclear arms race beyond the limits of the earth itself', whilst a 'global recession is steadily increasing unemployment in the upper side of the capitalist world, and spreading debt and famine in its underside'.[157] Meanwhile, wrote the editorial (only a little prematurely) to the one hundred and fiftieth issue of the *Review* in 1985, the 'world communist movement has passed away' and the 'labour movement in the West has been unable to resist the consolidation of regimes of the Anglo-American Right, or the emulation of their policies by governments of the Eurosocialist Left'.[158]

In its introduction to *Exterminism and Cold War*, the *Review* collectively argued for the centrality of a utopian dimension to the struggle for socialism: outlining and, in some sense, prefiguring a future socialist society would help to instil the necessary desire to make it a reality. Whereas there 'are structural reasons why the classical labour movement still remains the most steadfast component of anti-capitalist politics', it was the new social movements, wrote Anderson et al in 1984, that 'have … in recent years often shown themselves superior to the workers' movement in terms of ideal-political imagination and immediate capacity for moral mobilisation'.[159] What was required was 'an alliance between the older labour movements and the anti-capitalist elements in the new social movements, which alone can secure the goals of each'[160] – in effect, a combination of social power and moral mobilisation, sustained by a 'concrete utopianism'. The alliances made between the new social movements – women, in particular – and the striking British miners were, in this sense, exemplary.

The burgeoning revisionism on the Left, however, far from seeking a combination between the labour movement and the 'new social movements', counterposed them. This was, for example, the message carried by *Marxism Today*, reflecting a factional dispute that was to split and ultimately destroy the Communist Party. The 'modernisers' on the Right of the Party – grouped around *Marxism Today* – wielded the 'declassed' new social movements and a politics of 'identity' as a stick with which to beat the Left, whose principal focus was in the trade unions. The bitter internal contest for power gave control of the party to the former in 1983, an ascendancy cemented at a Special Congress in 1985. The ferocity of its purge of the Left outmatched Labour's own series of expulsions. 'Lee Pitcairn' – 'an opposition member of the Party who has been compelled to adopt a pseudonym'[161] – wrote a caustic account of these events for the *NLR* in 1985.[162] *Marxism Today* continued to enjoy a remarkable prominence as the most radical and outspoken (not to mention clamorously self-promoted) advocate of the 'new revisionism'. 'Although it is still billed as a discussion journal', wrote Pitcairn, 'its pages only seem available to those who wish to challenge the Party's established policies and perspectives'.[163] Samuel directed some well-aimed fire at the same target in the *Review* in a three-part history of 'The Lost World of British Communism'.[164] *Marxism Today*, he wrote, 'has a morbid – but very well informed – interest in fiascoes'; 'nothing seems to set the editorial adrenalin running, or the round tables humming, as a really good fiasco ... *Marxism Today* picks away at the sores'.[165] Moreover, these 'Filofax Marxists' and 'Designer Socialists'[166] displayed contempt and hostility towards working-class politics:

> taking its cue from feminism, it counterposed the 'new social forces' to the 'pre-historic' ones represented by the trade unions ... There is no doubt that much of this sentiment is not only anti-'workerist' but, at least by the traditional standards of the CP, anti-working class. Workers, at any rate male workers, appear as objects of contempt, 'racist' and 'sexist', beer-swilling and pot-bellied, loud-mouthed and according to *Marxism Today*'s fashion writers, the wearers of shapeless clothes.[167]

It appeared that the debate around *The Forward March of Labour Halted?*, 'at least so far as some of its participants were concerned', had 'acted to clear the ground for an increasingly outright repudiation of the very notion of an anti-capitalist working-class'.[168] So far as the 'new revisionists' and self-styled 'post-Marxists' were concerned, class was an insufficient basis for socialist politics. In championing the politics of the new social movements, the 'new revisionists' served to make them suspect in the eyes of the *NLR*.[169] In any event, by the mid-eighties the peace movement was in visible decline, and the women's movement fragmented. In 1984 Therborn wrote dismissively of the 'nebulous' concepts of 'New Social Movements', 'New Political Subjects' and 'New Subjectivities'.[170] The Left, he argued, should 'resist the fashions of the present': '[a]nti-welfare state, anti-union and anti-party ideologies have to be vigorously combated, even when they appear in "leftist" garb ... Whatever the intentions of their authors, these are now, as in the past, the voices of reaction and right-wing revanchism'.[171] Nervous of the revisionist contagion, the *Review* was increasingly wary of too radical a reformulation of socialist politics, heeding Timpanaro's warning: 'Whoever speaks of a socialism that must be "re-invented wholly anew" winds up inventing something very old: capitalism'.[172]

The first authoritative public statement of the *Review*'s determination to stand against the 'new revisionism' appeared in its one hundred and fiftieth issue in 1985 (which also marked twenty-five years of the *NLR*), prefacing Ralph Miliband's key-note article – 'The New Revisionism in Britain' – by unequivocally signalling that it 'takes its position with the critics, rather than the adherents, of the dominant wisdom that finds expression ... in such different publications as the "New Statesman", "Marxism Today" or the "Guardian".[173]

Miliband – who had drawn close to the *NLR* via the Socialist Society (in which he played a leading role), and had already entered the fray through an exchange with Eric Hobsbawm in the *Guardian* in February 1984[174] – maintained that the 'new revisionism', '[f]ar from offering a way out of the crisis, ... is another manifestation of that crisis, and contributes in no small way to the malaise, confusion, loss of confidence and even despair which have so damagingly affected the Left in recent years'.[175] He argued that 'the recomposition of the working class is not in the least synonymous with its disappearance as a class';[176] it had been in a constant state of recomposition since the nineteenth century, and the number of wage-earners was higher now than at any time in the past. At the heart of Miliband's argument was the centrality of the working class to the socialist project:

> the 'primacy' of organised labour in struggle arises from the fact that no other group, movement or force in capitalist society is remotely capable of mounting as effective and formidable a challenge to the existing structures of power and privilege as it is in the power of organised labour to mount. In no way is this to say that movements of women, blacks, peace activists, ecologists, gays, and others are not important, or cannot have effect, or that they ought to surrender their separate identity. Not at all. It is only to say that the principal ... 'gravedigger' of capitalism remains the organised working class. Here is the necessary, indispensable 'agency of historical change'. And if ... the organised working class will refuse to do the job, then the job will not be done; and capitalist society will continue, generation after generation, as a conflict-ridden, growingly authoritarian and brutalised social system.[177]

Mulhern had made much the same point in the *Review* the previous winter:

> [the] combination of interest, power and creative capacity distinguishes the working class from every other social and political force in capitalist society, and qualifies it as the indispensable agency of socialism ... [I]f it cannot regenerate itself, no outside intervention can do so. If that resource should, in some calamitous historical eventuality, be dispersed or neutralised, then socialism really will be reduced to a sectar-

ian utopia beyond the reach of even the most inspired and combative social movement.[178]

As the politics of the new revisionists became increasingly, and unambiguously, anti-socialist, the *Review* judged that in Britain, as in southern Europe, theoretical revision was rooted in the political setbacks of the period. Confidence in the strength of Anglo-Marxism, allied to a proto-socialist insurgency within the Labour Party in 1979-81, had provided the basis of the *Review*'s attempted reanchorage in the British Left. However, by 1985 the revisionist 'new consensus' was in the ascendant, and 'new realism' ruled the Labour Party. Finding itself more isolated than at any time since 1980, the *NLR* adopted a more defensive project: reanchorage had been superseded by retrenchment.

To this end witness – in addition to the Miliband and Mulhern texts – the trenchant defence of class politics in Norman Geras critique of Laclau and Mouffe's 'beautifully paradigmatic'[179] so-called 'post-Marxism'; Ellen Wood's *The Retreat from Class*; and Ernest Mandel's rejection of 'market socialism'.[180] It was perhaps symptomatic of the defensiveness of its engagement with the new revisionism that the *Review* was more forthright in its reassertion of basic tenets of classical socialism, than its resolution of the problems acknowledged to be confronting socialist strategy in the West. The *Review* had prefaced Geras' critique of Laclau and Mouffe by recognising that there 'are many reasons why it is necessary constantly to revise and renew socialist politics and historical materialist analysis', including 'the eruption of new emancipatory, egalitarian or socially redemptive programmes and movements'.[181] Marxism, it acknowledged, sometimes wrongly invited 'dogmatism and rigidity'.[182] However, in conducting its campaign against the contagion of the new revisionism, there was every danger that the *NLR* would indeed, as Anderson cautioned against, come to rest in an uncreative rejectionism.[183]

The *Review* noted that 'the leaders of the Labour Party have not shown the slightest capacity to identify and challenge capitalist decay' or – in the wake of the 1986 American bombing of Libya from bases in Britain – 'the perils of Atlanticism'.[184] However, it continued to maintain a close interest in the programmes and prospects of the Labour Left, in the misguided expectation of history repeating itself, and that a Kinnock government of the late eighties, treading the same path of crisis management as Wilson and Callaghan, would once again radicalise the disappointed Left inside and outside the Labour Party.[185]

One alternative, advocated by Mike Rustin and others, was for a '[r]adical democratisation' of the British state, involving proportional representation and regional and local decentralisation, enabling the development of a 'party of the left, in some combined shade of Green and Red, ... the opportunity to campaign openly for support, and to seek to reshape the political agenda',[186] and the experiments in municipal or 'city socialism' conducted by the GLC and other metropolitan county councils to flourish – experiments that provided, in Rustin's words, the 'greatest cause for hope' in what had otherwise been 'difficult years for the Left in Britain'.[187] Endorsing the need for a 'socialist micro-economics', Rustin argued that decentralised local and regional government was the most effective – and electorally popular – means of extending public provision and a socially responsible economy, as a radical alternative to both monetarism and Keynesianism. However, the *NLR* editorial prefacing Rustin's intervention was quick to reject any *counterposing* of municipal enterprise to national planning as 'an ingenuously coded retreat from socialisation', couched 'in libertarian tones'.[188] It argued that experiments in 'municipal socialism' would have no real chance of success unless they were 'sustained by central economic levers of public property'.[189] While Rustin argued that the Labour GLC represented just the alliance of the radical 'middle class', or 'new working class' (of 'cultural workers'), and traditional working class that the original New Left had sought and should still be seeking,[190] Ken Livingstone himself was viewed by Anderson with a certain suspicion, susceptible to being co-opted by the Labour leadership.[191] The *Review* thus found itself in the camp of the 'resolute left',[192] with such as Tony Benn and Arthur Scargill, and the left of the disintegrating Communist Party.

Indeed, largely on Ralph Miliband's initiative (and following on from his 'New Revisionism' article in *NLR*), Anderson, Blackburn and Tariq Ali took part in discussions of a 'think-tank' organised around Tony Benn: the 'Independent Left Corresponding Society'.[193] This orientation to the Campaign Group of Left Labour MPs[194] included, for example, the publication in the pages of the *Review* of the Campaign Group's 'A Strategy for Labour', presented by Tony Benn and Eric Heffer to the National Executive Committee of the Labour Party in 1986.[195]

However, with the party's 'soft-left', including many senior 'Bennites' of the early eighties, rallying to Kinnockite realism, Labour's 'resolute left' was being rapidly marginalised, and the 1987 election defeat passed with little comment in the *Review*. Having chosen 'a low and evasive profile' emptied of radical content, the Labour leadership had appeared more concerned with presentational style than political substance: 'Rarely', wrote the *Review*, 'can a defeated party have congratulated itself so much on its campaign as the British Labour Party did in 1987'.[196] That the Kinnock-Hattersley leadership, busying itself with wide-ranging 'policy reviews' and concentrating policy-making powers at the centre (at the expense of conference and the National Executive Committee), would embark on a further round of 'modernisation' was in little doubt.

The crisis of left-wing politics in Britain was due to no mere local or temporarily unfavourable turn of events. It affected the entire West European Left, north and south, social democrat and Communist alike, all busy 'dumping awkward commitments' and adjusting 'their sights downwards, confining themselves to ever more modest instalments of redistribution and promises to reduce unemployment, while having nothing to say about the organisation of production or the pattern of ownership'.[197] The 'checkmate of social Keynesianism in France' (in 1982-3), wrote Anderson in 1991, had been decisive, setting the boundaries for the Euro-Socialist experience in neighbouring countries.[198] When the French Socialist Party returned to power in 1988, the radicalism it had once espoused was entirely absent. The positioning of Michel Rocard's new government was unmistakable: 'an avowal that the Left can have no future except as part of a modern Centre for the management of the affairs of French capital'.[199]

In mapping the West European Left in this period[200] the *Review* had implicitly abandoned meaningful negotiation of the impasse facing socialist politics in the West, and focused entirely on the principal, if increasingly nominal, parties of the social democratic centre-Left: anti-capitalist parties and movements were conspicuously absent from their survey.[201] But by now even Keynesian social democracy was in crisis and retreat. With all prospects in the West at a premium, the *Review* looked East.

Chapter Five
The End of History?

1. The Cold War and the Second World

A central component of the global political and ideological offensive by a revanchist 'New Right' in the late seventies was a markedly more aggressive stance towards the Soviet Union. Détente had secured the SALT treaty of 1972 and the Helsinki accords of 1975 (recognizing Europe's post-1945 borders), yet, despite Nixon's bold diplomatic wooing of China, the overall perception of these years had been a relative weakening of American power. The economic success of capitalist rivals, especially Japan, had damaged American competitiveness, whilst American geo-political hegemony over western Europe was threatened by revolution in Portugal and the prospect of broad Left governments with Communist participation in France, Italy and Spain. OPEC's new-found strength and the rise of 'newly industrialised countries' in the Far East and elsewhere in the developing world presented an additional challenge, though of more immediate alarm to Washington was the dynamic of social revolution in the Third World – in Indo-China, southern Africa (the fall of the Portuguese colonial empire), the Horn of Africa and central America – which, whilst never instigated by Moscow, certainly looked to the Soviet Union for support, threatening an end to America's free hand in the global South, in the process damaging prospects for any understanding between Washington and Moscow based on maintaining the global status quo.

The advent of Reagan was presaged by the Carter administration's adoption of an increasingly bellicose stance on US-Soviet relations: the American Senate's refusal to ratify the SALT-2 agreement was followed by NATO's announcement in December 1979 that it would deploy a new generation of American short-range tactical nuclear missiles in Europe. The Soviet intervention in Afghanistan and the hostage crisis in Iran in the midst of a militantly anti-American 'Islamic revolution' (1979) lent weight to the sharp rightward and 'hawkish' turn in US politics, facilitating Reagan's Presidential victory (already signalled by a sharp shift to the right in Congressional elec-

tions) on a programme of domestic reaction and global confrontation with
the 'Evil Empire'.

Contrasting explanations of the origins and significance of this 'second'
Cold War were given considerable prominence in the *New Left Review*, once
the debate had been initiated by Edward Thompson in 1980. The spiralling
pursuit of nuclear stockpiles and parallel ideological polarisation were not,
in Thompson's estimate, the consequence of political competition subject
to rational, human determination. They were determined by the Cold War
itself, a dominant and pervasive 'system' with its own momentum: 'What is
known as the "Cold War" is the central human fracture, the absolute pole
of power, the fulcrum upon which power turns, in the world'.[1] The United
States and the Soviet Union were condemned as two symmetrical powers,
equally complicit in this escalating arms race: 'we must acknowledge not
one but two imperial formations';[2] and thus, he wrote, 'exterminism itself
is not a "class issue": it is a human issue'.[3] The exterminist momentum was,
in Thompson's bleak and urgent appeal, tending, through an irrational and
'messy inertia',[4] towards global annihilation: 'it is probable that exterminism will reach its historical destination'.[5] However, '[g]ive us victory in this',
Thompson concluded, 'and the world begins to move once more'.[6]

The urgency of the threat posed by this new course in world history, and
Thompson's commitment to meeting it, were not in any doubt. 'In Britain',
wrote the editorial collective of the *NLR* of the resurgence of the campaign
for nuclear disarmament, 'the prime intellectual stimulus for the revival
was given by Edward Thompson, in an act of public service with few comparisons in the recent history of any country'.[7] But they shared neither his
diagnosis of the conflict, nor his prescriptions for ending it. Mike Davis acknowledged that 'every socialist must unconditionally admire the optimism
of his will, and respond to the power of its summons to effective action
against the dangers of a new world war. But the pessimism of his intellect,
expressed no less powerfully, prompts critical reflection'.[8] The persistently
moralist and humanist imperative of Thompson's position had failed, in
Anderson's judgement, to 'generate any historical or materialist understanding of the international conflict'.[9]

The international response to Thompson's 'thunder-clap' provided 'the
organising focus for successive interventions on the new dangers of global
war',[10] comprising articles in the *Review* and a book, *Exterminism and Cold
War*, published by Verso in 1982. It encouraged the *New Left Review* to make
good its previous 'neglect or underestimate [of] the dynamic of the arms
race between East and West', and 'to bring its own socialist perspective to the
questions raised by Thompson'.[11] Equally, it marked a foray into the field of

international relations that was – for all the *Review*'s early recognition of the interplay between the First, Second, and Third Worlds – an area in which it had been 'traditionally very weak'.[12] 'Contemporary history', the *NLR* asserted, 'is ... *world* history, that of a globe now integrated into one vast field of inter-related conflicts.'[13]

In prefacing Thompson's essay, the *NLR* recognised that 'he is surely right to insist that nuclear weapons, pregnant with holocaust, cannot simply be analysed in terms of competing class forces or social systems, but also possess a menacing dynamic of their own'.[14] 'Advances' in weapons technology meant that there was effectively no longer any room for political control: 'in the mid-70s', wrote Thompson, 'the time required for the interhemispheric delivery of nuclear bombs had shrunk to about ten minutes, and it is now perhaps less'.[15] Any room for sanction by America's European allies, on whose territory the new tactical missiles would be based, had all but disappeared. Particularly menacing was the prospect of an accidental nuclear exchange; in 1984 Ken Coates warned that there had been '147 false alarms on North American early warning systems'[16] in the last eighteen months: '[i]f Man is ever obliterated from the earth by means of his own armaments, there will be no simple answer to the question: Did he fall or was he pushed?'[17] Nonetheless, the *NLR* was unwilling to apportion equal blame for this escalating threat: the Cold War was not, as Thompson suggested, merely the inertial consequence of an irrational competition between symmetrical power blocs. The *NLR* endorsed the Medvedevs' insistence 'on the central responsibility of American capitalism for the current international crisis ... in which every important step in the escalation of nuclear terror from Hiroshima to the Neutron Bomb has been initiated by the United States'.[18]

The *Review*'s response to Thompson came in two essays, by Mike Davis and Fred Halliday, which appeared alongside Thompson's initial intervention and subsequent reply to the debate in the 1982 Verso collection, *Exterminism and Cold War*.[19] Davis argued that it was necessary 'to reinstate the revolutionary Marxist conception of the modern epoch as an age of violent, protracted transition from capitalism to socialism ... [T]he true motor of the Cold War ... [is] the process of *permanent revolution* arising out of [the] uneven and combined development of modern capitalism ... [T]he major trend in modern history has been the tectonic action of ... elemental class struggles within and upon the international state system.'[20] Although Thompson balked at 'the way in which Davis offers to tidy up thirty years of history, and package it into categories',[21] this was, in essence, the *Review*'s perspective on the origins and character of the conflict. The Cold War was not essentially driven by an independent 'exterminist' mo-

mentum of its own: it would have ensued with or without nuclear weapons. The possession of such weapons, explained Halliday, 'at once dramatise
and endow with infinitely greater risk a conflict whose bases lie elsewhere
– above all in the conflict between capitalist and non-capitalist worlds ... It
is in the interaction of nuclear arms race with globalised social conflict that
the roots of the New Cold War lie'.[22] According to Halliday, the 'great contest' between the United States and the Soviet Union was much more than a
rivalry between two superpowers. It embodied, in however distorted a form,
the confrontation between rival social forces, overlain by state systems and
nuclear-armed alliances.

In Halliday's analysis, expanded in *The Making of the Second Cold War*
(published by Verso in 1983), the emergence of the Soviet Union as a world
power in 1945 constituted a watershed in international relations: thereafter global affairs were conducted in the context of the rivalry between
two opposing social formations. The first Cold War, which Halliday dated
from 1946 to 1954 (with the end of the Korean War and the Geneva accords on Indo-China), gave way to an uneasy, yet relatively stabilised, peace.
Throughout this period the United States and its allies maintained a considerable strategic advantage. With a global network of foreign bases, the
United States posed a constant threat to the security of the Soviet Union,[23]
and was not backward in deploying its strategic advantage in a calculated
policy of intimidation. The period of relatively stabilised peace that sub-
sisted through the sixties was one in which the greater military capacity, and
thus political and strategic superiority, of the United States could not be in
doubt. The defeat of the American war-machine in Vietnam came as a rude
shock, severely denting the standing of the United States and its own self-es-
teem. Meanwhile, the balance of America's nuclear lead, whilst still substantial, was reduced from 2:1 to 3:2 in the decade 1970 to 1980.[24] The relative
enhancement of the Soviet position should not be confused with the myth
of Soviet superiority or the manufactured claims in Washington about a
'missile gap'. Throughout the decade American military expenditure out-
stripped that of the Soviet Union; if other NATO countries and Japan and
China were included, the expenditure of the United States and its allies was
just over double that of the Soviet Union and Warsaw Treaty countries.[25]

Whilst the situation in Europe, certainly after the building of the Berlin
Wall in 1961, remained relatively frozen and stable, it was largely in the
Third World that the contest between the forces of capitalism and socialism (and national liberation) unfolded. The United States succeeded in
containing the great majority of these revolutions: between the victory of
the Chinese Revolution and the end of the Vietnam War, Cuba and Aden

(1967) provided embattled exceptions. Given the conservative cast of its bureaucratic dictatorship, and its military and strategic inferiority to the United States, the Soviet leadership was unwilling to offer anything but the most cautious support for revolutionary movements abroad. Nevertheless, American foreign policy followed a more circumscribed course after its defeat in Vietnam, and Halliday identified fourteen 'revolutionary upheavals' in the Third World between 1974 and 1980.[26] It was this, he argued, that had stirred the right-wing reaction in the United States and elsewhere: 'it is social revolution itself and the response to it which has triggered the counter-revolutionary drive that is so central to the Second Cold War'.[27] Halliday argued that the rise of an aggressive 'new Right' signalled a threefold offensive against the global post-war settlement, targeted at the domestic gains of the working class; at the USSR as a world power; and at the independence of the former colonial world. The anti-Soviet and Cold War mobilisation sought to roll back these gains, thus restoring the position of global capital and, concomitantly, the standing of the Western powers. 'The responsibility for Cold War II is shared between east and west ... but it is the west which, precisely because it has the upper hand, took the initiative in introducing a new level of competition which it believes will restore the primacy in world politics which recent developments have taken from it.'[28]

*Review*ing Halliday's *The Making of the Second Cold War* in 1984, Marten Ougaard argued that the 'centre-bourgeoisie' of the West was engaged on two separate fronts, East and South: against 'socialism' and anti-imperialism respectively. He calculated a relative *downturn* in Third World revolution after 1976, arguing that the sixties had witnessed a stronger challenge to the Western powers from that quarter. Ougaard thus drew an opposite conclusion from Halliday's account of the origins of the Second Cold War:

[C]risis and revolutionary pressure in the Third World contributed to the policies of detente, whereas the relative stabilisation of the periphery ... was supportive of the new cold war ... The dialectic between these two fronts is simply that when the pressure on one grows too strong, it becomes necessary to reduce tensions on the other. In order to deal with the mounting challenge of the Third World during the crisis of imperialism, the Western system had to seek detente, play the China card etc. ... When imperialism had cut its losses in the Third World, divided its remaining enemies and developed strategies to deal with them separately ... one of the conditions was established for a renewed offensive against the opposing social system.[29]

Replying to Ougaard in the same issue of the *Review*, Halliday reaffirmed his contention that the principal contradiction in global politics was between capitalism – both North *and* South – and social revolution:[30] inter-capitalist rivalries, between the bourgeoisies of the metropolitan core and the developing countries, certainly played some part in destabilising the global social order, but they were not the key dynamic. Whether the precise origins of the Second Cold War lay in the West's response to a heightened challenge in the Third World – Halliday's contention – or in the relative pacification of such a challenge – Ougaard's position – need not unduly detain us. The emphasis they shared was more central than the detail that divided them: 'Both Ougaard and Halliday insist that world politics must be grasped as the contradictory outcome of the clash of antagonistic social systems and forces'.[31]

    Halliday was undoubtedly expressing the collective position of the *NLR*, which in 1979 had insisted that the 'recrudescence of Cold War politics in the West … dates from the unwelcome shocks suffered by the world imperialist system from the triumph of the Vietnamese Revolution, to the consolidation of Angolan independence, the sustenance of the Ethiopian Republic [defeating a Somali invasion of the Ogaden region in 1977-8, and, more contentiously, resisting Eritrean separatism from 1978], the survival of South Yemen [Aden], and the overturn in Afghanistan – all facilitated or safeguarded by Soviet arms or assistance'.[32] The Cuban expedition to Angola in 1975 (thwarting a South African invasion force, and shifting the whole balance of power in southern Africa), for example, involving a military co-ordination across three continents, could not have been effected without the support of the Soviet Union, 'which spectacularly demonstrated the new military-diplomatic balance of forces in the Third World – the first time in history a socialist regime was able to lend decisive armed assistance to a beleaguered revolution across the divide of an ocean … The contrast, not merely with Spain in the 30's, but with Chile only two years earlier, was remarkable'.[33] These commitments served to demonstrate that, for all its cautious conservatism, the Soviet bureaucracy could be induced to play an actively progressive international role, and did not perceive itself to be as constrained in its actions as in the very recent past. Meanwhile, it was 'the revolutionary movements of Central America' that proved 'the storm-centres of the class struggle in the Western Hemisphere'.[34] Whilst the first socialist revolution in the English-speaking world (inaugurated in March 1979) was brought to an end when the United States invaded Grenada in 1983, the Sandinistas carried forward a broadly based social revolution in embattled

Nicaragua after the fall of the Somoza dictatorship in July 1979 – representing 'the most hopeful single victory of the past few years'.[35]

Conviction that the Cold War was a product of the global contest between capitalism and 'socialism' (or, at any rate, 'post-capitalism') led the *NLR* largely to reject Thompson's thesis on the nature of the conflict. The task before the peace movement was not simply to challenge a Cold War 'system' tending inexorably towards 'exterminism', in which both the United States and Soviet Union were equally culpable. If it was never quite to advocate active solidarity with one side in the conflict, the *Review* certainly sought to explain the asymmetrical character of the conflict itself, and identify the tasks facing the peace movement accordingly:

> The New Cold War … is the distorted product of the conflict between a militaristic capitalism and an involuted and bureaucratic socialism. It can only be transcended by a socialism that, whilst not equating these two international forces, seeks to be a historical alternative to both … [T]he strategic objectives of the European peace movement must now be two-fold – the disengagement of the Western half of the continent from the military system that represents the major seat of potential war, and the Eastern half from the political system that represents the major negation of civil liberties.[36]

'To build peace', argued Raymond Williams in the first response to Thompson in the *Review*, 'now more than ever, it is necessary to build more than peace':[37] it meant opposing global capital and the political power of the Western capitalist states which represented the principal threat to peace. 'It is impossible to eliminate the threat of nuclear war without eliminating the capitalist system', wrote Mandel: 'the criticism we make of the pacifists is not that they have "exaggerated" the danger of nuclear weapons but that they underestimate it'.[38] There was no doubting the scale of the mobilisation against the deployment of new missiles, bringing millions onto the streets of western Europe in protest – representing, in the eyes of the *NLR*, 'the greatest hope in European politics of the last few years'.[39] However, the conjuncture was peculiarly unfavourable for a breakthrough to socialist democracy East or West: 'the new possibility of global holocaust has altered the bases and terms of the prospect for socialism … making it overwhelmingly more urgent, yet practically more difficult, than ever before'.[40]

An integral part of the New Right's political and ideological mobilisation was a mounting campaign of anti-Sovietism. This 'contemporary Russophobia' was not confined to the Right, for it also infected broad sections of the Left: 'social-democratic periodicals which condoned the Moscow trials, Maoist zealots freshly awakened to the values of the Free World, Eurocommunist functionaries once supine before Stalin, can all be found today ventilating the most vulgar and ignorant anti-Soviet themes.'[41] Erstwhile Maoists made the most dramatic defections. Having pursued an unblinkingly reactionary foreign policy in the seventies, China was largely exempt from Western vilification, facilitating a rapid conversion from ultra-left anti-Sovietism to a more familiar right-wing version.[42] Maoism, of course, had little purchase in Britain; yet similar anti-Soviet phobias on the Left undoubtedly assisted the passage to anti-Communist and anti-socialist perspectives. It was just this slippage that the *NLR* sought to combat. At a minimum, a vigilant 'anti-anti-Sovietism'[43] was an almost unavoidable obligation. As the Second Cold War began in earnest, the *NLR* sought to counter the anti-Soviet offensive, soliciting, for example, Zhores Medvedev's 'Russia under Brezhnev' in 1979, commended as a balance sheet drawn with 're-markable calm and sobriety'[44] – qualities all too lacking in the 'gulagism' of the 'human rights' campaigns then being staged.

Whilst the bureaucratic confiscation of economic and political power was acknowledged and regretted, the post-capitalist character of the Soviet Union and its allies was nonetheless judged as constituting a positive factor in the configuration of global social forces. Despite this (on balance) favourable assessment, the tension between these negative and positive aspects of the Second World was central to the *Review*'s characterisation of the conjuncture. A 1978 editorial, for example, recognised that 'one central factor' in the rightward political drift consequent upon the escalation towards renewed Cold War was 'what might be termed a crisis of the prevailing models of socialism', given 'the cumulative evidence of the repressive and reactionary character of regimes which proclaim themselves to be socialist'.[45] Nevertheless, two issues later the *Review* praised the progressive character of Soviet foreign policy, with specific reference to Vietnam and Afghanistan.[46]

Symptomatic of the *Review*'s perspective was its assessment of the Soviet Union's involvement in Afghanistan – a pivotal moment at the outset of the Second Cold War. The seizure of power by the People's Democratic Party of Afghanistan (PDPA) – 'in effect the local Communist Party'[47] – in Kabul in April 1978 promised a sweeping programme of social reform. The *NLR* was quick to advise that socialists should welcome these developments,[48] despite their unpropitious context: 'at best, Afghan socialism will be constructed to a degree rare even in the history of twentieth-century struggles within the brutal realm of necessity'.[49] Unsurprisingly, the revolution was soon 'besieged by a fanatical counter-revolution',[50] sponsored and armed from without. A spiral of violence, compounded by bloody factional in-fighting within the ruling regime, presented an uncomfortable choice for the Soviet leadership (the situation on its southern borders already destabilised by the Islamic Revolution in Iran, raising the threat of American intervention): either complete abandonment or full engagement. Roy Medvedev, the socialist dissident, endorsed the Soviet intervention in defence of a progressive neighbouring government.[51] Fred Halliday, writing in the immediate aftermath of the entry of Soviet troops into Afghanistan, argued that the 'critical error of the Russians was less that they intervened in December 1979 than that they had allowed matters to reach such a point that they were confronted by the options then existing'.[52] The disastrous Amin regime was ousted, and Babrak Karmal installed – an attempt to avoid an impending civil war through a more conciliatory political approach. Halliday concluded that foreign intervention in support of revolution was acceptable on condition that the revolutionary forces enjoyed a genuine popular base, and that 'the international consequences, in terms of provoking imperialist retaliation, are not such as to outweigh the probable advantages'.[53] Whilst demonstrating the difficult choices before the Soviet leadership, Halliday calculated that the costs of the Soviet involvement did indeed seem to outweigh the likely gains: 'It is revolutionary forces across the world who will pay the price for the ravages of the Afghan counter-revolution, the authoritarian record of the PDPA leadership, the mistakes of Russian policy and the current imperialist offensive.'[54] Writing two years later, Halliday was even more forthright: the Soviet Union, 'even if it held an Islamic Vendée at bay in Afghanistan, ... has done substantial harm to the wider cause of peace and socialism'.[55]

Notwithstanding Halliday's conclusions with regard to the Soviet intervention in Afghanistan, the *Review* accepted a generally more positive account of the international role of the Soviet Union after 1978. In 1976 Anderson had written that 'Deutscher's optimism about the prospects for internal reform within the USSR after Stalin was unfounded';[56] and as late as 1978 the *Review* was, in the words of a confidential self-criticism, 'unwittingly appearing to lend comfort to ultra-left simplifications' in its characterisation of the Soviet Union.[57] However, by the beginning of the Second Cold War, the *Review* qualified its orthodox Trotskyite interpretation of the Soviet Union, tilting back towards the Deutscherite perspective it had held in the mid-sixties.[58]

This re-evaluation was reflected in Anderson's 1983 essay, in which he nevertheless began by acknowledging 'Trotsky's interpretation of Stalinism' as 'to this day the most coherent and developed theorisation of the phenomenon within the Marxist tradition'.[59] In Trotsky's analysis, Stalinism represented a bureaucratic degeneration of the Soviet state. But the bureaucracy did not constitute a new class; nor had it reversed the abolition of private property. It played a contradictory role at home, 'defending itself simultaneously against the Soviet working-class, from which it had usurped power, and against the world bourgeoisie, which sought to wipe out all the gains of the October Revolution and restore capitalism in Russia'.[60] Abroad, by contrast, the Soviet bureaucracy, in Trotsky's estimate, played an unambiguously counter-revolutionary role.

Anderson identified two main limitations to Trotsky's analysis of Stalinism. First, the Soviet bureaucracy played not an irredeemably counter-revolutionary role abroad, but, as at home, a 'contradictory' one. And secondly, the 'structures of bureaucratic power and mobilisation pioneered under Stalin proved to be both more dynamic and more general phenomenon on the international plane than Trotsky ever imagined'.[61] In other words, both the Soviet bureaucracy itself, and the parties that traced their descent from the Third International, had, contrary to Trotsky's expectations, performed revolutionary roles. For example, at the end of the Second World War capitalism had been abolished in half of Europe – albeit 'by bureaucratic fiat from above'.[62] Moreover, Stalinism – 'a workers state ruled by an authoritarian bureaucratic stratum – did not merely represent a *degeneration* from a prior state of (relative) class grace; it could also be a spontaneous *generation* produced by revolutionary class forces in very backward societies'.[63] Even socialist revolutions independent of Soviet initiative had proven to be Stalinist in character: in Yugoslavia, Albania, China, Vietnam and even Cuba. Stalinism became the standard model for all the 'post-capitalist' societies (indeed, something of an alternative development model for any number of radical bourgeois-nationalist regimes following decolonisation).

In line with this analysis, the *Review*'s 1983 Charter explained its duties thus: 'Today the Communist states ... represent a historic progress over the capitalist or pre-capitalist societies that preceded them, and a vital bulwark against imperialism. The review will defend them as such against every variety of capitalist attack, to which they are ceaselessly subject.'[64] Even North Korea, with an 'extraordinarily monolithic and regimented social order prostrated before the narcissistic cult of ... [its] Communist monarch',[65] elicited a sober and broadly favourable endorsement in Jon Halliday's 1981 essay. In spite of the United States' avowed desire to bomb the country back into the Stone Age during the 1950-3 war, real per capita income in 1974 was twenty times that of 1946: a social and material advance, reckoned Halliday, unprecedented in Korean history.[66]

Nonetheless, the negative aspects of 'actually existing socialism' were in-escapable. The Communist states, the Charter continued, exercised a 're-pressive tutelage over the working population', denying them 'fundamental rights of self-expression and self-determination', and thus generating 'popu-lar revolts against bureaucratic misrule'.[67] The main popular revolt in this period, and the one exception to the relative stability of the post-capitalist social order, was in Poland. The *NLR* had given considerable coverage to the strike-waves of 1970-1 and 1976, enthusing over the 'elemental directness and power of the *class consciousness* of the shipyard workers'.[68] The advent of Solidarity in August 1980 'took the anti-bureaucratic struggle of the Polish masses onto an altogether new and more organised plane',[69] and produced 'the most spectacular affirmation of the working-class capacity for self-or-ganisation seen in Europe since May 1968'.[70] However, with the Second Cold War in full swing, the political context of 1980-1 was quite different, ren-dering 'responsible Marxist intervention on Poland more complex than be-fore'.[71] 'The audacious militancy and superb solidary instincts' of the Polish working class remained to the fore, but the *Review* warily noted that the movement was 'constrained by a clerico-nationalist ideology symbolised by Walesa's genuflection before his Polish Pope':[72]

This time ... events in Poland rapidly became the focus of a gigantic ideological mobilisation in the West, of a clamorously anti-communist character – indeed for a time serving as the veritable pivot of the whole New Cold War waged by imperialism in this phase. This campaign, moreover, was not without popular echoes in the ranks of Solidarity itself, where strongly nationalist and vaguely pro-capitalist currents could coalesce in sentimental support for Reaganite rearmament against the USSR; more or less discreetly encouraged by the Vatican.[73]

Treading a delicate line, 'Oliver MacDonald' (Peter Gowan of the Fourth International, soon to join the *Review*'s editorial committee) argued that the best prospect for a socialist outcome had been in an alliance between reformist and grassroot groups within the Polish Communist Party – the PZPR – and Solidarity, in pursuit of a new relationship between the par-ty and working class. He judged that despite being infected by reaction-ary and nationalist currents, the Polish workers, in tandem with a renewed PZPR, could have advanced towards a genuine socialist democracy. In the event, Solidarity leaders failed to make common cause with the reformist 'Horizontal Movement' within the PZPR – even though a third of the par-ty's three million members belonged to the union.[74] Kania's replacement as prime-minister by Jaruzelski in February 1981 weakened the dim prospect of reform, and effectively paved the way for the imposition of martial law in December of the same year. Neither reform from within the ruling party, nor workers' revolution from without, nor even an articulation of the two, proved to be capable of resolving the Polish crisis. Instead, it was the most conservative forces within the party, seeking an accommodation with the Church under the auspices of the army, who stabilised their position with the advent of martial law.

Analysing the complex character of working class insurrection against a 'workers' state', MacDonald wrote that the 'fundamental feature of the Polish upheaval that has been so difficult for socialists (and anti-socialists) to grasp has been the fact that the Polish workers combine a tenacious political opposition to continued monopolistic rule by the Polish Communist party … with a no less tenacious defence of a group of rights never guaranteed by any capitalist state.'[75] In prefacing MacDonald's article, the *NLR* argued that the 'monolithicity of party rule involves a specific relationship to working-class organisation and rights: an arbitration between bureaucratic and class interests, in which the former is obliged to find some foothold in the latter'.[76] The concentration of political and economic power in the hands of the bureaucracy in modern industrial societies meant that it was peculiarly vulnerable to the challenge of a combative working class: while 'the proletariat of the capitalist world is disorganised and fragmented by economic crisis', continued the *Review*, hinting at its sense of the progressive potential inherent within the 'post-capitalist' social order, 'that of the East remains a massive and increasingly self-conscious social presence.'[77] However, in the context of renewed Cold War, the defensive preoccupations of the Soviet leadership meant that there was little chance of popular revolt being allowed to run its course in Poland or elsewhere in Eastern Europe. The most likely alternative to martial law in Poland was Soviet intervention.

The long life of the Stalinist model had, in Anderson's words, 'deeply tarnished the very idea of socialism in the advanced West, its absolute negation of proletarian democracy inhibiting the working class from an assault on capitalism within the structures of bourgeois democracy, and thereby decisively *strengthening* the bastions of imperialism in the late twentieth century'.[78] Fred Halliday cited the 'involution' of the post-capitalist states as one of the factors in the renewed the Cold War: by no measure could the Soviet Union be portrayed to the people of western Europe as an attractive alternative society. The abuses of human rights and the absence of even the rudiments of democracy gave a real grounding to the excesses of anti-Soviet propaganda. Where 'involution' turned to 'dementia',[79] as in the case of Pol Pot's 'Democratic Kampuchea', the consequences were more damning still.

The name of Communism was further tarnished by the equally ugly instances of war between 'socialist' countries. The Sino-Soviet schism of 1960 eventuated in armed border clashes in 1969 – easing Nixon's diplomatic coup of 1972 which resulted in 'People's China' becoming the staunchest of America's anti-Soviet allies in the seventies. The prospect of war between 'socialist' countries was raised again in 1979, with China's punitive military incursion into Vietnam following the latter's ejection of Pol Pot from Cambodia. 'This is not so much an epoch of capitalism riven by increasing contradictions and socialism marching triumphantly ahead', wrote Jon Halliday in 1980, 'as one of world capitalism relatively united while post-revolutionary societies are divided and battle over one another.'[80] None of this did anything to enhance either the lustre of 'actually existing socialism', or the geo-political standing of the Soviet Union vis-à-vis the West.

What, then, accounts for the *Review*'s more favourable reassessment of the post-capitalist societies? With the advent of the Second Cold War in 1978-9, the *Review* was quick to recognise that the conflict between the United States and the Soviet Union represented a contest between rival social systems and forces, 'manifestly' imposing 'new duties on the review'.[81] Meanwhile, expectations of a socialist revolution in one or more of the advanced capitalist countries – inaugurating socialist democracy in conditions of relative abundance and thus superseding the Eastern experience – had been dashed. The defeat of the Portuguese revolution in 1974-5, the failure of Euro-Communism, and the dismal record of social democracy and Latin 'Euro-Socialism', all served to underscore the intractability of effecting a transition to socialism in the West. Given that there was relatively little prospect of either a breakthrough to socialism in the West, or the overthrow of the bureaucratic dictatorships in the East, the *Review* was compelled to reflect that it was the bastardised 'socialism' of the 'post-capitalist' societies that offered the only effective 'bulwark against imperialism' for the foreseeable future.

2. The Fall in the East

In 1980 the *NLR* had confided, in an unpublished editorial report, that it may prove 'impossible to move towards socialism in the West until the USSR is itself democratised'.[82] That it considered having 'to accept a historical priority to progress in the East over advance in the West' a 'grim prospect',[83] said as much for the impasse of socialist strategy in the West as it did of the likelihood of democratisation in the Soviet Union. Events, however, were about to unfold at an unforeseen pace. The ascension of Mikhail Gorbachev to the leadership of the CPSU in 1985, and the quickening pace of reform thereafter, lent credibility to Deutscher's conviction (in opposition to orthodox Trotskyism) that a reform from above – from within the ranks of the party-bureaucracy – might facilitate progress towards socialist democracy in the Soviet Union.

At first there were few signs of radical initiative on Gorbachev's part. Zhores Medvedev offered a lukewarm assessment of the 27th Congress of the CPSU in 1986 and of Gorbachev himself, whom he described as a 'cautious type of person, with the limitations of a typical apparatchik, lacking Khrushchev's radicalism'.[84] However, the depth of the crisis facing the Soviet economy – the legacy of the long years of 'stagnation' under Brezhnev – in the context of intensified geo-political and military-technological competition with the West during the Second Cold War, left little room for caution.[85] Campaigns against corruption and alcoholism, under the slogan *perestroika* ('restructuring'), were not enough. *Glasnost* ('openness') had to be deployed in an attempt to weaken the dead hand of bureaucratic inertia. Roy Medvedev identified a radical turn by Gorbachev in 1986-7, combining a bold series of foreign policy initiatives with the recognition that limited domestic reforms were insufficient to the task in hand.[86] With the promise of democratisation, the *Review* could write in the summer of 1987 that Gorbachev's reform programme appeared to be 'going well beyond … the Khruschevite de-Stalinisation of the late fifties and early sixties'.[87] It hoped that 'glasnost and perestroika may be only the first, cautious words in a new vocabulary of socialist revival in the Soviet Union'.[88]

The formation of an independent Left, such as the Federation of Socialist Clubs in Moscow, and the work of individual socialists, such as Boris Kagarlitsky and the Medvedev brothers, were greeted by the *Review* as small signs of a tentative socialist renaissance in the USSR. Independent working class initiatives, such as the miners' strike in the summer of 1989, which broached the prospect of 'perestroika from below',[89] were potentially another. However, the principal dynamic of change lay in the contest between technocratic reformers – increasingly favouring market liberalisation – and separatist nationalists on the one hand, and conservatives and 'Great Russian' nationalists on the other. As the economy failed to respond to any of the measures designed to improve it, the centrifugal forces pulling the Union apart, such as ethnic tension in Trans-Caucasia and the Baltic, became ever stronger. In such circumstances, the technocratic liberals might, in Kagarlitsky's words, impose 'a hideous monster, a kind of negative con-

vergence' combining 'the worst features of both systems', which he designated 'market Stalinism'.[90]

Nonetheless, there was a moment when the promise of democratic reform held open the prospect of socialist renewal in the East, with all that
this might portend for a reinvigoration of socialist politics in the West. As
Tariq Ali put it to Yuri Afanasyev in an interview in the *NLR* in 1988: 'Many
of us who remain socialists in the West are beginning to regard the Soviet
Union once again as a country of hope. If you succeed, it could help in the
rebirth of mass socialism elsewhere in the world. In that sense the fight for a
socialist democracy is important not just for you but for us as well'.[91] Similar
sentiments were echoed in the *Review*'s introductory Themes early in 1989,
which considered that 'an alliance between the Western Left and socialist
reform forces in the East could throw back the neo-liberal offensive of the
past decade'.[92] Substantial hopes were thus invested in a transition to socialist democracy in the East at a time when, on other fronts, West and South,
socialists were in retreat. Indicative of the mood was Tariq Ali's *Revolution
From Above* (1988), a strikingly optimistic assessment of the chances of socialist renewal in the Soviet Union.[93]

The uncertain process of reform within the Soviet Union, and the diminishing prospects of a socialist outcome, were somewhat masked by the
dynamism of the Gorbachev leadership in the field of foreign affairs. 'The
lure of cutting a figure abroad', wrote Anderson in the *London Review of
Books* in 1991, 'generally exacts some domestic costs, but there is no other
modern case of such a gap between external adulation and internal repudiation as eventually opened up in Gorbachev's government of the Soviet
Union.'[94] Gorbachev's calculated appeals to Western public opinion – sparking a veritable 'Gorby-mania' – and a summit with Reagan, culminating in
the INF treaty signed at Washington in December 1987, brought the Second
Cold War to an end. More momentous still was the effective green light to
reformers within the ruling parties of Eastern Europe – and, no less, to dissident and public opinion at large.

Soon, however, events took a less hopeful turn. In the wake of the massacre
at Tiananmen Square in China in June 1989 – suppressing the student-led
democracy movement – the *Review* was compelled to acknowledge the 'deep
crisis of "actually existing socialism"',[95] whilst, more conclusively, Norberto
Bobbio wrote in the pages of the *Review* that the 'catastrophe of historical
communism stands literally before everyone's eyes'.[96] The crisis soon became a rout, for the accelerating pace of events during 1989 transformed the
entire post-war political landscape in Eastern Europe. The opening of the
Berlin Wall in November 1989 was perhaps the single most dramatic act of a

year of revolutions, as Communism's 'sclerotic ruling castes' fell like a house of cards.[97] The Velvet Revolution in Czechoslavakia symbolised the relative ease of the transition. Only in Romania was there a brief resort to arms to settle accounts with the old regime.

With the West European Left already in a state of crisis, and a deregulated and increasingly globalised capitalism in the ascendant, the fall of the Communist regimes in the East – long anticipated as a stimulus to socialist renewal – occurred at a peculiarly unfavourable moment for the Left. In 1989 the *Review* could write of Eastern Europe that 'a more or less protracted transition period lies ahead as social forces fight over alternative political programmes';[98] and that there were 'some grounds for hoping that the new post-Communist societies will carry forward into an uncharted future social forces and values at variance with actually-existing capitalism'.[99] Within a year, however, the *NLR* was compelled to acknowledge that 'identification with socialism in the region has dropped close to zero'.[100] The Left in Eastern Europe, from rightward-moving ex-Communists to refounded social democrats, almost everywhere went down to electoral defeat, in the aftermath of 1989, to a neo-liberal agenda of crash-course marketisation and privatisation. 'The peoples of Eastern Europe', wrote the *Review* in 1990, seem 'condemned to a capitalist purgatory, or limbo'.[101] Habermas described the transformation as 'a revolution that is to some degree flowing backwards',[102] clearing the ground for a period of capitalist development that had seemingly been by-passed. The *NLR* was reduced to drawing small crumbs of comfort. 'The chances of a socialist outcome in the East may be slender', noted an introductory Themes at the end of 1989, 'but if the transition to democracy is consolidated then at least more advantageous conditions for developing an anti-capitalist response will have been created'.[103] But even the transition to democracy was being jeopardised by the rising tides of nationalism. The disintegration of Yugoslavia provided an awful warning to the rest of the region.[104]

The fall of Communism in Eastern Europe was a geo-political triumph for the West: the *Review* had no doubt that the 'West has won the Cold War'.[105] Today's moribund 'Great Power Communism' was no spectre stalking the globe, wrote Blackburn in 1991, 'but an unhappy spirit, begging to be laid to rest'.[106] Thompson's 'exterminism' thesis of 1980 was shown to have been misjudged: it was not the case that the superpower elites, East and West, had been locked into an 'exterminist' logic. It was not the action of the peace movements, but a sudden change in the Soviet position – in a context of growing weakness – and the response of the Reagan administration, that promised to remove the recently installed missiles. The withdrawal of intermediate nuclear weapons from Europe, wrote Simon Bromley and Justin Rosenberg in 1988, 'will take place *after* the effective political defeat of anti-nuclear protest in every relevant European country'.[107] East and West did not, as Thompson argued, exist in a symbiotic relationship: the collapse of the one did not weaken, but strengthen, the other. Thompson insisted that opportunities for a 'third way' still existed, that in a post-Cold War Europe the fall of Communism in the East could be a stimulus to transformation in the West. Fred Halliday, in reply, doubted, in the context of Western triumphalism, that such an outcome was likely.[108]

Western economic and political pressure on Eastern Europe ensured that a 'third way' was not an available option. In 1990 Peter Gowan charted 'the central political role of the Western states in the internal affairs' of post-1989 Eastern Europe – a role 'made possible by the West's coercive power of exclusion from a world economy managed by political institutions in the hands of the leading capitalist states'.[109] Restructuring threatened to reduce the former Second World to the status of the Third, rather than raise it, as popular expectation had been led to believe, to the level of the First. In Poland, cited by Gowan by way of example, the IMF-imposed 'Balcerowicz Plan' had 'cut living standards by 40 per cent' in less than a year, 'an austerity drive of unparalleled scope in postwar international history'.[110] Where the potential for economic leverage was weakest, in Romania and Bulgaria, '[d]irect political intervention was ... used'.[111] 'The hope', wrote Gowan, 'seems to have been to apply Chancellor Kohl's tactics for the GDR elections, of in effect telling the voters to back the parties with access to Western funds: the Bulgarian opposition leader bluntly declared that he had been told by British Foreign Secretary Hurd that the Communist Party would not get a penny from the West if it won the elections. Whitehall's denial was unconvincing.'[112] The GDR, meanwhile, had been subjected, in Halliday's words, to 'the swift, decisive and methodical strangulation ... by the python of West German capitalism'.[113] It appeared, wrote the *Review* in 1990, that 'the post-Communist states will become a free-fire zone for a new species of booty capitalism'.[114]

The prospects for reform within the Soviet Union were hardly helped by Eastern Europe's colonisation by Western capitalism. Gorbachev's position had been weakened, and the hand of conservative caution strengthened, by the Soviet Union's geo-political retreat. Eastern Europe offered no model of a transition from Stalinism to socialist democracy, only a headlong flight to capitalism. A successful outcome to the reform process in the Soviet Union was becoming ever more doubtful:

Gorbachev must be given great credit for tolerating – in some cases more or less instigating – the settling of accounts with the Bourbons of Eastern Europe. Yet in the Soviet Union itself the Politburo and Central Committee have been indulgent to bureaucratic privilege and obstruction, credulous towards 'free market' technocrats, unimaginative in devising alternative socio-economic forms and, most dangerous of all, crudely bullying towards the national movements which challenge the central power.[115]

In both the Soviet Union and China, warned the *NLR* early in 1991, 'the security forces ... loom menacingly, propping up an ailing simulacrum of the old order'.[116]

Gorbachev's position was becoming increasingly precarious. It was the power of Boris Yeltsin – against whom Gorbachev had allied with conservatives in the winter of 1990-1 – that was waxing, a position strengthened with Yeltsin's victory in the first direct elections for the Presidency of the Russian Federation in June 1991. Gorbachev was finally and fatally undermined by the ill-starred coup of August 1991, the conservative plotters of the 'State Committee for the Emergency' being faced down in Moscow by Yeltsin's theatrical resistance. 'The August revolution defeated not only the coup but also Mikhail Gorbachev's reform project':[117] the Union was dissolved and the Party suppressed. Thereafter, the Yeltsin-Gaidar government of the Russian Federation accelerated the privatisation and marketisation of the ailing economy. R. W. Davies (a former collaborator of E. H. Carr) wrote that 'Trotsky's prediction' of capitalist restoration in the Soviet Union had 'unexpectedly turned from a wild misjudgement into an imaginative prophecy'.[118]

The *NLR* had already contemplated, in 1980, the possibility of capitalist restoration in the East. It seemed 'historically implausible' that there would be no individual cases of restoration, 'however jolting the prospect. After all, the bourgeois revolutions were followed by a number of absolutist restorations, even if these did not prove durable in character – 1660, 1815, 1824.'[119] Yugoslavia might be one such candidate for capitalist restoration, China 'possibly' another.[120] But capitalist restoration in the Soviet Union itself was a 'jolting prospect' indeed. It could not fail to be a traumatic experience for socialists the world over, for all their reservations and criticisms of its actual historical record and performance. 'It is true I was heavily critical of the Soviet Union', wrote G. A. Cohen in the *NLR*, 'but the angry little boy who pummels his father's chest will not be glad if the old man collapses.'[121]

The collapse of the Second World could not but have profound consequences for the *Review*'s geo-political perspective and its estimate of the
prospects for socialism. In the *Review*'s 1983 Charter, the Soviet Union and
the Second World had been designated 'post-capitalist' formations, 'bul-
warks against imperialism', engaged in a geo-political 'great contest' with
the capitalist West. Although far from being models of socialism, and performing at best a contradictory role in international politics, they nonetheless represented an historical advance upon capitalism. A social revolution
had taken place and a complementary political transformation might have
heralded the advent of a genuine socialist democracy.

The failure and defeat of Gorbachev spelt the end of such Deutscherite
hopes. Strong reformist currents had indeed emerged within the party-bureaucracy, but in Roy Medvedev's estimate, Gorbachev's reform programme
had been ill-thought-out and inconsistently pursued.[122] In the words of
the *Review*, Gorbachev had 'allowed a revolt to develop against the dead
weight of the party bureaucracy but failed to make himself its champion.
Gorbachev's fatal mistake was to have abstained from seeking a democratic
mandate at a time when he might still have won it.'[123] Arguably, the Soviet
Union was beyond salvation by the eighties: the intelligentsia was disaffect-
ed, the working class depoliticised, and the bureaucracy, where it had any
radical ambition, converted to marketisation – an elite 'demoralised by the
performance of the command economy but confident that its own skills
would be bankable in a market society'.[124] Gorbachev probably 'never had a
chance', wrote Alexander Cockburn, for the 'long narcolepsy of the Brezhnev
years' had 'irretrievably wrecked the Soviet Union's hopes of establishing
any successful rendez-vous with a modernised socialist economy'.[125]

3. The 'conjuncture of 1989'

The fall in the East was a decisive moment in the evolution of the *New Left
Review*: writing at the launch of the *Review*'s 'new series' in 2000, Anderson
precisely dates the 'current conjuncture' to 1989, the year of revolutions in
Eastern Europe.[126] Having already implicitly discounted the prospects for
socialism in the West, after the fall in the East the *Review* began to doubt
even the viability of reformist social democracy in the context of capitalist
'globalisation'. Significantly, the *NLR* was prepared to seriously contemplate
Francis Fukuyama's celebrated claim for 'the end of history ... that is, the
end point of mankind's ideological evolution and the universalisation of
Western liberal democracy as the final form of human government', the 'un-
abashed victory of economic and political liberalism' and 'the total exhaustion of viable systemic alternatives' to it;[127] judging that Fukuyama's thesis

'has a scope and thoughtfulness that sets it apart from simple Western triumphalism'.[128] (When an expanded version of Fukuyama's essay appeared as
The End of History and the Last Man in 1992, it received no fewer than three
reviews in the *NLR* – by Fred Halliday, Mike Rustin and Ralph Miliband
– and prompted a 100-page essay by Perry Anderson.)[129]

On the alert for signs of slippage so evident elsewhere on the Left amidst
so great a crisis of socialist politics, the SWP journal *International Socialism*
issued an 'open letter' critical of the *Review*'s response to the crisis in the
Gulf following Iraq's annexation of Kuwait in 1990. While acknowledging
their patent inconsistency,[130] the *Review* nonetheless judged that the sanctions applied against Iraq were 'appropriate and justified'.[131] Fred Halliday
(who had, one should remember, resigned from the editorial committee in
1983) wrote sympathetically in the same issue on the cause of Arab unity
and the revision of colonial borders (and for a wider share in the region's
oil wealth), but was quick to denounce Saddam Hussein's intervention as
'a clear case of aggression by a fascist state'.[132] However, he simultaneously
went one step further in *Marxism Today* in October 1990, arguing that military intervention to expel Iraq from Kuwait would be justified if sanctions
failed. At no point was this the position of the *NLR*, yet Halliday's stance,
and the *Review*'s 'neutralism', were taken to task by Alex Callinicos et al.,
who argued that the *Review* had mistakenly equated the 'little bully, Saddam
Hussein, with the much greater bully, US imperialism, as if a victory for the
one would be as bad for the peoples of the world as a victory for the other'.[133] The 'main enemy', they insisted, 'is in Washington'.[134] Yet, opposition
to America's war need not equate with any enthusiasm for Saddam Hussein,
and the *Review*'s position was not an indefensible one.[135] While some on
the Left rallied to military intervention in the Gulf, and later instances of
Western 'humanitarian' imperialism, the *Review* did not, as Callinicos et al.
feared, follow their lead.

What would distinguish the *Review* after the 'fall' of 1989-91, with the
geo-political and ideological triumph of the West being accompanied by the
on-going neo-liberal transformation of global capitalism, was not *apostasy*
– endorsement of neo-liberal 'realism' and US-led imperialism – but *pessimism* in the prospects of any alternative to the rule of capital. As recently as
1984 Göran Therborn had written reassuringly in the *Review* that social democracy's late electoral reversals were but temporary, conjunctural setbacks.
Discounting the challenge of the neo-liberal New Right, he judged that 'welfare state capitalism' was an 'irreversible development providing a fundamental basis for all future working-class struggles. The historic advances of
labour … constitute a historical conquest which cannot be undone by dem-

ocratic means'.[136] He concluded that the labour movement of the advanced capitalist countries was 'now clearly stronger and (moderately) more radical' than it was on the eve of social democracy's 'historical growth period which began in the middle of the 1960s'.[137] However, by 1992 Anderson was writing that '[t]he new reality is a massive asymmetry between the international mobility and organisation of capital, and the dispersal and segmentation of labour, that has no historical precedent'.[138] The 'globalisation of capitalism', far from drawing 'the resistances to it together', had 'scattered and outflanked them', resulting in 'a reduction in social capacities' to fight for an alternative to capitalism'.[139] In 1994 Anderson and Patrick Camiller judged that although social democracy 'may not be at an end … who can doubt that it is at an impasse?'[140] Internal divisions within the working class had 'unstitch[ed] the collective agencies required to challenge the status quo', making the 'task of *subjective* mobilisation for any radical change inherently harder',[141] while even 'more intractable' than the weakening of social democracy's constituency of support was 'the tightening of constraints that reduce the objective space for its traditional policies'.[142] Financial deregulation and the massive expansion of speculative international money markets had undermined traditional Keynesian policy tools, such as the control of interest and exchange rates, whilst the 'new tax aversion' had 'drastically narrowed' the 'limits of fiscal initiative'.[143] Thus, Anderson and Camiller concluded, '[t]rapped between a shifting social base and a contracting political horizon, social democracy appears to have lost its compass'.[144]

For Anderson, European social democracy was in danger of being remodelled on the lines of the Democratic Party in the United States: a notionally 'left' alternative, minus the instruments of Keynesian macro-economic management, and minus a commitment to the welfare state.[145] Such a 'left' politics would have only the most minimal ties to the – in any case – diminished institutions of organised labour. Similarly Therborn, previously so positive, had by 1992 radically revised his assessment of the prospects for social democracy. A 'post-modern', 'post-industrial' Left, he concluded, 'will be more in the image of the Left of the New Worlds of the Americas than in that of the classical Left of European industrial capitalism'.[146]

Chastened by the events of 1989-91, the *Review* began to articulate (without ever explicitly endorsing) a minimalist liberal-socialism[147] – involving an unacknowledged acceptance of key themes of the lately reviled new revisionism, and an abandonment of its erstwhile revolutionary politics without so much as a word of critical reflection. The *After the Fall* collection of essays led, significantly, with Norberto Bobbio, whose 'distinctive synthesis of liberalism and socialism'[148] had won Anderson's praise in the *NLR* in 1988:[149]

in the new conjuncture, wrote Anderson, Bobbio had come 'into his own'.[150] The collection contained not one essay from an identifiably revolutionary socialist perspective. Mandel, previously so prominent a contributor, was conspicuously absent, whereas Hobsbawm, only recently reprehended as an instigator of the new revisionism, contributed two essays, both reprinted from *Marxism Today*. For Blackburn, while the 'ruin of "Marxist-Leninist" Communism' had been 'sufficiently comprehensive to eliminate it as an alternative to capitalism', it had, moreover, compromised 'the very idea of socialism': the 'debacle of Stalinism has embraced reform-communism, and has brought no benefit to Trotskyism, or social democracy, or any socialist current'.[151] He now insisted that 'the Left must respect the complex structures of self-determination which the market embodies',[152] whilst Anderson and Camiller tabled such relatively modest reforms as basic income, stakeholding and industrial democracy.[153] (In 1991 Anderson even speculated that the 'Archimedean point' from which the 'social structures' of Western countries could be overturned – previously identified as 'the structural position occupied by the industrial working-class'[154] – might prove to be reform of the education system.)[155] On the plane of theory, always for the *Review*, of course, a key index of the health of socialist politics, Anderson was now sympathetically charting the rise of an indigenous 'Anglo-Weberian' historical sociology – specifically citing the work of Anthony Giddens, Michael Mann, W.G. Runciman and Ernest Gellner – and the explanatory challenge it presented to classical historical materialism in terms of societal development.[156]

Meanwhile, in the five years following Labour's 1987 election defeat, coverage of domestic politics all but disappeared. Labour's rightward course under Kinnock, the poll tax rebellion – save for an essay by Rodney Hilton on medieval tax revolts[157] – and the fall of Thatcher in 1990 all passed without comment. Returning instead to the broader historical themes of the Nairn-Anderson theses in 'The Figures of Descent' (1987), Anderson judged that it was the stubborn persistence of the 'old regime' – swept away in continental Europe in 1945 – that was the root cause of Britain's economic decline.[158] Dismissing the Thatcherite remedy – 'the logic of the market, left to itself tends to be *cumulative* rather than *corrective*', in the context of decline, '[d]eregulation … could only mean still more deindustrialisation' – Anderson was convinced that 'the modernisation of the state' was central to 'a reinvigoration of the economy'.[159]

Although doubtful of the chances of recovery – judging that the 'radical internationalisation' of the forces of production and circulation promised to render all 'national correctors, whatever their efficacy to date, increasingly tenuous in the future', thus concluding that 'perhaps the time in which' a solution to the 'British crisis' 'was possible, as a national recovery, has passed'[160] – it is thus unsurprising that Anderson endorsed Charter 88's programme of constitutional reform with considerable enthusiasm, describing it, in 1990, as the 'one bold attempt to break the log-jam left by the debacle of the Wilson-Callaghan years'.[161] In 1991 he wrote approvingly that it had proved the 'liveliest recent movement within civil society'[162] – pointedly ignoring the campaign of mass civil disobedience against the poll tax, a far livelier movement, and one which, moreover, could take no small credit for Thatcher's downfall (and the virtual elimination of the Conservative Party as a political force in Scotland).[163]

The renewed silence with regard to British politics was broken on the eve of the 1992 election. Such an intervention was itself unusual: not since 1964 had the *Review* pronounced upon an impending general election – a studied indifference, of the 'let it bleed' variety, was the usual stance. The message was unusual too, confirming the new-found moderation. Common to Perry Anderson's 'The Light of Europe' (1991) and Robin Blackburn's 'The Ruins of Westminster' (1992)[164] was the priority afforded to constitutional reform. Although the *Review* judged that 'constitutional reform is never going to suppress capitalism, it can help to furnish the democratic conditions where anticapitalist movements gain a wider hearing and greater possibilities for organisation',[165] with proportional representation the 'key'[166] to offering the opportunity for 'a New Left formation … to measure its support in elections and obtain appropriate representation'.[167] The apparently inexorable momentum towards European integration and national devolution within 'Ukania' was welcomed as potentially decisive factors in breaking the tenacious hold of the Westminster-Whitehall state.[168]

Recognising that the Liberal Democrats were firmer in their commitment to constitutional reform, Blackburn concluded that whilst there was 'no qualitative programmatic distinction' between the two principal opposition parties, there was 'a qualitative significance to democratic reforms'; and therefore argued that in the forthcoming election 'it will make sense to vote Labour or Liberal Democrat depending on which candidate is best placed to defeat the Conservative'.[169] Although the *Review* wrote that the preference for a Lib-Lab, rather than majority Labour, government 'does not necessarily represent the standpoint of the Editorial Committee as a whole',[170] Blackburn's advocacy of tactical voting in a key-note intervention certainly marked an abrupt departure on the part of the *NLR*. Prior to the previous election, Anthony Arblaster had written scathingly in the *Review* of Anthony Barnett's call for a pre-election deal between Labour and the then Liberal-SDP Alliance to defeat the Conservatives. Such a manoeuvre had been denounced by him in 1986 as evidence of an 'epidemic of pessimism' on the Left.[171] By 1992 the *Review*'s own expectations had been significantly lowered. In 1997 Blackburn cautiously welcomed Labour's victory as a 'Velvet Revolution'.[172]

Meanwhile, the *Review* was suffering from a certain internal dissolution. A relaunch, planned at an 'extraordinary Plenum' of the *NLR* in February 1985, had come to nought,[173] and by 1988 Anderson was writing privately that the *Review* no longer functioned as an intellectual collective, arguing that the *NLR* needed its own *perestroika*, the key to which lay in a complete renewal of the editorial committee.[174] This was duly achieved with the addition of a broad cross-section of individuals to the editorial committee in 1990,[175] the last and most ambitious attempt to establish a more direct engagement with broader currents of the domestic Left. However, very much in the spirit of the *Review*'s troubled internal life, the experiment ended acrimoniously within two short years in a sharp dispute over ownership and control of the journal.

An enlarged 27 member editorial board was instituted, comprising an expanded working editorial committee and more distant 'associate editors' – including Perry Anderson, who in 1989 had taken up an academic post at the University of California at Los Angeles. Patrick Wright judged the expansion 'a genuine attempt to reach beyond what Blackburn himself once described as the "steely Leninist core" that Anderson had given' the *NLR*.[176] Adverse financial accounts, disputed by some,[177] and the proposal to revert to two rather than three paid staff, were at the centre of the storm, and wider political issues seem to have played little part in the dispute. With a certain irony – though symbolic of the unacknowledged abandonment of its erstwhile revolutionary convictions – Blackburn suggested that at stake was 'defending the review's increasing open-minded approach to the present crisis of the left against those on the committee who were behaving like "gatekeepers" and generally carrying on as if NLR were "the last politburo" rather than a magazine of ideas'.[178]

Crucially, the new recruits had not been issued with shares in the *Review*, and as the conflict intensified, Blackburn reasserted his personal authority by recourse to the legal owners of the journal, the shareholders – including, ironically, ex-editors, many of whom had resigned in the course of past disputes, and a majority of whom had long ceased to have any direct connection with the *Review* (of the 27 shareholders, only 12 were currently on the editorial board). At the November 1992 AGM a majority of shares, and thus ultimate ownership, was vested in a new Trust, the trustees comprising

Perry Anderson, his brother Benedict, both now based in North America, and Ronald Fraser, who had resigned from the *Review* in 1977 and was now living in Spain.[179] In addition Quintin Hoare and Ellen Wood were ousted as company directors, replaced by Tariq Ali and Alexander Cockburn (who had been living and working in America for over twenty years). Production editor Robin Gable was duly dismissed, and 13 members of the editorial board resigned en bloc in February 1993 (longer-standing members Peter Dews, Quintin Hoare, Branka Magaš, and Ellen Wood, and new recruits from the 1990 intake Christopher Bertram, Ken Hirschkop, Monty Johnstone, Deniz Kandiyoti, Doreen Massey, Robin Murray, Mike Rustin, Kate Soper and Hilary Wainwright); five others (Patrick Camiller, Paul Cammack, Diane Elson, Norman Geras and Elizabeth Wilson) having already quit.[180]

The eight 'old guard' who remained – Perry Anderson, Tariq Ali, Robin Blackburn, Robert Brenner, Alexander Cockburn, Mike Davis, Peter Gowan and Michael Sprinker – were, in their majority, North American-based, re-inforcing the dislocation between the *NLR* and any anchorage in the British Left. The fact that there was to be no compensatory grounding of the *Review* on the far side of the Atlantic – other than academic[181] – served merely to accentuate its already pronounced extra-territoriality.

4. The Penalties of Olympianism:
Critical Reflections and Concluding Thoughts

On returning as editor-in-chief in 2000, Perry Anderson launched the 'new series' in a curiously uncertain vein, the shape and direction of the *NLR*'s intended 'overhaul' left very much in the air: the 'transition to another style of review', he writes, 'is not to be achieved overnight'.[182] If the future trajectory of the *Review* is unclear, this is but a belated acknowledgment of an uncertainty that has been evident for a decade or more, for it has become increasingly difficult to discern any guiding intellectual or political project. What is certain is that for the *NLR* the defeats of the recent past have raised a profound question-mark over the very viability of socialism. Moreover, the pursuit of a New Left politics via the *New Left Review*, the founding project of the 'new' New Left, has been quietly abandoned. In cautioning that his editorial is but 'a personal – and therefore provisional – statement: open to contradiction',[183] Anderson confirms the journal's 'normalisation', that it no longer enforces a particular line or speaks with a single voice.

What is striking about Anderson's 'Renewals' editorial is the valedictory tone and, above all, its ill-concealed pessimism.[184] For Anderson the 'conjuncture of '89' has sealed 'the virtually uncontested consolidation, and universal diffusion, of neo-liberalism', judging that for 'the first time since the Reformation, there are no longer any significant oppositions – that is, systemic rival outlooks – within the thought-world of the West.'[185] As we noted at the outset, Anderson appears to embrace the 'bitter conclusion' of 'a lucid recognition of the nature and triumph of the system, without either adaptation or self-deception, but also without any belief in the chance of an alternative to it'.[186]

While the *Review*'s Olympianism and distance from active politics was the principal theme of critics in the late seventies and early eighties, recent criticism has been drawn (in Gilbert Achcar's words) to Anderson's placing of the new series of the *New Left Review* 'under the sign of … an extreme defeatism … [and] pessimism'.[187] Achcar judges that 'Anderson seems more convinced of the omnipotence of neo-liberalism than most of its supporters!', pushing Anderson's "pessimism of the intellect" 'to surprising extremes'.[188] Elsewhere, James Petras denounces Anderson's 'manic defeatism',[189] while the bleakest interpretation is offered by Boris Kagarlitsky. For him, the new series is marked not so much by renewal as death: 'A familiar, well loved journal no longer exists. It has died, or more precisely, its own parents have killed it'.[190] However, *contra* Kagarlitsky, and notwithstanding the 'profound pessimism' of Anderson's position, Achar detects 'a new radicalisation in the journal noticeable since the war in Kosovo' – for Achar a '"defining moment" for the western intellectual left', judging that the '*NLR* came through this test, firmly on the side of the left and faithful to the tradition of its origins'.[191] Gregory Elliott's more extended and less polemical political biography of Perry Anderson (written prior to the 'new series') asserts the 'stoicism, rather than optimism or pessimism', of Anderson's increasingly 'precarious' and 'deracinated' position, underlining that 'Anderson has always taken the long view, played the long game', and exhibited the 'ability to *wait*'.[192] While the 'Andersonian turn is not in dispute', Elliott prefers to stress 'an enduring fidelity to the ideals of a lifetime; a modified yet undiminished zone of engagement in the cause of an international socialist culture and politics'.[193]

Pessimism, rather than 'capitulation' or apostasy, would appear the more fitting charge; a pessimism derived from a misreading of the current conjuncture (the 'conjuncture of 1989'), a misreading inscribed in, and, as I argued at the start, inexplicable without an understanding of the *Review*'s own history – assiduously avoided, given its resistance to critical self-reflection, by the *NLR* itself. A brief summary of that history, drawing out the *Review*'s principal character traits, is in order, by way of some concluding thoughts.

Disdaining the perceived 'populism' of the first New Left, the post-1962 *New Left Review*, 'Olympian' in tone and perspective, was from the outset committed to an unambiguously intellectual project. One important mark of the *Review*'s privileging of theoretical work has been its general reluctance to develop any organic links with the labour movement or other progressive social forces and currents on the British Left (compounded by an insistence that intellectual leadership must come from outside the working class).[194] A certain 'super-theoreticism'[195] may have its place in an intellectual division of labour within the culture of the Left, but the lack of 'control' that comes with a detached intellectualism has its penalties, not least the blockages in strategic thinking that result. Whilst the insights to be gained from a perspective that measures in terms of 'epochs and continents' are not to be doubted, the costs have been central to the *Review*'s evolution.

Reflecting, in former editorial board member Ellen Wood's words, the 'conviction that the central terrain of socialist struggle was … intellectual', the 'second' New Left suffered a 'loss of interest in popular struggles in general, and the labour movement in particular',[196] consistently overstating the role of ideas and underestimating – failing to analyse or engage with – social forces and movements on the ground. Anderson, for example, celebrated the naturalisation of continental Marxism in Britain and the development of an indigenous Anglo-Marxism (in a curiously 'bibliocentric'[197] account) – for which the *Review* could take no small credit – but the making of a socialist intelligentsia versed in Marxism failed either to advance the cause of winning a mass popular movement for socialism, or to resist the political and ideological challenge of the New Right. In Edward Thompson's words, 'a mountain of thought' failed to give 'birth to one political mouse'.[198] Similarly, in 'A Culture in Contraflow' Anderson's celebration of the radicalisation of the 'national culture' in the late eighties was entirely limited to its intellectual and academic, as opposed to its popular, dimension. He noted that 'academic dislike of the regime was so widespread that the level of Conservative support had fallen to less than a fifth of the lecturing body': '[o]nce pilloried from the Left', the world of higher education had 'become a bugbear of the Right'.[199] This counted for nought in resisting the consolidation of neo-liberalism under Thatcher and her successors. Conversely, the retreat of socialist *ideas* amongst the Western intelligentsia today accounts, in Kagarlitsky's judgement, for the *Review*'s current 'capitulation' to neo-liberal capitalism: '[f]or Anderson, the history of socialism is the history of ideas, and furthermore, of ideas that have gone out of fashion'.[200] Anderson registers the triumph of neo-liberalism – '[w]hatever limitations persist to its practice' – at the level of ideas: 'the most successful *ideology* in world history'.[201]

Crucially, in the years following 1968, the *Review* was amiss in its expectation that political practice would conform to its adopted revolutionary theory. Theoretical endeavour and strategic reflection have an important part to play in the making of a socialist politics, but only in a direct meaningful relationship with politics on the ground. Theoretical abstraction and a disdain for practice and popular experience actively deepen the division between theory and practice, hindering the development of a viable anti-capitalist politics.[202] Tellingly, no *concrete* revolutionary analysis, comparable to Perry Anderson's reformist 'Problems of Socialist Strategy' of 1965, was ever produced. Despite the efforts of some – the disparate grouping of 'libertarian leftists' associated with *Seven Days*, or those doubtful of Anderson's affiliation to Trotskyism in 1976 (in *Considerations on Western Marxism*) – and the more critical insight of most of those on the editorial committee in the seventies, in its heyday the *Review*'s perspective ultimately remained fixated on its romance with 1917. Having situated itself unambiguously within this tradition,[203] the *Review*'s search for an appropriate socialist strategy in the West proved unavailing, and by 1983 Anderson was compelled to acknowledge that the Trotskyist tradition had failed to provide a 'scenario for defeating capitalism in the West' – a 'blockage', he argued, which 'stemmed from too close an imaginative adherence to the paradigm of the October Revolution'.[204] It is a criticism that applies equally to the *Review* itself.

The ever-present tension between, on the one hand, a jealous guarding of the *Review*'s editorial and political independence and, on the other, recognition that this isolation from the wider Left has seriously disabled its strategic thinking and thwarted meaningful political intervention, would dog the journal down the years, though there is no doubt that independence has consistently won out over engagement. The result – two sides of the same coin – has been the preservation of the *Review*'s academic reputation, but frustration of its goal of answering the riddle of a strategy for socialism in the West.

The *Review*'s belated willingness to pursue reanchorage within the British Left after 1980 – including organisational collaboration in the Socialist Society – and respond to the issues raised by, amongst others, the women's movement, was a potentially fruitful moment, promising the thinking-through of a genuinely contemporary socialist politics. The moment, however, was lost. The sharp political defeats experienced during Thatcher's ascendancy – whose consequences still shape domestic politics – produced a bout of defeatism amongst Left intellectuals which, although sometimes passed off as innovative thinking, usually masked an accommodation to the rule of capital, a turn of events that induced the *Review* to retreat to the redoubt of its accustomed isolation. Failure to woo five socialist-feminists after the 1983 resignations ended with the recomposition of the editorial committee on more traditionalist lines. Engagement with the diminishing detachments of the 'resolute Left' continued through the mid-eighties, but soon, discounting the prospects for even a reformist social democracy in the West, everything was wagered, in a typically Olympian geo-political gesture, on the East. When the impasse of the Left in the West was compounded by the dramatic collapse of Communism in the East, the *Review* was unable to escape the general ruination of the Left, underlining its failure to articulate an alternative – sufficiently 'new' – New Left politics. The most recent attempt to anchor the *NLR* in the broader currents of the British Left, following the 'fall' of 1989-91, swiftly issued in the crisis and further resignations of 1992-3. Today, the *Review*'s extra-territoriality seems more firmly established than ever.

While age combined with academic seniority and respectability is one well-established road to political moderation, the case of the *New Left Review* deserves more searching explanation. Crucially, for all the damaging Olympianism of its detachment from popular politics, the *Review* has proved, paradoxically, insufficiently Olympian to escape either the general fate of Left intellectuals in periods of political defeat, or to stand outside its trans-Atlantic vantage point. Anderson's claim that for 'the first time since the Reformation, there are no longer any significant oppositions – that is, systemic rival outlooks – within the *thought-world* of the West'[205] captures the two principal vices of the *NLR*'s politics: the primacy of ideas over social forces and movements, and a one-sidedly Western perspective.

However much they may prefer to think of themselves as above the fray, intellectuals are imprisoned, like the rest of us, in their own biographical time and space, and those as sociated with the *NLR* are no exception. Indeed, intellectuals are perhaps peculiarly vulnerable to the moods of an evolving *zeitgeist*, weather vanes of profounder socio-economic and political winds of change. For intellectuals of the Left, political disappointment and defeat, particularly following previously high hopes, is a sure path to the right, witness the rapid turn of such as the 'New York intellectuals' of the forties, and the Parisian '*nouveaux philosophes*' of the seventies. 1968 (like 1956) had been a formative and defining moment, significantly over-determining the politics of the generation that was touched by it. If Thompson et al. barely escaped the moment of 1956, much the same might with equal justice be said of the second New Left – and many others – in relation to

1968: a moment of intense expectation, followed, ultimately, by sharp defeat. Disappointment and defeat have not turned the *NLR* to the right, but
they have induced a profound pessimism. For Gilbert Achar the parallels
with Western Marxism are 'striking':[206] the evolution of the *New Left Review*
since the eighties bears the stamp of defeat – deflating the hopes of the late
sixties and seventies – characterised by the 'academic emplacement of …
theory', itself reduced to 'an esoteric discipline', divorced 'from any popular practice', increasingly oriented to 'contemporary bourgeois culture', and
succumbing to a 'latent pessimism'.[207]

   Moreover, the *Review*'s reading of the current conjuncture is very much
from a Western perspective; indeed, more narrowly still, from an especially
American or British perspective, where neo-liberalism appears most entrenched. The French experience, notwithstanding the 'social-liberal' drift
of the Jospin government and the debacle of the 2002 presidential and parliamentary elections, has been quite different. 'Who from the French side
of the Channel', asks Achcar, 'could subscribe to Perry Anderson's diagnosis?'[208] The view from elsewhere in the world is very different again. In Latin
America, *contra* western Europe, the seventies were a period of appalling
repression, not a decade of expectations, while today, far from being marginalised and defeated, a radical, combative Left is undergoing growth and
renewal. This has fashioned no great innovation on the plane of theory to
suit the fads of Western academia, but has, more importantly, fired social
forces and produced popular movements at least the equal of southern
Europe a generation ago. The case of Brazil, a country close to Anderson's
heart,[209]amongst others, points, potentially, to a very different story than
neo-liberal triumphalism.

   While the retreat of Western socialist intellectuals is conventionally ascribed to the downturn of working-class struggles from the late seventies, Ellen Wood (writing in the 1995 *Socialist Register*, two years after her
departure from the *NLR*) prefers an alternative chronology in which the
'logic of intellectual trends on the left since the sixties is not so directly con-
nected to working class politics', but is rather a reflection of 'some major
epochal transformations', not least capitalist prosperity and the expansion
of an 'academic bourgeoisie' born of the massive growth in higher education.[210] The radicalisation of young intellectuals during the late sixties only
momentarily, and fortuitously, coincided with an upsurge in working-class
militancy; the trend of theoretical developments, Wood argues, was to stress
'the autonomy of political and ideological struggles' from class politics,
privileging 'the revolutionary efficacy of intellectuals, radical students, and
cultural revolution'.[211] The polemical point of her essay – championing the

first New Left's engagement with the labour movement against the second New Left's 'fairly extreme kind of intellectual substitutism'[212] – is to draw a 'direct evolutionary line from Maoism to post-modernism, and from "cultural revolution" to textural deconstruction',[213] indicting the post-1962 *NLR* in preparing the ground for the anti-socialist fads and fashions of contemporary post-modernism.[214]

Whether the retreat of socialist intellectuals should be ascribed to the defeats of the eighties or to the logic of intellectual trends originating in the sixties, or a combination of the two influences, can no doubt be ascribed as determinant in different individual cases. Certainly, the *Review* has consistently overstated the role of ideas, but it has not, as yet, arrived at the 'outer limits' of Wood's characterisation, never succumbing, for example, to intellectual fashion in the way of *Marxism Today* – Wood herself acknowledges that the '*New Left Review* has never explicitly "written off" the working class'.[215] While the *NLR* may have been caught in the intellectual currents Wood describes, it is the political defeats of the past twenty years that would seem to carry greater explanatory weight in understanding where the journal is today. As I have already argued, if unable to find any confidence in the prospects for socialism it has retained a deep antipathy to the reign of capital.

To its credit, the *Review* has not rushed to publish apologias for capitalism or pretended that all is now for the best in the best of all possible worlds; on the contrary, it has continued to be sharply critical of anti-socialist currents and critics.[216] But even if it were sufficient, as Anderson writes, for the *Review* 'to decipher the course of the world'[217] – leaving aside Marx's injunction that the point remains to change it – the *NLR*'s analysis, conditioned by its distance from, and disdain for, political practice, overstates the triumph of neo-liberalism and underestimates the scope of movements of resistance.

Today the making of a New Left remains unfinished, and pressing, business. It is a project that admits no short-cuts or easy answers. Although it will involve intellectual work, it cannot privilege it. In this respect, the post-1962 *New Left Review*'s project was flawed from the outset, for whilst socialist theory is an undeniably vital guide to political practice, it can only have effective purchase when developed in the context of, and engagement with, contemporary popular struggles.

While we should indeed endorse an uncompromising realism in preference to facile illusions in the prospects of radical social change, global capital is neither uncontested nor invincible. If extraordinarily dynamic, it remains inherently unstable. If, in its new series, the *New Left Review* is unlikely to abandon the undoubted advantages of its Olympian perspective, engaging with worldwide social and political movements that are actively contesting global capital in the task of making a New Left will help ensure that a salutary pessimism of the intellect is leavened by an equally necessary optimism of the will.

NOTES

Preface

1   In the wake of recent controversies surrounding the New Left, when hostile critics were eager to deride it as 'part of the old world', Robin Blackburn, was quick to defend, and effectively to claim, the heritage of the first New Left – of Thompson, Williams, Samuel et al. – insisting that the New Left 'remains a living force' ('Introduction: Revisiting the New Left', *NLR* 215, January/February 1996, p. 82. See also Blackburn's obituaries of key figures of the first New Left: 'Raymond Williams and the Politics of a New Left', *NLR* 168, March/April 1988, pp.12-22; 'Edward Thompson and the New Left', *NLR* 201, September/October 1993, pp. 3-9; 'Ralph Miliband 1924-1994', *NLR* 206, July/August 1994, pp. 15-22; and 'Raphael Samuel: The Politics of Thick Description', *NLR* 221, January/February 1997, pp. 133-8.) By the nineties, the *Review's* political perspective was arguably closer to that of the first New Left than it had ever been in the past, and in the thirtieth anniversary issue of the *Review* in 1990, the introductory editorial reflected that something of the 'original stance of opposition to Stalinism and Labourism has continued to define the NLR's politics ever since' (Themes, *NLR* 180, March/April 1990, p. 2) – a judgement that glibly glosses over the various turns in the second New Left's career and ignores, for example, the, albeit critical, support lent to the Soviet Union at the time of the Second Cold War. Whilst Michael Kenny rejects the 'notion of a complete break' (*The First New Left: British Intellectuals After Stalin*, Lawrence and Wishart, London, 1995, p. 4) between the two New Lefts, and Blackburn is keen to invoke the tradition of the early New Left, the concept of a 'generic', undifferentiated New Left is unhelpful. More cordial relations between the post-1962 *Review* and its forbears since the eighties should not obscure the fact that within the wider history of those tracing their intellectual and political ancestry to the moment of 1956, the second New Left has trodden a highly distinctive path.

2   The reference is to the Situationist International. See Peter Wollen, ed., *Raiding the Icebox: Reflections On Twentieth-century Culture*, Verso, London, 1993.

3   Lin Chun, *The British New Left*, Edinburgh University Press, 1993, p. xvi.

4   See Raymond Williams's categorisation of 'legitimating', 'academic' and 'operative' varieties of British Marxism ('Notes on British Marxism since the War', *NLR* 100, November 1976/January 1977, pp. 84ff.). Gregory Elliott stoutly defends 'the expressly "operative" character' of Anderson's Marxism (*Perry Anderson: The Merciless Laboratory of History*, University of Minnesota Press, Minneapolis and London, 1998, p. 31. Note also pp. 10-11).

5   'Renewals', *NLR* (II) 1, January/February 2000, p. 5.

6   Full back page advertisement, *Red Pepper*, September 2000 (and elsewhere).

7   'Renewals', p. 6.

8   Ibid., p. 10.

9   Ibid., p. 11.

10 Ibid., p. 17.

11 Ibid., pp. 13-14.

12 Ibid., p. 14.

13 Ibid., p. 13, n. 5.

14 Ibid.

15 Young writes that with the changeover in editorial control, 'the magazine was transformed in character into a narrower, more doctrinaire and mandarin journal of Marxist criticism ... [I]ts alignments and associations from then on were strictly "Old Left"' (*An Infantile Disorder? The Crisis and Decline of the New Left*, Routledge and Kegan Paul, 1977, p. 147).

16 John Saville, 'The Twentieth Congress and the British Communist Party', *Socialist Register 1976*, Merlin Press, London, 1976, pp. 1-23, and 'Edward Thompson, the Communist Party and 1956', *Socialist Register 1994*, Merlin Press, London, 1994, pp. 20-31; Mervyn Jones, 'Days of Tragedy and Farce', *Socialist Register 1976*, pp. 67-88; and Malcolm MacEwen, 'The Day the Party had to Stop', *Socialist Register 1976*, pp. 24-42. See also Mervyn Jones, *Chances*, Verso, London, 1987, and Malcolm MacEwen, *The Greening of a Red*, Pluto Press, London, 1991.

17 Robin Archer et al., eds, *Out of Apathy: Voices of the New Left Thirty Years On*, Verso, London and New York, 1989.

18 Some of the controversy aroused by these publications concerning the first New Left was reflected in the *Review* itself: see Fred Inglis, 'The Figures of Dissent'; Dorothy Thompson, 'On the Trail of the New Left'; and Jim McGuigan, 'Reviewing a Life. Fred Inglis's Biography of Raymond Williams', all in *NLR* 215, January/February 1996, pp. 83-92, 93-100, and 101-8, respectively; and Lin Chun, 'Reply to Dorothy Thompson and Fred Inglis', and Michael Kenny, 'Interpreting the New Left: Pitfalls and Opportunities', *NLR* 219, September/October 1996, pp. 133-37, 138-42, respectively.

19 See also Gregory Elliott, 'Olympus Mislaid? A Profile of Perry Anderson', *Radical Philosophy*, no. 71, May/June 1995, pp. 5-19, and 'Velocities of Change: Perry Anderson's Sense of an Ending', *Historical Materialism*, no. 2, 1998.

20 'The Two New Lefts', *International Socialism*, 17 August 1964, reprinted in David Widgery, ed., *The Left in Britain 1956-68*, Penguin, Harmondsworth, 1976, pp. 131-153: here p. 148.

21 Geoff Hodgson, 'The Antinomies of Perry Anderson', in *Socialism and Parliamentary Democracy*, Spokesman, Nottingham, 1977, pp. 105-37; Michael Rustin, 'The New Left and the Present Crisis', *NLR* 121, May/June 1980, pp. 63-89; Paul Hirst, 'Anderson's Balance Sheet', in *Marxism and Historical Writing*, Routledge and Kegan Paul, London, 1985, pp. 1-28; Ian Birchall, 'The Autonomy of Theory: A Short History of *New Left Review*', *International Socialism*, no. 10, Winter 1980/81, pp. 51-91; and Donald Sassoon, 'The Silences of *New Left Review*', *Politics and Power 3*, Routledge and Kegan Paul, London, 1981, pp. 219-254.

22 'A Chronology of the New Left and its Successors, or: Who's Old-Fashioned Now?', *Socialist Register 1995*, Merlin Press, London, 1995, pp. 22-49: here p. 35.

23 James Petras, 'Notes toward an understanding of revolutionary politics today', *Links*, no. 19, September to December 2001, pp. 5-34; Boris Kagarlitsky, 'The suicide of *New Left Review*', *International Socialism*, no. 88, Autumn 2000, pp. 127-33; and Gilbert Achcar, 'The "historical pessimism" of Perry Anderson', *International Socialism*, no. 88, Autumn 2000, pp. 135-41

24 'The Peculiarities of the English', *Socialist Register 1965*, Merlin Press, London, 1965, pp. 311-62 and *The Poverty of Theory and Other Essays* (1978), Merlin Press, London, 1980.

25 'The Left in the Fifties', *NLR* 29, January/February 1965, pp. 16-17.

26 Perry Anderson, 'Conspectus', unpublished document, 1964, p. i.

27 'NLR 1980-1983', unpublished editorial document, p. 55.

28 Gregory Elliott, *Perry Anderson: The Merciless Laboratory of History*, University of Minnesota Press, Minneapolis and London, 1998, p. xvii.

29 'Renewals', p. 6.

Chapter One: The Two New Lefts

1 Principally 'The Transition From Capitalism', in *New Fabian Essays*, ed., Richard Crossman (1952), and *The Future of Socialism* (1956).

2 In 1947 Communists 'were ousted or withdrew from the ruling coalitions of France, Italy, Norway, Belgium, Luxemburg and Austria. The Danish communists had already departed from government in 1945, while the Finns left in 1948. The Dutch communists had refused to take part in the national coalition because of the continuing Dutch colonial wars' (Donald Sassoon, *One Hundred Years of Socialism: The West European Left in the Twentieth Century*, I. B. Tauris, London, 1996, p. 97).

3 John Callaghan, *The Far Left in British Politics*, Basil Blackwell, Oxford, 1987, p. 49.

4 Francis Beckett, *Enemy Within: The Rise and Fall of the British Communist Party*, John Murray, London, 1995, p. 107.

5 Ibid. p. 117.

6 Editorial, *ULR* 1, Spring 1957, p. ii.

7 Stuart Hall, 'The "First" New Left: Life and Times', in Robin Archer et al., eds, *Out of Apathy: Voices of the New Left Thirty Years On*, Verso, London and New York, 1989, p. 13.

8 Ibid., p. 13.

9 Malcolm MacEwen remembers that 'Edward … typed the copy for the original *Reasoner*, 40,000 words, in four days' (*The Greening of a Red*, Pluto Press, London, 1991, p. 203). The title of the *Reasoner* was, according to Bryan Palmer, taken from an early nineteenth-century Jacobin-Radical journal, edited by John Bone (*E.P. Thompson: Objections and Oppositions*, Verso, London and New York, 1994, p. 74).

10 'It needs to be emphasised', wrote Saville in 1991, 'that the idea of resigning from the Communist Party was not in our minds when we began the *Reasoner* and it was only in the following months that we recognised, with great reluctance, the fundamental conservatism, not only of the leadership but of many of the rank and file': 'The Communist Experience: A Personal Appraisal',

Socialist Register 1991, Merlin Press, London, 1991, p. 22. See also, John Saville, 'Edward Thompson, The Communist Party and 1956', *Socialist Register 1994*, Merlin Press, London, 1994, p. 27.

11   John Saville, 'The Twentieth Congress and the British Communist Party', *Socialist Register 1976*, Merlin Press, London, 1976, p. 16.

12   'In June 1956 membership stood at 34,117 and by February 1958 it had declined to 24,670, a loss of 9,447 members or 27.7% of the membership' (Steve Parsons, '1956: What Happened inside the CPGB', *Our History: The Communist Party and 1956*, Socialist History Society Pamphlet 88, February 1993, p. 26).

13   Michael Kenny, *The First New Left*, Lawrence and Wishart, London, 1995, p. 23.

14   Edward Thompson, 'Revolution Again', *NLR* 6, November/December 1960, p. 18.

15   'Editorial', *NR* 5, Summer 1958, p. 1.

16   Peggy Duff, *Left, Left, Left*, Allison and Busby, London 1971, p. 128.

17   Edward Thompson, 'Outside the Whale', in Thompson et al., *Out of Apathy, Out of Apathy*, Stevens and Sons, London, 1960, p. 178.

18   'The Supply of Demand', *Out of Apathy*, pp. 95-6.

19   Editorial, *NLR* 1, January/February 1960, p. 3.

20   Edward Thompson, 'Revolution Again', p. 28.

21   Ibid.

22   The Fife Socialist League, led by Lawrence Daly (who had left the Communist Party in June 1956), was one of the most remarkable political achievements of the first New Left. Founded in 1957, and rooted in the coalmining villages of West Fife in Scotland, the League won council seats and trade union elections, and in 1958 Daly was elected to the county council for the mining village of Ballingry. In the general election of 1959 he took 11 per cent of the vote across the constituency (and finished ahead of the Communist candidate in a seat where Willie Gallacher had been MP from 1935 to 1950). The League, in Willie Thompson's judgement, comprised 'the oldest, most proletarian, best established and most politically successful element in the Scottish (or British) New Left' ('The New Left in Scotland', in Ian McDougall, ed., *Essays in Scottish Labour History*, John Donald, Edinburgh 1978, p. 221). The experience was, however, an isolated one. 'The Fife Socialist League was, of course, a unique departure, nothing resembling it appearing anywhere else in Britain, and its relatively large numerical basis, its organised structure and political activism remained an anomaly within the tendency of the New Left' (ibid., pp. 221-2). Daly wound up the League and joined the Labour Party in 1962.

23   Editorial, *NLR* 1, January/February 1960, p.1. A sentiment echoed by Stuart Hall, who stressed 'the necessity of challenging the conventional anti-intellectualism of the British labour movement and overcoming the traditional division between intellectuals and the working class' ('The "First" New Left', p. 35). To such an end the final *New Reasoner* promised that 'a monthly duplicated industrial bulletin really is on the way' ('Letter to Our Readers', *NR* 10, Autumn 1959, p. 131). The bulletin, *Searchlight*, ran to only four issues in 1960 and the Yorkshire-based 'Northern Industrial Committee' failed to get off the

ground (Kenny, op. cit., pp. 45-6). However, this anxiety, and the attachment of most of the British New Left to the working class as the principal agency of social change, puzzled C. Wright Mills: 'what I do not quite understand about some New Left writers is why they cling so mightily to "the working class" of the advanced capitalist countries as *the* historic agency, or even the most important agency, in the face of the really impressive historical evidence that now stands against this expectation ... Who is it that is thinking and acting in radical ways? All over the world ... the answer's the same: it is the young intelligentsia' ('Letter to the New Left', *NLR* 5, September/October 1960, p. 22). Mills' suspicion of the 'labour metaphysic' highlights something of the differences between the British New Left and its American counterpart.

24   Harold Silver, 'Left Clubs', *NLR* 4, July/August 1960, p. 70. New Leftist university publications included *New University* (Oxford), *Left* (Hull) and *Cambridge Forward*.

25   Raphael Samuel, 'Born-again Socialism', in Archer, Robin et al., eds, *Out of Apathy: Voices of the New Left Thirty Years On*, Verso, London and New York, 1989, p. 54, 45.

26   Peter Sedgwick, 'The Two New Lefts', originally published in *International Socialism*, 17 August 1964, and reprinted in David Widgery, *The Left in Britain 1956-68*, Penguin, Harmondsworth, 1976, p. 140.

27   'Notes for Readers', *NLR* 12, November/December 1961, p. i.

28   Minutes of the *NLR* Editorial Board, 9-10 October, 1960, quoted in Dennis Dworkin, *Cultural Marxism in Postwar Britain: History, the New Left, and the Origins of Cultural Studies*, Duke University Press, Durham (North Carolina) and London, 1997, p. 69.

29   Thompson, 'Revolution', in *Out of Apathy*, p. 287.

30   He later wrote that he 'was strongly opposed' to the merger ('Thirty Years of *The Socialist Register*', *Socialist Register 1994*, Merlin Press, London 1994, p. 1). See also Michael Newman, *Ralph Miliband and the Politics of the New Left*, Merlin Press, London, 2002, pp. 95-6. When the final vote on merger took place at a joint meeting of the two boards, Miliband 'was alone in opposing it' (Newman p. 98).

31   'On the Trail of the New Left', *NLR* 215, January/February 1996, 159, p. 99. 'Both boards were increasingly preoccupied with the struggle to sustain the financial and commercial viability of two journals. Even more pressing was the cost in human capital. For many of us, normal life had more or less been suspended in 1956. Some had not stopped running round in circles since ... and were by then in a state of extreme political exhaustion' (Stuart Hall, 'The "First" New Left', p. 22). 'I regretted the merger', wrote Mervyn Jones, 'and saw that Edward and Dorothy did too, but producing a journal from Holly Bank [the Thompson's Halifax home] was too much even for their dedication and energy' (*Chances*, Verso, London 1987, p. 165).

32   Editorial, *NLR* 1, January/February 1960, p. 1.

33   'Notes for Readers', *NLR* 12, November/December 1961 (inside covers, un-numbered).

34   Kenny lays much of the blame for these tensions at the feet of Edward Thompson, who, as chair of the executive committee of the board, bombarded Hall with correspondence. Kenny writes of Thompson's 'increasingly oppositional behaviour', (op. cit., p. 36) and 'the conspiratorial and fractious discourse into which Thompson collapsed during this period' (ibid., p. 37). This would appear an excessively negative characterisation of the relationship between Thompson and Hall, whose personal friendship apparently survived intact (interview with Dorothy Thompson, 12 November 1996, Worcester).

35   Kenny, op. cit., p. 32.

36   See John Saville, 'A Note on West Fife', *NR* 10, Autumn 1959, pp. 9-13. Kenny reckoned that support for Daly in the 1959 general election 'constituted one of the most controversial decisions the New Left ever took': op. cit., p. 25.

37   'The British Left', *NLR* 30 March/April 1965, pp. 25-6.

38   'The New Left as a Social Movement', in Robin Archer et al., eds, *Out of Apathy*, p. 127.

39   'Letter to Our Readers', *NLR* 2, March/April 1960, p. 70.

40   'Notes for Readers', *NLR* 12, November/December 1961 (inside covers, unnumbered).

41   'For a year or two CND seemed to be carrying all before it … so the reversal of the vote on nuclear disarmament in 1961 came as an astonishing blow' (Raymond Williams, *Politics and Letters: Interviews with New Left Review*, New Left Books, London, 1979, p. 365).

42   'The crisis', argued Mervyn Jones, 'was the greatest single political reason why the Campaign sank into insignificance' (op. cit., p. 179).

43   'Our attitude towards the Labour Party was particularly mistaken', wrote Raymond Williams on reflection. 'It was never taken seriously enough. There was a general sense that given its integration into the world of NATO capitalism, it was a negligible organisation: while the marches were so big, and left clubs were springing up all over the country, this outdated institution could be left to expire' (*Politics and Letters*, p. 365). Perhaps reflecting this perception of Labour's relative weakness, analysis of the Labour Party by the New Left was surprisingly thin: the first substantive analysis was Miliband's *Parliamentary Socialism* in 1961.

44   In February 1956 party membership stood at 33,095, falling to 26,742 in 1957. By 1964, it was 34,281 (Willie Thompson, *The Good Old Cause: British Communism 1920-1991*, Pluto Press, London, 1992, p. 218).

45   MacEwen, op. cit., p. 205. Kenny paints a bleak picture, where '[p]ersonal squabbles were frequent' and 'the board had degenerated into competing factions' (op. cit., p. 37).

46   MacEwen, op. cit., p. 29.

47   Minutes of the board meeting, 7 April 1963, cited Dennis Dworkin, *Cultural Marxism in Postwar Britain: History, the New Left, and the Origins of Cultural Studies*, Duke University Press, Durham (North Carolina) and London, 1997, p. 112.

48   'Statement', *NLR* 24, March/April 1964, p. 112.

49   'A Decennial Report', unpublished editorial document, 1974, p. 3.

50   Williams, *Politics and Letters*, p. 366.

51   Perry Anderson, *Arguments Within English Marxism*, Verso, London 1980, pp. 135-36

52   Quoted in Widgery, op. cit., p. 131.

53   Ralph Miliband, 'Thirty Years of *The Socialist Register*', p. 1.

54   Perry Anderson, 'Conspectus', unpublished document, October 1964, p. i.

55   Anderson's charge that the original New Left offered 'no articles, ideas or assistance … (Edward provided the only exception)' ('Conspectus', unpublished document, October 1964, p. i), is unfounded: the nine issues for 1962-63 included pieces by Barratt Brown, Daly, Hughes, Jones, MacEwen, Miliband, Thompson and Williams – though no doubt many of these articles had been prepared prior to the change in editorship. Direct reference to the changeover was not made in the *Review* until an uninformative 'Statement' appeared in *NLR* 24, March/April 1964, p. 112.

56   'A Decennial Report', p. 4, p. 3.

57   Dworkin cites a fall in circulation from 10,000 to just 3,500 by 1962-3 (Dworkin, op. cit., p. 76). The *Review* itself reported that the first issue had a print-run of 9,000 copies ('Letter to Our Readers', *NLR* 2, March/April 1960, p. 69). An internal memorandum gives circulation figures of 2,500 for the *New Reasoner*, and 7,500 for the *ULR* just prior to the merger ('Suggestions for Speakers and Organisers at Meetings where the New Left Review is Launched', unpublished document, no date (1959), Thompson papers).

58   Patrick Wright, 'Beastly Trials of the Last Politburo', *Guardian*, 17 July 1993, p. 29.

59   Dworkin, op. cit., pp. 76-7. Perry Anderson, Benedict Anderson and Ronald Fraser were the 'three donors who had put the review's finances on a sound footing in the sixties' (Robin Blackburn, letter to 'Contributors and Friends', 19 March 1993).

60   On Anderson's family background, see Benedict Anderson, introduction to *Language and Power*, Cornell University Press, Ithaca, 1990. Note also the Harry Kreisler interview, 'Reflections on the Left from the Left: Conversation with Perry Anderson', 27 April 2001, which can be found at http://globetrotter.berkeley.edu/Elberg/Anderson. Benedict considered his 'own country' to be Ireland ('Western Nationalism and Eastern Nationalism', *NLR* [II] 9, May/June 2001, p. 34), and Perry appears distinctly disappointed to have been born in England: 'by accident, I was born in London, but I was conceived in China, so I should have been born in China': Harry Kreisler interview.

61   Juliet Mitchell, born in New Zealand in 1940, author of the seminal feminist text 'Women, the Longest Revolution', *NLR* 40, November/December 1966, pp. 11-37, later becoming a central figure in the women's movement, and writing key socialist-feminist texts such as *Woman's Estate*, 1971 and *Psychoanalysis and Feminism*, 1974. On the editorial committee, 1963-83.
      Roger Murray wrote largely on Africa. E/c, 1962-83.
      Gabriel Pearson, a veteran of *Universities and Left Review*. From a London, Jewish, Communist background. Read English at Balliol, and contributed mostly on literary themes. E/c, 1962-7.

Mike Rustin, who remained on board for a brief couple of years, but would be involved again in the early nineties. Like others, came to the *Review* via the *New University* at Oxford. Today co-editor (with Stuart Hall and Doreen Massey) of *Soundings*, and Professor of Sociology at the University of East London. E/c, 1962-4 and 1990-3.

Tom Wengraf, today Senior Lecturer in Sociology and Social Research Methods at Middlesex University. E/c, 1962-70.

Anthony Barnett. Founding Director of Charter 88, author of *This Time: our constitutional revolution* (1997). E/c, 1966-83.

Ben Brewster wrote the introductions to the series on Western Marxists. E/c, 1966-71.

Alexander Cockburn (born 1941), Oxford educated, son of the well-known Communist journalist Claud Cockburn, worked at the *Times Literary Supplement* and *New Statesman* before moving to the United States in 1973, where he has continued to work as a journalist. Today co-editor of the radical American Newsletter *Counterpunch*. E/c, 1965-present.

Ronald Fraser (born in Hamburg, where his father was in business, in 1930), a pioneering oral historian, overseeing the long-running series on 'Work' in the *NLR*, and author of *Blood of Spain* (1979). He would play a pivotal role in New Left Books before a falling out in 1977. Later one of the three-member Trust in which ownership of the *Review* would be vested in 1992. E/c, 1964-77.

Quintin Hoare, General editor of the Marx Pelican Library (eight volumes, published by *NLR* and Penguin Books), and co-editor and translator of Gramsci's *Prison Notebooks* (1971) and *Political Writings* (two volumes, 1977 and 1978), remained at the *Review* until the 1992-3 dispute. Today Director of the Bosnian Institute, a London-based educational charity. E/c, 1964-93.

Gareth Stedman Jones (born London, 1942), also came to the *Review* via Oxford and the student journal *New University*. An historian with a special interest in nineteenth century labour, and an important figure in the History Workshop movement. Author of *Outcast London* (1971). Today Professor in Modern History at Cambridge University. E/c, 1965-83.

Nicolas Krassó (born in Hungary, 1930; died 1986: see Robin Blackburn, 'Nicolas Krassó 1930-86', *New Left Review* 155, January-February 1986, pp. 125-8). A pupil of Lukács, he left Hungary for England in 1956. E/c, 1966-86.

Branka Magaš. Croatian-born. Has written widely on the former Yugoslavia, including *The Destruction of Yugoslavia* (1993) and, as co-author, *The War in Croatia and Bosnia-Herzegovina 1991-5* (2001). E/c, 1967-93.

Bob Rowthorn (born 1943). Today Professor in Economics at Cambridge University. E/c, 1967-83.

Peter Wollen (born London, 1938), writing (initially under the pseudonym 'Lucien Rey') on art, aesthetics and cinema. Author of *Signs and Meanings in the Cinema* (1968). Today Chair of Critical Studies at UCLA. E/c, 1964-83.

62   'A Decennial Report', p. 11.

63   Ibid., p. 23.

64   Perry Anderson, 'The Left in the Fifties', *NLR* 29, January/February 1965, pp. 16-17

65   'A Decennial Report', p. 6.

66   Perry Anderson, 'Conspectus', unpublished document, p. i.

67   '[T]he magazine was transformed in character into a narrower, more doctri-
      naire and mandarin journal of Marxist criticism ... its alignments and associa-
      tions from then on were strictly "Old Left"': *An Infantile Disorder? The Crisis
      and Decline of the New Left*, Routledge and Kegan Paul, London, 1977, p. 147.

68   The SDS was in contact with the British New Left, inspired, claims Ronald
      Fraser, by the *Out of Apathy* collection, through which it adopted the name
      Neue Linke: Ronald Fraser et al., *1968: A Student Generation in Revolt*, Chatto
      and Windus, London, 1988, p. 49.

69   'The Two New Lefts', p. 148.

70   'A Decennial Report', p. 4.

71   Gregory Elliott, 'Olympus Mislaid?', *Radical Philosophy*, no. 71, May/June 1995,
      p. 7.

72   'A Decennial Report', p. 18.

73   For example, Rex Malik, *What's Wrong with Industry?* and Andrew Hill and
      Anthony Whichelow, *What's Wrong with Parliament?* Prominent works in
      the *genre* included Michael Shanks' *The Stagnant Society* (1961) and Anthony
      Sampson's *Anatomy of Britain* (1962).

74   Tom Nairn, 'The Future of the British Crisis', *NLR* 113-4, January/April 1979,
      p. 46.

75   Anderson, 'Origins of the Present Crisis', p. 15. Anderson later reflected that the
      controversies surrounding these interventions had missed this very question
      of the *origins* of the 'present crisis', the 'central problem at stake' in the debate:
      'The Figures of Descent', *NLR* 161, January/February 1987, p. 21. The essays
      that make up the original 'theses' comprise: Anderson's 'Origins of the Present
      Crisis', *NLR* 23, January/February 1964, pp. 26-53; 'Problems of Socialist
      Strategy', in Anderson and Blackburn, eds, *Towards Socialism*, Fontana/*NLR*,
      London 1965, pp. 221-90; 'Socialism and Pseudo-Empiricism', *NLR* 35,
      January/February 1966, p. 2-42; and 'Components of the National Culture',
      NLR 50, July/August 1968, pp. 3-57 (to be examined in the following chapter);
      and Nairn's 'The British Political Elite', *NLR* 23, January/February 1964, pp.19-
      25; 'The English Working Class', *NLR* 24, March/April 1964, pp. 43-57; 'The
      Nature of the Labour Party', *NLR* 27, September/October 1964, pp. 38-65 and
      NLR 28, November/December 1964, pp. 33-62; 'Labour Imperialism', *NLR* 32,
      July/August 1965, pp. 3-15, and 'The Fateful Meridian', *NLR* 60, March/April
      1970, pp. 3-35. The earliest intimation of the outlook expounded in them may
      be found in Nairn's review 'Landed England', *NLR* 20, Summer 1963, pp. 116-
      19.

76   Colin Leys, *Politics in Britain: From Labourism to Thatcherism*, Verso, London
      and New York, 1989, p. 14.

77   Gramscian themes were also deployed by Anderson and Nairn against the 'cul-
      turalist humanism' of Thompson and Williams: see David Forgács, 'Gramsci
      and Marxism in Britain', *NLR* 176, July/August 1989, pp. 70-88. The Nairn-
      Anderson theses, according to Forgács, 'had a source in the long note on
      the Risorgimento ... where Gramsci discusses the different routes by which

the bourgeoisie came to power in France, Germany, Italy and Britain': ibid., p. 75. (The relevant passage appears in Quintin Hoare and Geoffrey Nowell Smith, eds and trans., *Selections from Prison Notebooks*, Lawrence and Wishart, London, 1971, pp. 82-3.)

78 Perry Anderson, *English Questions*, Verso, London and New York, 1992, p. 3.
79 'Decennial Report', p. 16.
80 Anderson, *English Questions*, p. 3. The *New Left Review*'s 'theoretical lineage', wrote Anderson in 1966, lay in 'Western European Marxism' – and particularly in the work of Lukács, Gramsci and Sartre: 'Socialism and Pseudo-Empiricism', p. 31.
81 Perry Anderson, 'Origins of the Present Crisis', in *English Questions*, p. 17. (All quotations are from the 1992 reprint, unless otherwise indicated.)
82 Ibid.
83 Ibid., pp. 18, 21.
84 Ibid., p. 20.
85 Ibid.
86 Nairn, 'The British Political Elite', p. 25.
87 Ibid., p. 20.
88 Anderson, 'Socialism and Pseudo-Empiricism', p. 29.
89 Anderson, 'Origins of the Present Crisis', p. 22.
90 Ibid., p. 24.
91 Ibid., p. 27.
92 Anderson, 'Socialism and Pseudo-Empiricism', p. 19.
93 Anderson, 'Origins of the Present Crisis', p. 20.
94 Nairn, 'The British Political Elite', p. 21.
95 Anderson, 'Socialism and Pseudo-Empiricism', p. 41.
96 Tom Nairn, 'The Fateful Meridian', p. 11. Utilitarianism was too readily dismissed in the Nairn-Anderson theses. Donald Sassoon has argued that the 'Bentham-Webb axis … has operated over the last hundred years as the authentic ideological pillar of the British state', inspiring the development of the welfare state by the 'collective intellectual' of 'politicians, academics, chairmen of Royal Commission, pamphleteers, functionaries, broadcasters, journalists and government advisers' ('The Silences of *New Left Review*', *Politics and Power 3*, Routledge and Kegan Paul, London, 1981, pp. 225, 229). 'This collective theorist', continued Sassoon, with reference to Anderson's concept of an 'absent centre' at the heart of British culture, 'has obviously not produced a "total theory of man", nor a "classical sociology". It has produced something better: political hegemony' (ibid., p. 229).
97 'Socialism and Pseudo-Empiricism', p. 22.
98 'Origins of the Present Crisis', p. 34.
99 Nairn, 'The British Political Elite', p. 21.
100 Nairn has written that the Cold War marked for Britain 'a renewed cult of ancient Constitutional Liberty and wise pragmatism: an especially holy wayside shrine of the Free World' (*The Break-up of Britain*, Verso, London, 1981, p. 67).

101 'By the fifties, the most efficient firms in Britain were found to be mainly en-
    terprises which were either started by foreigners (refugees) since 1940, control-
    led by minorities (Quakers, Jews), or branches of international corporations
    (mainly American). The conquering entrepreneurs of the mid nineteenth cen-
    tury had become mediocre executives in the mid twentieth' ('Origins of the
    Present Crisis', p. 44).

102 The restraining hands of John Saville and Ralph Miliband, editors of the
    Socialist Register, cut the most inflammatory passages from the published text.
    All quotations from Thompson's text are cited from the unexpurgated version
    of the essay, first published in *The Poverty of Theory and Other Essays* (1978),
    Merlin Press, London, 1980, pp. 35-91. The first issue of the *Socialist Register*
    in 1964 received a warm welcome in the pages of the *Review*: see Tom Wengraf,
    'The *Socialist Register*', NLR 26, July/August 1964, pp. 90-93.

103 Thompson, 'Peculiarities', p. 45. Thompson argued that to deploy the term
    'aristocracy' was misleading, suggesting an unwarranted feudal connotation
    – though Anderson and Nairn did not dispute the fact that the landed class
    had long since been transformed into agrarian *capitalists*. While Nairn spe-
    cifically denied that the aristocracy was feudal – the aristocracy had a 'basi-
    cally capitalist structure ... and ... absence of legal definition as a privileged
    estate' ('The British Political Elite', p. 20) – there are nonetheless references to
    a 'pseudo-feudal' colouration that suggest a certain slippage from an agrarian
    (and commercial) capitalism to something more emphatically archaic.

104 'At the Point of Decay', in *Out of Apathy*, pp. 9-10.

105 Thompson, 'Peculiarities', p. 56.

106 Ibid., p. 35.

107 Ibid., p. 38.

108 Ibid., p. 87.

109 Ibid., p. 88.

110 Anderson, 'Socialism and Pseudo-Empiricism', pp. 2-3.

111 However, Anderson did later accept Thompson's objection to fixing the French
    Revolution as the yardstick – a 'model which concentrates attention upon one
    dramatic episode ... *the* Revolution', insisting 'upon an ideal type' ('Peculiarities',
    p. 47) of revolution – by which the transition to bourgeois modernity in
    England might be disparagingly measured (just as Gramsci had judged the
    Italian *Risorgimento*) as 'premature' and 'incomplete'. 'One can almost hear the
    stretching of historical textures', Thompson wrote, 'as the garment of English
    events ... is strained to cover the buxom model of *La Révolution Francaise*'
    ('Peculiarities', p. 78). In 'The Notion of Bourgeois Revolution' (presented at
    Cambridge in 1976, but unpublished until 1992) Anderson concluded that
    'none of the great turbulences of the transition to modernity has ever con-
    formed to the simple schema of a struggle between a feudal aristocracy and in-
    dustrial capital of the sort presupposed in the traditional Marxist vocabulary
    ... [T]he exception was the rule – every one was a bastard birth' ('The Notion
    of Bourgeois Revolution' (1976), in *English Questions*, pp. 112-3). Of the most
    obvious examples, one might cite from as diverse a group as the American
    Revolution (and the later triumph of the Union over the Confederacy), the

Italian *Risorgimento*, the unification of Germany under Bismarck, and the 'Meiji Restoration' in Japan.

112 See Hinton, 'The Labour Aristocracy', *NLR* 32, July/August 1965, pp. 72-7.

113 'Socialism and Pseudo-Empiricism', p. 32.

114 Nicos Poulantzas, 'Marxist Political Theory in Great Britain', *NLR* 43, May/June 1967, pp. 57-74.

115 Ibid., p. 65.

116 Whilst it is the case that throughout the nineteenth-century the personnel of the central state – the focus of Anderson and Nairn's attentions – were largely recruited from the patrician elite, it should also be remembered that at the level of local government the industrial middle class was asserting itself in the wake of such reforms as the New Poor Law of 1834 and the Municipal Corporations Act of 1835. It was to reach energetic heights of municipal bourgeois pride in the spate of town halls, galleries, libraries, parks and other more prosaic improvements – such as street lighting and sanitation – that proliferated as the century progressed.

117 'Peculiarities', pp. 53-4.

118 'Barrington Moore, Perry Anderson and English Social Development', in Stuart Hall, Dorothy Hobson, Andrew Lowe and Paul Willis, eds, *Culture, Media, Language*, Hutchinson, London, 1984, p. 62.

119 Anderson, 'Origins of the Present Crisis', p. 47.

120 Richard Johnson judged that Anderson and Nairn's 'analysis points to "radical liberal" solutions', 'like all good "social democrats", we become mere "modernisers"': Johnson, 'Barrington Moore, Perry Anderson and English Social Development', pp. 69, 70.

121 Enoch Powell: The New Right', *NLR* 61, May/June 1970, pp. 3-27; 'British Nationalism and the EEC', *NLR* 69, September/October 1971, pp. 3-28; 'The European Problem', *NLR* 75 (Special Issue: 'The Left Against Europe?'), September/October 1972, pp. 5-120; 'Scotland and Europe', *NLR* 83, January/February 1974, pp. 57-82; 'The Modern Janus', *NLR* 94, November/December 1975, pp. 3-29; 'The Twilight of the British State', *NLR* 101/2, January/April 1977, pp. 3-61; *The Break-up of Britain: Crisis and Neo-Nationalism*, New Left Books, London, 1977; 'The Future of Britain's Crisis', *NLR* 113/114, January/April 1979, pp. 43-69; 'The Crisis of the British State', *NLR* 130, November/December 1981, pp. 37-44; *The Enchanted Glass*, Radius, London, 1988; 'The Sole Survivor', *NLR* 200, July/August 1993, pp. 41-7. Increasingly frustrated by the congenital corporatism of British labour, Nairn would seek new agencies of change to detonate the UK state : Scots and Welsh nationalism from within and European integration from without.

122 'The Figures of Descent' *NLR* 161, January/February 1987, pp. 20-77.

123 Robert Looker, 'Perry Anderson's Changing Account of the Pattern of English Historical Development', in Colin Barker and David Nicholls, eds, *The Development of British Capitalist Society: A Marxist Debate*, Northern Marxist Historians Group, Manchester, 1988, p. 8. The landed aristocracy, notes Robert Looker, had 'their character progressively re-written and marginalised', whilst the 'financial and commercial bourgeoisie' enjoyed 'a corresponding acces-

sion of attention', and took 'the leading role in the climacteric act set in the late nineteenth century' (ibid.) 'Re-weighting' there may be, but not perhaps quite so 'radical' as Looker contends. Nairn's 'Labour Imperialism' of 1965, for example, focused on this very issue of the City's predominance – albeit in a context where the City was seen as a fixture of a non-productive gentlemanly, archaic and, indeed, 'aristocratic' world.

124 Acknowledging the strength of Arno Mayer's argument in *The Persistence of the Old Regime* (1981), Anderson recognised that the landowning class had re-mained politically and culturally dominant in every European country down to the First World War, thus threatening to demolish the singularity Anderson and Nairn had ascribed to Britain. If Mayer's continental comparisons had made the descriptions offered in the original theses 'more readily plausible', it had, in Anderson's words, left 'their explanatory function apparently more questionable' ('The Figures of Descent', p. 27). The search for the sources of British economic decline had therefore to be found 'not in the general phe-nomenon of landowner persistence ... but in the particular patterns' this had taken, the distinct character of its ruling bloc, and the state 'which embodied' its rule (ibid., p. 57.).

Anderson's 're-weighting' also drew significantly upon Geoffrey Ingham's *Capitalism Divided?* (1984), charting the dominance of commercial interests over those of domestic industrial capital. Anderson described it as 'perhaps the most important single contribution to a better understanding of the British fate to have appeared in the eighties' (ibid., p. 33 n. 43). Ingham's work was also endorsed in Colin Leys' favourable review, 'The Formation of British Capital', *NLR* 160, November/December 1986, pp. 114-20 – which appeared in the is-sue of the *NLR* immediately prior to 'The Figures of Descent'. (See also Leys' assessment of the subordinate character of industrial capital in 'Thatcherism and British Manufacturing: A Question of Hegemony', *NLR* 151, May/June 1985, pp. 5-25). In response to these interventions, the *Review* carried two substantive critiques of the perspective presented by Anderson, Ingham, and Leys: Michael Barratt Brown, 'Away With All the Great Arches: Anderson's History of British Capitalism', *NLR* 167, January/February 1988, pp. 22-51; Alex Callinicos, 'Exception or Symptom? The British Crisis and the World System', *NLR* 169, May/June 1988, pp. 97-106.

When the landowners divided on ideological lines during the Civil War that 'sealed their conversion to capitalist forms of development' ('The Figures of Descent', p. 32), it was the City merchants who tilted the balance in favour of the parliamentary forces. Thus, whilst capital's 'first historical incarnation in England was agrarian', argued Anderson, its 'second was mercantile' (ibid): the modern foundations of the City, namely the Bank of England and Stock Exchange, were laid following the Revolution of 1688, developments that were crucial to Britain's pioneering industrial revolution. However, as 'historical first-comer' Britain paid a profound penalty, for its 'industrialisation arrived without deliberate design, and triumphed without comparable competitors' (ibid., pp. 71-2), distinguished by the almost complete absence of any state sponsorship or support. Even though they were 'old regimes', the continental

states were conspicuously more interventionist, spawning professional bureaucratic cadres committed to a 'modernisation' (that carried an increasingly
nationalist and militarist inflection). In Britain, '[j]ust because industrialisation came as a spontaneous, molecular process, after a long prior build-up,
there was no occasion for official intervention to promote or guide it from
above' (ibid., p. 37). It was this very lead 'that fixed the path of subsequent
Victorian involution' (ibid., p.72).

In continental Europe, as the economic power of the landed elite waned, it was
industrial manufacturing, in close alliance with bank or – in Hilferding's classical study – 'finance' capital, that emerged to fill its place. (In Hilferding's analysis, banks and other financial institutions began to exert control of industry
with the latter's concentration, somewhere around the turn of the century in
the most advanced capitalist economies. This marked the phase of 'monopoly
capital', of industrial rationalisation, tending also to forms of state intervention, and culminating in what might be termed 'state-monopoly' or 'organised'
capitalism. Despite some tentative signs of such a development in the thirties,
it was, Ingham argued in *Capitalism Divided?*, precisely this stage of rationalisation that was so markedly absent in Britain.) In Britain, by contrast, when
'agrarian property lost its weight it was not industry but finance [more properly, commerce] which became the hegemonic form of capital' ('The Figures
of Descent', p. 57). The commercial bourgeoisie of the City remained distant
from the concerns of industrialists, being politically, socially and culturally
closer to the traditional agrarian elite. Moreover, in the age of empire and *Pax
Britannica*, they were firmly oriented to overseas investment – a perspective
reinforced by a state that combined 'a Treasury determined to minimise government at home, and a Foreign Office of vice-regal horizons abroad' ('The
Figures of Descent', p. 57). Britain's economic fortunes were sealed in this City-
Treasury-Bank of England nexus. Its priorities of sustaining free trade and an
international role for sterling operated, in an age of increased competition,
to the detriment of domestic manufacturing; a dominance symbolised by the
defeat of Joseph Chamberlain's campaign for imperial protection.

125 'Origins of the Present Crisis', p. 35.
126 'At the Point of Decay', p. 11.
127 'Origins of the Present Crisis', p. 37.
128 'The tragedy of the first proletariat ... was that it was in a critical sense premature' (Anderson, 'Origins of the Present Crisis', p. 23). 'The formation of
the English working class was a major tragedy' (Nairn, 'The English Working
Class', p. 52).
129 'Origins of the Present Crisis', p. 23.
130 Ibid.
131 'The Peculiarities of the English', p. 71.
132 Ibid.
133 'Origins of the Present Crisis', p. 37.
134 Nairn, 'The Nature of the Labour Party', reprinted in *Towards Socialism*,
Cornell University Press, Ithaca, 1966, p. 160.
135 Ibid., p. 179.

136 Ibid., p. 176.
137 'Origins of the Present Crisis', p. 23.
138 'The Nature of the Labour Party', p. 204.
139 'Problems of Socialist Strategy', in *Towards Socialism*, p. 241.
140 Ibid., p. 265.
141 Perry Anderson, 'The Limits and Possibilities of Trade Union Action', in Robin Blackburn and Alexander Cockburn, eds, *The Incompatibles: Trade Union Militancy and the Consensus*, Penguin/*New Left Review*, Harmondsworth, 1967, p. 266. Anderson considered university lecturers to be 'perhaps the most important single group of intellectuals in the country' ('Problems of Socialist Strategy', p. 275).
142 Nairn, 'The English Working Class', p. 53.
143 Ibid., pp. 53, 57.
144 'Problems of Socialist Strategy', p. 237.
145 Ibid., p. 234.
146 Ibid., p. 228.
147 Ibid., p. 230.
148 'Origins of the Present Crisis', p. 30. Anderson gave particular emphasis to the cultural dimension of hegemony in the British context – 'the extreme importance of cultural institutions in the British pattern of hegemony' (ibid., p. 41) – given the limited bureaucratic and military character of the British state.
149 'Problems of Socialist Strategy', p. 244.
150 Ibid., p. 279.
151 Peter Sedgwick, 'The Two New Lefts', p. 149.
152 'Conspectus', pp. ii-iii.
153 'Problems of Socialist Strategy', p. 265.
154 Nairn, 'The English Working Class', p. 57.
155 'The Left in the Fifties', p. 17.
156 NLR, 'On Internationalism', *NLR* 18, January/February 1963, p. 4.
157 See, for example, R. D. Laing, 'Series and Nexus in the Family', *NLR* 15, May/June 1962, pp. 7-14; a review of Marcuse's *One-Dimensional Man*, *NLR* 26, July/August 1964, pp. 78-80; and 'What is Schizophrenia?', *NLR* 28, November/December 1964, pp. 63-8; Ralph Miliband's obituary, 'C. Wright Mills', *NLR* 15, May/June 1962, pp. 15-20 and Michael Rustin, 'The Relevance of Mills' Sociology', *NLR* 21, October 1963, pp. 92-116; and Edmund Leach, 'Claude Lévi-Strauss – Anthropologist and Philosopher', *NLR* 34, November/December 1965, pp. 12-27.
158 Themes, *NLR* 37, May/June 1966, p. 1.
159 Georg Lukács, 'Technology and Social Relations', *NLR* 39, September/October 1966, pp. 27-34; Walter Benjamin, 'Paris, Capital of the 19th Century', *NLR* 48, March/April 1968, pp. 77-88; and Antonio Gramsci, 'Soviets in Italy', *NLR* 51, September/October 1968, pp. 28-58.
160 Louis Althusser, 'Contradiction and Overdetermination', *NLR* 41, January/February 1967, pp. 15-35.
161 'The Peculiarities of the English', p. 73.
162 'A Decennial Report', p. 15.

163 Ibid., p. 14.
164 Ibid., p. 15. These were rehearsals of Anderson's critical appraisal of Gramsci's work in 1977: 'The Antinomies of Antonio Gramsci', *NLR* 100, November 1976/January 1977, pp. 5-78.
165 Nicos Poulantzas, 'Marxist Political Theory in Great Britain', *NLR* 43, May/June 1967, p. 70. Thus, in Poulantzas' judgement, Nairn and Anderson were amiss in attempting 'to delimit the "dominant class" by *assuming* ... that it possesses a specific and coherent class consciousness' (ibid., p. 63).
166 Barrington Moore, Perry Anderson and English Social Development', p. 63.
167 'The British Left', *NLR* 30, March/April 1965, p. 19.
168 Joan Robinson, 'The Final End of Laissez-Faire', *NLR* 26, July/August 1964, pp. 3-9.
169 Serge Mallet, 'Continental Capitalism and the Common Market', *NLR* 19, March/April 1963, p. 22.
170 Barbara Castle, 'The Lessons of French Planning', *NLR* 24, March/April 1964, pp. 33-42; Lelio Basso, 'The Centre-Left in Italy', *NLR* 17, Winter 1962, pp. 9-16; Ernest Mandel, 'The Dialectic of Class and Region in Belgium', *NLR* 20, Summer 1963, pp. 5-31; Giorgio Fanti, 'The Resurgence of the Labour Party', *NLR* 30, March/April 1963, pp. 27-44; and John Hughes, 'The British Economy: Crisis and Structural Change', *NLR* 21, October 1963, pp. 3-20, and 'An Economic Policy for Labour', *NLR* 24, March/April 1964, pp. 5-32.
171 'The Two New Lefts', p. 151.
172 The prominence afforded to social democratic 'names' was perhaps understandable in promotional terms: Anderson's 1964 'Conspectus' sought to excuse the fledgling new model *NLR* on this score ('Conspectus', p. iii).
173 'A Decennial Report', p. 15.
174 'Critique of Wilsonism', *NLR* 27, September/October 1964, pp. 4, 22.
175 Ibid., pp. 11, 20.
176 Wilson, quoted in ibid., p. 11
177 'Origins of the Present Crisis', p. 47.
178 Ibid.
179 'Critique of Wilsonism', p. 21.
180 Themes, *NLR* 32, July/August 1965, p. 1. Its foreign policy record was lamentable: 'In every major under-developed zone in the world today ... British troops are in the firing-line, imposing armed neo-imperialism on the coloured and dispossessed peoples of the Third World' (Themes, *NLR* 31, May/June 1965, p. 1).
181 NLR, 'Divide and Conquer', *NLR* 28, November-December 1964, pp. 1-3.
182 Anderson, 'Conspectus', p. iii.
183 Whilst for Nairn and Anderson France provided the model of bourgeois development, in terms of 'the labour movements that emerged within the capitalist states thereafter ... it was at least as much the Italian party and class ..., as anything this side of the Alps, which provided the coded contrast for us' (Anderson, *English Questions*, p. 6). Whilst emphasising that it must 'modernise and destalinise', the PCI was, in Anderson's 1962 estimate, 'the most lucid in the world communist movement', combining 'fluent modernity and

lability in the domestic Italian situation and intransigent militancy on colonial issues' ('Introduction to the Debate of the Central Committee of the Italian Communist Party on the 22nd Congress of the CPSU', *NLR* 13-14, January/ April 1962, p. 160). Anderson commended the PCI's policy of 'presence', favourably contrasting it with the isolationism of its French sister-party (for example, the latter's purely negative position on the Common Market), and its conviction 'that absolute segregation of "reforms" from "revolution" was abstract and undialectical' (ibid.).

184　'Once again the economy is being sacrificed on the altar of the pound sterling, but this time it is a Labour high priest who is performing the ceremony' – the disillusioned words of Richard Pryke, assistant to Wilson's economic adviser Thomas Balogh, in 'The Predictable Crisis', *NLR* 39, September/October 1966, p. 15.

185　The debate, initiated by Ken Alexander and John Hughes in 1959 with their pamphlet, 'A Socialist Wages Plan', continued during the early period of the Labour government. Bob Rowthorn's 'The Trap of an Incomes Policy', *NLR* 34, November/December 1965, pp. 3-11, was itself a reply to a series of *Tribune* articles, principally by Michael Barratt Brown and Royden Harrison. It in turn elicited further responses from Alexander and Hughes, 'A Defence of the Incomes Policy Strategy', *NLR* 36 March/April 1966, pp. 92-4, and Barratt Brown and Harrison, 'Incomes Policy – A Reply', *NLR* 37, May/June 1966, pp. 86-94.

186　The Yugoslav experiment with market reforms was being treated with suspicion by the proponents of workers' control even at this early stage: it was acknowledged that in a successful socialist economy local autonomy would have to be matched by co-ordinated planning. '[I]t is not impossible that we may yet regard that country [i.e. Yugoslavia] as an object-lesson in pitfalls, rather than the brave new pilot which it looked like being in the beginning' (Coates, 'Democracy and Workers' Control', p. 315).

187　'Critique of Wilsonism', *NLR* 27, September/October 1964, p. 25. See also Fred Singleton and Tony Topham, 'Yugoslav Workers' Control', *NLR* 18, January/ February 1963, pp. 73-84; Tony Topham, 'Shop Stewards and Workers' Control', *NLR* 25, May/June 1964, pp. 3-16; and Ken Coates, 'Democracy and Workers' Control', pp. 291-316.

188　'A Decennial Report', p. 26. In the same year an *NLR* delegation comprising Anderson, Anthony Barnett, Jon Halliday, Peter Wollen and Quintin Hoare visited Sweden for 'an official colloquy' with the Swedish Communist Party (ibid., p. 26).

189　Themes, *NLR* 42, March/April 1967, p. 1.

190　'A Decennial Report', p. 25.

191　Robin Blackburn and Alexander Cockburn, eds, Introduction to *The Incompatibles*, p. 10.

192　Ibid., p. 11.

193　'The Nature of the Labour Party', p. 179.

194　'The Limits and Possibilities of Trade Union Action', pp. 267, 271.

195　'Problems of Socialist Strategy', pp. 260, 265.

196 'The Role of Militancy' (interview), *NLR* 46, November/December 1967, pp. 3-15.

197 'A Decennial Report', p. 4.

198 Gregory Elliott, 'Olympus Mislaid?', *Radical Philosophy*, no.71, May/June 1995, p. 7.

199 'On Internationalism', *NLR* 18 (January/February 1963, p. 3.

200 NLR, 'Introduction to Mandel', *NLR* 20, Summer 1963, p. 3.

201 Perry Anderson, 'Portugal and the End of Ultra-Colonialism', Parts 1-3, *NLR* 15, May/June 1962, pp. 83-102, *NLR* 16, July/August 1962, pp. 88-123, and *NLR* 17, Winter 1962, pp. 85-114; Lucien Rey, 'Persia in Perspective', Parts 1-2, *NLR* 19, March-April 1963, pp. 32-55, and *NLR* 20, Summer 1963, pp. 69-98; Roger Murray and Tom Wengraf, 'The Algerian Revolution', *NLR* 22, December 1963, pp. 14-65; and Ernest Mandel, 'The Dialectic of Class and Region in Belgium', *NLR* 20, Summer 1963, pp. 5-31.

202 'Introduction to Mandel', p. 3.

203 Ibid.

204 'Conspectus', p. vi.

205 Ibid.

206 *NLR* 13-14, January/April 1962, p. 154.

207 See, for example, Stanley Mitchell, 'Impressions of Russia', *NLR* 18 January/February 1963, pp. 51-9 – a personal recollection of a recent 'cultural trip' for British teachers; and E. H. Carr, 'Revolution from Above', *NLR* 46, November/December 1967, pp. 17-27, on the turn to the collectivisation of agriculture in 1929.

208 'Three Currents in Communism', *NLR* 23, January/February 1964, pp. 3-18, and 'The Unfinished Revolution', *NLR* 43, May/June 1967, pp. 27-39 (an extract from the book of the same title); and the two interviews 'On the Arab-Israeli War', *NLR* 44, July/August 1967, pp. 30-45 and 'Germany and Marxism', published posthumously, in *NLR* 47, January/February 1968, pp. 61-9.

209 'The Unfinished Revolution', p. 33.

210 Ibid., p. 34.

211 Ibid., p. 39.

212 'On the Israeli-Arab War', p. 35.

213 'Three Currents in Communism', p. 15.

214 Deutscher's withering condemnation of the Cultural Revolution, written within a couple of months of its launch, went unheeded by the *Review*. 'Its effect on China's spiritual and intellectual life', he wrote, 'is, in all probability, going to be just as devastating and lasting as were the consequences of the Stalinist witch-hunts' ('The Meaning of the "Cultural Revolution"' (1966), reprinted in *Marxism, Wars and Revolutions*, Verso, London, 1984, p. 213). 'Mao has been in one person China's Lenin and Stalin. But at the end of his road he shows more and more similarity to Stalin; and the latest orgy of his personality cult underlines the likeness. It is as if he had outlived himself and is already a relic of the past, an embodiment of China's backwardness and isolationism' (ibid., p. 217).

215 The generally favourable, though rather sketchy, attitude to China was re-
    flected in the *NLR* by, for example, Jan Myrdal, 'A Chinese Village', *NLR* 30,
    March/April 1965, pp. 60-72; Joan Robinson, 'The Communes and the Great
    Leap Forwards', *NLR* 37, May/June 1966, pp. 69-72; and Bill Jenner, 'History in
    the Manufacture', *NLR* 41, January/February 1967, pp. 84-96.

216 'A Decennial Report', p. 8.

217 'On Internationalism', p. 3. In the period 1962-3, coverage of the Third World
    accounted for a quarter of the *Review*'s output ('A Decennial Report', p. 124).

218 'The Third World: Its Emergence and Contours', *NLR* 18, January/February
    1963, pp. 5-23 and 'Bingo or UNO?', *NLR* 21, October 1963, pp. 21-9.

219 'The Third World: Its Emergence and Contours', pp. 6, 16.

220 'Bingo or UNO?', p. 28.

221 Ibid., p.29.

222 The *Review* later reflected critically on Sartre's Third Worldist influence at this
    time, and particularly 'his famous texts on Fanon and Nizan' ('A Decennial
    Report', pp. 5-6).

223 Jean-Paul Sartre, Preface to Frantz Fanon, *The Wretched of the Earth* (1961),
    Penguin, Harmondsworth, 1978, pp. 12, 22.

224 Fanon, op. cit., pp. 251-2.

225 'Third World or Third Force?', *NLR* 20, Summer 1963, pp. 32-36, and 'After
    Imperialism', *NLR* 25, May/June 1964, pp. 17-25.

226 'Conspectus', p. vi.

227 'Third World or Third Force?', p. 35.

228 'The New Nation-States', *NLR* 30, March /April 1965, pp. 86-95.

229 Robin Blackburn, 'Putting the Hammer down on Cuba', *NLR* [II] 4, July/
    August 2000, p. 20, n. 11.

230 'Prologue to the Cuban Revolution', *NLR* 21, October 1963, pp. 52-91.

231 'Second Thoughts on Ghana', *NLR* 42, March/April 1967, pp. 25-6. Note also
    Murray's 'Militarism in Africa', *NLR* 38, July/August 1966, pp. 35-59, and the
    disillusioned introductory Themes of that issue: 'The past two years have seen
    a massive wave of military interventions and counter-revolution throughout
    the Third World ... Nowhere is this more so than in Africa', where the 'end
    of "African Socialism" may be the beginning of the struggle for socialism in
    Africa' (*NLR* 38, July/August 1966, p. 2).

232 'Second Thoughts on Ghana', p. 27.

233 Documented in Lucien Rey, 'Dossier of the Indonesian Drama', *NLR* 36,
    March/April 1966, pp. 26-40; Hamza Alavi, 'Indian Capitalism and Foreign
    Imperialism', *NLR* 37, May/June 1966, pp. 77-85; James Petras, 'Co-ordinated
    Counter-Revolution: Latin America's New Phase', *NLR* 38, July/August 1966,
    pp. 60-4 and 'Dominican Republic: Revolution and Restoration', *NLR* 40,
    November/December 1966, pp. 76-84 and *NLR* 41, January/February 1967,
    pp. 64-69; and Oswald Stack, 'Indian Realities', *NLR* 42, March/April 1967, pp.
    40-3.

234 NLR, 'The Marxism of Régis Debray', *NLR* 45, September/October 1967, pp.
    8-12.

235 Themes, *NLR* 33, September/October 1965, p. 1. 'The earlier "Third Worldism" of NLR thus received a new and powerful transfusion, of a much more aggressively revolutionary character, at a time when its own traditional concern with the colonial and ex-colonial world was decreasing' ('A Decennial Report', p. 21).

236 The 'stagist' strategy of the Latin American Communist Parties – involving an 'alliance of four classes', including the 'national bourgeoisie', in carrying forward a 'national democratic revolution' as a necessary prelude to socialism – was denounced by Debray as fatally mistaken: the 'national bourgeoisie' had taken fright in the wake of the Cuban revolution and gone over to the US imperialist camp, under the banner of the 'Alliance for Progress'. Writing in 1963, Blackburn had underlined Fanon's conviction that the bourgeoisie of the Third World was but the enfeebled shadow of the once dynamic and revolutionary Western bourgeoisie: 'It imitates the Western bourgeoisie in its negative and decadent period without having made the initial efforts of exploration and invention which themselves created this Western bourgeoisie ... It is already senile without ever having known the impatience, fearlessness and the voluntarism of youth and adolescence' ('Prologue to the Cuban Revolution', p. 62). Rejected, too, was the 'Trotskyite' strategy of 'dual power', which Debray considered dangerously passive: even where Bolivian miners or Colombian peasant communities were locally armed for self-defence, they had proven all too vulnerable to attack once the equilibrium of class forces nationally had swung against them.

237 'Latin America: The Long March', *NLR* 33, September/October 1965, p. 23.

238 *Revolution in the Revolution?* (1967), Penguin, Harmondsworth, 1968, p. 85.

239 Ibid. p. 75.

240 'A Decennial Report', pp. 5-6.

241 'Problems of Socialist Strategy', p. 290. In Anderson's words, the two zones were 'divided by all the immense distance of different historical time' (ibid.)

242 Michael Kenny, 'Communism and the New Left', in Geoff Andrews, Nina Fishman and Kevin Morgan, eds, *Opening the Books: Essays on the Social and Cultural History of the British Communist Party*, Pluto Press, London, 1995, p. 205.

243 Kenny, *The First New Left*, p. 4.

244 In judging that from the beginning the *New Left Review* had more of the flavour of the *ULR* than the *New Reasoner*, Kenny goes so far as to assert that '[f]or those who had been associated with the *New Reasoner*, the new journal was an intense disappointment' (*The First New Left*, p. 77).

245 Though not all shared Thompson's impatience: Ralph Miliband, for example, recognised that socialism was not on the immediate agenda, and stressed, like Raymond Williams, the politics of 'the long haul': 'The Transition to the Transition', *NR* 6, Autumn 1958, pp. 35-48.

246 'The Left in the Fifties', p. 17.

247 'The Peculiarities of the English', p. 37.

248 A weakness subsequently acknowledged by Anderson in the Foreword to *English Questions*, Verso, London and New York, 1992, p. 5.

249 'Barrington Moore, Perry Anderson and English Social Development', p. 61.

250 See the chapter on 'Internationalism', pp. 130-56.

251 'Socialism and Pseudo-Empiricism', pp. 35, 34.

252 John Callaghan, op. cit., p. 167.

253 *Arguments Within English Marxism*, p. 147.

254 Ibid.

255 Newman, op. cit., p. 96.

256 A perspective Trotsky attributed to Lenin, and Gregory Elliott in turn to Perry Anderson ('Olympus Mislaid? A Profile of Perry Anderson', *Radical Philosophy*, no.71, May/June 1995, p. 5).

257 Ian Birchall, 'The Autonomy of Theory: A Short History of *New Left Review*', International Socialism, no.10, Winter 1980/81, p. 60.

258 'The Antinomies of Antonio Gramsci', *NLR* 100, November 1976/January 1977, p. 27 n. 48.

259 'A Decennial Report', p. 18: thus 'the opportunity for a *revolutionary* critique of the Nairn-Anderson theses was lost'.

260 Kenny, *The First New Left*, pp. 6, 137. A selection of Gramsci's work, *The Modern Prince and Other Writings* (edited by Louis Marks), had been published by Lawrence and Wishart in 1957 and reviewed by Christopher Hill in *New Reasoner* 4, Spring 1958, pp. 107-13. A more comprehensive edition of the *Notebooks* did not appear in English until 1971.

261 Although Nairn, while rejecting British national identity as irredeemably the elite-nationalism of the imperial UK state, did later see in Scottish and Welsh national-popular identity a potent means of dissolving the UK state.

262 Others of the Historians' Group who left the party after 1956 included Royden Harrison, Christopher Hill, Rodney Hilton, Victor Kiernan, George Rudé and Raphael Samuel (Willie Thompson, 'Historiography and the British Marxist Historians', *Socialist History*, no. 8, 1995, p. 10).

263 Bill Schwarz, '"The People" in History: the Communist Party Historians Group', in Richard Johnson, Gregor McLennan, Bill Schwarz and David Sutton, eds, *Making Histories*, Hutchinson, London, 1982, p. 54.

264 'Peculiarities of the English', p. 64.

Chapter Two: The Moment of 1968

1   Themes, *NLR* 44, July/August 1967, p. 1.

2   See Raymond Williams, ed., *May Day Manifesto 1968*, Penguin, Harmondsworth, 1968. The manifesto was originally drafted in the summer of 1966; its contributors included – alongside Williams – Michael Barratt Brown, Stuart Hall, Mike Rustin and Edward Thompson of the first New Left.

3   Ronald Fraser et al., *1968: A Student Generation in Revolt*, Chatto and Windus, London, 1988, p. 2.

4   Todd Gitlin, *The Sixties: Years of Hope, Days of Rage*, Bantam Books, Toronto, 1987, p. 13.

5   André Glucksmann, 'Strategy and Revolution in France 1968', *NLR* 52 November/December 1968, p. 88.

6   Temperamentally, the leading figures at the *NLR*, such as Anderson, were not particularly well-disposed to the counter-culture, with its tendency to excessively self-indulgent apoliticism. However, Robin Blackburn, Nicolas Krassó and Juliet Mitchell all lectured at the short-lived Anti-University of London, founded in the wake of the 1967 Dialectics of Liberation Conference at the Roundhouse, Chalk Farm, London.

7   Gareth Stedman Jones, Anthony Barnett and Tom Wengraf, 'Student Power: What is to be Done?' pp. 4-5.

8   Fraser, op. cit., p. 64.

9   Ernest Mandel, 'Where is America Going?', *NLR* 54, March/April 1969, p. 5.

10   Tariq Ali, *1968 and After*, Blond and Briggs, London, 1978, p. xxxiii.

11   David Caute, *Sixty Eight: The Year of the Barricades*, Paladin Books, London, 1988, p. 3. Vietnam also served to demarcate the new revolutionary Left from the older Left: the *NLR* (like the Vietnam Solidarity Campaign with which it was closely involved) called for the 'unambiguous and total solidarity' of Western socialists with the Democratic Republic of Vietnam and the National Liberation Front (Themes, *NLR* 47, January/February 1968, p. 1), in contrast, for example, to the Communist Party's more ambiguous call for 'peace'.

12   Ibid., p. 123.

13   Ronald Fraser, op. cit., p. 164.

14   Caute, op. cit., p. 122.

15   Gitlin, op. cit., p. 311.

16   Ibid., p. 326.

17   Fraser, op. cit., p. 283.

18   Ibid., p. 295.

19   Gitlin, op. cit., p. 242.

20   Ibid., p. 221.

21   Fraser, op. cit., p. 165.

22   Eric Hobsbawm, 'May 1968' (1969), in *Revolutionaries*, Quartet Books, London, 1982, p. 234.

23   Tom Nairn, 'Why it Happened', in Angelo Quattrocchi and Tom Nairn, *The Beginning of the End*, Panther, London, 1968, p. 104.

24   André Glucksmann, op. cit., p.67.

25   Introduction, *NLR* 52, November/December 1968, pp. 4, 5.

26   Ibid., p. 4.

27   Ibid., p. 5.

28   Themes, *NLR* 52, November/December 1968, p. 5.

29   Themes, *NLR* 100, November 1976/January 1977, p. 1.

30   Unparalleled in central and eastern Europe, Czechoslovakia had enjoyed parliamentary democratic government throughout the inter-war years. The Communist Party had a strong popular base: in the first post-war elections in 1946 it had received 38 per cent of the vote and, together with its Social Democratic allies, enjoyed a clear majority of seats in the National Assembly.

31   Note for example the sharp break with Deutscherite perspectives presented in Lucio Colletti 'The Question of Stalin', *NLR* 61, May/June 1970, pp. 61-81.

32   'Document B: Ten Theses', unpublished editorial document, 1968-9, pp. 5, 1.

33 Perry Anderson, *Arguments Within English Marxism*, Verso, London, 1980, p. 152.
34 'From Petrograd to Saigon', *NLR* 48, March/April 1968, p. 5.
35 Ibid.
36 Ibid., p. 6. 'The tremendous Vietnamese victories not only revealed the truth of the military situation. They also dramatically revealed, on TV screens throughout the world, the truth about the American occupation of Vietnam: images of terror and oppression that are the lineal descendants of those of the German occupation of Europe - public shooting of prisoners, deliberate rasing of towns, looting by collaborationists and mass bombing' (Themes, *NLR* 48, March/April 1968, p. 1).
37 Therborn, 'From Petrograd to Saigon', p. 6.
38 Ibid., p. 3. Arguing in similar terms in an interview conducted by Perry Anderson, Ronald Fraser and Quintin Hoare, Sartre judged 'that the origins of [the French] May lie in the Vietnamese Revolution' (Jean-Paul Sartre, 'Itinerary of a Thought', *New Left Review* 58, November/December 1969, p. 62).
39 Marilyn Young, *The Vietnam Wars, 1945-1990*, Harper Collins, New York, 1991, p. 255.
40 Introduction, *NLR* 52, November/December 1968, p. 5.
41 C. Wright Mills, 'Letter to the New Left', *NLR* 5, September/October 1960, p. 22.
42 Caute, op. cit., p. 386.
43 Themes, *NLR* 43, May/June 1967, p. 1.
44 Ben Brewster and Alexander Cockburn, 'Revolt at LSE', *NLR* 43, May/June 1967, p. 25
45 'A Decennial Report', pp. 39, 27.
46 'Revolutionary Socialist Students' Federation, Manifesto', *NLR* 53, January/February 1969, p. 21. In constituting itself 'as an extra-parliamentary opposition', the RSSF argued 'that new, participatory mass-based organisations are required to overthrow capitalism', given 'that existing political parties and trade unions cannot either structurally or politically sustain revolutionary programmes' (ibid., pp. 21-2).
47 Introduction, *NLR* 52, November/December 1968, p. 7.
48 Cited Fraser, op. cit., p. 10.
49 Themes, *NLR* 59, January/February 1970, p. 2.
50 NLR, 'Presentation of Blanqui' and Auguste Blanqui, 'Instructions for an Uprising', *NLR* 65, January/February 1971, pp. 27-9 and pp. 30-34, respectively. 'Insurrection is an art: the conquest of power cannot be left wholly to spontaneity. If for this reason alone, revolutionary Marxism has reason to pay homage to Blanqui' ('Presentation of Blanqui', p. 29).
51 In 1972 Tariq Ali – closely associated with members of the *New Left Review* in the RSSF, *Black Dwarf*, and the International Marxist Group; later a member of the *Review*'s editorial committee – could go so far as to 'visualise a situation … where a city like Liverpool could witness an armed insurrection by sections of the proletariat' (*The Coming British Revolution*, Jonathan Cape, London, 1972, p. 230).

52   'We were full of our revolutionary toughness', recalls Sheila Rowbotham, 'a stance which infuriated our elders.' By contrast, the first New Left's *Mayday Manifesto* 'looked too respectable, too safe': *Promise of a Dream: Remembering the Sixties*, Penguin, London, 2001, p. 175.

53   See Tom Nairn, *The Hornsey Affair*, Penguin, Harmondsworth, 1969.

54   'A Decennial Report', p. 40.

55   'Revolutionary Socialist Students' Federation, Manifesto', *NLR* 53 January/February 1969, pp. 22, 21.

56   'Revolutionary Socialist Students' Federation, Manifesto', p. 22. Its 'Action Programme' called for an 'end to bourgeois ideology – masquerading as education – in courses and lectures' (ibid).

57   James Wilcox, 'Two Tactics', *NLR* 53, January/February 1969, pp. 23-4.

58   James Wilcox, 'Two Tactics', pp. 23-32; David Triesman, 'The Impermanent Stronghold', pp. 33-5; David Fernbach, 'Strategy and Struggle' pp. 37-42; and Anthony Barnett, 'A Revolutionary Student Movement', pp. 43-53, *NLR* 53, January/February 1969.

59   'Strategy and Struggle', p. 42.

60   'Two Tactics', p. 26.

61   Ibid., p. 27.

62   Cited Chris Harman, *The Fire Last Time: 1968 and After* (1988), Bookmarks, London, Chicago, Sydney, 1998, p. 156.

63   The *NLR*'s 'red bases' line was accepted with some reluctance by the International Socialists in the interest of compromise (Harman, op. cit., p. 376, n. 45).

64   Rowbotham, op. cit., p. 176.

65   Harman, op. cit., p. 150

66   Fred Halliday, born Dublin, 1946, was then a student at the University of London's School of Oriental and African Studies. Today he is a recognised expert on the politics of Middle East and Professor of International Relations at the LSE. On the editorial committee 1968-83.

67   'A Decennial Report', p. 40.

68   Ibid., p. 41.

69   'Verso Constitution', unpublished document, no date (1983), p. 1.

70   'The Unknown Marx', *NLR* 48, March/April 1968, p.43. '*Capital*', he wrote, 'is painfully unfinished, like a mystery novel which ends before the plot is unravelled. But the *Grundrisse* contains the author's plot-outline as a whole' (ibid., p. 55).

71   Introduction to Alexander Cockburn and Robin Blackburn, eds, *Student Power*, Penguin/*New Left Review*, Harmondsworth, 1969, p. 7.

72   Ibid., p. 8.

73   Ibid., p. 9.

74   Ibid., p. 8.

75   'Revolutionary Socialist Students' Federation, Manifesto', p. 21. Writing in the *Review* in 1970, Lucio Magri argued that the radically altered character of contemporary capitalism – conditions of relative abundance – required new forms of politics: 'For the first time, the fundamental contradiction of the system moves to the forefront: the contradiction between use value and exchange

value, or production as an end in itself and the reification of man, labour and consumption' ('Problems of the Marxist Theory of the Revolutionary Party', *NLR* 60, March/April 1970, p. 117).

76 Introduction, *NLR* 52, November/December 1968, p. 8.
77 'Why It Happened', pp. 118, 119.
78 Ibid., p. 115.
79 Ibid., p. 160.
80 Between September 1969 and May 1970 there were some 250 major bombings: Gitlin, op. cit., p. 401.
81 'A Decennial Report', p. 44.
82 Introduction, *NLR* 52, November/December 1968, p. 7.
83 Gregory Elliott, *Perry Anderson: The Merciless Laboratory of History*, University of Minnesota Press, Minneapolis and London, 1998, p. xiv.
84 'The Founding Moment', unpublished manuscript, 1969, p. 134.
85 Themes, *NLR* 50, July/August 1968, p. 1.
86 'Components of the National Culture', *NLR* 50, July/August 1968, p. 57. See also Robin Blackburn, 'A Brief Guide to Bourgeois Ideology', in Cockburn and Blackburn, eds, *Student Power*, pp. 163-213.
87 'Components of the National Culture', p. 6.
88 Ibid., p. 12.
89 Ibid., pp. 56, 57.
90 Sunil Khilnani, *Arguing the Revolution: The Intellectual Left in Postwar France*, Yale University Press, New Haven and London, 1993, p. 78.
91 'Components of the National Culture', p. 12.
92 Ibid., p. 13.
93 Quoted in ibid., p. 18.
94 Ibid., p. 19.
95 Ibid., p. 48.
96 Ibid., p. 50.
97 Ibid., p. 51.
98 Ibid., p. 56.
99 Ibid., p. 4. Albeit now with a revolutionary twist, this culturalist emphasis was consistent with Anderson's thinking in 1964, when he wrote: 'The struggle for a liberated culture today is not in any sense a secondary or supplementary one. It is inseparable from the notion of socialism itself ... In the advanced capitalist countries of our time, *consciousness* is the condition of any meaningful social change' ('Critique of Wilsonism', *NLR* 27, September/October 1964, p. 27).
100 'The *Coupure* of May', p. 8.
101 Ibid., p. 11.
102 Ibid., p. 4.
103 Ibid., p. 8.
104 Ibid., p. 9.
105 Ibid.
106 Nairn, 'Why It Happened', pp. 129, 130.
107 'The *Coupure* of May', p. 10.
108 Ibid.

109 Ibid., p. 11.

110 'Ten Theses', p. 7.

111 Ibid., p. 8.

112 Ibid., p. 7. Despite recognising that analysis of the Cultural Revolution was 'rendered difficult by the extreme paucity of reputable information of the most basic kind' (Themes, *NLR* 53, January/February 1969, p. 2), such illusions were reflected by the *Review* in, for example, Bill Jenner's 'The New Chinese Revolution', *NLR* 53, January/February 1969, pp. 83-96. See also John Collier, 'The Cultural Revolution in Canton', *NLR* 48, March/April 1968, pp. 63-71 and 'Canton: March-May 1968', *NLR* 50, July/August 1968, pp. 93-104; and Mao Tse-tung, 'Talk on Strategic Dispositions', *NLR* 54, March/April 1969, p. 33-40.

113 Ibid.

114 Perry Anderson, Ronald Fraser, Quintin Hoare, interview with Jean-Paul Sartre, 'Itinerary of a Thought', *NLR* 58, November/December, p. 62.

115 'Ten Theses', p. 8.

116 'A Decennial Report', p. 32.

117 'The *Coupure* of May', p. 11.

118 Themes, *NLR* 44, July/August 1967, p. 2.

119 Nicolas Krassó, 'Trotsky's Marxism', *NLR* 44, July/August 1967, p. 79.

120 Ibid., p. 72.

121 Ibid., p. 76.

122 Ibid.

123 Ibid.

124 This was why, when Stalin effectively adopted key elements of the programme of the Left Opposition in the 'great turn' of 1928-9, most of Trotsky's followers resigned themselves to Stalin's leadership.

125 Ibid., p. 77.

126 Ibid., pp. 64-5.

127 Ernest Mandel, 'Trotsky's Marxism: an Anti-Critique', *NLR* 47, January/February 1968, p. 38.

128 Ibid., p. 40.

129 Quoted in ibid., p. 39.

130 Ibid., p. 40.

131 Ibid., p. 36.

132 Leon Trotsky, *The Revolution Betrayed*, Faber and Faber, London, 1937, p. 104.

133 'Trotsky's Marxism: an Anti-Critique', p. 50.

134 *The Revolution Betrayed*, p. 241.

135 'Reply to Ernest Mandel', *NLR* 48, March/April 1968, p. 103.

136 'A Decennial Report', p. 30.

137 Ibid., p. 32.

138 'Reply to Mandel', p.102. The fact that the Soviet bureaucracy exported social revolution to Eastern Europe after 1945, and that parties of the Third International were themselves capable of making revolution – in China, Yugoslavia, Vietnam, etc. – suggested that Trotsky had been wrong to identify

the Soviet Union and Comintern as politically bankrupt. It caused controversy within the Fourth International, allowing, for example, Michel Pablo to voice a more favourable assessment of the parties of the Third International: see Pablo, 'Where Are We Going' (1951), in *Struggle in the Fourth International: International Secretariat Documents 1951-1954*, Pathfinder Press, New York, 1974.

139 'Reply to Mandel', p. 102.

140 'A Decennial Report', p. 31.

141 Ibid.

142 Tariq Ali, *Street Fighting Years: An Autobiography of the Sixties*, Collins, 1987, p. 151. Aside from the call for making 'red bases' of the universities in 1968, note also, for example, Blackburn's otherwise laudatory introduction to Debray's *Strategy for Revolution*, 1970, in which all criticisms are in Maoist accents; including three direct quotations from Mao, and other references, in just 17 pages.

143 Themes, *NLR* 61, May/June 1970, p. 1. 'The top men of the system', wrote Tamara Deutscher in 1970, 'have no initiative and no self-confidence. They seem to sit on an ice floe which is cracking dangerously – they are afraid of rocking it; they can neither direct it, nor stop it, nor step off it' ('Soviet Oppositions', *NLR* 60, March/April 1970, p. 55).

144 'Ten Theses', p. 5. The *Review* was eager to recognise the socialist opposition in the Soviet Union, heralding Roy Medvedev's 1974 essay, 'Problems of Democratisation and Detente' (*NLR* 83, January/February 1974, pp. 27-40), as 'without question one of the most important political statements to emerge from within the Soviet Union in recent years' ('Introduction to Medvedev', p. 25). However, the *Review* did not share Medvedev's conviction that 'any shift towards a more consistent democratisation ... is at present possible in the USSR only as a result of certain initiatives "from above" supported "from below", but not as a sheer result of pressure "from below"' (p. 33). It prefaced Medvedev's article with the assertion that: 'Marxists outside the USSR ... will respect this view and the depth of experience behind it; but they will not share either its prediction or preference' ('Introduction to Medvedev', p. 26). Tamara Deutscher's observations in 1970 were closer to those of the editorial collective ('Soviet Fabians and Others', *NLR* 62, July/August 1970, pp. 45-54). Distant from the cautious approach of Varga and Medvedev, and liberals such as Sakharov, she discerned in them a perennial failing of the Russian intelligentsia: their unease at the potentially explosive entry of the masses into politics. However, writing again six years later, she too voiced a similar disquiet: the Soviet working class, with no recent revolutionary or democratic experience, might be capable only of a destructive intervention ('Intellectual Opposition in the USSR', *NLR* 96, March/April 1976, pp. 101-13). Solzhenitsyn, the most prominent dissident, expounded a reactionary, religious nationalism, not uncommon in oppositional intellectual circles: a phenomenon that struck Tamara Deutscher 'as a symptom of terrible sickness and trauma' ('USSR: Democratic Alternatives', *NLR* 104, July/August 1977, p. 115). Nonetheless, Solzhenitsyn's achievements were recognised by the socialist oppositionists:

reviewing *The Gulag Archipelago*, Medvedev acknowledged that 'Solzhenitsyn has dealt a heavy blow to Stalinism and neo-Stalinism ... None of us has done more than Solzhenitsyn in this respect' ('On Gulag Archipelago', *NLR* 85, May/June 1974, p. 31). Even Robin Blackburn, reviewing Solzhenitsyn's earlier *The First Circle* in 1970, was moved to write that it represented 'in some ways the first socialist realist novel ever to have been written' ('The First Circle', *NLR* 63, September/October 1970, p. 57).

145 Themes, *NLR* 72, March/April 1972, p. 2.

146 'Polish Document – Presentation', *NLR* 72, March/April 1972, p. 32.

147 Themes, *NLR* 69, September/October 1971, pp. 1-2. See also Tariq Ali, 'Bangla Desh: Results and Prospects', *NLR* 68, July/August 1971, pp. 27-48; and Fred Halliday, 'The Ceylonese Insurrection', *NLR* 69, September/October 1971, pp. 55-90.

148 'Chou En-Lai's Message to Sirimavo Bandaranaike', *NLR* 69, September/October 1971, p. 91. See also 'Chou En-lai's Message to Yahya Khan', pledging Chinese support to Pakistan in opposition to Bangladeshi independence, in *NLR* 68, July/August 1971, p. 46.

149 'A Decennial Report', p. 63.

150 Ben Brewster, 'Communication', *NLR* 70, November/December 1971, pp. 110-111.

151 A 'pogrom of the intelligentsia', in Deutscher's damning contemporary assessment ('The Meaning of the "Cultural Revolution"' (1966), *Marxism, Wars and Revolution*, Verso, London, 1984, p. 213).

152 Gilbert Padoul, 'China 1974: Problems not Models', *NLR* 89, January/February 1975, pp. 73-84. In the same issue, see also Claude Aubert, 'People's Communes – How to Use a Standard Visit', pp. 86-96.

153 'A Decennial Report', p. 63

154 'Marxist Analysis and Post-Revolutionary China', *NLR* 100, November 1976/January 1977, pp. 165-192.

155 See, for example, Göran Therborn, 'A Critique of the Frankfurt School', *NLR* 63, September/October 1970, pp. 65-96; Gareth Stedman Jones, 'The Marxism of the Early Lukács: An Evaluation', *NLR* 70, November/December 1971, pp. 27-64; and Norman Geras, 'Althusser's Marxism: An Account and Assessment', *NLR* 71, January/February 1972, pp. 57-86. In 1977 NLB published *Western Marxism: A Critical Reader*, collecting these and other texts. Parallel with this more critical appraisal was a new emphasis on a more classical Marxist 'materialism', given that Western Marxism had often 'bent the stick' in an idealist direction. Especially significant in this respect was Sebastiano Timpanaro's 'Considerations on Materialism' (*NLR* 85, May/June 1974, pp. 3-22), whose influence on Anderson et al. may be gauged by the *Review*'s description of it as 'one of the most original philosophical essays to have been written by a Marxist in the last decade' (Themes, *NLR* 85, May/June 1974, p. 1). Timpanaro, in defence of a maligned Engelsian perspective, asserted not merely the determining weight of the socio-economic 'base' over the political and cultural 'superstructures', but the equally determining priority 'of the physical level over the biological level, and of the biological level over the socio-economic level;

both in the sense of chronological priority … and in the sense of the conditioning which nature *still* exercises on man and will continue to exercise at least for the foreseeable future': 'Considerations on Materialism', p. 7.

156 *Considerations on Western Marxism* (1976), Verso, London, 1989, p. 101.
157 Ibid., pp. 95-6, 96.
158 Ibid., p. 96.
159 Ibid., p. 100.
160 Ibid., p. viii.
161 Elliott, *Perry Anderson*, p. 105.
162 *Considerations on Western Marxism*, p. 109.
163 Ibid., p. 100.
164 Ibid.
165 Ibid., p. 101.
166 Ibid., p. 103.
167 Ibid., p. 100.
168 Gareth Stedman Jones, 'Comment', unpublished document, no date, p. 9.
169 'Comments on Western Marxism: An Introduction', unpublished document, 10 October 1974, p. 6. Nairn's identification of 1914 as 'the critical date in the narrative of modern socialism' led him to study nationalism. For Anderson the critical date was 1917 – leading him to study Absolutism, whose 'last bulwark' the Russian revolution had destroyed: Perry Anderson, Foreword to *English Questions*, Verso, London and New York, 1992, p. 7.
170 'Comments on Western Marxism', p. 11.
171 *Considerations on Western Marxism*, p. 113. Eric Hobsbawm judged that in the 'Afterword' Anderson 'retracted much of the first 90 per cent of his essay': 'Look Left', *New Statesman*, 24 September 1976, p. 410.
172 Considerations on Western Marxism, p. 114.
173 Ibid., p. 117.
174 Ibid., p. 113.
175 In raising 'a number of possible doubts' as to the 'economic architecture of *Capital* itself' (ibid., p. 115), Anderson wrote that the 'most hazardous conclusions that the system of *Capital* yielded were the general theorem of the falling rate of profit, and the tenet of an ever-increasing class polarisation between bourgeoisie and proletariat. Neither has yet been adequately substantiated' (ibid.). See also Geoffrey Hodgson, 'The Theory of the Falling Rate of Profit', *NLR* 84, March/April 1974, pp. 55-82. In the words of the *Review*'s preface, Hodgson argued that Marx's theory of the falling rate of profit was 'theoretically misconceived, empirically unsubstantiated and politically redundant': Themes, *NLR* 84, March/April 1974, p. 2.
176 'Marx assumed that capitalism would progressively mitigate and annul nationality in a new universalism: in fact, its development summoned and reinforced nationalism' (*Considerations on Western Marxism*, p. 115).
177 *Considerations on Western Marxism*, p. 121.
178 See Anthony Barnett, 'Introduction to Western Marxism: Some Preliminary Comments', unpublished document, 24 July 1974, p. 4; Fred Halliday, 'Comment on Western Marxism', unpublished document, no date, p. 3; Nairn,

'Comments on Western Marxism: An Introduction', p. 12; and Stedman Jones, 'Comment', p. 10. The comments of Norman Geras (letter to Anderson, 26 June 1974) were more affirmative.

179 Pre-publication flyer.

180 'A Decennial Report', p. 63.

181 'NLR 1975-1980', pp. 4-5.

182 Anna Coote and Beatrix Campbell, *Sweet Freedom: The struggle for women's liberation*, Picador, London, 1982, p. 17.

183 Juliet Mitchell, 'Women: The Longest Revolution', *NLR* 40, November/ December 1966, pp. 11-37. Note also Quintin Hoare's response and Juliet Mitchell's reply, under 'discussion', *NLR* 41, January/February 1967, pp. 78-83.

184 'NLR 1975-80', p. 74

185 David Fernbach, an activist in the Gay Liberation Front, would later define his own politics as an attempt 'to integrate the radical perspective of the gay movement together with the established ideas of socialism and the other new insights of ecology and the counterculture' (*The Spiral Path: a gay contribution to human survival*, Alyson, Boston and Gay Men's Press, London, 1981, back cover).

186 John Callaghan, *The Far Left in British Politics*, Blackwell, Oxford, 1987, p. 159.

187 Caute, op. cit., p. 236. Note Stokeley Carmichael's infamous reply to being questioned on the position of women in the movement: "prone". Yet the women's movement also learnt from black liberation notions of 'cultural oppression', and its emphasis on consciousness-raising borrowed from the Maoist injunction to 'speak bitterness', recorded in William Hinton's *Fanshen: A Documentary of Revolution in a Chinese Village*, first published by Monthly *Review* Press in the USA in 1966.

188 Rowbotham, op. cit., p. 117 and elsewhere. On the emergence of the women's movement from within and against the movements inspired by the sixties revolt, note also Naomi Jaffe and Bernadine Dohrn, 'The Look is You', *New Left Notes* (the newsletter of the American SDS), March 1968.

189 'A Decennial Report', p. 54.

190 'NLR 1975-80', p.3.

191 The internal editorial report, 'NLR 1975-80', cites a core *aktiv* of '7/8' (p. 76). Elliott identifies seven active members, excluding Magaš from the eight cited here (*Perry Anderson*, p. 111).

192 The IMG was a small organisation, whose 'membership stood at 40 in 1968, 400 in 1972 and around 800 by 1978' (John Callaghan, *British Trotskyism: Theory and Practice*, Basil Blackwell, Oxford, 1984, p. 157).

193 By 1983 Mandel had contributed more to the *Review* than anyone apart from Anderson and Nairn: no less than 13 articles and 250 pages ('NLR 1980-1983', appendix p. xi).

194 The book's purpose was spelt out in Jon Rothschild's introduction: 'to present a comprehensive synopsis of the Fourth International's analysis of the contemporary world scene and the opportunity it affords for a revolutionary

breakthrough to socialist democracy' (*Revolutionary Marxism Today*, New Left
Books, London, 1979, p. x).

195 'A Decennial Report', p. 54.
196 Ibid.
197 Ibid., p. 78.
198 'NLR 1975-1980', pp. 3-4.
199 'A Decennial Report', p. 72.
200 'NLR 1975-80', p. 78
201 'A Decennial Report', p. 73. 'The unity of NLR ... has always been directly re-
     lated to the productivity of its working collective' (ibid.)
202 '"Ever since the late sixties, the NLR editorial committee had thought of itself
     as a kind of Leninist central committee." This pattern of behaviour persisted
     "long after the game was up"': Tariq Ali, cited in Patrick Wright, 'Beastly Trials
     of the Last Politburo', *Guardian*, 17 July 1993.
203 Melodramatically characterised by Patrick Wright as exhibiting the 'morbid
     pathology' of a 'Leninist psychodrama', involving 'ruthless comradely criti-
     cism' of submitted manuscripts (Wright, art. cit.)
204 'NLR 1975-80', p. 7; an intended reply on Hoare's part never materialised,
     ibid.
205 'NLR 1975-80', pp. 6-10.
206 Ibid., p. 8.

Chapter Three: Revolutionary Expectations

1   Themes, *NLR* 72, March/April 1972, p. 1.
2   'Late Capitalism', *NLR* 98 July/August 1976, pp. 59-83.
3   In presenting Karl Kautsky's 1914 text 'ultra-imperialism', the *NLR* affirmed
     that it judged 'international anarchy' to be the fundamental characteristic of
     the capitalist mode of production (*NLR* 59, p. 40. n. 174).
4   Themes, *NLR* 96, March/April 1976, p. 1. The year before, the *Review* had writ-
     ten that the end of the long post-war boom had placed the 'world capitalist
     economy' in a 'profound crisis' (Themes, *NLR* 90, March/April 1975, p. 1).
5   NLR, 'Victory in Indochina', *NLR* 91, May/June 1975, pp. 1-2. 'In 1968 the Tet
     offensive helped to detonate the May events in France. The immediate rever-
     berations of the liberation of Indochina cannot yet be seen, but they will al-
     ready be silently making history' (ibid., p. 2).
6   Quoted in Themes, *NLR* 91, May/June 1975, p. 1.
7   'On the Twenty Second Congress of the French Communist Party', *NLR* 104,
     July/August 1977, p. 4.
8   Themes, *NLR* 96, March/April 1976, p. 1.
9   'The Founding Moment', unpublished manuscript, 1969, p. 3.
10   Paul Ginsborg, *A History of Contemporary Italy: Society and Politics 1943-1988*,
     Penguin Books, London, 1990, p. 298.
11   Ibid., p. 313.
12   Jean-Marie Vincent, 'The PCF and its History', *NLR* 52, November/December
     1968, pp. 39-46; Ilios Yannakakis, 'The Greek Communist Party', *NLR* 54,

March/April 1969, pp. 46-54; Pertii Hynynen, 'The Popular Front in Finland', *NLR* 57, September/October 1969, pp. 3-20; Göran Therborn, 'Swedish Communism – End of an Interlude', *NLR* 58, November/December 1969, pp. 37-42; Bill Warren, 'The Programme of the CPGB – A Critique', *NLR* 63, September/October 1970, pp. 7-41; Lucio Magri, 'Italian Communism in the Sixties', *NLR* 66, March/April 1971, pp. 37-52; and Fernando Claudin, 'The Split in the Spanish Communist Party', *NLR* 70, November/December 1971, pp. 75-99.

13 'The Founding Moment', p. 20.

14 Ibid., p.36.

15 Succeeding the sectarian 'Third Period' that had led to the debacle of the German workers' movement and Hitler's rise to power (see Eric Hobsbawm, 'Confronting Defeat: the German Communist Party', *NLR* 61, May/June 1970, p. 84). Nonetheless, Hobsbawm wrote that the left turn of 1928 was enthusiastically endorsed by the majority of the KPD: it had always tended towards 'heroic illusions' and 'a residuum of ultra-radicalism' (ibid., p. 84), and carried out with 'zeal' the 'suicidal line of 1929-33' (ibid., p. 88). It had, after all, experienced first hand the counter-revolutionary predilections of the SPD: 'a passionately and viscerally anti-revolutionary and governmental Social-Democracy' (ibid., p. 84).

16 The PCF had effectively initiated the Popular Front tactic in 1934, a year prior to its official adoption by the Comintern (though no doubt with Moscow's sanction), in response to Hitler's coup and the threat of French fascism – in particular the 6 February 1934 assault on parliament.

17 Fernando Claudin, 'Spain – The Untimely Revolution', *NLR* 74, July/August 1972, p. 32. Claudin argued that an appeal to the revolutionary élan of the masses, rather than an accommodation with the political Centre involving a demobilisation of the spirit of 1936, could have saved Spain from fascism.

18 On Greece, see Ilios Yannakakis (above), and, more especially, George Catephores, 'The Kapetanios', *NLR* 79, May/June 1973, pp. 50-9. On the Philippines, see Jonathan Fast, 'Imperialism and Bourgeois Dictatorship in the Philippines', *NLR* 78, March/April 1973, pp. 69-96 and William Pomeroy, 'On the Philippine Huk Struggle', *NLR* 81, September/October 1973, pp. 93-100.

19 Although, in introducing Claudin's reflections on the Spanish Civil War, the *Review* argued that in 'the contemporary world the sacrifice of revolutionary possibilities to the alleged dictates of diplomacy underlines the continuing relevance of the Spanish case' (Themes, *NLR* 74, July/August 1972, pp. 1-2), by the seventies the Western Communist Parties in fact exercised considerable independence from Moscow. They met the invasion of Czechoslovakia, for example, with almost universal condemnation.

20 The conversion of most Western Communist Parties to a parliamentary road to socialism was in certain significant respects conditioned by this international affiliation, for their distancing from both the Bolshevik model of revolution and the Soviet model of 'socialism' was justified on the grounds of different 'national roads to socialism' – permitting them to revise their strategic perspectives without directly condemning the specificities of the Soviet experience.

Their democratic commitment was thus necessarily couched in parliamentary terms, for to advocate a direct democracy from below would have entailed an overt criticism of the Soviet Union. Ernest Mandel was keen to stress the links between Stalinism and Euro-Communism – see his *From Stalinism to Eurocommunism: The Bitter Fruits of Socialism in One Country* (1977), trans. Jon Rothschild, New Left Books, London, 1978. Stalin had acknowledged that a different route to socialism was applicable in the West, approving the adoption of the non-Leninist *British Road to Socialism* in 1951.

21   'The Founding Moment', p. 56.

22   Ibid., p. 123.

23   Ibid., p. 17.

24   There was significant opposition to effecting a break with the old workers' parties even amongst revolutionaries: 'in March 1919 the newly formed German Communist Party at Luxemburg's urgings rejected the formation of a new International' (ibid., p. 10).

25   Ibid., p. 51.

26   Ibid., p. 127.

27   Kyle Steenland, 'Two Years of 'Popular Unity' in Chile: A Balance Sheet', *NLR* 78, March/April 1973, p. 4. The *Review* warned that the destruction of the 'repressive armoury of the bourgeois State machine' was an 'indispensable precondition for the liberation of the exploited classes from the reign of capital … [S]oviet-type institutions' were an urgent necessity if there was 'to be any chance of a socialist revolution in Chile' (Themes, *NLR* 78, March/April 1973, p. 1).

28   First published in three instalments in *Rinascita*, September-October 1973, and reproduced in English translation in *Marxism Today*, February 1974, pp. 39-50

29   'Reflections after the events in Chile', p. 47.

30   *Eurocommunism and Socialism* (1977), trans. John Wakeham, New Left Books, London, 1978, p. 66.

31   *Eurocommunism and the State*, Lawrence and Wishart, London, 1977, p. 40.

32   'The Italian Road to Socialism', *NLR* 106, November/December 1977, p. 44.

33   A sociological corollary was appended by Nicos Poulantzas, who justified the search for such alliances on the basis that the working class in modern capitalist societies comprised only a minority of the population. This he deduced from a narrow definition of the proletariat, discounting all but those directly engaged in 'productive labour'. The consequence of such a designation was a swollen and heterogeneous 'intermediate strata', lumping together in a single category the old petty-bourgeoisie (peasant farmers and craftsmen, i.e., small proprietors) and the 'new petty-bourgeoisie' – 'white-collar' and professional workers (who, in selling their labour, are, in objective terms, a fraction of the working class): Nicos Poulantzas, 'On Social Classes', *NLR* 78, March/April 1973, pp. 27-54, and *Classes in Contemporary Capitalism*, New Left Books, London, 1975. Responding to Poulantzas' analysis in the *Review* in 1976, Erik Olin Wright proposed a more satisfactory solution to the problem of 'class boundaries in advanced capitalist societies', deploying the concept of 'contradictory class

locations' ('Class Boundaries in Advanced Capitalist Societies', *NLR* 98, July/ August 1976, p. 26). Categories based on objective relations to the means of production delivered the classic tripartite division between bourgeoisie, petty-bourgeoisie and proletariat. But, argued Wright, these were not clear-cut, easily identified demarcations. A grey area, or 'contradictory location', existed on the boundaries, determined by more subjective factors. 'The more contradictory is a position within social relations of production, the more political and ideo-logical relations can influence its objective position within class relations. The more a position coincides with the basic antagonistic class relations at the level of social relations of production, the less weight political and ideological forces have in determining its class position' (ibid., p. 40). Thus, for example, the de-gree of unionisation amongst teachers or nurses will affect their allegiance to the working class and socialist politics. The 'ideological' nature of some jobs, such as the police, would tend in the opposite direction. In sum, Wright argued that the strength of the attraction of socialist politics was itself a significant factor in consolidating the unity and purpose of the proletariat, and in win-ning the allegiance of those in contradictory, yet adjacent, class locations, thus retaining the commitment to a policy of political coalition-building within a new hegemonic bloc.

34   'The Strategic Option: Some Questions', in André Liebich, ed., *The Future of Socialism in Europe?*, Interuniversity Centre for European Studies, Montréal, 1978, p. 22.

35   Ibid., p. 25.

36   Robin Blackburn (ed.), *Revolution and Class Struggle: A Reader in Marxist Politics*, Fontana, Glasgow, 1977, p. 19.

37   Ibid.

38   'Communist Party History', in Raphael Samuel, ed., *People's History and Socialist Theory*, Routledge and Kegan Paul, London, 1981, p. 155. On the Portuguese revolution, see Robin Blackburn, 'The Test in Portugal', *NLR* 87-8, September/December 1974, pp. 5-46.

39   Ginsborg, op. cit., p. 372.

40   'On the Twenty Second Congress of the French Communist Party', p. 9.

41   Ibid.

42   Themes, *NLR* 96, March/April 1976, p. 1.

43   Themes', *NLR* 103, May/June 1977, p. 1.

44   'On the Twenty Second Congress of the French Communist Party', p. 9.

45   'The Antinomies of Antonio Gramsci', *NLR* 100, November 1976/January 1977, p. 78. Anderson observed in 1992 that this had been '[w]ritten in the wake of the Portuguese Revolution' as an attempt to 'draw a balance-sheet of the last great strategic debate of the international labour movement, for strug-gles still pending' (*A Zone of Engagement*, Verso, London and New York, 1992, p. xi).

46   This was a view initially shared by Gramsci, who, however, endorsed rather than rejected Lenin's voluntarism, describing October as a 'revolution against *Capital*' (*Selections from Political Writings 1910-1920*, Lawrence and Wishart, London, 1977, pp. 34-7).

47 'Democracy and Dictatorship in Lenin and Kautsky', *NLR* 106, November/December 1977, p. 75.

48 Themes, *NLR* 82, November/December 1973, p. 2. Note Norman Geras' two articles, 'Rosa Luxemburg: Barbarism and the Collapse of Capitalism', *NLR* 82, November/December 1973, pp. 17-37, and 'Rosa Luxemburg after 1905', *NLR* 89, January/February 1975, pp. 3-46, and his *The Legacy of Rosa Luxemburg*, published by New Left Books in 1976.

49 In a famous passage in the *Prison Notebooks* Gramsci had written that '[i]n Russia the state was everything, civil society primordial and gelatinous; in the West, there was a proper relation between state and civil society, and when the state trembled a sturdy structure of civil society was at once revealed' (*Selections from Prison Notebooks*, eds and trans. Quintin Hoare and Geoffrey Nowell-Smith, Lawrence and Wishart, London, 1971, p. 238).

50 'The Antinomies of Antonio Gramsci', p. 27. More 'persistently and coherently' than Lenin, for instance: see *Considerations on Western Marxism*, p. 117.

51 Themes, *NLR* 65, January/February 1971, p. 2. See also Giuseppe Fiori, *Antonio Gramsci: Life of a Revolutionary*, New Left Books, London, 1970.

52 Themes, *NLR* 82, November/December 1973, p. 2.

53 Note the concluding remarks by both Poulantzas and Miliband: For Poulantzas the issue of socialist transformation 'remains open' ('The Problem of the Capitalist State', *NLR* 58, November/December 1969, p. 78); whilst for Miliband it 'raises very large and complex questions' ('The Capitalist State: Reply to Nicos Poulantzas', *NLR* 59, January/February 1970, p. 60).

54 *Considerations on Western Marxism*, p. 103.

55 See Perry Anderson, *Passages from Antiquity to Feudalism* and *Lineages of the Absolute State*, both New Left Books, London, 1974. Anderson concluded that the '*Russian Revolution was not made against a capitalist state at all.* The Tsarism that fell in 1917 was a feudal apparatus: the Provisional Government never had time to replace it with a new or stable bourgeois apparatus. The Bolsheviks made a *socialist revolution*, but from beginning to end they never confronted the *central enemy* of the workers' movement in the West. Gramsci's deepest intuition remained – after the October Revolution – a *new* political object for Marxist theory, and revolutionary practice' (*Lineages*, p. 359). This posed problems 'which have still to be theoretically and practically solved in the second half of the twentieth century' (p. 360). Gregory Elliott describes *Passages* and *Lineages* as 'orphaned volumes', judging that the failure to complete planned volumes on the subsequent bourgeois and socialist revolutions 'possibly constitutes the single most important fact about Anderson's intellectual career to date', 'the "absent centre" of his theoretical-political oeuvre' (*Perry Anderson: The Merciless Laboratory of History*, University of Minnesota Press, Minneapolis and London, 1998, p. 78).

56 In 'Antinomies' Anderson developed themes first advanced in 1968, in which he highlighted the central weakness of Gramsci's perspective in the period 1919-20: the absence of a theory of insurrection against the bourgeois state ('Introduction to Gramsci 1919-20', *NLR* 51, September/October 1968, pp. 22-27).

57   'The Antinomies of Antonio Gramsci', p. 72.

58   Ibid., p. 26.

59   Ibid., p. 27. Anderson cited his own 1965 'Problems of Socialist Strategy' as representative of such illusions (ibid., p. 27 n. 48).

60   Elsewhere in the *Notebooks* Gramsci tended to define 'hegemony' as a combination of coercion and consent, equally distributed between state and civil society. This Anderson swiftly discounted: coercion was the exclusive property of the state; in Weber's classic definition, it enjoyed 'a monopoly of legitimate violence over a given area'. A third interpretation could be read as conflating state and civil society. This, in Anderson's estimate, was an equally inadmissible error, dangerously concealing the very real distinction between fascism and bourgeois democracy – an error that occurred in the thinking of both Althusser and the Frankfurt School. 'The boundaries of the State', he argued, 'are not a matter of indifference to Marxist theory or revolutionary practice' (ibid., p. 36).

61   Ibid., p. 29.

62   Ibid., pp. 29-30.

63   Ibid., p. 55.

64   Ibid., p. 69.

65   Ibid., p. 70.

66   Ibid., p. 78.

67   Ibid.

68   'The Antinomies of Perry Anderson', in *Socialism and Parliamentary Democracy*, Spokesman Press, Nottingham, 1977, p. 132.

69   'The Test in Portugal', p. 41.

70   'Revolutionary Strategy in Europe – A Political Interview', *NLR* 100, November 1976/ January 1977, p. 98.

71   Ibid., pp. 97-8.

72   'The Antinomies of Antonio Gramsci', p. 78.

73   'Document B: Ten Theses', unpublished editorial document, 1968/9, p. 18.

74   'The Strategic Option', p. 28.

75   'Armed Insurrection and Dual Power', *NLR* 66, March/April 1971, p. 68.

76   'The Strategic Option', p.28. Later, in 1999, Blackburn would reflect that the 'vision of ... a workers' democracy virtually neutralising and hence by-passing representative democracy' was the 'central flaw' in Ernest Mandel's strategic thinking ('The Unexpected Dialectic of Structural Reforms', in *The Legacy of Ernest Mandel*, Gilbert Achcar (ed.), Verso, London and New York, 1999, p. 21). By then he preferred to pursue the democratisation of representative institutions in tandem with 'forms of self-administration in civil society' (ibid., p.22).

77   'The State in the Transitional Period', *NLR* 113/114, January/April 1979, p. 117.

78   For a lucid British version of Left Euro-Communism see Hodgson's *Socialism and Parliamentary Democracy*. He insisted that there was no 'Chinese Wall between "bourgeois" and "proletarian" democracy' (p. 12); and proposed what was, in effect, a parliamentary road to socialism reinforced by a popular mobi-

lisation and institutionalisation from below, in a 'mutually reinforcing dialectic' (p. 9).

79   Henri Weber, 'Eurocommunism, Socialism and Democracy', *NLR* 110, July/August 1978, p. 13. The Euro-Communists conception of the transition to socialism 'postulates action without reaction, a working class without a bourgeois class, socialism without capitalists and victory without struggle' (Régis Debray, quoted in ibid., p. 14 n. 18).

80   *Arguments Within English Marxism*, Verso, London, 1980, p. 195.

81   'Towards a Democratic Socialism', *NLR* 109, May/June 1978, p. 87.

82   'Eurocommunism, Socialism and Democracy', p. 5.

83   Ibid., p. 9.

84   Ibid., p. 14.

85   See, for example, Claudin's *Eurocommunism and Socialism*, and Mandel's *From Stalinism to Eurocommunism*, published by New Left Books in quick succession in 1977 and 1978.

86   'NLR 1975-1980', p. 19.

87   'NLR 1975-1980', p. 47. Anderson's unpublished manuscript dates from 1970; 'The Antinomies of Antonio Gramsci' was extracted from it in 1976-77.

88   'The Strategic Option', pp. 27-28.

89   'Italian Communism in the Sixties', *NLR* 66, March/April 1971, p. 50.

90   Ginsborg, op. cit., p. 334

91   'NLR 1975-1980', p. 41.

92   Ibid., pp. 42, 41.

93   Themes, *NLR* 109, May/June 1978, p. 1.

94   Themes, *NLR* 108, March/April 1978, p. 1.

95   A crisis announced by Louis Althusser in a speech in Venice in November 1977 at a conference organised by *Il Manifesto*. The article was reproduced in English as 'The Crisis of Marxism', in *Marxism Today*, July 1978, pp. 215-27. Althusser's denunciation of the leadership of the PCF for its role in the March defeat, 'What Must Change in the Party', was translated in the *Review* in 1978. He wrote that its 'deep-rooted, tenacious and inveterate distrust of the masses' had been especially damaging ('What Must Change in the Party', *NLR* 109, May/June 1978, p. 43). The PCF's calculated manouevering against its Socialist Party allies – an alliance that was itself the result not of a popular mobilisation, but a pact from above – confirmed 'a reflux of rejection when faced by anything not controlled by the apparatus' (ibid., p. 41).

96   Cited in Callaghan, *The Far Left*, p. 128

97   Themes, *NLR* 75, September/October 1972, p. 1.

98   Robin Blackburn, 'The Heath Government: A New Course for British Capitalism', *NLR* 70, November/December 1971, pp. 3-26 and Anthony Barnett, 'Class Struggle and the Heath Government', *NLR* 77, January/February 1973, pp. 3-41.

99   Themes, *NLR* 76, November/December 1972, p. 1.

100 Ibid.

101 *Considerations on Western Marxism*, p. 95.

102 Themes, *NLR* 70, November/December 1971, p.1.

103 Arthur Scargill, 'The New Unionism', *NLR* 92, July/August 1975, pp.3-33.

104 'The Antinomies of Perry Anderson', p. 137.

105 'The New Left and the Present Crisis', *NLR* 121, May/June 1980, p. 70. Similarly, in 1981 Ian Birchall wrote that whilst in the sixties the *Review*, 'whatever its weaknesses, attempted to engage strategically with contemporary events', by the seventies it 'increasingly remained aloof' ('The Autonomy of Theory: A Short History of *New Left Review*', *International Socialism*, no.10, 1980-81, p. 71).

106 'Anderson's Balance Sheet', in Paul Hirst, *Marxism and Historical Writing*, Routledge and Kegan Paul, London, 1985, p. 5. Privately the *NLR* acknowledged the problem (while doing nothing to correct it): 'the lack of any close or binding relationship to political practice has allowed the review to elude responsibility for its own errors, in a way that no periodical linked to an organisational form could do' ('A Decennial Report' p. 78).

107 'The Autonomy of Theory', p. 70. At least privately, the *Review* recognised that this propensity to abandon previous positions 'as though they had never existed' was a serious flaw; acknowledging that '[p]erspectives falsified by events were silently relinquished rather than explicitly disavowed. New positions incompatible with former attitudes would then typically emerge at a later stage without reference to them' ('Decennial Report', unpublished editorial document, 1974, p. 80).

108 'The Silences of *New Left Review*', *Politics and Power 3*, Routledge and Kegan Paul, London, 1981, p. 251.

109 Ibid.

110 'Anderson's Balance Sheet', p. 8.

111 Branka Magaš and Robin Blackburn, 'Comment on Lucien Rey', *NLR* 67, May/June 1971, p. 111.

112 Branka Magaš, 'Women's Liberation', *NLR* May/June 1970, pp. 31-4.

113 Branka Magaš, 'Sex Politics: Class Politics', *NLR* 66, March/April 1971, p. 91.

114 Ibid.

115 Lucien Rey, 'Comment', *NLR* 66, March/April 1971, p. 96.

116 'Communication', Fred and Jon Halliday, Lucien Rey and Gareth Stedman Jones, *NLR* 90, March/April 1975, p. 112. The 1980 editorial report also noted Fred Halliday and Anthony Barnett's criticism of the 'absence of any attention to the recruitment of women to the e[ditorial]/c[ommittee' (*NLR* 1975-80, p. 75).

117 'Comment on Lucien Rey', p. 110.

118 Ibid.

119 Ibid., p. 111.

120 Though note the debate on the question of domestic labour: Wally Seccombe, 'The Housewife and Her Labour under Capitalism', *NLR* 83, January/February 1974, pp. 3-24; Jean Gardiner, 'Women's Domestic Labour', and Margaret Coulson, Branka Magaš and Hilary Wainwright, '"The Housewife and Her Labour under Capitalism": A Critique', *NLR* 89, January/February 1975, pp. 47-58 and 59-71, respectively; a brief 'Communication' from Fred and Jon Halliday, Lucien Rey and Gareth Stedman Jones, *NLR* 90, March/April 1975, p.

112; Wally Seccombe, 'Domestic Labour: Reply to Critics', *NLR* 94, November/December 1975, pp. 85-96; and Maxine Molyneux, 'Beyond The Domestic Labour Debate', *NLR* 116, July/August 1979, pp. 3-27.

121 Themes, *NLR* 55, May/June 1969, p. 1.

122 Liam Baxter, Bernadette Devlin, Michael Farrell, Eamon McCann and Cyril Toman, 'People's Democracy: a Discussion on Strategy', *NLR* 55, May/June 1969, pp. 3-19. See also Peter Gibbon, 'The Dialectic of Religion and Class in Ulster', *NLR* 55, May/June 1969, pp. 20-41 and 'Ireland – Split in Sinn Fein', *NLR* 60, March/April 1970, pp. 49-52; and Alexander Cockburn, 'Introduction to Cathal Goulding', and Cathal Goulding, 'The New Strategy of the IRA', *NLR* 64, November/December 1970, pp. 50-1, pp. 51-61 respectively.

123 'A Decennial Report', p. 61

124 With Ellen Hazelkorn and Henry Patterson's 'The New Politics of the Irish Republic, *NLR* 207, September/October 1994, pp. 49-71.

125 *The Coming British Revolution*, , Jonathan Cape, London, 1972, p. 229.

126 Callaghan, *The Far Left in Britain*, p. 136. When the silence was finally broken, Robin Blackburn, demonstrating a certain scepticism towards IRA-Republicanism, would argue for the need to address 'what might be demanded by joint self-determination for the two main communities' ('Ireland and the *NLR*', *NLR* 212, July/August 1995, p. 155).

127 'British Nationalism and the EEC', *NLR* 69, September/October 1971, p. 8.

128 'The European Problem', *NLR* 75, September/October 1972, pp. 5-120.

129 Themes, *NLR* 75, September/October 1972, p. 2.

130 Ibid.

131 See Andrew Glynn and Bob Sutcliffe, 'The Critical Condition of British Capital', *NLR* 66, March/April 1971, pp. 3-33, and 'Labour and the Economy', *NLR* 76, November/December 1972, pp. 91-6; and David Yaffe, 'The Crisis of Profitability: a Critique of the Glyn-Sutcliffe Thesis', *NLR* 80, July/August, pp. 45-62.

132 'The European Problem', p. 71.

133 Ibid., p. 73.

134 Ibid., p. 118. Note, by way of contrast, Edward Thompson's patriotic fulminations against the Common Market. '[T]he great British middle class thinks "Europe" is about … the belly. A market is about consumption' ('Going into Europe' (*Sunday Times*, 27 April 1975), reprinted in *Writing by Candlelight*, Merlin Press, London, 1981, p. 85). 'This Eurostomach is the logical extension of the existing eating-out habits of Oxford and North London' (ibid., p. 84). Thompson did balance his near-xenophobia with a measured political calculation: 'Some sillies in the labour movement suppose the Market will facilitate socialist and trade-union unity. It will do the opposite. It will put the bourgeoisie twenty years ahead at one throw' (ibid., p. 87). At the heart of Thompson's analysis was a deep-rooted conviction, quite at odds with the perspective of the post-1962 *NLR*, that Britain was ripe for socialism: 'Utterly without self-confidence, hemmed in at every side by the defensive organisations of a humane working class (the "English disease"), the British bourgeoisie prepares, as its last hope of survival, to surrender its identity to the larger

rapacity of the European bourgeoisie. It may not survive itself: but at least it will make sure that Money does ... As British capitalism dies above and about us, one can glimpse, as an outside chance, the possibility that we could effect here a peaceful transition – for the first time in the world – to a democratic socialist society' (ibid., pp. 86-88). If this was indeed so, it was a reasonable estimate that joining the Common Market would serve to weaken such a prospect. The *NLR* held no such expectations. On the contrary, it calculated that a 'corporatist' British labour movement offered an insufficient challenge to the UK state. However, there was no simple division between the first and second New Lefts on this issue: Raymond Williams, for example, was closer to Tom Nairn on the question of Europe and nationalism.

135 *The Break-Up of Britain* (1977), Verso, London, 1981, p. 42 (from 'The Twilight of the British State', originally published in *NLR* 101-2, February/April 1977, pp. 3-61).

136 'The Three Dreams of Scottish Nationalism', *NLR* 49, May/June 1968, p. 4.

137 'Enoch Powell: The New Right', p. 8.

138 *The Break-Up of Britain*, pp. 79-80.

139 Ibid., p. 329 (from 'The Modern Janus', originally published in *NLR* 94, November/December 1975, pp. 3-29).

140 Themes, *NLR* 94, November/December 1975, p. 1.

141 Themes, *NLR* 105, September/October 1977, p. 1.

142 *Considerations on Western Marxism*, p. 115.

143 'Marxists and the National Question', *NLR* 96, March/April 1976, p. 81.

144 'The Modern Janus', pp. 335-36.

145 Ibid., p. 340.

146 Ibid.

147 Ibid., p. 353.

148 Ibid., pp. 347-48.

149 Ibid., p. 359.

150 'The Modern Janus' was a text with which Quintin Hoare and Robin Blackburn 'in particular ... stressed a strong divergence' ('NLR 1975-1980', p. 7).

151 'Some Reflections on "The Break-Up of Britain"', *NLR* 105, September/October 1977, p. 6.

152 Ibid., p. 17.

153 Ibid., p. 11.

154 Ibid., p. 12.

155 Ibid., p. 14. By contrast, Régis Debray argued, in the same issue of the *Review*, that the national dimension was paramount: 'I believe the revolution will never win in France until it recovers the national heritage for its own ends' ('Marxism and the National Question', *NLR* 105, September/October 1977, p. 39).

156 'Some Reflections on "The Break-Up of Britain"', p. 23.

157 'NLR 1975-1980', p. 12.

158 Ibid., p. 13.

159 Ibid.

160 *Arguments Within English Marxism*, pp. 2-3.

161 Donald Sassoon, 'The Silences of *New Left Review*', *Politics and Power 3*, Routledge and Kegan Paul, London, 1981, p. 221.

162 *Arguments Within English Marxism*, p. 128.

163 E. P. Thompson, *The Poverty of Theory and Other Essays* (1978), Merlin Press, London, 1980, p. 374.

164 Ibid., p. 323.

165 Translated and reproduced in *NLR* 109, May/June 1978, pp. 19-45.

166 *Arguments Within English Marxism*, p. 113.

167 Norman Geras, 'Althusser's Marxism: An Account and Assessment', *NLR* 71, January/February 1972, pp. 57-86; André Glucksmann, 'A Ventriloquist Structuralism', *NLR* 72, March/April 1972, pp. 68-92; Pierre Vilar, 'Marxist History, A History in the Making: Towards a Dialogue with Althusser', *NLR* 80, July/August 1973, pp. 65-106; and Valentino Gerratana, 'Althusser and Stalinism', *NLR* 101-2, February/April 1977, pp. 110-21.

168 *The Poverty of Theory*, p. 366. Pointedly, the volume included 'The Peculiarities of the English', the 1965 riposte to the 'Nairn-Anderson theses', with the original cuts restored.

169 Postscript to *William Morris: Romantic to Revolutionary*, Pantheon, New York, 1976, pp. 763-810. The postscript appeared as 'Romanticism, Moralism and Utopianism: The Case of William Morris' in *NLR* 99, September/October 1976, pp. 83-111.

170 *The Poverty of Theory*, p. 265.

171 Ibid., p. 271.

172 Ibid., p. 195.

173 Ibid., p. 376.

174 Ibid., pp. 377, 379.

175 Raphael Samuel, 'Editorial Note', in Samuel, ed., *People's History and Socialist Theory*, Routledge and Kegan Paul, London, 1981, p. 376.

176 'Althusser thinks the relation between Marxist theory and the working class movement as one of exteriority: the former is produced outside the latter, and must be imported into it … Its … effect is to make the relation between Marxist theory and the working class a unilateral and purely pedagogic one: the intellectuals "give" the class the knowledge it needs. This is only the final consequence of every idealism: elitism. When knowledge celebrates its autonomy, the philosophers celebrate their dominance' ('Althusser's Marxism: An Account and Assessment', pp. 83-4).

177 *The British New Left*, Edinburgh University Press, Edinburgh, 1993, p. xvi. Witness the following passage, in which Anderson indicts Western Marxism for fashioning theory divorced from political practice, which reads like something of a self-parody. Its central criticism can be made with equal force of the *Review* itself: 'the extreme difficulty of language characteristic of much of Western Marxism in the twentieth century was never controlled by the tension of a direct or active relationship to a proletarian audience. On the contrary, its very surplus above the necessary minimum quotient of verbal complexity was the sign of its divorce from any popular practice. The peculiar esotericism of Western Marxist theory was to assume manifold forms: in Lukács, a cumber-

some and abstruse diction, freighted with academicism; in Gramsci, a painful and cryptic fragmentation, imposed by prison; in Benjamin, a gnomic brevity and indirection; in Della Volpe, an impenetrable syntax and circular self-reference; in Sartre, a hermetic and unrelenting maze of neologisms; in Althusser, a sybilline rhetoric of elusion.' (*Considerations on Western Marxism* (1976), Verso, London, 1989, p. 54).

178 'A Chronology of the New Left and its Successors, or: Who's Old-Fashioned Now?', *Socialist Register 1995*, Merlin Press, London, 1995, p. 29. Underlining the second New Left's detachment from popular politics, Sheila Rowbotham has written: 'While I was friendly with some of the group around *New Left Review* after 1963, I could not understand how they could be socialists and not bother about being personally remote from working-class people. This made them very different from the initiators of the New Left' ('The Women's Movement and Organising for Socialism', in Sheila Rowbotham, Lynne Segal and Hilary Wainwright, *Beyond the Fragments: Feminism and the Making of Socialism* (1979), Merlin Press, London, 1981, p. 26).

179 *The Poverty of Theory*, p. 383.

180 Michael Rustin, 'The New Left and the Present Crisis', *NLR* 121, May/June 1980, pp. 63-89; Donald Sassoon, 'The Silences of *New Left Review*', *Politics and Power 3*, Routledge and Kegan Paul, London, 1981, pp. 219-254; and Paul Hirst, 'Anderson's Balance Sheet', in Hirst, *Marxism and Historical Writing*, Routledge and Kegan Paul, London, 1985, pp. 1-28.

181 *Arguments Within English Marxism*, p. 103.

182 Ibid., p. 204. 'If there is a "Marxism" of the contemporary world which Marx or Engels would have recognised instantly as an idealism, Althusserian structuralism is this. The category has attained to a primacy over its material referent; the conceptual structure hangs above and dominates social being' (ibid., p. 205).

183 Thompson's notion of class consciousness in *The Making of the English Working Class*, for example, was considered by Anderson to be 'far too voluntarist and subjectivist' (*Arguments Within English Marxism*, p. 40).

184 Ibid., p.58.

185 Ibid.

186 *The Poverty of Theory*, p. 280.

187 Ibid., p. 216.

188 *Arguments Within English Marxism*, pp. 129-30.

189 Ibid., p. 22.

190 '[W]hat marxism might do, for a change, is sit on its own head a little in the interests of socialism's heart. It might close down one counter in its universal pharmacy, and cease dispensing potions of analysis to cure the maladies of desire' (Postscript to *William Morris*, p. 807; 'Romanticism, Moralism and Utopianism: The Case of William Morris', *NLR* 99, September/October 1976, p. 108).

191 *Arguments Within English Marxism*, p. 206.

192 Ibid., p. 135.

193 Ibid.

194 Ibid., p. 120.
195 Ibid., p. 118.
196 See Ernest Mandel, *From Stalinism to Eurocommunism* (1977), New Left Books, London, 1978. Thompson remained by and large implicitly committed to the perspective of the CPGB's 1951 *British Road to Socialism*. With specific reference to Thompson's 1960 essay 'Revolution', Anderson argued that the 'degree of continuity with the main strategic perspectives of the CPGB from the mid-50s onwards is unmistakable' (*Arguments Within English Marxism*, p. 191).
197 *Arguments Within English Marxism*, p. 106. In a direct response to Anderson and co., Thompson wrote: 'the critique which the "second" NLR has offered to the provincialism of the British intellectual Left, and to its complacent anchorage in a particular national heritage, has been altogether healthy and challenging. In many areas it has become possible to opt for co-existence' ('Romanticism, Moralism and Utopianism: The Case of William Morris', p. 110). However, Thompson doubted the 'orthodoxy' 'that the absence of something called a "mature sociology" was disabling in British intellectual traditions. I have never been convinced of this, and would not wish to trade German philosophy and sociology for English poetry and moral criticism' (ibid.).
198 'Those who think that they can deal with our present system in this piece-meal way very much underrate the strength of the tremendous organisation under which we live … Nothing but a tremendous force can deal with this force: it will not suffer itself to be dismembered, nor to lose anything which really is its essence without putting forth all its force in resistance; rather than lose anything which it considers of importance it will pull down the roof of the world upon its head' (William Morris, 'Whigs, Democrats and Socialists' (1886), quoted in *Arguments Within English Marxism*, p. 178).
199 *Arguments Within English Marxism*, p. 178.
200 Ibid., p. 177.
201 Ibid., p. 206.
202 Ibid., p. 156.
203 Ibid., p. 207.
204 'Diary', *London Review of Books*, 21 October 1993, pp. 24-5. However, Thompson's intervention – and the History Workshop debate at Oxford in 1979 in particular – provoked fractures elsewhere in the New Left, principally between Thompson and Stuart Hall's endeavours at the Centre for Contemporary Cultural Studies.

Chapter Four: From Rethinking to Retrenchment

1   'A Decennial Report', unpublished editorial document, 1974, p. 85.
2   'NLR 1975-1980', unpublished editorial document, 1980, p. 33.
3   Ibid., p. 40.
4   *In the Tracks of Historical Materialism*, Verso, London, 1983, p. 32.
5   'NLR 1975-1980', p. 47.

6   *In the Tracks of Historical Materialism* comprised a series of lectures delivered in America the previous year. Significant passages were rehearsed in the editorial report, 'NLR 1975-1980'.
7   *In the Tracks of Historical Materialism*, p. 33.
8   Ibid., p. 35.
9   Ibid., p. 34.
10 Ibid., p. 37.
11 Ibid., p. 38.
12 Ibid., p. 55.
13 Ibid.
14 Ibid., p. 56.
15 'NLR 1975-80', p. 45
16 'NLR 1980-3', unpublished editorial document, 1982, p. 44
17 Ibid.
18 'NLR 1975-1980', p. 42.
19 Ibid., p. 23.
20 Ibid., p. 42.
21 *In the Tracks of Historical Materialism*, p. 76.
22 Ibid.
23 '"Teachers, Writers, Celebrities": Intelligentsias and Their Histories', *NLR* 126, March/April 1981, p. 53, n. 13.
24 Armstrong, Philip, Andrew Glyn and John Harrison, *Capitalism Since World War II: The making and break-up of the long boom*, Fontana, London, 1984, p. 381.
25 'The Rise and Decline of Southern European Socialism', *NLR* 146, July/August 1984, p. 42.
26 Initially the leftist radical-patriotic PASOK movement, which swept to power in Greece in 1981, proved an exception to this rule, but by 1987 James Petras could write that the 'Papandreou government has virtually turned its back on popular sections of its electoral clientele, pursuing pro-big business policies of a consistency and ruthlessness that would be hard to outmatch anywhere in Europe' ('The Contradictions of Greek Socialism', *NLR* 163, May/June 1987, p. 21).
27 Themes, *NLR* 146, July/August 1984, p. 2.
28 *In the Tracks of Historical Materialism*, p. 24.
29 Ibid., p. 67. Anderson acknowledged that the *Review*'s previous dismissal of Habermas had been 'a major error of appreciation' (ibid., p. 59). See also the 'Introduction to Jürgen Habermas', *NLR* 115, May/June 1979, p. 72, and Themes, p. 3, prefacing Jürgen Habermas, 'A Philosophico-Political Profile', *NLR* 151, May/June 1985, pp. 75-105.
30 *Considerations on Western Marxism*, p. 103. Despite serious reservations about Western Marxism, the *Review* could justifiably claim that 'the critical reception and diffusion of the corpus of Western Marxism' which it had sponsored, 'helped to prepare the way for the emergence of a lively and many-sided Anglophone Marxist culture' (Themes, *NLR* 150, March/April 1985, p. 1).
31 'NLR 1975-1980', p. 49.

32   *In the Tracks of Historical Materialism*, p. 25.

33   Ibid., p. 20.

34   Ibid., p. 68.

35   'NLR 1975-1980', p. 51.

36   Themes, *NLR* 123, September/October 1980, p. 1.

37   *In the Tracks of Historical Materialism*, p. 27.

38   Gregory Elliott, 'Olympus Mislaid? A Profile of Perry Anderson', *Radical Philosophy*, no. 71, May/June 1995, p. 14 (adapted from Kate Soper, *Humanism and Anti-Humanism*, Hutchinson, London, 1986, p. 117, n. 79).

39   'NLR 1980-1983', p. 45.

40   Ibid., pp. 52, 53.

41   'A Problem in Defining the Socialist Society', unpublished document, 1981, p. 1.

42   *In the Tracks of Historical Materialism*, p. 68.

43   Ibid.

44   Ibid., p. 80.

45   Ibid. 'If capital could visit such destruction on even so poor and small an outlying province of its empire as Vietnam, to prevent its loss, is it likely that it would suffer its extinction meekly in its own homelands? The lessons of the past sixty-five years or so are in this respect without ambiguity or exception: there is no case ... where the existence of capitalism has been challenged, and the furies of intervention, blockade and civil strife have not descended in response' (ibid., p. 103).

46   *Considerations on Western Marxism*, p. 100.

47   *In the Tracks of Historical Materialism*, p. 79. At least in private, the *NLR* was expressing reservations about Trotskyism as early as 1980. Trotskyism's 'capacity to generate a sustained and creative alternative Marxism' had proved 'disappointingly limited ... Symbolically, Mandel was unable to produce a promised strategic study of *Revolution in Western Europe*, whilst the '"crisis of Marxism"' elicited no counter-statement of memorable force' ('NLR 1975-1980', pp. 47-8).

48   *In the Tracks of Historical Materialism*, p. 79.

49   Ibid., p. 80.

50   *Considerations on Western Marxism*, pp. 100-1.

51   *In the Tracks of Historical Materialism*, p. 79.

52   Ibid., p. 87.

53   Ibid., pp. 86-7.

54   Ibid., p. 105.

55   Ibid., p. 88.

56   'NLR 1975-1980', p. 68. The work of Anthony Giddens, for example, was presented in the *NLR* as 'an appreciative critique by a non-Marxist of the Marxist tradition in social theory': Erik Olin Wright, 'Giddens' Critique of Marxism', *NLR* 138, March/April 1983, p. 11.

57   *In the Tracks of Historical Materialism*, p. 83.

58   Ibid., p. 84.

59   Ibid., p. 83.

60 Ibid., p. 84. In terms of the transition from capitalism to socialism, the issue of ecological sustainability challenged what Cohen called the 'developmental thesis' of historical materialism. A technological-determinist reading of the transition from capitalism to socialism, warranted, for example, by Marx's 1859 *Preface*, had never much found favour with either of the two New Lefts. Even Cohen, in his defence of an 'orthodox' Marx, was moved to write that 'the promise of abundance is not an endless flow of goods, but a sufficiency produced with a minimum of unpleasant exertion' (G. A. Cohen, *Karl Marx's Theory of History: A Defence*, quoted in Andrew Levine and Erik Olin Wright, 'Rationality and Class Struggle', *NLR* 123, September/October 1980, p. 61) – points emphasised by both Ellen Wood and Kate Soper in the pages of the *Review*. Ellen Wood wrote that 'socialism will liberate the creative capacities of humanity from the imperatives of exploitation and specifically from the compulsions of capitalist self-expansion – which is something different from simply continuing capitalist development by permitting an even more "un-conditional" revolutionising of productive forces of the kind that capitalism has set in train' ('Marxism and the Course of History', *NLR* 147, September/ October 1984, p. 106). This was vital, Wood continued, because otherwise a misunderstanding could arise, which 'not only puts in question the liber-ating effects of socialist production but also, among other things, creates a suspicion among people increasingly sensitive to environmental dangers that Marxism, no less than capitalism, is an invitation to ecological disaster' (ibid., p. 106). Kate Soper expressed similar sentiments: 'It is not "putting the clock back" to want to secure a just and reasonably enjoyable future; and to be sure now of any future at all, we need to become less scornful of those evoking the old-fashioned notion of plenitude as the feast of sufficiency' ('A Difference of Needs', *NLR* 152, July/August 1985, p. 117).

61 NLR, Foreword to *Exterminism and Cold War*, Verso, London, 1982, p. viii.

62 Ibid.

63 *In the Tracks of Historical Materialism*, p. 92.

64 Ibid., p. 95.

65 Ibid., p. 94.

66 Ibid., p. 105.

67 Ibid.

68 'NLR 1975-1980', p. 62.

69 Foreword, *Exterminism and Cold War*, p.ix, adding that such agencies and strategies 'will inevitably be more complex than those envisaged by Marx and Engels in their time' (ibid).

70 Ibid.

71 *In the Tracks of Historical Materialism*, p. 99.

72 Ronald Aronson, 'Historical Materialism, Answer to Marxism's Crisis', *NLR* 152, July/August 1985, p. 76.

73 Ibid.

74 Ibid., p. 82.

75 Ibid., p. 84.

76   'NLR 1980-83', p. 53; comparable, in its own estimate, to the relationship of the *Economist* 'to British bourgeois politics', ibid.

77   Ibid., p. 54. Since the late sixties, between a half and two-thirds of the *Review*'s readers have been overseas, with a particular concentration in North America, northern Europe, Australia and Japan ('Notes for Meeting 21/1/84', unpublished editorial document, p. 3).

78   'NLR 1975-1980', pp. 54-5.

79   Ibid., p. 54.

80   Ibid., p. 56.

81   Ibid., p. 57.

82   Stuart Hall, 'Nicos Poulantzas: State, Power, Socialism', *NLR* 119, January/February 1980, pp.60-9; Raymond Williams, 'Beyond Actually Existing Socialism' and Raphael Samuel, 'British Marxist Historians, 1880-1980: Part One', both in *NLR* 120, March/April, pp. 3-19 and pp. 21-96, respectively; Edward Thompson, 'Notes on Exterminism, the Last Stage of Civilisation', and Michael Rustin, 'The New Left and the Present Crisis', both in *NLR* 121, May/June 1980, pp. 3-31 and pp. 63-89, respectively; and Raymond Williams again, 'The Politics of Nuclear Disarmament', *NLR* 124, November/December 1980, pp. 25-42.

83   A controversy sparked by Terry Eagleton's critique of Williams in 1976, and Williams's own piece, 'Notes on British Marxism Since the War' in *NLR* 100, led directly to *Politics and Letters*, published by New Left Books in 1979, and the conscious policy of 'reanchorage' ('NLR 1975-1980', p. 16). Reflecting on the divergent careers of the two New Lefts, Mike Rustin acknowledged that there had been 'indispensable contributions in recent years even from tendencies with whose overall political direction I have strongly disagreed ... What are now required', he wrote – much in the spirit of Anderson's call to Thompson to 'explore new problems together' – 'are new initiatives, drawing on the whole of our political experience' ('The New Left and the Present Crisis', *NLR* 121, May/June 1980, pp. 63-4).

84   'Iron Britannia', *NLR* 134, July/August 1982, p. 51.

85   Themes, *NLR* 129, September/October 1981, p. 1.

86   Donald Sassoon, *One Hundred Years of Socialism: The West European Left in the Twentieth Century*, I.B.Tauris, London, 1996, p. 696.

87   'NLR 1980-1983', p. 18. In this the *Review* proved 'consistent with its own past, in which it had always sought to establish critical contact or support for whatever force appeared to threaten the status quo most immediately in national politics' – namely Wilsonism, trade unions, students, Scots and Welsh nationalism, and European integration (ibid).

88   Ibid., p. 12.

89   Perry Anderson, 'A Problem in Defining the Socialist Society', unpublished document, p.1. Thus garning a membership that included Tony Benn and the Labour Left.

90   'NLR 1980-1983', p. 12. Blackburn's reservations were expressed in 'Notes on the English Political Crisis', unpublished document, no date (but 1981), p. 2.

91   'Labourism and the Transition to Socialism', *NLR* 129, September/October 1981, pp. 3-22.

92   'On the Political Economy of the Socialist Transformation', *NLR* 133, May/June 1982, pp. 52-66.

93   David Coates, 'Space and Agency in the Transition to Socialism', *NLR* 135, September/October 1982, p. 52. See also Leo Panitch, 'Trade Unions and the Capitalist State', *NLR* 125, January/February 1981, pp. 21-43; Francis Cripps, 'The Britsh Crisis – Can the Left Win?'; and Geoff Hodgson, 'Communication', *NLR* 128, July/August 1981, pp. 93-7, 97, respectively.

94   Themes, *NLR* 122, July/August 1980, p. 1

95   Adam Przeworski, 'Social Democracy as a Historical Phenomenon', *NLR* 122, July/August 1980, p. 56.

96   Leo Panitch and Colin Leys, *The End of Parliamentary Socialism: From New Left to New Labour*, Verso, London and New York, 1997, p. 207.

97   'The advances of the left within the Labour Party', wrote Blackburn, 'and the encouraging results of the local elections of May 1981 might be thought to represent a reversal of the trends that culminated in the debacle of the last Labour government' (in Eric Hobsbawm et al., *The Forward March of Labour Halted?*, Verso/*Marxism Today*, London, 1981, p. 159).

98   Tariq Ali and Quintin Hoare, 'Socialists and the Crisis of Labourism', *NLR* 132, March/April 1982, p. 78. This failure to construct a revolutionary party accounts for the revision of Ali's 1972 assessment that '[t]he destruction of the Labour Party by the revolutionary left is an event which the revolutionary movement has long been waiting for and which will be greeted with much re-joicing' (*The Coming British Revolution*, Jonathan Cape, London, 1972, p. 73).

99   Ibid., p. 81.

100 Ibid., p. 61.

101 *Parliament, People and Power*, Verso, London, 1982, p. 35.

102 Ibid.

103 Ibid., pp. 124, 123.

104 'Labourism and the Transition to Socialism', *NLR* 129, September/October 1981, p. 16.

105 Anderson's advocacy of proportional representation was based not on liberal-democratic grounds, but on its precedent in the party-list system of early Soviet elections: Letter (unpublished) to *NLR*, 5 October 1983, p. 3. The *Review* judged that the Labour Left seek an 'Alternative Political Strategy' to match its 'Alternative Economic Strategy' ('NLR 1980-1983', p. 41).

106 'NLR 1980-1983', p. 41.

107 Panitch and Leys, op. cit., p. 163.

108 Themes, *NLR* 133, May/June 1982, p. 3.

109 'NLR 1980-1983', p. 20.

110 'Iron Britannia', p. 72.

111 Ibid., p. 51.

112 Ibid., p. 54.

113 Ibid., pp. 7-8.

114 Ibid., p. 54.

115 Ibid., p. 55.

116 Ibid.

117 Ibid., p. 8.

118 Panitch and Leys, op. cit., p. 207.

119 Themes, *NLR* 134, July/August 1982, p. 1. In contrast, for example, to *Marxism Today*, which had raised the spectre of Thatcherism since before the 1979 election, the *Review*'s interest in the subject was initially remarkably slight. It was not until 1984 that the *Review* carried its first substantive analysis of 'Thatcherism'. Whereas Hall and Jacques argued that Thatcherism had 'altered the whole post-war balance of social forces' (*The Politics of Thatcherism*, Lawrence and Wishart/*Marxism Today*, London, 1983, p. 12), Jessop et al. countered that it had 'neither produced a new, national-popular consensus nor created a new, organic power bloc' (Bob Jessop, Kevin Bonnett, Simon Bromley and Tom Ling, 'Authoritarian Populism, Two Nations and Thatcherism', *NLR* 147, September/October 1984, p. 41). It should be seen 'less as a monolithic monstrosity and more as an alliance of disparate forces around a self-contradictory programme' (ibid., p. 38). They concluded that Hall's presentation of Thatcherism misrecognised the 'fluidity of the current situation', ignored the 'opportunities thereby created', and therefore produced 'inadequate strategic recommendations' (ibid., p. 59). The Left should not, they argued, bemoan the passing of the post-war Keynesian consensus of the political centre-ground, nor popular discontent with certain aspects of the workings (but not the general principles) of the welfare state: it should present a radical alternative of its own.

120 'NLR 1980-1983', p. 48.

121 Ibid., p. 50.

122 Ibid., p. 45.

123 'Such is the thinness of the Labour Party's political culture', wrote Rustin in 1989, 'that *Marxism Today* has ... become more or less the theoretical organ of Labour revisionism too' ('The Politics of Post-Fordism: or, The Trouble with "New Times"', *NLR* 175, May/June 1989, p. 56).

124 'NLR 1980-1983', p. 17.

125 Ibid., p. 45.

126 Ibid., p. 46. Citing texts by Jacques, Rowthorn, Hobsbawm, Aaronovitch, Bloomfield, Devine, Lane and others, Anderson wrote that the Communist Party had been instrumental in promoting revisionist perspectives ('Notes on the Current Outlook', unpublished document, April 1985, p. 2).

127 Notes on the Current Outlook', unpublished document, April 1985, p. 6.

128 'NLR 1980-1983', p. 12. See also Nairn's critique of Hobsbawm's advocacy of Labour's 'broad church', 'The Crisis of the British State', *NLR* 130, November/December 1981, pp. 37-44.

129 Hobsbawm, *The Forward March of Labour Halted?*, p. 173.

130 Ibid.

131 'Some way of uniting the majority of the British people which is opposed to Thatcherism must be found': 'Labour's Lost Millions', *Marxism Today*, October

1983 (reprinted in *Politics for a Rational Left*, Verso/*Marxism Today*, London and New York, 1989, p. 67).

132 'NLR 1980-3', p. 47. During the early nineteen-forties, Earl Browder had advocated disbanding the Communist Party of the United States in favour of joining the broad church of the New Deal Democratic Party.

133 'NLR 1975-80', p. 83

134 Ibid., pp. 90-92.

135 Letter to Robin Blackburn, 4 August 1983; and Letter to *NLR*, 5 October 1983.

136 'NLR 1980-1983', p. 55.

137 Themes, *NLR* 142, November/December 1983, p. 4.

138 'NLR 1980-83', p. 57

139 In all, Davis contributed nine substantive essays on the history and politics of the USA between 1980 and 1988, the most important of which were collected as *Prisoners of the American Dream* by Verso in 1986, constituting something akin to an American equivalent of the Nairn-Anderson thesis. In the three years covered by the 1982 editorial report, articles emanating from North America accounted for over a quarter of the *Review*'s total output (a substantial increase from a previous norm of around 6 per cent): 'NLR 1980-1983', Appendix 5. *The Year Left*, an annual publication covering the politics of the American Left, was first published by Verso in 1986 (see Paul Buhle's review of its first three years, 'Between Bad Times and Better', *NLR* 175, May/June 1989, pp. 95-110); whilst the parallel 'Haymarket Series' – commemorating the centenary of the martyrs of the first American May Day – was launched under the general editorship of Michael Sprinker and Mike Davis.

140 Quintin Hoare and Branka Magaš though by now largely 'passive', remained on board: *NLR* 1980-83, p. 55.

141 Tariq Ali, 'Labourism and the Pink Professors', in Ali and Ken Livingstone, *Who's Afraid of Margaret Thatcher?*, Verso, London, 1984, p. 2.

142 'NLR 1980-1983', pp. 51, 52.

143 Themes, *NLR* 140, July/August 1983, p. 1.

144 Raymond Williams, 'Problems of the Coming Period', pp. 7-18; Jenny Taylor, 'Canvassing for Socialism', pp.19-22; Ken Livingstone, 'Why Labour Lost', interview with Tariq Ali, pp. 23-39; and Eric Heffer, 'Socialists and the Labour Party', pp. 40-9, all in *NLR* 140, July/August 1983.

145 Cited – alongside the Italian PdUP, of a more directly '68 vintage – by the *NLR* interviewers in Benn, *Parliament, People and Power*, p. 123. Jesse Jackson's 'Rainbow Coalition' in the 1984 primaries was another prospective model: see Manning Marable, 'Jackson and the Rise of the Rainbow Coalition', *NLR* 149, January/February 1985, pp. 3-44.

146 'NLR 1975-1980', p. 66.

147 *In the Tracks of Historical Materialism*, p. 90.

148 Ibid.

149 Ibid., p. 91.

150 Ibid., p. 92.

151 *NLR* 'Charter', no date (but 1983), p. 10.

152 Cathy Porter, Lynne Segal, Barbara Taylor and Hilary Wainwright, (unpublished) letter to NLR, 6 February 1984. Mulhern's was an isolated voice arguing for acceptance of the women's demands ('NLR's Charter: Socialism and Feminism', unpublished document, no date, 1984).

153 Kate Soper, who had also been invited onto the editorial committee, was critical of the manner in which the demands were tabled (letter (unpublished) to the *NLR*, 20 February 1984). Nonetheless, she too felt unable to join the editorial committee.

154 Angela Weir and Elisabeth Wilson, 'The British Women's Movement', *NLR* 148, November/December 1984, pp. 74-103. Note also Johanna Brenner and Maria Ramas, 'Rethinking Women's Oppression', *NLR* 144, March/April 1984, pp. 33-71, a critique of Michèle Barrett's *Women's Oppression Today* (published by Verso in 1980); and Michèle Barrett's responses, 'Rethinking Women's Oppression: a Reply to Brenner and Ramas', *NLR* 146, July/August 1984, pp. 123-8; and 'Weir and Wilson on Feminist Politics', *NLR* 150, March/April 1985, pp. 143-7.

155 It covered the diverse experience of women in Cambodia, Britain, Spain, India, West Germany, Greece, the Arab countries, Ireland, Japan, Bangladesh, Brazil, France, the Soviet Union and Norway. There is no doubting either the breadth of this survey, or the greater coverage of feminist issues in the *Review* in the eighties. However, it was largely descriptive in character, and offered little by way of a reformulation of socialist politics. 'Even today', wrote Frigga Haug in 1986, feminism 'remains … unclear how far the oppression of women is crucial to this society's survival and, conversely, whether women's liberation would necessarily revolutionise the structure of society as a whole – and how that can be done' ('The Women's Movement in West Germany', *NLR* 155, January/February 1986, p. 74).

156 Themes, *NLR* 150, March/April 1985, p. 1.

157 Ibid.

158 Ibid.

159 Perry Anderson, Fölker Fröbel, Jürgen Heinrichs, Otto Kreye, 'On Some Postulates of an Anti-Systemic Policy in Western Europe', Starnberg Institute for the Study of Global Structures, Developments and Crises, 1984, pp. 17, 18.

160 Ibid., p. 18.

161 Themes, *NLR* 153, September/October 1985, p. 2. (Lee Pitcairn had been the pseudonym adopted by the Communist journalist Claud Cockburn in the thirties.)

162 'Crisis in British Communism: an Insider's View', *NLR* 153, September/October 1985, pp. 102-20.

163 'Crisis in British Communism', p. 109.

164 'The Lost World of British Communism', *NLR* 154, November/December 1985, pp. 3-53, 'Staying Power: The Lost World of British Communism, Part Two', *NLR* 156, March/April 1986, pp. 63-113, 'Class Politics: The Lost World of British Communism, Part Three', *NLR* 165, September/October 1987, pp. 52-91.

165 'The Lost World of British Communism', pp. 22, 25.

166 'Class Politics: The Lost World of British Communism, Part Three', pp. 76, 83.

167 Ibid., pp. 90-1.

168 'NLR 1980-1983', p. 46.

169 In prefacing Werner Hülsberg's 1985 essay, 'The Greens at the Crossroads', the *NLR* warily noted that in 'Britain, the rhetoric of "new social movements" often screens older forms of accommodation to the established order' (Themes, *NLR* 152, July/August 1985, p. 1). It did, however, recognise that in West Germany the 'Greens, who embody the genuine substance of such movements, have shown a more decisive spirit' (ibid.).

170 'The Prospects of Labour and the Transformation of Advanced Capitalism', *NLR* 145, May/June 1984, p. 5. A first draft of Therborn's text received a 'detailed critique' from Anderson (ibid., p. 6, footnote).

171 Ibid., p. 37.

172 *On Materialism*, Verso, London, 1980, p. 261.

173 Themes, *NLR* 150, March/April 1985, p. 2.

174 Michael Newman, *Ralph Miliband and the Politics of the New Left*, Merlin Press, London, 2002, pp. 278-9. Note also Miliband's *Socialist Register 1983* article, 'Socialist Advance in Britain', pp. 103-20.

175 'The New Revisionism in Britain', *NLR* 150, March/April 1985, p. 6.

176 Ibid., p. 9.

177 Ibid., p. 13.

178 'Towards 2000, or News From You-Know-Where', *NLR* 148, November/December 1984, p. 22.

179 Ellen Wood, *The Retreat From Class*, Verso, London, 1986, p. 47 (quoted in Norman Geras, 'Post-Marxism?', *NLR* 163, May/June 1987, p. 43).

180 Norman Geras, 'Post-Marxism?', *NLR* 163, May/June 1987, pp. 40-82, and 'Ex-Marxism Without Substance: Being a Real Reply to Laclau and Mouffe', *NLR* 169, May/June 1989, pp. 34-61; Ernest Mandel, 'In Defence of Socialist Planning', *NLR* 159, September/October 1986, pp. 5-37, and 'The Myth of Market Socialism', *NLR* 169, May/June 1988, pp. 108-20; and Ellen Wood, *The Retreat From Class: A New 'True' Socialism*, Verso, London, 1986.

181 Themes, *NLR* 163, May/June 1987, pp. 1-2.

182 Ibid., p. 2.

183 'NLR Perspectives', unpublished document, 1985, p. 2. In a rejectionist vein, see also Gregory Elliott, 'The Odyssey of Paul Hirst', *NLR* 159, September/October 1986, pp. 81-105.

184 Themes, *NLR* 157, May/June 1986, p. 2.

185 Perry Anderson, 'Notes on the Current Outlook', unpublished document, 1985, p. 4.

186 'Restructuring the State', *NLR* 158, July/August 1986, pp. 52, 53. Proportional representation was also proposed by contributors to the *Review* as varied as Hilary Wainwright ('The Limits of Labourism: 1987 and Beyond', *NLR* 164, July/August 1987, pp. 34-50, here p. 49) and Arthur Scargill ('Proportional Representation: A Socialist Concept', *NLR* 158, July/August 1986, pp. 76-80).

187 'Lessons of the London Industrial Strategy', *NLR* 155, January/February 1986, p. 75. See also John Palmer, 'Municipal Enterprise and Popular Planning', *NLR* 159, September/October 1986, pp. 117-24.

188 Themes, *NLR* 155, January/February 1986, p. 2.

189 Ibid.

190 'The New Left as a Social Movement', in Robin Archer et al., eds, *Out of Apathy*, Verso, London, 1989, p. 128

191 'Notes on the Current Outlook', p. 2.

192 Themes, *NLR* 155, January/February 1986, p. 2.

193 Newman, op. cit., p. 300. Others took part from the Socialist Society, notably Hilary Wainwright and John Palmer; and there were contributions from such as Andrew Glyn, Laurence Harris, and Robin Murray at a session on economics.

194 Leading to the Chesterfield Conferences, the first in October 1987, and the launch of the Socialist Movement.

195 'A Strategy for Labour: Four Documents', *NLR* 158, July/August 1986, pp. 60-75. Note also Andrew Glyn (author of the Campaign Group sponsored *One Million Jobs a Year*), 'Capital Flight and Exchange Controls', *NLR* 155, January/February 1986, pp. 37-49. Glyn's proposals – 'implying … a break with the logic of capitalism' – were well received by the *Review* (Themes, *NLR* 155, January/February 1986, p. 2).

196 Themes, *NLR* 164, July/August 1987, p. 2.

197 Themes, *NLR* 165, September/October 1987, p. 1.

198 'The Light of Europe'(1991), in *English Questions*, Verso, London and New York, 1992, p. 318.

199 Themes, *NLR* 171, September/October 1988, p. 1.

200 In a series of essays beginning in 1984, and collected and published by Verso a decade later: *Mapping the West European Left*, Verso, London, 1994.

201 The sole exception was Werner Hülsberg's examination of the West German Green Party, though this was not included in the *Mapping the West European Left* collection: 'The Greens at the Crossroads', *NLR* 152, July/August 1985, pp. 5-29.

Chapter Five: The End of History

1   'Notes on Exterminism, The Last Stage of Civilisation', *NLR* 121, May/June 1980, p. 6.

2   Ibid.

3   Ibid., p. 29. Thompson's perspective bore affinities with that of Rudolf Bahro, former dissident in the GDR and by the time of the Second Cold War a leading figure in the West German Green Party. 'The fracture dividing the world … into two systems', he wrote, 'no longer represents any kind of positive perspective, … it no longer shows any trace of a boundary between revolution and counter-revolution, socialism and anti-socialism, world proletariat and world bourgeoisie' ('A New Approach for the Peace Movement in Germany', in *NLR*, ed., *Exterminism and Cold War*, Verso, London, 1982, p. 93).

4   'Notes on Exterminism', p. 3.
5   Ibid., p. 27.
6   Ibid., p. 31.
7   *NLR*, Foreword to *Exterminism and Cold War*, p. ix.
8   'Nuclear Imperialism and Extended Deterrence', in *Exterminism and Cold War*, p. 35.
9   *Arguments Within English Marxism*, Verso, London, 1980, p. 148.
10 'NLR 1980-1983', unpublished document, 1982, p. 23.
11 Ibid., p. 24.
12 Ibid.
13 Foreword to *Exterminism and Cold War*, p. ix.
14 Themes, *NLR* 121, May/June 1980, pp. 1-2.
15 Thompson, 'Notes on Exterminism', p. 10.
16 'The Peace Movement and Socialism', *NLR* 145, May/June 1984, p. 106.
17 Peter Sedgwick, *ULR* 7, Autumn 1959, quoted in Thompson, 'Notes on Exterminism', p. 4.
18 Themes, *NLR* 130, November/December 1981, p. 1.
19 Halliday notes that both his essay and subsequent book 'drew heavily on the ideas and advice of the NLR editorial board members' (Preface, unnumbered page, *The Making of the Second Cold War*, Verso, London, 1983).
20 'Nuclear Imperialism and Extended Deterrence', p. 44.
21 Thompson, 'Europe, the Weak Link in the Cold War', in *Exterminism and Cold War*, p. 342. 'I distrust … those', wrote Thompson, 'who (after Cambodia, after Solidarity and Polish martial law) are satisfied with the old categories and who offer to explain overmuch' (ibid., p. 348).
22 'The Sources of the New Cold War', in *Exterminism and Cold War*. pp. 291-2.
23 It was only in 1957 that the Soviet Union could, with its newly developed missile systems, target America at all; and not until the sixties that Soviet delivery systems were in any way comparable to those of the United States.
24 *The Making of the Second Cold War* (1983), second edition, Verso, London, 1986, p. 71.
25 Ibid., pp. 56-7.
26 Ibid., p. 92.
27 Ibid., p. 63.
28 Ibid., p. 45.
29 'The Origins of the Second Cold War', *NLR* 147, September/October 1984, pp. 73-4.
30 'The Conjuncture of the Seventies and After: A Reply to Ougaard', *NLR* 147, September/October 1984, pp. 76-83.
31 Themes, *NLR* 147, September/October 1984, p. 2.
32 Themes, *NLR* 117, September/October 1979, p. 1.
33 'NLR 1975-1980', unpublished document, 1980, p. 33.
34 Themes, *NLR* 135, September/October 1982, p. 1.
35 'NLR 1975-1980', p. 39.
36 'The Sources of the New Cold War', pp. 327, 322.

37 'The Politics of Nuclear Disarmament', *NLR* 124, November/December 1980, p. 42. The point was reiterated and quoted in both Themes, *NLR* 131, January/February 1982, p. 1, and Perry Anderson, *In the Tracks of Historical Materialism*, Verso, London, 1983, p. 96.

38 'The Threat of War and the Struggle for Socialism', *NLR* 141, September/October 1983, p. 49. Opposition to war, wrote Lucio Magri, was too limited a goal: 'Two thirds of humanity lives on the edge of physical starvation and social brutalisation, in the first instance because gigantic planetary resources are absorbed by military spending and the largest part of scientific research is devoted to means of death rather than life ... What kind of peace is it ... that condemns millions of people to death by hunger every year?' ('The Peace Movement and European Socialism', *NLR* 131, January/February 1982, p. 11).

39 Themes, *NLR* 130, November/December 1981, p. 1. There was also a far from inconsiderable peace movement in the United States itself, charted in the *Review* in Alexander Cockburn and James Ridgway, 'The Freeze Movement versus Reagan', *NLR* 137, January/February 1983, pp. 5-21.

40 NLR, Foreword to *Exterminism and Cold War*, p. vii.

41 Themes, *NLR* 117, September/October 1979, p. 1. The distinguished non-Marxist historian E. H. Carr, interviewed in the *Review* upon completion of his *History of Soviet Russia*, was moved to protest against the anti-Sovietism of the 'human rights' campaigns: 'An outburst of national hysteria on this scale is surely the symptom of a sick society ... I am sorry that so much of the Left has been engulfed in the flood' ('The Russian Revolution and the West', *NLR* 111, September/October 1978, p. 31).

42 China's foreign policy, wrote the *Review* in 1980, was characterised by 'its un-hinged anti-Sovietism; its crude alignment with the far right of imperialism; its cynical alliance with Pol Pot; and its disgraceful invasion of Vietnam' (*NLR* 122, July/August 1980, p. 2).

43 Gregory Elliott, *The Merciless Laboratory of History: Aspects of Perry Anderson*, forthcoming 1998, manuscript, p. 209.

44 Themes, *NLR* 117, September/October 1979, p. 1; see Zhores Medvedev, 'Russia under Brezhnev', *NLR* 117, September/October 1979, pp. 3-29. For an equally sobering account, see Alec Nove, 'The Soviet Economy: Problems and Prospects', *NLR* 119, January/February 1980, pp. 3-19. Whereas Medvedev highlighted the social and legal improvements in the lot of the Soviet people in the seventies, Nove warned of the increasing inefficiencies evident in the 'command economy'.

45 Themes, *NLR* 108, March/April 1978, p. 1.

46 Themes, *NLR* 110, July/August 1978, p. 1.

47 Themes, *NLR* 112, November/December 1978, p. 1.

48 Ibid.

49 'Revolution in Afghanistan', *NLR* 112, November/December 1978, p. 5.

50 Themes, *NLR* 119, January/February 1980, p. 1.

51 'The Afghan Crisis', *NLR* 121, May/June 1980, pp. 91-6.

52 'War and Revolution in Afghanistan', *NLR* 119, January/February 1980, p. 38.

53 Ibid., p. 41.

54   Ibid.
55   'The Sources of the New Cold War', p. 311.
56   *Considerations on Western Marxism*, New Left Books, London, 1976, p. 100.
57   'NLR 1975-1980', p. 23. The guilty 'evidence' comprised 'a maladroit Themes'
     (ibid.), quoted above, which had argued that 'a central factor' in the recent
     'rightward shift at the ideological level' was 'the cumulative evidence of the
     repressive and reactionary character of regimes which proclaim themselves to
     be socialist' (Themes, *NLR* 108, March/April 1978, p. 1).
58   Moreover, Gregory Elliott argues that parallels may be drawn between Sartre's
     alignment with the PCF in the fifties, and Anderson's with the USSR in the
     eighties, substituting, 'amid the global class struggle of the second Cold War',
     the Soviet Union 'as locum tenens' for both absent *party* and *class* (*Perry
     Anderson: The Merciless Laboratory of History*, University of Minnesota Press,
     Minneapolis and London, 1998, p. 30).
59   'Trotsky's Interpretation of Stalinism', *NLR* 139, May/June 1983, p. 49. The pa-
     per was delivered as a lecture in Paris the previous year.
60   Ibid., p. 51.
61   Ibid., p. 56.
62   Ibid.
63   Ibid., p. 57.
64   'Charter', unpublished draft, no date (1983), p. 5.
65   Themes, *NLR* 127, May/June 1981, p. 2.
66   'The North Korean Enigma', *NLR* 127, May/June 1981, p. 51. Jon Halliday ar-
     gued that a genuinely popular socialist revolution had been carried forward
     in 1945-6, and that the foundations of Kim Il-Sung's unrivalled personality
     cult were a consequence of the traumatised state of the country following the
     devastating war of 1950-3.
67   'Charter', p. 5.
68   'Polish Document – Presentation', *NLR* 72, March/April 1972, p. 32.
69   'NLR 1980-1983', p. 31.
70   Themes, *NLR* 139, May/June 1983, p. 2.
71   'NLR 1980-1983', p. 32.
72   Themes, *NLR* 125, January/February 1981, p. 2.
73   'NLR 1980-1983', pp. 31-2.
74   Daniel Singer, *The Road to Gdansk: Poland and the USSR*, Monthly *Review*
     Press, New York, 1982, p. 256.
75   'The Polish Vortex: Solidarity and Socialism', *NLR* 139, May/June 1983, p. 6.
76   Themes, *NLR* 139, May/June 1983, p. 1.
77   Ibid.
78   'Trotsky's Interpretation of Stalinism', p. 57.
79   Ibid.
80   'Capitalism and Socialism in East Asia', *NLR* 124, November/December 1980,
     p. 20.
81   'NLR 1975-1980', p. 24.
82   Ibid., p. 71.
83   Ibid.

84 'Innovation and Conservatism in the New Soviet Leadership', *NLR* 157, May/June 1986, p. 15.

85 Brezhnev's 'historic compromise' was characterised by Kagarlitsky thus: 'The rulers guarantee the masses a certain degree of social stability while the masses, in return, are obliged to give up the struggle for their rights. The rulers guarantee that there will be no return to Stalinism, but do not carry out any further liberalisation. The slogan of the era is "neither reaction nor reform". Its ideal is stability, understood as meaning immobility' (*The Thinking Reed: Intellectuals and the Soviet State, 1917 to the Present*, Verso, London and New York, 1988, p. 211).

86 'Soviet Power Today', *NLR* 179, January/February 1990, pp. 65-80.

87 Themes, *NLR* 164, July/August 1987, p. 1.

88 Ibid., p. 2.

89 Theodore Friedgut and Lewis Sigelbaum, 'Perestroika from Below: The Soviet Miners' Strike and its Aftermath', *NLR* 181, May/June 1990, pp. 5-32.

90 'The Importance of Being Marxist', *NLR* 178, November/December 1989, p. 33.

91 'Yuri Afanasyev on the 19th Conference of the CPSU' (interview), *NLR* 171, September/October 1988, p. 86.

92 Themes, *NLR* 175, May/June 1989, p. 1.

93 Ali revealingly affirmed: 'My own political formation has been greatly influenced by the writings of Isaac Deutscher, Leon Trotsky and Ernest Mandel (in that order)' (*Revolution From Above*, Hutchinson Radius, London, 1988, p.ix). Although publicly reticent, Anderson wrote with a guarded optimism as to the prospects of a 'liberal socialism' in the USSR in a letter (unpublished) to Norberto Bobbio, 12 December 1988, p. 3.

94 'August in Moscow', *London Review of Books*, 26 September 1991, p. 6.

95 Themes, *NLR* 177, September/October 1989, p. 1.

96 'The Upturned Utopia', *NLR* 177, September/October 1989, p. 37.

97 Themes, *NLR* 174, March/April 1989, p. 1.

98 Ibid.

99 Themes, *NLR* 178, November/December 1989, p. 2.

100 Themes, *NLR* 182, July/August 1990, p. 1.

101 Ibid., p. 2.

102 'What Does Socialism Mean Today? The Rectifying Revolution and the Need for New Thinking on the Left', *NLR* 183, September/October 1990, p.4. Thus, 'a peculiar characteristic of this revolution' was 'its total lack of ideas that are either innovative or oriented towards the future' (ibid., p. 7).

103 Themes, *NLR* 178, November/December 1989, p. 2. In its previous issue the *Review* had denounced the suppression of the democracy movement in China, arguing that democratisation offered a 'social learning process which can alone offer a hope of advance towards genuine democracy and socialism' (Themes, *NLR* 177, September/October 1989, p. 1).

104 Writing in the *Review* in 1992, Branka Magaš pinned the chief blame for the break-up of the Yugoslav federation on the aggressive nationalism of the leadership of the Serb Republic, first evidenced in the suspension of Tito's 1974

constitution and the suppression of autonomy in Kosovo in 1989. Of the Milošević regime in Belgrade, she wrote that it was 'a racially based, proto-fascist formation that can survive only by creating new sources of war and conflict' ('The Destruction of Bosnia-Hercegovina', *NLR* 196, November/December 1992, p. 110).

105 Themes, *NLR* 182, July/August 1990, p. 1.
106 'Fin de Siècle: Socialism after the Crash', *NLR* 185, January/February 1991, p. 5.
107 'After Exterminism', *NLR* 168, March/April 1988, p. 67. Anderson doubted that the peace movement had contributed significantly to the ending of the Cold War: 'Between the ideals of END and the realities of Soviet breakdown was a large gap. It is not a belittlement of the advocates of the end of the Cold War to distinguish them from its agents. The First World War was not terminated by the Zimmerwald Left or the Stockholm Appeal, but by the victory of the Entente. We do not honour them the less for that' ('Diary', *London Review of Books*, 21 October 1993, p. 25).
108 For the exchange between Halliday and Thompson, see Fred Halliday, 'The Ends of the Cold War', *NLR* 180, March/April 1990, pp. 5-23; Edward Thompson, 'The Ends of the Cold War', and Fred Halliday, 'A Reply to Edward Thompson', *NLR* 182, July/August 1990, pp. 139-46, 147-50 respectively. See also Mary Kaldor, 'After the Cold War', *NLR* 180, March/April 1990, pp. 25-37.
109 'Western Economic Diplomacy and the New Eastern Europe', *NLR* 182, July/August 1990, p. 81.
110 Ibid., p. 76.
111 Ibid., p. 77.
112 Ibid.
113 'The Ends of the Cold War', p. 14.
114 Themes, *NLR* 179, January/February 1990, p. 1.
115 *Ibid.*, p. 2.
116 Themes, *NLR* 185, January/February 1991, p. 3.
117 Themes, *NLR* 189, September/October 1991, p. 1.
118 'Gorbachev's Socialism in Historical Perspective', *NLR* 179, January/February 1990, p. 23.
119 'NLR 1975-1980', p. 70.
120 Ibid.
121 'The Future of a Disillusion', *NLR* 190, November/December 1991, p. 10.
122 'Politics after the Coup', *NLR* 189, September/October 1991, pp. 91-109.
123 Themes, *NLR* 189, September/October 1991, p. 1.
124 Ibid.
125 'Radical as Reality', in *After The Fall*, p. 167. 'It is perhaps only today, in a context of mounting contradictions in Eastern Europe', wrote the *Review* in 1989, 'that we can fully appreciate the severity of the blow dealt to international socialism by the Soviet-led occupation of Czechoslovakia in August 1968. By blocking democratisation in a country with one of the oldest and most solid organised workers' movements in the world, the "normalisers" ensured that socialist forces would be in a weak and compromised position throughout

Eastern Europe when Brezhnevite normality became impossible to maintain' (Themes, *NLR* 176, July/August 1989, p. 1). Kagarlitsky was similarly convinced, dating the abandonment of faith in Soviet socialism amongst the intelligentsia to the invasion of Czechoslovakia: 'On the morning of 21 August 1968 the entire ideology of Soviet liberalism collapsed in a few minutes, and all the hopes aroused by the Twentieth Congress fell to the ground. Whereas previously liberal intellectuals had comforted themselves with the thought that, on the whole, our society has a sound foundation, that it has not lost its socialist character, that … the revolution was sick but not dead, the events of 1968 scattered those illusions. It was not a matter of "the excesses of Stalinism" but of the system itself' (*The Thinking Reed*, p. 200).

126 'Renewals', *NLR* (II) 1, January/February 2000, p. 9.

127 'The End of History?', reprinted in Kenneth Jensen, ed., *A Look at the End of History?*, United States Institute of Peace, Washington DC, 1990, p. 2.

128 Themes, *NLR* 193, May/June 1992, p. 2

129 Fred Halliday, 'An Encounter with Fukuyama', pp. 89-95; Michael Rustin, 'No Exit From Capitalism?', pp. 96-107; Ralph Miliband, 'Fukuyama and the Socialist Alternative', pp. 108-13, all in *NLR* 193, May/June 1992; and Perry Anderson, 'The Ends of History', in *a Zone of Engagement*, Verso, London and New York, 1992, pp. 279-375.

130 The United States itself had 'recently invaded Panama and Grenada and bombed Libya, while abetting Israeli incursions and annexations … There should have been UN sanctions against Israel as strong as this, instead of the lavish US aid that was actually forthcoming' (Themes, *NLR* 184, November/December 1990, p. 1).

131 Ibid.

132 'The Crisis of the Arab World: The False Answers of Saddam Hussein', *NLR* 184, November/December 1990, p. 73.

133 Alex Callinicos, Paul Foot, Mike Gonzalez, Chris Harman and John Molyneaux, 'An Open Letter to *New Left Review*', *International Socialism*, no.50, Spring 1991, p. 103.

134 Ibid.

135 For Robert Brenner, 'the long-held but debilitating illusion that "the enemy of my enemy is my friend"' must be abandoned ('Why is the United States at War with Iraq?', *NLR* 185, January/February 1991, p. 123). Such a characterisation 'could not be *less* true' in the case of the Iraqi regime, whose 'accomplishments' included 'the systematic physical extermination of virtually the entire Iraqi Left' (ibid.). When war commenced, with the 'largest bombing onslaught since the Vietnam War' (Themes, *NLR* 185, January/February 1991, p. 1) proving enough to expel the conscript Iraqi army from Kuwait, the *Review* unequivocally condemned the West's military action: Saddam Hussein's 'brutal invasion and occupation of Kuwait did justify international action', argued the *Review*, 'but not this horrendous slaughter' (Themes, *NLR* 186, March/April 1991, p. 1). Kuwait, meanwhile, had been returned to its 'royal rowdies', whilst the fortunes of the democratic opposition in Kuwait and Iraq counted for nothing in Western calculations (ibid.).

136 'The Prospects of Labour and the Transformation of Advanced Capitalism', p. 25.

137 Ibid., p. 15.

138 'The Ends of History', in *A Zone of Engagement*, p. 366.

139 Ibid.

140 Introduction to Anderson and Patrick Camiller, eds, *Mapping The West European Left*, Verso, London and New York, 1994, p. 7.

141 Ibid., p. 14. They counted 'five axes of differentiation': between manual and clerical labour, between secure and casualised work, and on the bases of age, gender and ethnicity (ibid., p. 12).

142 Ibid., p. 14.

143 Ibid., p. 15.

144 Ibid. While others have doubted the impact of 'globalisation', the *Review*'s analysis of the prospects for social democracy largely accept that the 'unforgiving context' of globalisation 'has rendered obsolete historical strategies of reform and amelioration based on the existing capacities of nation states' (Themes, *NLR* 204, March/April 1994, p. 1).

145 'The Light of Europe', p. 324; the neo-liberal path pursued by the Australian and New Zealand Labour Parties in the eighties: see, for example, Bruce Jesson, 'The Disintegration of a Labour Tradition: New Zealand Politics in the 1980s', *NLR* 192, March/April 1992, pp. 37-54.

146 'The Life and Times of Socialism', *NLR* 194, July/August 1992, p. 32.

147 As early as 1988, with 'classic liberal ideals in question in the West and democratic ferment in the East', the *Review* was arguing that 'the project of a liberalised socialism, or of a socially responsible and authentic liberalism, may well appear to hold out the best of both worlds' (Themes, *NLR* 170, July/August 1988, p. 1).

148 Perry Anderson, *A Zone Of Engagement*, p. xii.

149 Perry Anderson, 'The Affinities of Norberto Bobbio', *New Left Review* 170 July/August 1988, pp. 3-36.

150 *A Zone Of Engagement*, p. xii. Socialists, Ralph Miliband argued, must recognise the value of liberal systems of representative government, for socialism could not 'entail the wholesale rejection of traditional liberal principles in the conduct of government, but rather their radical extension, far beyond anything that was ever dreamt of by liberal thinkers' ('Reflections on the Crisis of the Communist Regimes', *NLR* 177, September/October 1989, p. 35).

151 'Fin de Siècle: Socialism after the Crash', *NLR* 185, January/February 1991, p. 5.

152 Robin Blackburn, Preface to Blackburn (ed.) *After The Fall: The Failure of Communism and the Future of Socialism*, Verso, London and New York, 1991, p.xvi. Marx, Trotsky and Guevara were cited in support of a 'socialised market', on the model proposed by Diane Elson in the *Review* in 1988 ('Market Socialism or Socialisation of the Market?', *NLR* 172, November/December 1988, pp.3-44). 'The need to monitor optimisation with the use of market indicators', wrote Blackburn, 'is a lesson of Soviet and Chinese experience that can certainly not be ignored by socialists who wish to suppress capitalism in its

global strongholds' ('Fin de Siècle' p.48); whilst the decentralised and market-oriented success enjoyed by the Chinese economy was held up for admiration. In the first issue of the *NLR* to appear after the August 1991 coup in Moscow – devoted entirely to the fall of Communism and, more tentatively, the future of socialism – Blackburn's was the only contribution from a member of a twenty-six strong editorial committee ('Russia Should Be Looking East, not West', *NLR* 189, September/October 1991, pp. 137-40). Given the evident dynamism of the Chinese economy, with its decentralised ownership in labour collectives and municipal authorities, Blackburn considered 'that the eventual settling of accounts with China's gerontocracy' might be achieved without the 'economic devastation and social regression' of other ex-Communist countries (Preface to *After the Fall*, p. xv). The diminished scale of Blackburn's prospectus may be judged by his discussion of social ownership, in which, *inter alia*, the New Zealand Dairy Board, the employee-owned John Lewis Partnership, and Taiwan's state banks were cited approvingly ('Fin de Siècle' p.50). '[M]arkets yes, … capitalism no', was Therborn's summary ('Vorsprung durch Rethink', in *After the Fall*, p. 300). Significantly, perhaps, an article co-authored by Pat Devine, who had been (confidentially) identified by Anderson as one of the exemplars of the 'new revisionism' in 1985 ('Notes on the Current Outlook', unpublished document, 1985, p. 2), offered, in contrast to Blackburn and co.'s enthusiasm, a left-wing critique of market socialism (Fikret Adaman and Pat Devine, 'On the Economic Theory of Socialism', *NLR* 221, January/February 1997, pp. 54-80). Note also, in contrast to Blackburn's relative optimism (see, for example, 'Russia Should Be Looking East, not West', *NLR* 189, September/ October 1991, pp. 137-40), Richard Smith's critical account of the social and ecological cost of China's transition to capitalism. Smith argued that 'it would be helpful if intellectuals who call themselves socialists stopped pandering to the prevalent market idolatry', and 'abandoned such oxymorons as "market socialism"' ('Creative Destruction: Capitalist Development and China's Environment', *NLR* 222, March/April 1997, p. 41). More innovative has been Blackburn's ongoing development of the concept of a 'pension socialism' in conditions of a 'grey capitalism'. Arguing for workers' ownership of financial and pension funds, with the capacity to invest in socially identified priorities (and thus more effective than workers' control at factory level), Blackburn judges that the coordination of capitalism takes place at the financial level and must be challenged there: 'The New Collectivism: Pension Reform, Grey Capitalism and Complex Socialism', *NLR* 233, January/February 1999, pp. 3-65.

153 Introduction to Anderson and Patrick Camiller, eds, *Mapping The West European Left*, Verso, London and New York, 1994, p. 19-22.
154 *In The Tracks of Historical Materialism*, p. 94.
155 'The Light of Europe', p. 352. Anderson cited Paul Auerbach, 'On Socialist Optimism', *NLR* 192, March/April 1992, pp. 5-35. Auerbach asserted the priority of 'cultural revolution' (p.5), rejecting the classical Marxist emphasis on the economic substructure, 'Saint-Simonian fantasies', and 'adventurist … experiments' (p. 34). It 'seems indisputable now', he argued, 'that had the 1945

Labour government concentrated on rewriting the 1944 Education Act and reconstructing the university system, a genuine and lasting cultural transformation of the society may well have been possible' (p. 10). In Western Europe, Auerbach continued, 'radical approaches to social transformation were dislocated by schemes for taking the 'commanding heights' of industry. In the process, much intellectual and political energy has been dissipated by being distracted from the task of social transformation and the central battlegrounds for this transformation: the schools and other social institutions concerned with the upbringing of children. It is in these institutions that a radical transformation of society will take place, if it is to take place at all' (p. 35). See also James Donald, 'Dewey-Eyed Optimism: The Possibility of a Democratic Education', *NLR* 192, March-April 1992, pp. 133-44, and Krishan Kumar, 'Socialist Reconstruction of Schooling: A Comment', *NLR* 195, September/October 1992, pp. 118-23.

156 See, in particular, *A Zone of Engagement.*

157 'Unjust Taxation and Popular Resistance', *NLR* 180, March/April 1990, pp. 177-84.

158 It was defeat in war that brought bourgeois democracy to the German Federal Republic and Italy, whilst universal suffrage accompanied liberation in France. By contrast, '[n]o "gale of creative destruction" had blown through the creaking political timbers of the United Kingdom for nearly three centuries when the victorious powers met at Potsdam' ('The Figures of Descent', *NLR* 161, January/February 1987, p. 48).

159 'The Figures of Descent', pp. 72, 73, 48. A precondition for economic renewal, wrote Anderson, was 'a centralising force capable of regulating and counteracting the spontaneous molecular movements of the market' (ibid., p. 73), delineating 'three major types of such a regulative intelligence in advanced capitalism' since the war (ibid., p. 71.). A technocratic bureaucracy had successfully effected the modernisation of post-war French capitalism, whilst in West Germany it was primarily the banks that had directed a similar economic 'miracle'. Japan had benefited from a combination of the two: both a strongly interventionist state and a supportive bank structure. A third – social democratic/corporatist – model had been implemented in Sweden and Austria, where 'labour has played an institutional role comparable to that of bureaucracy or banking elsewhere' (ibid., p. 74). British singularity resulted from the absence of 'any of these three possible correctors, once the process of decline became manifest': the '*fainéant* industrial bourgeois of modern British history found no understudies for their role' (ibid., p. 76).
In one of the more telling critiques of Anderson's analysis, David Coates has argued that over-emphasising the fault-line between commercial and financial capital on the one hand, and industrial capital on the other, and downplaying the deeper divide that separates capital, in all its forms, from labour, can tend to a position prescribing capitalist modernisation rather than socialism. That Anderson should return to such themes in the late eighties, with the abandonment of expectations aroused after 1968, is itself significant. Coates writes: 'What Anderson sees as the industrial consequences of failed capitalist ratio-

nality might more properly be grasped as the local consequence of the stead-fast rationality of the entire British capitalist class. Industrial decline has not happened here because the local capitalist class did not do its job properly. Industrial decline has happened here because it did, and continues to do, that job extremely well. Capital goes where the pickings are largest and easiest; and that is fixed not primarily by divisions of interest between capitalists, but by the division of interests between capital and labour. Of all the contradictions on which the Anderson searchlight settles in the pursuit of causal "figures of descent", that is the one over which his torch sweeps with the greatest speed' ('In Pursuit of the Anderson thesis', in Colin Barker and David Nicholls, eds., *The Development of British Capitalism: A Marxist Debate*, Northern Marxist Historians Group, Manchester, 1988, p. 75).

160 'The Figures of Descent', p. 77.

161 'A Culture in Contraflow – II', *NLR* 182, July/August 1990, p. 136. Anderson and Blackburn – alongside Nairn, Miliband, Rustin et al. – were founding sig-natories of Charter '88, whilst its co-ordinator was Anthony Barnett, an active member of the *Review*'s editorial committee until 1983. Indeed, Blackburn judged that 'the impulse behind the Charter ... reflected the politics of the New Left' ('The Ruins of Westminster', *NLR* 191, January/February 1992, pp. 11-12). Michael Kenny is sometimes too eager to downplay the distinction between the two New Lefts. He writes, for example, that 'Thompson's belief in the creation of a new, morally conscious citizenry' was a 'precursor for the ideas of the Charter '88 group' (*The First New Left: British Intellectuals After Stalin*, Lawrence and Wishart, London, 1995, p. 78). Thompson never signed the Charter. His perspective entailed the *defence* of threatened existing rights and liberties, not the making of a written constitution or a Bill of Rights. The 'undermining of democracy is certainly going on, and at an inflationary rate': it was left to 'the defenders of civil liberties to uphold the constitution [sic.] and the rule of law' (*Writing by Candlelight*, Merlin Press, London, 1979, p. 210).

162 Perry Anderson, 'The Light of Europe', in *English Questions*, Verso, London and New York, 1992, p. 347

163 Recognising, in Anthony Arblaster's words, that 'Britain turns out to be a far less deeply and securely liberal polity than has been popularly supposed' ('Taking Monarchy Seriously', *NLR* 174, March/April 1989, p. 110), the Charter called for 'a new constitutional settlement' that would include a Bill of Rights; a writ-ten constitution; freedom of information and open government; proportional representation; abolition of the House of Lords; and 'an equitable distribution of power' between the nations of the UK, and between local, regional and cen-tral government – a programme 'carefully brokered', in Rustin's account, to at-tract both Liberal Democrats and independent socialists of a largely New Left provenance ('Citizenship and Charter 88', *NLR* 191, January/February 1992, p. 40). It remained a somewhat elitist body of 'left-liberal notables', largely com-prising 'journalists, lawyers, writers and academics' (ibid., p. 40); and its own organisation operated with a certain 'democratic deficit' (ibid., p. 41). In con-trast to the Anti-Poll Tax Federation (or, for example, the CND mobilisations

of the early eighties), Charter 88 had no mass organisational presence: by 1992 it had won a modest thirty thousand signatories (ibid.).

164 Perry Anderson, 'The Light of Europe', in *English Questions*, pp. 302-53; and Robin Blackburn, 'The Ruins of Westminster', *NLR* 191, January/February 1992, pp. 5-35. Blackburn's conclusion was the same as Anderson's in 'The Figures of Descent': Britain missed 'the moment of democratic renovation that accompanied the defeat of fascism in Europe', permitting the UK state 'to inhabit a providential Shangri-la, appearing vigorous and well-preserved despite its advanced years' ('The Ruins of Westminster', p. 7).

165 Themes, *NLR* 191, January/February 1992, p. 1.

166 Anderson wrote that 'electoral reform remains, as it has always been, the key to any qualitative change': 'The Light of Europe', p. 347.

167 'The Ruins of Westminster', p. 23.

168 Perry Anderson and Patrick Camiller judged that implementing effective macro-economic policy in the future would require 'the construction of a true federal framework in Europe', arguing that the 'West European Left will acquire new contours only when this crux is resolved' (*Mapping The West European Left*, p. 22). 'Such a Union', Anderson wrote in 1992, 'is the only kind of general will that can contest the new power of the invisible hand as the arbiter of collective destinies' ('The Ends of History', in *A Zone of Engagement*, p. 365).

169 'The Ruins of Westminster', p. 23.

170 Themes, *NLR* 191, January/February 1991, p. 2.

171 'Labour's Future and the Coalition Debate', *NLR* 157, May/June 1986, pp. 56.

172 Robin Blackburn, 'Reflections on Blair's Velvet Revolution', *NLR* 223 May/June 1997, pp. 3-16.

173 Perry Anderson, (unpublished) letter to Ellen Wood, Patrick Camiller and Robin Blackburn, 17 November 1988, p. 1.

174 Perry Anderson, (unpublished) letter to Ellen Wood, Patrick Camiller and Robin Blackburn, 17 July 1988, p. 1.

175 New members included Christopher Bertram, Paul Cammack, Diane Elson, Ken Hirschkop, Monty Johnstone, Deniz Kandiyoti, Doreen Massey, Robin Murray, Mike Rustin (previously on the editorial committee 1962-4), Kate Soper, Hilary Wainwright and Elizabeth Wilson.

176 Patrick Wright, 'Beastly Trials of the Last Politburo', *Guardian*, 17 July 1993, p. 29.

177 Those who resigned considered the *Review*'s purported financial predicament to be based on 'a highly controversial assessment' ('Resignations from the Editorial Board of New Left *Review*', Christopher Bartram et al., 24 February 1993, p. 2).

178 Wright, *art. cit.* Quintin Hoare worried that the *Review* might be drifting towards an 'eclectic directionlessness', but Blackburn, 'who has always been more pluralist than some of his colleagues', insisted that "[w]e are not ... a journal for recycling an already established truth" (ibid).

179 Perry Anderson, Benedict Anderson and Ronald Fraser had been the 'three donors who had put the review's finances on a sound footing in the sixties' (Robin Blackburn, letter to 'Contributors and Friends', 19 March 1993).

180 Blackburn admitted to having 'acted in a high-handed way', pleading 'a "fierce survival instinct" and a determination that his journal should not go the way of *Marxism Today*, *New Socialist*, *Spare Rib*, and other defunct publications of the left' (Wright, *art. cit.*).

181 At the beginning of 1995 the *NLR* acknowledged 'its appreciation for the on-going collaboration of the Center for Social Theory and Comparative History at UCLA', having recently published no less than five essays 'which were previously presented at the Center's annual colloquium series' (*NLR* 209, January/February 1995, p. 109), undoubtedly a consequence of Anderson's tenure there.

182 'Renewals', p. 6. Whilst Anderson judges that the journal has reached the point, as it enters its fifth decade, where its life must be extended 'beyond the conditions' and 'generations that gave rise to' it, ('Renewals', p. 6) acknowledging 'a radical discontinuity in the culture of the Left' – in which '[v]irtually the entire horizon of reference in which the generation of the sixties grew up has been wiped away .... For most students, the roster of Bebel, Bernstein, Luxemburg, Kautsky, Jaurès, Lukács, Lenin, Trotsky, Gramsci have become names as remote as a list of Arian bishops' (ibid., p. 17) – there is, in fact, no evidence of generational renewal, and established names so far dominate the new series.

183 Ibid.

184 Ironically, Anderson criticises Eric Hobsbawm and *Marxism Today* for optimism! 'As late as 1998, Eric Hobsbawm and former *Marxism Today* writers were still hopefully proclaiming the end of neo-liberalism' ('Renewals', p. 10).

185 'Renewals', pp. 10, 17.

186 Ibid., p. 13, n.5.

187 Achcar, Gilbert, 'The "historical pessimism" of Perry Anderson', *International Socialism*, no. 88, Autumn 2000, p. 138.

188 Ibid., pp. 137, 136.

189 Petras, James, 'Notes toward an understanding of revolutionary politics today', *Links*, no. 19, September to December 2001, p. 34.

190 'The suicide of *New Left Review*', *International Socialism*, no.88, Autumn 2000, p. 133.

191 Achcar, op. cit., p. 140. The *Review* has also, if in a somewhat sketchy and journalistic way, begun to address the politics of anti-globalisation in the series, 'A Movement of Movements?' (though note the qualifying question mark).

192 *Perry Anderson: The Merciless Laboratory of History*, University of Minnesota Press, Minneapolis and London, 1998, pp. 240, xv, xiii.

193 Ibid., pp. 192, xiv. Elliott is keen to draw parallels with Issac Deutscher: 'Like Deutscher before him, his fortitude amid the collapse of so many edifices of the Left, is arresting' (ibid., p. 191).

194 Because, wrote Anderson in 1965, 'the relationship between the working class and culture, decisive for its consciousness and ideology is *inevitably* mediated through intellectuals, the only full tenants of culture in a capitalist society' ('Problems of Socialist Strategy' in Perry Anderson and Robin Blackburn, eds., *Towards Socialism* (1965), Cornell University Press, Ithaca, New York, 1966, p. 241). Again, two years later, he was writing that 'intellectuals and petit bour-

geois ... alone can provide the essential *theory* of socialism' (Perry Anderson, 'The Limits and Possibilities of Trade Union Action', in Robin Blackburn and Alexander Cockburn, eds., *The Incompatibles: Trade Union Militancy and the Consensus*, Penguin & *New Left Review*, Harmondsworth, 1967, p. 266).

195 Lin Chun, *The British New Left*, Edinburgh University Press, 1993, p. xvi.

196 'A Chronology of the New Left and its Successors, or: Who's Old-Fashioned Now?', *Socialist Register 1995*, Merlin Press, London, 1995, p. 29.

197 Gregory Elliott, 'Olympus Mislaid? A Profile of Perry Anderson', *Radical Philosophy*, no.71, May/June 1995, p. 14.

198 Edward Thompson, *The Poverty of Theory and Other Essays* (1978), Merlin Press, London, 1980, p. 383.

199 'A Culture in Contraflow – I', *NLR* 180, March/April 1990, pp. 46, 42.

200 Kagarlitsky, op.cit., p. 129.

201 'Renewals', p. 17 (my italics).

202 In Ian Birchall's reckoning, '[p]erhaps ... the most serious indictment of the *Review* that can be made is that, by its style and manner, it has turned working-class militants away from theory by convincing them that it is irrelevant and inaccessible' ('The Autonomy of Theory: A Short History of *New Left Review*', *International Socialism*, no.10, Winter 1980/81, p.85). A charge addressed at length in the *Review*'s 1983 Charter (though ultimately underlining the centrality afforded to intellectual endeavour). The *NLR*, it noted, 'acknowledges that the division of labour within advanced capitalist societies, as in all prior class societies, stratifies culture in such a way that its highest reaches are typically reserved for the privileged, and reflect such privilege in their structure. Prior to the advent of communism, this link cannot be broken completely or cleanly. The production of socialist thought within a capitalist society – one designed to abolish such privilege – will therefore itself necessarily be marked by the division of labour and culture characteristic of capital. The resulting tension between quality and complexity, on the one hand, and availability and popularity on the other, is one that has to be negotiated by all publications of the Left, according to their different purposes and functions, and every resolution has its price. No unitary register is possible, in such a divided society; nor can any publication command all registers at once. In these conditions of inevitable diversification, NLR finds its place at the more demanding – thereby also more restrictive – end of the intellectual spectrum: that is, committed to intensive rather than extensive development of socialist culture, accepting all the limitations of readership that this realistically involves' ('Charter', unpublished editorial document, no date (but 1983), pp. 2-3).

203 'The political tradition in which NLR situates itself starts in this century from the October Revolution' ('Charter', p. 4).

204 'Trotsky's Interpretation of Stalinism', *NLR* 139, May/June 1983, p. 57.

205 'Renewals', p. 17, my italics.

206 Achcar, op.cit., p. 136.

207 Achcar, citing Anderson's own characterisation of Western Marxism in *Considerations on Western Marxism* (ibid., pp. 136-7).

208 Ibid., p. 139.

209 A 'long-standing and passionate interest' according to Elliott (*Perry Anderson*, p. 239).

210 'A Chronology of the New Left and its Successors, or: Who's Old-Fashioned Now?', *Socialist Register 1995*, Merlin Press, London, 1995, pp. 23, 38.

211 Ibid., pp. 32, 34.

212 Ibid., p. 35.

213 Ibid., p. 31.

214 Previously, Ian Birchall similarly argued that the 'journal's style did much to create a milieu in which Marxist theory became the pursuit of the latest fashionable thinker' (op. cit., p. 67). Donald Sassoon has drawn similar conclusions. The importation of Western Marxism, he argued, 'paved the way for the growing influence of French thinkers in American and British universities: Roland Barthes, Michel Foucault, Jacques Derrida, Jacques Lacan and others. The subsequent and paradoxical outcome of this importation was the eventual disengagement of many intellectuals from Marxism' (*One Hundred Years of Socialism: The West European Left in the Twentieth Century*, I.B.Tauris, London, 1996, p. 385).

215 Wood, op. cit., p. 43.

216 Nor has it simply refused to recognise the current crisis of socialist politics – the head-in-the-sands-Marxism (in former editorial committee member Norman Geras' words) of the 'shouting sects' ('Democracy and the Ends of Marxism', *NLR* 203, January/February 1994, p. 106).

217 'Renewals', *NLR* (II) 1, January/February 2000, p. 5.

Bibliography

Books and Articles

Abse, Tobias, 'Judging the PCI', *NLR* 153, September/October 1985, pp.5-40

Achcar, Gilbert, 'The "historical pessimism" of Perry Anderson', *International Socialism*, no.88, Autumn 2000, pp.135-41

Aglietta, Michel, 'World Capitalism in the Eighties', *NLR* 136, November/December 1982, pp.5-41

Ali, Tariq, *The Coming British Revolution*, Jonathan Cape, London, 1972
  - *1968 and After*, Bland & Briggs, London, 1978
  - and Quintin Hoare, 'Socialists and the Crisis of Labourism', *NLR* 132, March/April 1982, pp.59-81
  - ed., *The Stalinist Legacy*, Penguin, Harmondsworth, 1984
  - and Ken Livingstone, *Who's Afraid of Margaret Thatcher?*, Verso, London, 1984
  - *Street Fighting Years: An Autobiography of the Sixties*, Collins, 1987
  - *Revolution From Above*, Hutchinson, London, 1988

Althusser, Louis, 'Contradiction and Overdetermination', *NLR* 41, January/February 1967, pp.15-35
  - 'On the Twenty-Second Congress of the French Communist Party', *NLR* 104, July/August 1977, pp.3-22
  - 'What Must Change in the Party', *NLR* 109, May/June 1978, pp.19-45
  - 'The Crisis of Marxism', *Marxism Today*, July 1978, pp.215-27

Anderson, Perry, 'Origins of the Present Crisis', *NLR* 23, January/February 1964, pp.26-53
  - 'A Critique of Wilsonism', *NLR* 27, September/October 1964, pp.3-27
  - 'Conspectus', unpublished document, 1964
  - 'The Left in the Fifties', *NLR* 29, January/February 1965, pp.3-18
  - and Robin Blackburn, eds., *Towards Socialism* (1965), Cornell University Press, Ithaca, New York, 1966
  - 'Problems of Socialist Strategy', in Anderson and Blackburn, eds, *Towards Socialism*, pp.221-90
  - 'Socialism and Pseudo-Empiricism', *NLR* 35, January/February 1966, pp.2-42
  - 'Components of the National Culture', *NLR* 50, July/August 1968, pp.3-57
  - 'The Founding Moment', unpublished manuscript, 1969
  - *Passages From Antiquity to Feudalism* (1974), Verso, London, 1978
  - *Lineages of the Absolute State* (1974), Verso, London, 1989
  - *Considerations on Western Marxism* (1976), Verso, London, 1989
  - 'The Antinomies of Antonio Gramsci', *NLR* 100, November 1976/January 1977, pp.5-78

- 'The Strategic Option: Some Questions', in André Liebach, ed., *The Future of Socialism in Europe?*, Interuniversity Centre for European Studies, Montréal, 1978, pp.21-9
- 'Notes on *The Poverty of Theory*', unpublished document, 1979
- *Arguments Within English Marxism*, Verso, London, 1980
- 'Notes on "Why the American Working Class is Different"', unpublished document, 1980
- 'Communist Party History', in Raphael Samuel, ed., *People's History and Socialist Theory*, Routledge and Kegan Paul, London, 1981 pp.145-56
- 'A Problem in Defining the Socialist Society', unpublished document, 1981
- "Imperialism - Pioneer of Capitalism", unpublished document, 1981
- Letter (unpublished) to Johanna Brenner and Maria Ramas, 27 January 1983
- 'Trotsky's Interpretation of Stalinism', *NLR* 139, May/June 1983, pp.49-58
- Letter (unpublished) to Robin Blackburn, 4 August 1983
- Letter (unpublished) to *NLR*, 5 October 1983
- *In The Tracks of Historical Materialism*, Verso, London, 1983
- 'Memo on Socialism and Feminism', unpublished document, 12 February 1984
- 'Notes on the Current Outlook', unpublished document, 1985
- 'NLR Perspectives', unpublished document, 1985
- 'Figures of Descent', *NLR* 161, January/February 1987, pp.20-77
- Letter (unpublished) to Ellen Wood, Patrick Camiller and Robin Blackburn, 17 July 1988
- Letter (unpublished) to Ellen Wood, Patrick Camiller and Robin Blackburn, 17 November 1988
- 'A Culture in Contraflow - I', *NLR* 180, March/April 1990, pp.41-78
- 'A Culture in Contraflow - II', *NLR* 182, July/August 1990, pp.85-137
- 'August in Moscow', *London Review of Books*, 26 September 1991, pp.5-8
- *A Zone of Engagement*, Verso, London and New York, 1992
- 'The Ends of History', in *A Zone of Engagement*, pp.279-375
- *English Questions*, Verso, London and New York, 1992
- 'The Light of Europe', in Anderson, *English Questions*, pp.302-53
- 'Diary', *London Review of Books*, 22 October 1993, pp.24-5
- 'Maurice Thomson's War', *London Review of Books*, 4 November 1993, pp.13-17
- and Patrick Camiller, eds, *Mapping the West European Left*, Verso, London and New York, 1994
- 'Under the Sign of the Interim', *London Review of Books*, 4 January 1996, pp.13-17
- 'The Europe to Come', *London Review of Books*, 25 January 1996, pp.3-8
- 'A Sense of the Left' (1996), *NLR* 231, September/October 1998, pp.73-81
- 'A Reply to Norberto Bobbio', *NLR* 231, September/October 1998, pp.91-3
- *The Origins of Postmodernity,* Verso, London and New York, 1998
- 'Renewals', *NLR* (II) 1, January/February 2000, pp.5-24
Arblaster, Anthony, 'Labour's Future and the Coalition Debate', *NLR* 157, May/June 1986, pp.45-60
Archer, Robin et al., eds, *Out of Apathy: Voices of the New Left Thirty Years On*, Verso, London and New York, 1989

Aronson, Ronald, 'Historical Materialism, Answer to Marxism's Crisis', *NLR* 152, July/August 1985, pp.74-94

Armstrong, Philip, Andrew Glyn and John Harrison, *Capitalism Since World War II: The making and break-up of the long boom*, Fontana, London, 1984

Arrighi, Giovanni, 'Marxist Century, American Century: The Making and Remaking of the World Labour Movement', *NLR* 179, January/February 1990, pp.29-63

 - 'World Income Inequalities and the Future of Socialism', *NLR* 189, September/October 1991, pp.39-65

 - *The Long Twentieth Century: Money, Power, and the Origins of Our Times*, Verso, London and New York, 1994

Bahro, Rudolf, 'The Alternative in Eastern Europe', *NLR* 106, November/December 1977, pp.3-37

 - *The Alternative in Eastern Europe*, trans. David Fernbach, New Left Books, London, 1978

 - *From Red to Green*, trans. Gus Fagan, Verso, London, 1984

Barker, Colin and David Nicholls, eds., *The Development of British Capitalism: A Marxist Debate*, Northern Marxist Historians Group, Manchester, 1988

Barnett, Anthony, 'A Revolutionary Student Movement', *NLR* 53, January/February 1969, pp.43-53

 - 'Class Struggle and the Heath Government', *NLR* 77, January/February 1973, pp.3-41

 - 'Introduction to Western Marxism: Some Preliminary Comments', unpublished document, 24 July 1974

 - 'Raymond Williams and Marxism: A Rejoinder to Terry Eagleton', *NLR* 99, September-October 1976, pp.47-64

 - 'Iron Britannia', *NLR* 134 (Special Issue), July/August 1982, pp.5-96

 - 'The Empire State', in Barnett, ed., *Power and the Throne: The Monarchy Debate*, Vintage/Charter 88, London, 1994

Barratt Brown, Michael, 'Third World or Third Force?', *NLR* 20, Summer 1963, pp.32-36

 - 'Away With All the Great Arches: Anderson's History of British Capitalism', *NLR* 167, January/February 1988, pp.22-51

Barrett, Michèle, *Women's Oppression Today*, Verso, London, 1980

Beckett, Francis, *Enemy Within: The Rise and Fall of the British Communist Party*, John Murray, London, 1995

Benn, Tony, *Parliament, People, Power*, Verso, London, 1982

Berlinguer, Enrico, 'Reflections after the events in Chile', *Marxism Today*, February 1974, pp.39-50

Berman, Marshall, 'The Signs in the Street', *NLR* 144, March/April 1984, pp.114-23

Birchall, Ian, 'The Autonomy of Theory: A Short History of *New Left Review*', *International Socialism*, no.10, Winter 1980/81, pp.51-91

Blackburn, Robin, 'Prologue to the Cuban Revolution', *NLR* 21, October 1963, pp.52-91

- and Alexander Cockburn, eds., *The Incompatibles: Trade Union Militancy and the Consensus*, Penguin/*New Left Review*, Harmondsworth, 1967

- 'A Brief Guide to Bourgeois Ideology', in Alexander Cockburn and Robin Blackburn, eds, *Student Power*, Penguin/*New Left Review*, Harmondsworth, 1969, pp.163-213

- 'Introduction' to *Strategy for Revolution*, Regis Debray (ed. Robin Blackburn), Jonathan Cape, London, 1970, pp.7-23

- 'Let It Bleed: Labour and the General Election', *Red Mole*, Vol. 1, no.3, April 1970

- 'The Heath Government: A New Course for British Capitalism', *NLR* 70, November/December 1971, pp.3-26

- 'The Test in Portugal', *NLR* 87/88, September/December 1974, pp.5-46

- 'Marxism: Theory of Proletarian Revolution', *NLR* 97, May/June 1976, pp.3-35

- 'Preface' to *Revolution and Class Struggle: A Reader in Marxist Politics*, Robin Blackburn (ed.), Fontana, Glasgow, 1977, pp.9-21

- 'Raymond Williams and the Politics of a New Left', *NLR* 168, March/April 1988, pp.12-22

- 'A Brief History of New Left Review 1960-1990', in *Thirty Years of the New Left Review: Index to Numbers 1-184 (1960-1990)*, London, 1992, pp.v-xi

- 'Fin de Siècle: Socialism after the Crash', *NLR* 185, January/February 1991, pp.5-66

- ed., *After The Fall: The Failure of Communism and the Future of Socialism*, Verso, London and New York, 1991

- 'The Ruins of Westminster', *NLR* 191, January/February 1992, pp.5-35

- 'Edward Thompson and the New Left', *NLR* 201, September/October 1993, pp.3-9

- 'Ralph Miliband 1924-1994', *NLR* 206, July/August 1994, pp.15-22

- 'Raphael Samuel: The Politics of Thick Description', *NLR* 221, January/February 1997, pp. 133-8.

- 'Ernest Mandel 1923-1995', *NLR* 213, September/October 1995, pp.96-100

- 'Reflections on Blair's Velvet Revolution', *NLR* 223, May/June 1997, pp.3-16

- 'The Unexpected Dialectic of Structural Reforms', in *The Legacy of Ernest Mandel*, Gilbert Achar (ed.), Verso, London and New York, 1999, pp.16-23

- 'The New Collectivism: Pension Reform, Grey Capitalism and Complex Socialism', *NLR* 233, January/February 1999, pp.3-65

- 'Kosovo: The War of NATO Expansion', *NLR* 235, May/June 1999, pp.107-23

Blackledge, Paul, *Perry Anderson, Marxism and the New Left*, Merlin Press, London, 2004

Bobbio, Norberto, 'The Upturned Utopia', *NLR* 177, September/October 1989, p.37-9

- 'At the Beginning of History', *NLR* 231, September/October 1998, pp.82-90

Brenner, Johanna and Maria Ramas, 'Rethinking Women's Oppression', *NLR* 144, March/April 1984, pp.33-71

Brenner, Robert, 'The Origins of Capitalist Development: A Critique of Neo-Smithian Marxism', *NLR* 104, July/August 1977, pp.25-92

- 'Why is the United States at War with Iraq?', *NLR* 185, January/February 1991, pp.122-37

- and Mark Glick, 'The Regulation Approach: History and Theory', *NLR* 188, July/August 1991, pp.45-119

- 'Uneven Development and the Long Downturn: The Advanced Capitalist Economies from Boom to Stagnation, 1950-1998', *NLR* 229 (Special Issue: 'The Economics of Global Turbulence), May/June 1998, pp.1-265

Brewster, Ben, 'Armed Insurrection and Dual Power', *NLR* 66, March/April 1971, pp.59-68

- 'Communication', *NLR* 70, November/December 1971, pp.110-11

- and Alexander Cockburn, 'Revolt at the LSE', *NLR* 43, May/June 1967, pp.11-25

Cain, P. J. and A. G. Hopkins, *British Imperialism: Innovation and Expansion 1688-1914*, Longman, London, 1993

- *British Imperialism: Crisis and Deconstruction 1914-1990*, Longman, London, 1993

Callaghan, John, *British Trotskyism*, Blackwell, Oxford, 1984

- *The Far Left in British Politics*, Blackwell, Oxford, 1987

- *Socialism in Britain Since 1884*, Blackwell, Oxford, 1990

- 'The Road to 1956' *Socialist History*, no.8, 1995 pp.13-21

Callinicos, Alex, 'Perry Anderson and "Western Marxism"', *International Socialism*, no.23, Spring 1984, pp.113-28

- 'Exception or Symptom? The British Crisis and the World System', *NLR* 169, May/June 1988, pp.97-106

- *Trotskyism*, Open University Press, Buckingham, 1990

- et al., 'An Open Letter to *New Left Review*', *International Socialism*, no. 50, Spring 1991, pp.101-3

Camiller, Patrick, 'Spanish Socialism in the Atlantic Order', *NLR* 156, March/April 1986, pp.5-36

- 'Beyond 1992: The Left and Europe', *NLR* 175, May/June 1989, pp.5-17

Carrillo, Santiago, *Eurocommunism and the State*, trans. Nan Green and A. M. Elliott, Lawrence and Wishart, London, 1977

Carr, E. H., 'Revolution From Above', *NLR* 46, November/December 1967, pp.17-27

- 'The Russian Revolution and the West', *NLR* 111, September/October 1978, pp.25-36

Castellina, Luciana, '*Il Manifesto* and Italian Communism', *NLR* 151, May/June 1985, pp.26-42

Caute, David, *Sixty Eight: The Year of the Barricades*, Paladin Books, London, 1988

Chun, Lin, *The British New Left*, Edinburgh University Press, Edinburgh, 1993

- 'Reply to Dorothy Thompson and Fred Inglis', *NLR* 219, September/October 1996, pp. 133-7

Claudin, Fernando, *The Communist Movement, From Comintern to Cominform: Part One, The Crisis of the Communist International*, trans. Brian Pearce, Monthly Review Press, New York and London, 1975

- *The Communist Movement, From Comintern to Cominform: Part Two, The Zenith of Stalinism*, Monthly Review Press, New York and London, 1975

- 'Democracy and Dictatorship in Lenin and Kautsky', *NLR* 106, November/December 1977, pp.59-76

- *Eurocommunism and Socialism* (1977), trans. John Wakeham, New Left Books, London, 1978

Coates, David, 'Labourism and the Transition to Socialism', *NLR* 129, September/October 1981, pp.3-22

- 'Space and Agency in the Transition to Socialism', *NLR* 135, September/October 1982, pp.49-63

Coates, Ken, 'How Not to Reappraise the New Left', *Socialist Register 1976*, Merlin Press, London, 1976, pp.111-27

- 'The Choices Before Labour', *NLR* 131, January/February 1982, pp.32-43

- 'The Peace Movement and Socialism', *NLR* 145, May/June 1984, pp.88-121

Cockburn, Alexander and Robin Blackburn, eds, *Student Power*, Penguin/*New Left Review*, Harmondsworth, 1969

Cohen, G. A., *Karl Marx's Theory of History: A Defence*, Oxford University Press, Oxford, 1978

Colletti, Lucio, 'A Political and Philosophical Interview', *NLR* 86, July/August 1974, pp.3-28

Communist Party, *The British Road to Socialism*, London, 1951

- *The British Road to Socialism*, London, 1977

- *Facing up to the Future*, supplement to *Marxism Today*, September 1988

- *Manifesto for New Times*, London, 1989

Coote, Anna and Beatrix Campbell, *Sweet Freedom: The struggle for women's liberation*, Picador, London, 1982

Coulson, Margaret, Branka Magaš and Hilary Wainwright, 'The Housewife and her Labour under Capitalism - A Critique', *NLR* 89, January/February 1975, pp.59-71

Croft, Andy, 'Writers, the Communist Party and the Battle of Ideas, 1945-50', *Socialist History*, no.5, Summer 1994, pp.2-25

- 'Mapless in the Wilderness: Randall Swingler and 1956', *Socialist History*, no.19, 2001, pp.44-70

Crosland, Anthony, *The Future of Socialism* (1956), Jonathan Cape, London, 1985

Crossman, Richard, ed., *New Fabian Essays*, Turnstile Press, London, 1952

Curran, James, *The Future of the Left*, Polity Press/*New Socialist*, Cambridge, 1984

Davis, Mike, 'Nuclear Imperialism and Extended Deterrence', in *NLR*, ed., *Exterminism and Cold War*, Verso, London, 1982, pp.35-64

- *Prisoners of the American Dream: Politics and Economy in the History of the US Working Class*, Verso, London, 1986

Debray, Régis, 'Latin America: The Long March', *NLR* 33, September/October 1965, pp.17-58

- 'Problems of Revolutionary Strategy in Latin America' (1965), *NLR* 45, September/October 1967, pp.13-41

- *Revolution in the Revolution?* (1967), trans. Bobby Ortiz, Penguin, Harmondsworth, 1968

- 'A Modest Contribution to the Rites and Ceremonies of the Tenth Anniversary' (1978), *NLR* 115, May/June 1979, pp.45-65

Deutscher, Isaac *Stalin: A Political Biography* (1949), Penguin, Harmondsworth, 1974
  - *The Prophet Armed - Trotsky: 1879-1921*, Oxford University Press, Oxford, 1954
  - *The Prophet Unarmed - Trotsky: 1921-1929* (1959), Oxford University Press, Oxford, 1982
  - *The Prophet Outcast - Trotsky 1929-1940* (1963), Oxford University Press, Oxford, 1987
  - 'Three Currents in Communism', *NLR* 23, January/February 1964, pp.3-18
  - 'The Unfinished Revolution: 1917-67', *NLR* 43, May/June 1967, pp.27-39
  - *Marxism, Wars and Revolutions: Essays from Four Decades*, ed. Tamara Deutscher, Verso, London, 1984
Duff, Peggy, *Left, Left, Left*, Allison and Busby, London, 1971
Dworkin, Dennis, *Cultural Marxism in Postwar Britain: History, the New Left, and the Origins of Cultural Studies*, Duke University Press, Durham (North Carolina) and London, 1997

Eagleton, Terry, 'Criticism and Politics: The Work of Raymond Williams', *NLR* 95, January/February 1976, pp.3-23
Elliott, Gregory, *Labourism and the English Genius*, Verso, London and New York, 1993
  - 'Missing Ingredients', *Radical Philosophy*, no.68, Autumn 1994, pp 45-8
  - 'Olympus Mislaid? A Profile of Perry Anderson', *Radical Philosophy*, no. 71, May/June 1995, pp.5-19
  - 'Velocities of Change: Perry Anderson's Sense of an Ending', *Historical Materialism*, no.2, 1998
  - *Perry Anderson: The Merciless Laboratory of History*, University of Minnesota Press, Minneapolis and London, 1998
Elson, Diane, 'Market Socialism or Socialisation of the Market?', *NLR* 172, November/December 1988, pp.3-44
Emmanuel, Arghiri, 'State and Transition to Socialism', *NLR* 113-4, January/April 1979, pp.111-31

Fanon, Frantz, *The Wretched of the Earth* (1961), trans. Constance Farrington, Penguin, Harmondsworth, 1978
Forgács, David, 'Gramsci and Marxism in Britain', *NLR* 176, July/August 1989, pp.70-88
Fraser, Ronald et al., *!968: A Student Generation in Revolt*, Chatto and Windus, London, 1988
Fukuyama, Francis, *The End of History and the Last Man* (1992), Penguin, Harmondsworth, 1993

Geras, Norman, 'Althusser's Marxism: An Account and Assessment', *NLR* 71, January/February 1972, pp.57-86
  - 'Rosa Luxemburg: Barbarism and the Collapse of Capitalism', *NLR* 82, November/December 1973, pp.17-37
  - 'Rosa Luxemburg after 1905', *NLR* 89, January/February 1975, pp.3-46

- *The Legacy of Rosa Luxemburg*, New Left Books, London, 1976
- 'Literature of Revolution', *NLR* 113-114, January-April 1979, pp.3-41
- 'Post-Marxism?', *NLR* 163, May/June 1987, pp.40-82
- 'Ex-Marxism Without Substance: Being a Real Reply to Laclau and Mouffe', *NLR* 169, May/June 1989, pp.34-61
- 'Democracy and the Ends of Marxism', *NLR* 203, January/February 1994, pp.92-106
Ginsborg, Paul, *A History of Contemporary Italy: Society and Politics 1943-1988*, Penguin Books, London, 1990
Gitlin, Todd, *The Sixties: Years of Hope, Days of Rage*, Bantam Books, Toronto, 1987
Glucksmann, André, 'Strategy and Revolution in France 1968', *NLR* 52, November/December 1968, pp.67-121
Gorz, André, *Farewell to the Working Class* (1980), trans. Mike Sonenscher, Pluto Press, London, 1982
- 'The New Agenda', *NLR* 184, November/December 1990, pp.37-46
Gowan, Peter, 'Western Economic Diplomacy and the New Eastern Europe', *NLR* 182, July/August 1990, pp.63-82
- 'The Gulf War, Iraq and Western Liberalism', *NLR* 187, May/June 1991, pp.29-70
- 'Neo-Liberal Theory and Practice for Eastern Europe', *NLR* 213, September/October 1995, pp.3-60
Gramsci, Antonio, *Selections from the Prison Notebooks* (1971), eds and trans. Quintin Hoare and Geoffrey Nowell Smith, Lawrence and Wishart, London, 1982

Hall, Stuart, and Martin Jacques, eds, *The Politics of Thatcherism*, Lawrence and Wishart/*Marxism Today*, London, 1983
- 'Authoritarian Populism: A Reply to Jessop et al.', *NLR* 151, May/June 1985, pp.115-24
- *The Hard to Renewal: Thatcherism and the Crisis of the Left*, Verso/*Marxism Today*, London, 1988
- and Martin Jacques, eds, *New Times: The Changing Face of Politics in the 1990s*, Lawrence and Wishart/*Marxism Today*, London, 1989
- 'The "First" New Left: Life and Times', in Robin Archer et al., eds, *Out of Apathy*, pp.11-38
- et al., 'Then and Now: A Re-evaluation of the New Left', in Robin Archer et al., eds, *Out of Apathy*, pp.143-70
Halliday, Fred, 'Comment on Western Marxism', unpublished document, no date
- 'Marxist Analysis and Post-Revolutionary China', *NLR* 100, November 1976/January 1977, pp.165-92
- 'Revolution in Afghanistan', *NLR* 112, November/December 1978, pp.3-44
- 'The War and Revolution in Afghanistan', *NLR* 119, January/February 1980, pp.20-41
- 'The Sources of the New Cold War', in *NLR*, ed., *Exterminism and Cold War*, pp.289-328
- *The Making of the Second Cold War* (1983), second edition, Verso, London, 1986
- 'The Ends of Cold War', *NLR* 180, March/April 1990, pp.5-23

- 'The Crisis of the Arab World: The False Answers of Saddam Hussein', *NLR* 184, November/December 1990, pp.69-74

Harman, Chris, *The Fire Last Time: 1968 and After* (1988), Bookmarks, London, Chicago, Sydney, 1998

Heinemann, Margot, '1956 and the Communist Party', *Socialist Register 1976*, Merlin Press, London, 1976, pp.43-57

Hinton, James, 'The Labour Aristocracy', *NLR* 32, July/August 1965, pp.72-7.

 - *Labour and Socialism: A History of the British Labour Movement 1867-1974*, Wheatsheaf, Brighton, 1983

 - *Protests and Visions: Peace Politics in 20th Century Britain*, Radius, London, 1989

Hinton, William, *Fanshen: A Documentary of Revolution in a Chinese Village*, Penguin, Harmondsworth, 1972

Hirst, Paul, 'Anderson's Balance Sheet' in Hirst, *Marxism and Historical Writing*, Routledge and Kegan Paul, London, 1985, pp.1-28

Hobsbawm, Eric, *Industry and Empire* (1968), Penguin, Harmondsworth, 1971

 - *Revolutionaries* (1973), Quartet Books, London, 1982

 - 'Look Left', *New Statesman*, 24 September 1976, pp.409-11

 - 'Some reflections on "The Break-up of Britain"', *NLR* 105, September/October 1977, pp.3-23

 - et al., *The Forward March of Labour Halted?*, Verso/*Marxism Today*, London, 1981

 - *Politics for a Rational Left: Political Writing 1977-1988*, Verso/*Marxism Today*, London, 1989

 - *Age of Extremes: The Short Twentieth Century 1914-1991* (1994), Abacus, London, 1995

 - 'Identity Politics and the Left', *NLR* 217, May/June 1996, pp.38-47

Hodgson, Geoff, *Socialism and Parliamentary Democracy*, Spokesman, Nottingham, 1977

Hülsberg, Werner, *The German Greens*, Verso, London, 1988

Hutton, Will, *The State We're In*, Jonathan Cape, London, 1995

Ingham, Geoffrey, *Capitalism Divided? The City and Industry in British Social Development*, Macmillan, London and Basingstoke, 1984

 - 'Commercial Capital and British Development', *NLR* 172, November/December 1988, pp.45-65

Inglis, Fred, *Raymond Williams*, Routledge, London, 1995

 - 'The Figures of Dissent', *NLR* 215, January/February 1996, pp.83-92

Jacoby, Russell, *The Last Intellectuals: American Culture in the Age of Academe*, Basic Books, New York, 1987

Jameson, Fredric, 'Postmodernism, or The Cultural Logic of Late Capitalism', *NLR* 146, July/August 1984, pp.53-92

Jessop, Bob et al., 'Authoritarian Populism, Two Nations, and Thatcherism', *NLR* 147, September/October 1984, pp.32-60

 - et al., 'Thatcherism and the Politics of Hegemony: A Reply to Stuart Hall', *NLR* 153, September/October 1985, pp.87-101

- et al., 'Popular Capitalism, Flexible Accumulation and Left Strategy', *NLR* 165, September/October 1987, pp.104-122

- et al., 'Farewell to Thatcherism? Neo-Liberalism and 'New Times'', *NLR* 179, January/February 1990, pp.81-102

Johnson, Richard, 'Barrington Moore, Perry Anderson and English Social Development', (1980), in Stuart Hall *et al.*, eds, *Culture, Media, Language*, Hutchinson, London, 1984

Johnstone, Monty, '1956 and 1989 - The Legacy', *Our History Pamphlet 88: The Communist Party and 1956*, February 1993, pp.39-47

Jones, Gareth Stedman, Anthony Barnett and Tom Wengraf, 'Student Power: What is to be Done?', *NLR* 43, May/June 1967, pp.3-9

- 'Comment' (on manuscript of Anderson's 'Western Marxism'), unpublished document, no date

Jones, Mervyn, 'Days of Tragedy and Farce', *Socialist Register 1976*, Merlin Press, London, 1976, pp.67-88

- *Chances*, Verso, London, 1987

Kagarlitsky, Boris, *The Thinking Reed: Intellectuals and the Soviet State from 1917 to the Present*, trans. Brian Pearce, Verso, London, 1988

- *The Dialectic of Change*, trans. Rick Simon, Verso, London, 1990

- 'The suicide of *New Left Review*', *International Socialism*, no.88, Autumn 2000, pp.127-33

Katsiaficas, George, *The Imagination of the New Left: A Global Analysis of 1968*, South End Press, Boston, 1987

Kaye, Harvey J., and Keith McClelland, eds, *E.P. Thompson: Critical Perspectives*, Temple University Press, Philadelphia, 1990

Kayman, Martin, *Revolution and Counter-Revolution in Portugal*, Merlin Press, London, 1987

Kenny, Michael, 'Communism and the New Left', in Geoff Andrews, Nina Fishman and Kevin Morgan, eds, *Opening the Books: Essays on the Social and Cultural History of the British Communist Party*, Pluto Press, London, 1995, pp.195-209

- *The First New Left: British Intellectuals After Stalin*, Lawrence and Wishart, London, 1995

- 'Interpreting the New Left: Pitfalls and Opportunities', *NLR* 219, September/October 1996, pp. 138-42.

Khilnani, Sunil, *Arguing the Revolution: The Intellectual Left in Postwar France*, Yale University Press, New Haven and London, 1993

Kozak, Marion, 'How it all Began: A Footnote to History', *Socialist Register 1995*, Merlin Press, London, 1995, pp.264-85

Krassó, Nicolas, 'Trotsky's Marxism', *NLR* 44, July/August 1967, pp.64-86

- 'Reply to Ernest Mandel', *NLR* 48, March/April 1968, pp.90-103

Laclau, Ernesto, *New Reflections on the Revolution of Our Time*, Verso, London and New York, 1990

- and Chantal Mouffe, *Hegemony and Socialist Strategy* (1985), Verso, London and New York, 1990

- and Chantal Mouffe, 'Post-Marxism without Apologies', *NLR* 166, November/December 1987, pp.79-106

Lenin, Vladimir, *The State and Revolution* (1917), Foreign Languages Press, Peking, 1970

- *The Proletarian Revolution and the Renegade Kautsky* (1918), Foreign Languages Press, Peking, 1970

- *"Left-Wing" Communism, An Infantile Disorder* (1920), Foreign Languages Press, Peking, 1970

Leys, Colin, *Politics in Britain: From Labourism to Thatcherism* (1983), second edition, Verso, London and New York, 1989

- 'Thatcherism and British Manufacturing', *NLR* 151, May/June 1985, pp.5-25

- 'The Formation of British Capital', *NLR* 160, November/December 1986, pp.114-20

- 'Still a Question of Hegemony', *NLR* 181, May/June 1990, pp.119-28

- 'A Radical Agenda for Britain', *NLR* 212, July/August 1995, pp.3-13

Liebman, Marcel, *Leninism under Lenin*, trans. Brian Pearce, Merlin Press, London, 1975

Lipietz, Alain, 'Towards Global Fordism?', *NLR* 132, March/April 1982, pp.33-47

- 'Marx or Rostow?', *NLR* 132, March/April 1982, pp.48-58

- 'How Monetarism has Choked Third World Industrialisation', *NLR* 145, May/June 1984, pp.71-87

- *Miracles and Mirages: The Crises of Global Fordism*, trans. David Macey, Verso, London, 1987

- 'The Debt Problem, European Integration and the New Phase of World Crisis', *NLR* 178, November/December 1989, pp.37-50

Löwy, Michael, *The Politics of Combined and Uneven Development: The Theory of Permanent Revolution*, Verso, London, 1981

MacEwen, Malcolm, 'The Day the Party had to Stop', *Socialist Register 1976*, Merlin Press, London, 1976, pp.24-42

- *The Greening of a Red*, Pluto Press, London, 1991

McCarney, Joseph, 'The True Realm of Freedom: Marxist Philosophy after Communism', *NLR* 189, September/October 1991, pp.19-38

McKenzie, Norman, ed., 'The Insiders', *ULR* 6, Winter 1958, pp.i-iv and 25-64

- ed., *Conviction*, McGibbon and Kee, London, 1959

McGuigan, Jim, 'Reviewing a Life. Fred Inglis's Biography of Raymond Williams', *NLR* 215, January/February 1996, pp.101-8

Magaš, Branka, 'Sex Politics: Class Politics', *NLR* 66, March/April 1971, pp.69-92

Magri, Lucio, 'Problems of the Marxist Theory of the Revolutionary Party' (1963), *NLR* 60, March/April 1970, pp.97-128

- 'The May Events and Revolution in the West' (1968), *Socialist Register 1969*, Merlin Press, London, 1969, pp.29-53

- 'Italian Communism in the Sixties' (1970), *NLR* 66, March/April 1971, pp.37-52

- 'The Peace Movement and European Socialism', *NLR* 131, January/February 1982, pp.5-19

- 'The European Left between Crisis and Refoundation', *NLR* 189, September/
October 1991, pp.5-18

Mandel, Ernest, 'Trotsky's Marxism: An Anti-Critique', *NLR* 47, January/February
1968, pp.32-51

- 'Lessons of May', *NLR* 52, November/December 1968, pp.9-31
- 'Trotsky's Marxism: A Rejoinder', *NLR* 56, July/August 1969, pp.69-96
- *Late Capitalism* (1972), trans. Joris de Bres, New Left Books, London, 1975
- 'Revolutionary Strategy in Europe – A Political Interview', *NLR* 100, November
1976/ December 1977, pp.97-132
- *From Stalinism to Eurocommunism: The Bitter Fruits of 'Socialism in One
Country'* (1977), trans. Jon Rothschild, New Left Books, London, 1978
- 'On the Nature of the Soviet State' (interview), *NLR* 108, March/April 1978,
pp.23-45
- *The Second Slump: A Marxist Analysis of Recession in the Seventies* (1978), Verso,
London, 1980
- *Trotsky: A Study in the Dynamic of his Thought*, New Left Books, London, 1979
- *Revolutionary Marxism Today*, New Left Books, London, 1979
- 'The Threat of War and the Struggle for Socialism', *NLR* 141, September/
October 1983, pp.23-50
- 'In Defence of Socialist Planning', *NLR* 159, September/October 1986, pp.5-37
- 'The Myth of Market Socialism', *NLR* 169, May/June 1988, pp.108-20

Mayer, Arno J., *The Persistence of the Old Regime: Europe to the Great War*, Croom
Helm, London, 1981

Marx, Karl, *The Revolutions of 1848*, Penguin/*New Left Review*, Harmondsworth,
1973

- *Surveys From Exile*, Penguin/*New Left Review*, Harmondsworth, 1974
- *The First International and After*, Penguin/*New Left Review*, Harmondsworth,
1974
- *Early Writings*, Penguin/*New Left Review*, Harmondsworth, 1975
- *Capital Volume 1*, Penguin/*New Left Review*, Harmondsworth, 1976

Miliband, Ralph, 'The Sickness of Labour', *NLR* 1, January/February 1960, pp.5-9

- *Parliamentary Socialism* (1961), second edition, Merlin Press, London, 1979
- *The State in Capitalist Society* (1969), Quartet Books, London, 1982
- 'The Capitalist State: Reply to Nicos Poulantzas', *NLR* 59, January/February
1970, pp.53-60
- 'Poulantzas and the Capitalist State', *NLR* 82, November/December 1973, pp.83-
92
- 'The Coup in Chile', *Socialist Register 1973*, Merlin Press, London, 1974, pp.451-
74
- *Marxism and Politics*, Oxford University Press, Oxford, 1977
- 'State Power and Class Interests', *NLR* 138, March/April 1983, pp.57-68
- *Class Power and State Power*, Verso, London, 1983
- 'The New Revisionism in Britain', *NLR* 150, March/April 1985, pp.5-26
- 'Reflections on the Crisis of Communist Regimes', *NLR* 177, September/
October 1989, pp.27-36

- 'Thirty Years of *The Socialist Register, Socialist Register 1994*, Merlin Press, London, 1994, pp.1-19
  - 'The Plausibility of Socialism', *NLR* 206, July/August 1994, pp.3-14
Mills, C. Wright, 'Letter to the New Left', *NLR* 5, September/October 1960, pp.18-23
Mitchell, Juliet, 'Women: The Longest Revolution', *NLR* 40, November/December 1966, pp.11-37
  - *Woman's Estate* (1971), Penguin, Harmondsworth, 1973
  - *Psychoanalysis and Feminism* (1974), Penguin, Harmondsworth, 1979
Mulhern, Francis, *The Moment of Scrutiny* (1979), Verso, London, 1981
  - 'Towards 2000, or News from You-Know-Where', *NLR* 148, November/December 1984, pp.5-30
  - 'A Welfare Culture? Hoggart and Williams in the Fifties', *Radical Philosophy*, no. 77, May/June 1996, pp.26-37

Nairn, Tom, 'The British Political Elite', *NLR* 23, January/February 1964, pp.19-25
  - 'The English Working Class', *NLR* 24, March/April 1964, pp.43-57
  - 'The Nature of the Labour Party - 1', *NLR* 27, September/October 1964, pp.38-65
  - 'The Nature of the Labour Party - 2', *NLR* 28, November/December 1964, pp.33-62
  - 'Labour Imperialism', *NLR* 32, July/August 1965, pp.3-15
  - 'The Three Dreams of Scottish Nationalism', *NLR* 49, May/June 1968, pp.3-18
  - 'Why It Happened', in Angelo Quattrocchi and Tom Nairn, *The Beginning of the End: France, May 1968*, Panther Books, London, 1968
  - 'The Fateful Meridian', *NLR* 60, March/April 1970, pp.3-35
  - 'Enoch Powell: The New Right', *NLR* 61, May/June 1970, pp.3-27
  - 'British Nationalism and the EEC', *NLR* 69, September/October 1971, pp.3-28
  - 'The European Problem', *NLR* 75 (Special Issue: 'The Left Against Europe?'), September/October 1972, pp.5-120
  - 'Scotland and Europe', *NLR* 83, January/February 1974, pp.57-82
  - 'Comments on Western Marxism: An Introduction', unpublished document, 10 October 1974
  - 'The Modern Janus', *NLR* 94, November/December 1975, pp.3-29
  - 'The Twilight of the British State', *NLR* 101/2, January/April 1977, pp.3-61
  - *The Break-up of Britain: Crisis and Neo-Nationalism* (1977), revised edition, Verso, London, 1981
  - 'The Future of Britain's Crisis', *NLR* 113/114, January/April 1979, pp.43-69
  - 'The Crisis of the British State', *NLR* 130, November/December 1981, pp.37-44
  - *The Enchanted Glass*, Radius, London, 1988
  - 'The Sole Survivor', *NLR* 200, July/August 1993, pp.41-7
  - 'Reflections on Nationalist Disasters', *NLR* 230, July/August 1998, pp.145-52
Newman, Michael, *Ralph Miliband and the Politics of the New Left*, Merlin Press, London, 2002
NLR, 'On Internationalism', *NLR* 18, January/February 1963, pp.3-4
  - ed., *Western Marxism: A Critical Reader*, New Left Books, London, 1977

- ed., *Exterminism and Cold War*, Verso, London, 1982
- 'Introduction, Revisiting the New Left', *NLR* 215, January/February 1996, p.82
Nove, Alec, *The Economics of Feasible Socialism*, Allen and Unwin, London, 1983
- 'Markets and Socialism', *NLR* 161, January/February 1987, pp.98-104

Palmer, Bryan D., *E. P. Thompson: Objections and Oppositions*, Verso, London and New York, 1994
Panitch, Leo, 'Ralph Miliband, Socialist Intellectual, 1924-1994', *Socialist Register 1995*, Merlin Press, London, pp.1-21
- and Colin Leys, *The End of Parliamentary Socialism: From New Left to New Labour*, Verso, London and New York, 1997
Pitcairn, Lee, 'Crisis in British Communism: An Insider's View', *NLR* 153, September/October 1985, pp.102-20
Petras, James, 'Notes toward an understanding of revolutionary politics today', *Links*, no.19, September to December 2001, pp.5-34
Pontusson, Jonas, 'Behind and Beyond Social Democracy in Sweden', *NLR* 143, January/February 1984, pp.69-96
- 'Radicalisation and Retreat in Swedish Social Democracy', *NLR* 165, September/October 1987, pp.5-33
Poulantzas, Nicos, 'Marxist Political Theory in Britain', *NLR* 43, May/June 1967, pp.57-74
- 'The Problem of the Capitalist State', *NLR* 58, November/December 1969, pp.67-78
- 'On Social Classes', *NLR* 78, March/April 1973, pp.27-54
- 'The Capitalist State: A Reply to Miliband and Laclau', *NLR* 95, January/February 1976, pp.63-83
- *State, Power, Socialism*, trans. Patrick Camiller, New Left Books, London, 1978
- 'Towards a Democratic Socialism', *NLR* 109, May/June 1978, pp.75-87
Przeworski, Adam, 'Social Democracy as a Historical Phenomenon', *NLR* 122, July/August 1980, pp.27-58

Robinson, Joan, *The Cultural Revolution in China*, Penguin Books, Harmondsworth, 1969
Ross, George, *Workers and Communists in France: From Popular Front to Eurocommunism*, University of California Press, Berkeley, Los Angeles and London, 1982
- and Jane Jenson, 'Strategy and Contradiction in the Victory of French Socialism', *Socialist Register 1981*, (eds) Ralph Miliband and John Saville, Merlin Press, London, 1981, pp.72-103
- and Jane Jenson, 'The Tragedy of the French Left', *NLR* 171, September/October 1988, pp.5-44
Rowbotham, Sheila, 'Women's Liberation and the New Politics', Spokesman pamphlet no.17, Nottingham, 1971
- *Promise of a Dream: Remembering the Sixties*, Penguin, London, 2001
- and Lynne Segal and Hilary Wainwright, *Beyond the Fragments: Feminism and the Making of Socialism* (1979), Merlin Press, London, 1981

Rowthorn, Bob, 'Late Capitalism', *NLR* 98 July/August 1976, pp.59-83

Rustin, Michael, 'The New Left and the Present Crisis', *NLR* 121, May/June 1980, pp.63-89

 - 'Different Conceptions of Party: Labour's Constitutional Debates', *NLR* 126, March/April 1981, pp.17-42

  - *For a Pluralist Socialism*, Verso, London, 1985

  - 'The New Left as a Social Movement', in Robin Archer et al., eds, *Out of Apathy*, pp.117-28

  - 'The Politics of Post-Fordism: Or, The Trouble with "New Times"', *NLR* 175, May/June 1989, pp.54-77

  - 'Citizenship and Charter 88', *NLR* 191, January/February 1991, pp.37-42

Samuel, Raphael, '"Bastard" Capitalism', in E. P. Thompson et al., *Out of Apathy*, Stevens and Sons, London, 1960, pp.19-55

 - 'British Marxist Historians 1880-1980: Part One, *NLR* 120, March/April 1980, pp.21-96

 - ed., *People's History and Socialist Theory*, Routledge and Kegan Paul, London, 1981

 - 'The Lost World of British Communism', Parts 1-3, *NLR* 154, November/December 1985, pp.3-53; *NLR* 156, March/April 1986, pp.63-113; and *NLR* 165, September/October 1987, pp.52-91

 - 'Born-again Socialism', in Robin Archer et al., eds, *Out of Apathy*, pp.39-57

Sartre, Jean-Paul, Preface to Frantz Fanon,*The Wretched of the Earth* (1961), Penguin, Harmondsworth, 1978, pp.7-26

 - 'Itinerary of a Thought', *New Left Review* 58, November/December 1969, p.43-66

 - 'Socialism in One Country', *NLR* 100, November 1976/December 1977, pp.143-163

Sassoon, Donald, 'The Silences of *New Left Review*', *Politics and Power 3*, Routledge and Kegan Paul, London, 1981, pp.219-254

 - *One Hundred Years of Socialism: The West European Left in the Twentieth Century*, I.B.Tauris, London, 1996

Saville, John, 'The Twentieth Congress and the British Communist Party', *Socialist Register 1976*, Merlin Press, London, 1976, pp.1-23

 - 'The Communist Experience: A Personal Appraisal', *Socialist Register 1991*, Merlin Press, London, 1991, pp.1-27

 - 'Edward Thompson, the Communist Party and 1956', *Socialist Register 1994*, Merlin Press, London, 1994, pp.20-31

Schwarz, Bill, '"The People" in History: The Communist Party Historians' Group, 1946-1956', in Richard Johnson et al., eds, *Making Histories: Studies in History-Writing and Politics*, Hutchinson, London, 1982, pp.44-95

Seale, Patrick and Maureen McConville, *French Revolution 1968*, William Heinemann and Penguin Books, London and Harmondsworth, 1968

Seccombe, Wally, 'The Housewife and her Labour under Capitalism', *NLR* 83, January/February 1974, pp.3-24

Sedgwick, Peter, 'The Two New Lefts', *International Socialism*, no.17, Summer 1964, pp.15-23, reprinted in David Widgery, ed., *The Left in Britain 1956-68*, Penguin, Harmondsworth, 1976, pp.131-153
 - 'Pseud Left Review', *International Socialism*, no.15, Summer 1966, pp.18-19
Segal, Lynne, 'The Silence of Women in the New Left', in Robin Archer et al., eds, *Out of Apathy*, pp.114-16
Singer, Daniel, *The Road to Gdansk*, Monthly Review Press, New York, 1982
Soper, Kate, 'The Socialist Humanism of E. P. Thompson', in *Troubled Pleasures: Writings on Politics, Gender and Hedonism*, Verso, London, 1990, pp.89-125
Spriano, Paolo, *Stalin and the European Communists* (1983), trans. Jon Rothschild, Verso, London, 1985

Taylor, Charles, 'Marxism and Socialist Humanism', in Robin Archer *et al.*, eds, *Out of Apathy*, pp.59-78
Therborn, Göran, 'From Petrograd to Saigon', *NLR* 48, March/April 1968, pp.3-11
 - 'The Prospects of Labour and the Transformation of Advanced Capitalism', *NLR* 145, May/June 1984, pp.5-38
 - 'The Life and Times of Socialism', *NLR* 194, July/August 1992, pp.17-32
Thompson, Dorothy, 'The Personal and the Political' (interview), *NLR* 200, July/August 1993, pp.87-100
 - 'On the Trail of the New Left', *NLR* 215, January/February 1996, pp.93-100
Thompson, Duncan, 'Pessimism of the Intellect? The *New Left Review* and the "conjuncture of 1989"', *Socialist History 20*, Rivers Oram Press, London, Sydney and New York, 2002, pp.19-39
Thompson, E. P., *William Morris: Romantic to Revolutionary* (1955), revised edition, Pantheon, New York, 1976
 - 'Through the Smoke of Budapest', *Reasoner*, no.3, November 1956 (supplement), pp.1-7
 - 'Socialism and the Intellectuals', *Universities and Left Review*, no.1, Spring 1957, pp.31-6
 - 'Socialist Humanism: An Epistle to the Philistines', *New Reasoner*, no.1, Summer 1957, pp.105-43
 - 'Agency and Choice - I', *New Reasoner*, no.5, Summer 1958, pp.89-106
 - 'The New Left', *New Reasoner*, no.9, Summer 1959, pp.1-17
 - 'A Psessay in Ephology', *New Reasoner*, no.10, Autumn 1959, pp.1-8
 - 'Revolution', *NLR* 3, May/June 1960, pp.3-9
 - et al., *Out of Apathy*, Stevens and Sons, London, 1960
 - 'At the Point of Decay', in Thompson *et al.*, *Out of Apathy*, pp.3-15
 - 'Outside the Whale', in Thompson et al., *Out of Apathy*, pp.141-94
 - 'Revolution Again!', *NLR* 6, November/December 1960, pp.18-31
 - *The Making of the English Working Class* (1963), Penguin, Harmondsworth, 1982
 - 'The Peculiarities of the English', *Socialist Register 1965*, Merlin Press, London, 1965, pp.311-62
 - 'An Open Letter to Leszek Kolakowski', *Socialist Register 1965*, Merlin Press, London, 1965, pp.1-100

- 'Romanticism, Utopianism and Moralism: The Case of William Morris', *NLR* 99, September/October 1976, pp.83-111
  - *The Poverty of Theory and Other Essays* (1978), Merlin Press, London, 1980
  - 'The Politics of Theory' (1979), in Raphael Samuel, ed., *People's History and Socialist Theory*, Routledge and Kegan Paul, London, 1981, pp.396-408
  - *Writing By Candlelight*, Merlin Press, London, 1980
  - 'Notes on Exterminism, the Last Stage of Capitalism', *NLR* 121, May/June 1980, pp.3-31
  - 'Europe, the Weak Link in the Cold War', in *NLR* ed., *Exterminism and Cold War*, Verso, London, 1982, pp.329-49
  - 'The Ends of the Cold War', *NLR* 182, July/August 1990, pp.139-46
Thompson, Willie, 'The New Left in Scotland', in Ian MacDougall, ed., *Essays in Scottish Labour History*, John Donald, Edinburgh, 1978, pp.207-24
  - *The Good Old Cause: British Communism 1920-91*, Pluto Press, London, 1992
  - *The Left in History: Revolution and Reform in Twentieth-Century Politics*, Pluto Press, London, 1997
Threlfall, Monica, ed., *Mapping the Women's Movement: Feminist Politics and Social Transformation in the North*, Verso, London and New York, 1996
Timpanaro, Sebastiano, *On Materialism* (1970), trans. Lawrence Garner, Verso, London, 1980
Trotsky, Leon, *The Third International After Lenin* (1929), trans. John G. Wright, Pathfinder Press, New York, 1970
  - *The Permanent Revolution and Results and Prospects* (1931), trans. John G. Wright and Brian Pearce, Pathfinder Press, New York, 1978
  - *The Revolution Betrayed: What is the Soviet Union and Where is it Going?*, trans. Max Eastman, Faber and Faber, London, 1937
  - *In Defense of Marxism: The Social and Political Contradictions of the Soviet Union* (1942), Pathfinder Press, New York, 1990

Wainwright, Hilary, 'The Limits of Labourism: 1987 and Beyond', *NLR* 164, July/August 1987, pp.34-50
  - *Arguments for a New Left: Answering the Free Market Right*, Blackwell, Oxford and Cambridge (MA), 1994
Wald, Alan M., *The New York Intellectuals: The Rise and Decline of the anti-Stalinist Left from the 1930s to the 1980s*, University of North Carolina Press, Chapel Hill (NC), 1987
Warren, Bill, 'The Programme of the C.P.G.B. – A Critique', *NLR* 63, September/October 1970, pp.27-41
  - 'Imperialism and Capitalist Industrialisation', *NLR* 81, September/October 1973, pp.3-44
  - *Imperialism: Pioneer of Capitalism*, ed. John Sender, New Left Books, London, 1980
Weber, Henri, 'Eurocommunism, Socialism and Democracy', *NLR* 110, July/August 1978, pp.3-14
Wengraf, Tom, 'An Essay on the Early New Left Review', unpublished MA thesis, University of Birmingham, 1979

Werskey, Gary, *The Visible College*, Allen Lane, Penguin, London, 1978
Widgery, David, *The Left in Britain 1956-68*, Penguin, Harmondsworth, 1976
Wilcox, James, 'Two Tactics', *NLR* 53, January/February 1969, pp.23-32
Williams, Raymond, *Culture and Society 1780-1950* (1958), Penguin, Harmondsworth, 1985
 - *The Long Revolution* (1961), Penguin, Harmondsworth, 1984
 - 'The British Left', *NLR* 30, March/April 1965, pp.18-26
 - ed., *May Day Manifesto 1968*, Penguin, Harmondsworth, 1968
 - 'Base and Superstructure in Marxist Cultural Theory', *NLR* 82 November/December 1973, pp.3-16
 - 'Notes on British Marxism Since the War', *NLR* 100, November 1976/January 1977, pp.81-94
 - *Marxism and Literature*, Oxford University Press, Oxford, 1977
 - 'Problems of Materialism', *NLR* 109, May/June 1978, pp.3-17
 - *Politics and Letters: Interviews with New Left Review*, New Left Books, London, 1979
 - 'Beyond Actually Existing Socialism', *NLR* 120, March/April 1980, pp.3-19
 - 'The Politics of Nuclear Disarmament', *NLR* 124, November/December 1980, pp.25-42
 - *Towards 2000*, Chatto and Windus, London, 1983
 - 'Problems of the Coming Period', *NLR* 140, July/August 1983, pp.7-18
 - *Resources of Hope: Culture, Democracy, Socialism*, ed. Robin Gable, Verso, London and New York, 1989
Wilson, Elizabeth and Angela Weir, 'The British Women's Movement', *NLR* 148, November/December 1984, pp.74-103
Wollen, Peter, ed., *Raiding the Icebox: Reflections On Twentieth-century Culture*, Verso, London, 1993
Wood, Ellen Meiksins, *The Retreat From Class: A New 'True' Socialism*, Verso, London, 1986
 - 'Capitalism and Human Emancipation', *NLR* 167, January/February 1988, pp.3-20
 - *The Pristine Culture of Capitalism: A Historical Essay on Old Regimes and Modern States*, Verso, London and New York, 1991
 - 'A Chronology of the New Left and its Successors, or: Who's Old-Fashioned Now?', *Socialist Register 1995*, Merlin Press, London, 1995, pp.22-49
Wood, Neal, *Communism and British Intellectuals*, Victor Gollancz, London, 1959
Worsley, Peter, 'Revolution of the Third World', *NLR* 12, November/December 1961, pp.18-25
Wright, Erik Olin, 'Class Boundaries in Advanced Capitalist Societies', *NLR* 98, July/August, 1976, pp.3-41
Wright, Patrick, 'Beastly Trials of the Last Politburo', *Guardian*, 17 July 1993, p.29

Young, Marilyn, *The Vietnam Wars, 1945-1990*, Harper Collins, New York, 1991
Young, Nigel, *An Infantile Disorder? The Crisis and Decline of the New Left*, Routledge and Kegan Paul, London, 1977

Journals (other than the *New Left Review*)
New Reasoner, nos.1-10, 1957-59
The *Reasoner*, nos.1-3, 1956
Seven Days, nos.1-20, October 1971-March 1972, and Special Issue, May 1972
Universities and Left Review, nos.1-7, 1957-59

Unpublished *NLR* editorial documents
'Document A: Theory and Practice: The *Coupure* of May', 1968/9
'Document B: Ten Theses', 1968/9
'A Decennial Report', 1974
'NLR 1975-1980', 1980
'NLR 1980-1983', 1982
'Charter', no date (but 1983)

Index

Achcar, Gilbert, xi, 158, 162

Afghanistan, 140-1

Althusser, Louis, 23, 60, 64, 74, 81, 99-103, 107

Ali, Tariq, 37, 54, 66, 95, 118-9, 131, 147, 157

Amendola, Giorgio, 79

Anderson, Benedict, 9, 157

Anderson, Perry, new series viii-ix, 157-60; two New Lefts, xi, 7-8, 9-10, 39-42; background, 9; structural reform, 27-30, 32; Bolivia 1967, 37; Third Worldism, 38; 'Components of the National Culture', 58-60; Krassó-Mandel exchange, 65; *Considerations on Western Marxism*, 66-9; conflictual behaviour, 71, 72, 124; contrasting southern & northern Europe, 74-5; Western Communist Parties, 76-9; 'Antinomies of Antonio Gramsci', 83-5; direct democracy, 86-8; British labour militancy (early seventies), 92; response to 'Poverty of Theory', 99-105; *In the Tracks of Historical Materialism*, 107-110; 'riddle of Sphinx' (socialist strategy, early eighties), 110-15, 124, 127; Anglophone Marxism, 110-11, 114; stepping down as editor (1983), 123-4; Independent Left Corresponding Society, 131; on Trotskyism, 141-2; post-Soviet fall, 153-5; reweighting of Nairn-Anderson theses, 154-5, 177-8, 226-7; failed e/c enlargement (1990-2), 156-7; pessimism, 157-8

Aronson, Ronald, 114

Ayer, Alfred, 6

Barnett, Anthony, 10, 53-4, 55, 69, 71, 72, 91, 92, 120-1, 124, 155

Barratt Brown, Michael, 35

Benn, Tony (and Bennism), 116-7, 119, 131

Bertram, Christopher, 157

Birchall, Ian, xi, 41, 93

Black Dwarf, 54-5, 69

Blackburn, Robin, on *NLR*, x, 165; background, 9; *The Incompatibles*, 29; Cuban Revolution, 35-6; Bolivia 1967, 37; 1968, 53-5; Maoism, 65; IMG, 66, 71; on Nairn & nationalism, 72; 'parliamentary Cretinism', 86; 1970 election & Heath government, 91; on feminism, 94; Socialist Society, 117; editor, 123-4, 156-7; Independent Left Corresponding Society, 131; Soviet 'fall', 148, 154; 1992 election, 155-6

Blackledge, Paul, x

Bobbio, Norberto, 147, 153-4

Brenner, Robert, 157

Brewster, Ben, 10, 53, 66, 70, 87

Brittain, Victoria, 126

Britten, Keith, 34-5

Buchanan, Keith, 34-5

Butt, Dennis, 7-8

Callinicos, Alex, 152

Camiller, Patrick, 126, 153, 157

Cammack, Paul, 157

Carillo, Santiago, 79, 90

Centre for Contemporary Cultural Studies, 8, 41

Charter 88, 18, 155

Chile, 78, 79-80

Chun, Lin, x, 102

Claudín, Fernando, 83, 87, 107

CND (Campaign for Nuclear Disarmament), 3-4, 6, 7, 34, 105

Coates, David, 117-8, 119
Coates, Ken, 135
Cockburn, Alexander, 10, 55, 69, 70, 151, 157
Cohen, G.A., 110, 150
Conference of Socialist Economists, 73
CPGB (Communist Party of Great Britain), 1, 2, 29, 40, 122, 127, 131
CPGB Historians' Group, 2, 41
Crosland, Anthony, 1

Daly, Lawrence (& Fife Socialist League), 5-6, 168
Davis, Mike, 124, 134-5, 157
Debray, Régis, 36-8, 102
Deutscher, Isaac, 32-4, 38, 63, 68
Dews, Peter, 126, 157
Duff, Peggy, 4
Dworkin, Dennis, x

Eagleton, Terry, 72, 110
Elliott, Gregory, x, 158, 165
Elson, Diane, 157
Euro-Communism, 77-9, 82, 87-9, 108
Euro-Socialism, 109-10, 127, 132

Falkland's War, 120-1
Fanon, Frantz, 35
feminism, 112-3, 125-6
Fernbach, David, 53, 54, 55, 66, 70
Forgács, David, 41
Fourth International, 26, 52, 62, 71, 76, 89, 112
France ('crisis of Marxism', 1978), 107-9
Fraser, Ronald, 10, 55, 70, 72, 157
French May (1968), 46-9, 52
Fukuyama, Francis, 151-2

Gable, Robin, 157
Gay Liberation, 66, 69
Geras, Norman, 70-1, 72, 101, 124, 130, 157
German Revolution (1918-23), 83
Gorbachev, Mikhail, 146-7, 149-51
Gowan, Peter, 126, 143-4, 149, 157

Gramsci, Antonio, 12, 23, 24, 41-2, 60
Greece, 75, 80
Gulf War 1991, 152

Habermas, Jürgen, 110, 148
Hall, Stuart, x, 2, 3, 4, 6, 7, 8, 101, 115, 119-20
Halliday, Fred, 54-5, 66, 69, 70-1, 94, 95, 124, 135-8, 141, 144, 149, 152
Halliday, Jon, 94, 124, 142, 145
Heffer, Eric, 125, 131
Hirschkop, Ken, 157
Hirst, Paul, xi, 92-3, 101
History Workshop Journal, 8, 41
Hoare, Quintin, 10, 55, 66, 71, 72, 118-9, 157
Hobsbawm, Eric, 98-9, 110, 122-3, 154
Hodgson, Geoff, xi, 92, 101, 117-8
Hoggart, Richard, 8
Hungary 1956, 2

Idiot International, 69
IMG (International Marxist Group), 52, 55, 66, 70, 71, 118
Inglis, Fred, x
Institute for Workers Control, 25, 93
International Socialists/SWP (Socialist Workers' Party), 54, 152
IRA, 95
Ireland, 94-5
Italy, 57, 75, 89-90, 91, 109

Johnson, Richard, 18, 25, 40, 68, 101
Johnstone, Monty, 157
Jones, Mervyn, x, 7

Kagarlitsky, Boris, xi, 146, 158-9
Kandiyoti, Deniz, 157
Kenny, Michael, x, 3, 39, 41
Khruschev, Nikita, 2
Krassó, Nicolas, 10, 62-5

Labour Party, 1, 3, 4, 6, 7, 26-9, 96, 116-20, 126, 130, 131-2
Leavis, F.R., 59-60
Left Clubs, 5-6

Livingstone, Ken, 118, 124, 131
Löwy, Michael, 97

MacEwen, Malcolm, x
Magaš, Branka, 10, 66, 71, 94, 157
Mandel, Ernest, 26, 28, 33, 63-5, 68, 71, 73, 86, 89, 110, 130, 154
Maoism, 33, 58-9, 60-2, 64-5, 108-9
Marcuse, Herbert, 53
Marxism Today, 122, 123, 127-8, 129, 152, 154, 163
Massey, Doreen, 157
Mayday Manifesto, 8, 43, 73, 92
Merrington, John, 124
Mills, C. Wright, 23, 52, 169
Miliband, Ralph, 5, 8, 39, 84, 110, 116, 117, 128-9, 131, 152
Mitchell, Juliet, 10, 70, 124
Mitterand, François, 91, 109
Morris, William, 100, 104-5
Mulhern, Francis, 70-1, 109, 110, 124, 129-30
Murdoch, Iris, 6
Murray, Robin, 157
Murray, Roger, 10, 124

Nairn, Tom, 10, 47-8, 53, 56, 61, 68, 69, 70, 71, 95-9, 124
Nairn-Anderson theses, 11-25, 154
New Left, first New Left, 2-9; new New Left, 9-11; contrasting two New Lefts, 39-42
New Left Books/Verso, 53, 55, 72, 110
New Left Review, foundation, 2, 5-6; Wilsonism and structural reform, 26-30; latent Third Worldism, 30-9; revolutionary turn 1968, 44-51, 57-8, 60-2; state and revolution in West, 81-91; re-anchorage, 115-6; 1983 election, 121-3; retrenchment, 123-32; *Exterminism and Cold War*, 134-9; reinterpretation of Second World, 139-51; failed enlargement 1990-2, 156-7; new series, 157; pessimism, 157-64
New Reasoner, 2, 3, 39-41

Newman, Michael, x

Palmer, Bryan, x
PCF (French Community Party), 47-8, 77-8, 81, 88, 90-1, 100
PCI (Italian Communist Party), 28, 42, 76-7, 81, 89-90
Pearson, Gabriel, 3, 7, 10
People's Democracy, 95
Petras, James, xi, 158
Poland, 66, 143-4
Porter, Cathy, 125-6
Portuguese revolution, 75, 80-1, 90
Poulantzas, Nicos, 17, 24-5, 84, 87, 107, 110
Prague Spring, 49

Reasoner, 3
Red Mole, 55, 91
Rowbotham, Sheila, 70
Rowthorn, Bob, 10, 73, 124
RSSF (Revolutionary Socialist Students' Association), 52-4, 56
Rustin, Michael, x, xi, 6, 10, 92, 101, 115, 131, 152, 157

Samuel, Raphael, x, 3, 5, 7-8, 115, 127-8
Sartre, Jean-Paul, xi, 10, 33, 38, 53, 58-9
Sassoon, Donald, xi, 93, 101
Saville, John, x, 2, 3, 8, 39
Scanlon, Hugh, 29, 30
Scargill, Arthur, 92, 131
Schwarz, Bill, 41
Second Cold War, 109, 133-41, 147
Sedgwick, Peter, xi, 5, 11, 22, 26-7, 30
Segal, Lynne, 125-6
Seven Days, 69-70, 160
Socialist Register, 8, 39
Socialist Society, 116-7, 160
Soper, Kate, 157
Stedman Jones, Gareth, 10, 69, 94, 124
student revolt 1968, 44-8, 52-4
Suez 1956, 2

Taylor, Barbara, 92, 125-6
Taylor, Charles, x, 3

Thatcherism, 116, 154

Therborn, Göran, 50-1, 110, 128, 152, 153

Thompson, Dorothy, 5

Thompson, Edward, on second New Left, xi, 39-42, 92, 99-105, 115; first New Left, 2-8; critique of Nairn-Anderson theses, 16-18, 24; Second Cold War, 134-6, 149

Trotsky/Trotskyism, 60-9, 112, 141-2, 160

Universities and Left Review, 2, 3, 5, 39-41

USA, New Left, 10, 45-6, 51, 52

Vietnam War, 45-6, 50-1, 75

VSC (Vietnam Solidarity Campaign), 48, 53

Wainwright, Hilary, 125-6, 157

Weber, Henri, 87, 88-9

Wengraf, Tom, 10

Western Marxism, 60, 61, 66-8, 162

Williams, Raymond, viii, 6, 8, 25, 60, 72, 103, 110, 115-6, 117, 124, 139

Wilson, Elizabeth, 157

Wollen, Peter, 10, 69, 70, 94, 124

Women's Liberation Movement, 94, 95

Women's Liberation Workshop, 69

Wood, Ellen, xi, 102, 126, 157, 159, 162-3

Young, Nigel, x